a handbook of
world trade

a handbook of
world trade

2nd edition

a strategic guide to
trading internationally

Consultant Editor:
Jonathan Reuvid

PUBLISHING SA
An affiliate of the International Chamber of Commerce
The world business organization

**KOGAN
PAGE**

London and Sterling, VA

First published in 2001 by Kogan Page Limited
Second edition published in Great Britain and the United States in 2004 by Kogan Page Limited

Kogan Page Limited
120 Pentonville Road
London N1 9JN
UK

Kogan Page US
22883 Quicksilver Drive
Sterling VA 20166-2012
USA

www.kogan-page.co.uk

© Kogan Page and contributors 2001, 2004

ISBN 0 7494 4143 7

British Library Cataloguing in Publication Data

A CIP record for this book is available from the British Library.

Library of Congress Cataloging-in-Publication Data

Reuvid, Jonathan.
   A handbook of world trade / Jonathan Reuvid.-- 2nd ed.
     p. cm.
Previous ed. entered under title has subtitle: A strategic guide to trading internationally.
   ISBN 0-7494-4143-7
   1. International trade--Handbooks, manuals, etc. I. Title.
HF 1379.H366 2004
382--dc22
                       2003026740

Typeset by JS Typesetting, Wellingborough, Northants
Printed and bound in Great Britain by Cambrian Printers Ltd, Aberystwyth, Wales

Contents

About the Editor

Jonathan Reuvid graduated in economics at Oxford and was employed as an economist by the French national oil company, Total, at the time of its UK market entry. From there he moved into investment banking, financial consultancy and marketing strategy. After seven years working for the engineering division of the US multinational Barnes Group with European general management responsibility, he engaged in the development of joint ventures and technology transfers in Northern China, where he remains involved. In 1989 Jonathan embarked on a new career in business publishing, editing and writing a series of international business books with Kogan Page. He has a developing interest in the delivery of business briefings and adult learning on the Internet.

List of Contributors

Richard Bate joined ICC United Kingdom as director at the beginning of 1992. He has wide marketing experience, including CEO level, with well-known companies including Wilkinson Sword, Wyeth Laboratories, Nicholas International, Gallaher, l'Oreal and Gillette. Although he has lived mainly in the UK, he has broad international business experience.

Maria Livanos Cattaui was appointed Secretary General of the International Chamber of Commerce (ICC) in 1996. As chief executive of the world business organization, she is responsible for overseeing global policy formulation and representing the interests of world business to governments and international organizations.

Before joining ICC, Ms Cattaui was the Managing Director of the World Economic Forum (WEF), responsible for its annual meeting in Davos, Switzerland. She was educated in the United States and is an Honours graduate of Harvard University.

For the last eight years **George Curmi** has been consulting on trade and project finance to international companies in Europe, the USA and the Far East. He was formerly deputy general manager of a Belgian Bank in London, specializing in trade finance. He stayed 22 years with that bank following an earlier career in commerce and six years with the foreign department of a UK clearing bank.

Since 1951 **Derrick Edwards** has been helping exporters and importers to use financial techniques which can add considerable profit or competitiveness without speculation. In the 1960s he struggled to bring them together by way of an Export Bank. In 1968 he saved one exporter £78,000, and was put in business to form Export Finance Consultants Ltd, and subsequently Forextec Ltd. His autobiography was published in 1998 and describes his six years in the Royal Navy, the ferocity of war at sea and a sinking ship; also his family background in the theatre ending with his work alongside Laurence Olivier at the Old Vic.

Michaela Eglin was the permanent representative to the United Nations and other international organizations of the International Chamber of Commerce in Geneva. One of her main activities was to follow developments in the WTO. Her previous career includes eight years at the World Bank in Washington as an editor and several consultancies at Geneva-based UN organizations. She has written on China's accession to the WTO for Chatham House and other specialized organizations and edited a volume on the results of the Uruguay Round of multilateral trade negotiations. She holds a BA degree in journalism from the University of Maryland and studied international economics at the Graduate Institute in Geneva.

After a career in the motor industry, both in manufacturing and retailing, **Gordon Hutt** joined SGS in 1977. Although based in the UK, he travelled extensively and worked in East and Central Africa, Australia, Latin America and the USA, eventually becoming director of the Global Trade Solutions Division in the UK. Now retired, he maintains contact with Africa through the WABA.

Amy Jackson was admitted as a solicitor in 1999 after training with Laytons in Bristol. She was then seconded to Bufete Mullerat in Barcelona and also worked for a law firm in Sydney before returning to join the company and commercial department of Laytons, London. Amy specializes in commercial agency and distribution matters and international trade and customs law. Laytons is a commercial law firm whose focus is commercial and finance, property and construction and personal.

John Merrett, an English solicitor, was a legal advisor in the Royal Dutch/ Shell Group for 27 years. He worked in many jurisdictions on dispute problems in the oil and chemicals businesses. Since retirement in 1996 he has become an arbitrator and the UK representative of the ICC International Court of Arbitration. He is a member of the ICC Commission which was responsible for drafting the ICC ADR Rules in 2000 and of the governing bodies of several international law institutions.

Fiona Mucklow was educated at Bristol University and the LSE and qualified as a solicitor in 2001. She specializes in international environmental law, and joined Clyde & Co in 1999 after serving with several international environmental agencies.

Kevin Newbold is a senior manager in the Deloitte & Touche Customs and International Trade Group. He has been a consultant since 1989, having previously worked with Customs & Excise for six years. He now advises multinational companies on the customs implications of the movement of goods globally.

Åke Nilson's professional specialization is e-commerce for trade. He holds an LL.M from Uppsala. After work in the London marine insurance market, he founded Marinade Limited, an e-commerce consultancy, in 1988, and Allagraf Limited, a software company in 2000. He has chaired the ICC's electronic commerce project since 1995.

Stephen Orava is a partner in the International Trade Group at King & Spalding International LLP in London. He represents clients on international trade regulatory matters in the European Union, the United States, and other countries. He also advises public and private clients on the negotiation and enforcement of WTO rules, and on market access strategy. Mr Orava has substantial experience before WTO dispute settlement panels and the Appellate Body, including the first cases under the WTO Anti-Dumping Agreement and the Safeguards Agreement.

Philippe Ruttley was educated at Oxford University and was called to the Bar in 1980 and later admitted as a solicitor in 1991. He is a partner and head of the EC and WTO Group at the leading international law firm of Clyde & Co, London. He specializes in EC competition law, public international law and WTO law. Since 1997, he has been secretary of the World Trade Law Association and has published extensively on EC and WTO issues. He is the co-author and editor of *The WTO and International Trade Regulation* (1998), *Liberalisation and Protectionism in the World Trading System* (1999) and *Due Process in WTO Dispute Resolution* (2001).

Stephen Tricks was educated at Oxford and has practised at Clyde & Co since 1980, becoming a partner in 1986. He specializes in international trade law, particularly dispute resolution. He lectures regularly for the ICC UK, international trade associations and London University.

Marc Weisberger was educated at Cambridge University, and was called to the Bar in 1998. He practises in the EC & WTO Group at Clyde & Co, London, where he specializes in all aspects of EC competition law, WTO law and public international law. His previous publications include *Due Process in WTO Dispute Settlement*, the 3rd Yearbook of the World Trade Law Association.

Foreword

Richard Bate, Director, ICC, UK

I was very pleased when Kogan Page and Jonathan Reuvid asked me to become involved in this *Handbook of World Trade* because the subject goes to the very core of why the ICC was founded in 1919. The world was just emerging from the horrors of World War I and a group of business people came together to found an organization that would work in the interests of international trade, in the hope that greater trade between nations would prevent a repeat of the war. This objective clearly did fail, but the organization that was created, the ICC, has grown from strength to strength. The ICC stands for free trade and, among the many things that we do in the interests of trade, we write the rules that enable international trade to take place.

The ICC was also partly responsible for the founding of the GATT, the predecessor to the World Trade Organization. Since 1946, we have worked closely with the GATT, and now the WTO, and it is even more appropriate, therefore, for us to be involved with this excellent publication. There are many well-known and skilled contributors. Michaela Eglin used to be the ICC's representative in Geneva, and she has unrivalled knowledge of the workings of the WTO, and we still maintain very close working relationships with the WTO in Geneva.

The technical aspects to conducting international trade are so important, and our three contributors are well-known experts in their field. Dispute resolution is the key activity of the ICC International Court of Arbitration, and John Merrett is our arbitration expert in ICC UK.

Managing foreign currencies is one of the issues that tends to frighten the smaller traders, so Derrick Edwards' contribution will be of particular interest to many readers. Part Four gets down to the important basics of being paid, and how to ensure that payment is timely. George Curmi has worked with the ICC for many years and is an expert in the ICC rules for documentary credits – UCP 500 (incorporating eUCP), and other aspects of trade finance.

In Part Five there are several articles on how to go about the physical part of international trade, what the pitfalls are and how best to avoid them. Finally, we deal with e-commerce. Åke Nilson was the Chairman of the ICC E-commerce project when it was first created, and he is now co-chair of the ICC's Special Advisory Group on e-related issues.

Some case histories and useful appendices make this handbook a 'must have' for all those who are involved in international trade. I would like to congratulate Jonathan Reuvid in bringing together so many experts so that we can all share in their knowledge and hopefully trade more successfully and less stressfully than before this handbook was produced.

Foreword

Adriaan Vickery FIEx, National Chairman,
The Institute of Export

In the beginning there was barter, followed by export and import, later defined as international trade. Bilateral relations became multilateral, which created trading blocs who supported their own with subsidies and technical and trade barriers, obscuring weakness in the competitive arena, creating unearned wealth, and depriving the nascent and latent of the opportunity to make a valid contribution. These became known as the developed.

Technology brought globalization, with communication, education, innovation and an awareness of the availability of emancipation, equality, and level playing fields. The uninformed found knowledge and began to form friendships with others of similar origins and backgrounds. The benefits of technology were used, in cultural terms, not to invent the wheel but to create a new grouping, ready to stake its claim to its share of the dream known as free trade. These were known as the developing.

Over the years, it became obvious that global considerations transcend imposed national narrowness in the creation of wealth. The importance of trade and the need for economic well being was common to all and, gradually, a global will evolved in an effort to resolve issues and differences on the road to the dream known as free trade. Thus the developed and the developing agreed to work towards all that the dream implied, no support for the unnecessary, the useless, the uncompetitive. On the other hand, free access to all trading places for all was deemed essential and certainly desirable. Each agreed the need to examine demands, both demanding and demanded, and it was agreed to arrive at a conclusion many years ahead – in 2004.

It swiftly became evident that those that had were reluctant to give it up, and that those that didn't had a lot that they were reluctant to give up. Thus subsidies might not be cut, nor would there be an end to corruption, excessive bureaucracy, improved investment rules, or tariff cuts. Political might, misjudgement, impatience, intolerance, pride, even arrogance became an issue, pushing more achievable multilateral and bilateral arrangements back to the fore. Despite this, the plan and the hope would always be for consensus – in the end, there was always barter.

Meanwhile, world trade continued, with all the attendant regulations, rules, tariffs and duties. Cultural and language differences abounded, as did all the variations in quality and safety standards. There were new demands, inherent to the globalization process, for greater corporate responsibility and concern for the environment, diversity, sustainability, health and safety, community, fair trade, and human rights values, all of which were now perceived as areas in which multinational and global organizations have influence and accountability.

The Institute of Export is delighted to be invited to be involved in this most useful source of reference and advice. Having worked with Jonathan Reuvid on previous occasions, we have come to know and respect him as a Sinologist, internationalist and strategy consultant. As an educationalist, and of particular interest to the Institute, he is engaged in the design and delivery of academically accredited educational business and management programmes. As an editor and publisher, he has involved himself in a variety of international trade and business books of the highest quality.

This particular work is intended for the practising international or global trader, as well as students of international trade operations and management, with many interesting and informative chapters written by experts in their own fields. It details, in context, the issues and processes referred to above, and achieves and informs in a thought provoking and valuable style, which is both useful and enjoyable.

Preface

Maria Livanos Cattaui, Secretary General, ICC

WHY THE DOHA ROUND MUST SUCCEED

How soon the logjam impeding the Doha trade round can be removed is anybody's guess. Deadlocks – followed by dramatic breakthroughs – have been par for the course in previous rounds. Still, this handbook went to press in February 2004, there were some hopeful signs. Both Robert Zoellick, the United States Trade Representative and European Union Trade Commissioner Pascal Lamy pushed for resumption of the negotiations. We shall see what we shall see.

The World Trade Organization must persevere in the search for final agreement, even if this takes longer than planned. No issue in world economic policy is more important than bringing the negotiations to a successful conclusion and thereby strengthening the multilateral trading system that has served the world well for more than half a century.

The official name for the round 'The Doha Development Agenda', reflects the resolve of the WTO governments, when they launched the round in November 2001, to take decisive action to open markets, especially to the agricultural products of the developing world. In the interest of a more stable world, this intention to bring hope and opportunity to the developing countries must not be disappointed.

Governments should not get too preoccupied with the 1 January 2005 deadline for completing the round, which has always seemed unrealistic. What matters is restoring momentum lost through the setback at the Cancún ministerial meeting in September, and that the final package represents a further significant advance in world trade liberalization.

All WTO governments must be ready to compromise, because the price of failure is too high for everyone. Resurgent protectionism is the last thing the still fragile world economy needs. Public confidence in effective international cooperation would be severely dented if the Doha round does not get off the ground.

A further danger is that governments might turn away from the multilateral trading system, with its disciplines that protect the weak and restrain the strong, and focus instead on bilateral and regional agreements that discriminate against countries that are excluded. There is ample evidence that this is already happening.

Such agreements give the partner with the strongest economic clout obvious advantages. Moreover, having to contend with a patchwork of such arrangements makes life even more complicated for businesses engaged in international trade.

The International Chamber of Commerce insists on the primacy of multilateral agreements as the most effective means to liberalize international trade. It sees bilateral or regional agreements as useful building blocks as long as they are in conformity with WTO rules.

With the presidential election looming in the United States and the European Union preoccupied with enlargement and selecting a new Commission, trade negotiators need to put aside political grandstanding and buckle down to securing genuine progress, the more unobtrusively the better. Results are what count, not headlines.

The much vaunted political will to succeed, often evoked by political leaders, must be translated into genuine give and take at the negotiating table among the WTO member governments for the common good of all.

The key to a successful Doha round will be the willingness of the United States, the European Union and Japan to roll back agricultural protection. The aim must be to reduce trade-distorting agricultural support, thereby liberalizing agricultural trade and improving market access. The text agreed in Doha foresaw countries accepting an end date for phasing out all agricultural subsidies.

ICC has suggested that the WTO governments concentrate on key outstanding issues, building as a starting point on the draft ministerial text that was submitted at Cancún. The priorities should be:

- agreement on agriculture;
- agreement on market access for industrial products, with greater attention paid to non-tariff barriers;
- progress on each of the so-called Singapore issues – competition, investment, trade facilitation and transparency in government procurement – on their own merit and at their own pace.

Estimates abound that show the benefits trade liberalization brings to the world economy. According to the University of Michigan, removing all barriers to trade would add $1.9 trillion to the global economy. While liberalization to that extent is plainly unattainable, the study also estimates that reducing barriers by one third would raise output by about $613 billion – about the size of the Canadian economy.

The Doha round remains an opportunity to win benefits for rich and poor nations alike and to build a trading system in harmony with the global economy of the 21st century. It is an opportunity that must not be missed.

Introduction

Jonathan Reuvid

This second edition of *A Handbook of World Trade* sets out to cover the same broad canvass of content as the first edition and is fully updated to the third quarter of 2003. As before, the twin objectives are to offer practical business guidance to companies seeking to expand their international trading activities and to provide a comprehensive background briefing on the evolution of the World Trade Organization (WTO) and its leading role in the development of freer global markets within the framework of WTO rules.

CONTENTS

The book is arranged in five distinct parts, which address both corporate readers and those engaged in the study of international trade.

Part One focuses on the WTO, the pivotal role of the International Chamber of Commerce (ICC) and the macro-statistics of world trade. For corporate strategists and traders who, like myself prior to the development of this book are largely ignorant of WTO history and its functions, the first four chapters provide important background knowledge. We are especially grateful to Steve Orava of King & Spalding International, who attended the ministerial meeting of the WTO in Cancun in September 2003 and has contributed a new chapter covering China's WTO entry in December 2001 and the status of the present Doha round.

Chapter 1.6 on the patterns and trends in international trade has been updated to include detailed statistics for 2001 and headline data through to mid-2003.

Part Two is of a more technical nature, covering the regulatory issues and conflicts in international trade, how disputes between WTO members arise and are processed within WTO rules and general dispute resolution. In chapter

2.1, Kevin Newbold of Deloitte & Touche provides an overview of customs duties and tax. In the following six chapters Philippe Ruttley and his colleagues at Clyde & Co., London, the leading law firm specializing in EC competition law, public international law and WTO law, provide detailed briefings, mainly from an EC perspective, on the key issues which give rise to disputes within the WTO and conflict between companies in respect of WTO rules. In the last chapter of Part Two, John Merrett, an associate of ICC's London office, has updated his guidance on disputes resolution through arbitration mechanisms.

Part Three, devoted to the management of foreign exchange in international trade, is written by Derrick Edwards, a doyen of the subject, who has been promoting the cause of effective currency management without risk for more than forty years. The numerous worked examples in the text demonstrate how additional profits can be won by structuring transactions in the supplier's, the customer's or a neutral currency and making forward provision for foreign exchange settlement.

Since almost half the world's exports are still denominated in US dollars, not even the foreign trade of Eurozone members is immune from these issues.

Part Four is a detailed guide to the the alternative forms of trade finance commonly available and their accompanying documentation. Written by George Curmi, an acknowledged expert in trade finance and the ICC rules for documentary credits, this section of the book emphasises the necessity of getting right the minutiae of documentation for all trade transactions. Chapter 4.7 on legal precedents, previously tabled as an appendix, is co-authored by Stephen Tricks of Clyde & Co. and George Curmi; it highlights the penalties of ambiguity and how heavy the costs are of getting it wrong. An additional section on political risk has been included in this edition, also written by George Curmi and edited by Paul Sweasey of Benfield Limited, a specialist in this field. These chapters are essential reading for all those engaging in international trade or exploring alternative financing mechanisms.

Part Five discusses some of the key practical issues in the development of international trade from researching markets and the appointment of agents and distributors through freight and logistics to trading online and directors' liabilities. Written by experienced practitioners, this section of the book revisits and updates conventional processes in the context of today's communications technology and open access to global information.

The text is supported in the Appendices by reference data, contact lists, examples of trade documentation and reading lists for those wishing to explore specific topics or the processes of international trade in greater depth.

I am indebted to our co-publishers, ICC Publishing SA, for the provision of much of this background material.

Finally, my thanks to Maria Livanos Cattaui, Secretary General of the ICC for her Preface and to Richard Bate, Director of ICC (UK) and Adriaan Vickery, National Chairman of the UK's Institute of Export, for their Forewords. Their continuing support for the book since its inception has been a great source of encouragement.

THE CURRENT OUTLOOK FOR WORLD TRADE

Our book goes to print three months after the collapse of the Cancun ministerial meeting and immediately following this month's meeting in Geneva at which little progress was made. The immediate outlook for the WTO and world trade itself is depressing. There is no shortage of candidates for the role of villain in the inevitable blame session that has ensued. Large high-profile ministerial meetings are hardly the most promising forum to reach agreement on detailed trade issues where perceived national self-interest rules and some alternative way forward must now be found.

The facts of life in international trade are that the top 20 importers account for 80 per cent of merchandise trade, counting the EU as a single state. If the concept of an outcome binding on every WTO member were to be abandoned, a negotiation among about 30 countries (again including the EU as one unit) with commitment to any agreement would be more likely to produce a positive result. In the meantime, in the absence of general agreement, bilateral deals will probably proliferate.

List of Abbreviations and Acronyms

AAA	American Arbitration Association
ADR	alternative dispute resolution
AoA	Agreement on Agriculture
ASEAN	Association of South-East Asian Nations
B2B	business-to-business
BIFA	British International Freight Association
BS	British Standards
CA	Certification Authority
CAP	Common Agricultural Policy
CEMA	HM Customs and Excise Management Act 1979
CFI	EC Court of First Instance
CIC	Credit Industriel et Commercial
CIF	Cost Insurance Freight
CITES	Convention against the International Trade in Endangered Species
CMB	China Merchants Bank
CRF	clean report of findings
DDA	Doha Development Agenda
DG Trade	Directorate-General for External Relations
DSB	Dispute Settlement Body
DSM	Dispute Settlement Mechanism
DSU	Dispute Settlement Understanding
EC	European Community
ECGD	Export Credit Guarantee Department
ECJ	European Court of Justice
ECP	Electronic Commerce Project (ICC)
ECU	European currency unit
EDI	electronic data interchange
EEC	European Economic Community
EFTA	European Free Trade Area

EMS	European Monetary System
EU	European Union
EUROFER	European Confederation of Iron and Steel Industries
FEDERTESSILE	Italian Textile Foundation
FCA	Free Carrier
FIATA	International Federation of Freight Forwarders Association
FOB	Free on Board
GATS	General Agreement on Trade in Services
GATT	General Agreement on Tariffs and Trade
GSP	General System of Preferences
GUIDEC	General Usage for Internationally Digitally Ensured Commerce (ICC)
ICC	International Chamber of Commerce
IFIA	International Federation of Inspection Agencies
IFIA	International Federation of Inspection Agencies
ILSA	Iran and Libya Sanctions Act
IMF	International Monetary Fund
IOE	Institute of Export
ISBP	International Standard Banking Practice
ISO	International Standards
ISP	International Standby Practices
ITO	International Trade Organization
LCIA	London Court of International Arbitration
LDC(s)	less developed country/countries
LIFFE	London International Financial Futures Exchange
MFA	Multifibre Arrangement
MFN	most favoured nation
NAFTA	North American Free Trade Agreement
NVOC	non-vessel owning carrier
OECD	Organization for Economic Cooperation and Development
OEM	original equipment manufacturer
OMA	orderly marketing arrangement
OPEC	Organization of the Petroleum Exporting Countries
PKI	public key infrastructure
Pofec	Principles of Fair Electronic Contracting (ICC)
PSI	pre-shipment inspection service
QR	quantitative restrictions

RTA	regional trade agreement
SGS	Société Générale de Surveillance SA
SPS	Agreement on Sanitary and Phytosanitary Measures
SWIFT	Society for Worldwide Interbank Financial Telecommunication
TBR	Trade Barriers Regulation
TBT	technical barriers to trade
TIMS	Trade-related Investment Measures Agreement
TRIPS	Agreement on Trade-Related Aspects of Intellectual Property Rights
TPRM	Trade Policy Review Mechanism
UCP 400	earlier version: Uniform Customs and Practice for Documentary Credits
UCP 500	Uniform Customs and Practice for Documentary Credits
UNCITRAL	United Nations Commission on International Trade Law
UNCTAD	United Nations Conference on Trade and Development
URC	Uniform Rules for Collection
URCB	Uniform Rules for Contract Bonds
URDG	Uniform Rules for Demand Guarantees
VAT	value added tax
VER	voluntary export restraint
WCF	World Chambers Federation
WCN	World Chambers Network
WIPO	World Intellectual Property Organization
WTO	World Trade Organization

Part 1

The Origins and Nature of the World Trade Organization

The Development of Multilateral Trade Agreements

Michaela Eglin, formerly ICC, Geneva

INTRODUCTION

The rules-based multilateral trading system as we know it today is relatively young and had its origins in the middle of the 20th century. It arose from the ashes of World War II in reaction to the protectionist tariff walls and quota restrictions that had been steadily erected (with some reprieve) since the end of the 19th century. Together with the financial crisis and depression of the 1930s, these barriers had brought international trade to a virtual standstill.

Between 1948 and 1994, multilateral trade in goods was governed by the General Agreement on Tariffs and Trade (GATT). Eight successive rounds of multilateral trade negotiations achieved not only a remarkable reduction in restrictive border measures (from double-digit tariffs to an average of 4 per cent on industrial goods) and non-tariff barriers, but also an ever-increasing acceleration in the growth of world trade. The Uruguay Round, which lasted from 1986 to 1993, for the first time incorporated trade in services, agriculture, intellectual property rights and textiles into the process of liberalization. It also provided for the creation of a new institution, the World Trade Organization (WTO), which was established in January 1995. The GATT, its underlying principles, provisions and disciplines, as amended and complemented over time, continue to be an integral part of the WTO Agreements. This historical overview looks at the antecedents to multilateral trade, the main elements of the treaty framework, the major developments that inspired and impeded the objectives of governments, and the challenges that remain at the outset of the third millennium.

ANTECEDENTS TO THE GATT

The GATT began as a chapter in the larger design for an International Trade Organization (ITO) that was to be the third pillar of the neo-liberal post-war institutions together with the World Bank and the International Monetary Fund (IMF). However, the ITO never came into being because the US Congress refused to ratify it. This did not prevent the USA from spearheading multilateral tariff negotiations and masterminding the drafting of a multilateral treaty governing commercial relations among participating countries. The role of the USA was then, and continues to be, crucial in moving countries along the path of trade liberalization, albeit not always in a consistent manner.

In the early part of the 20th century the USA pursued a high tariff policy (including the prohibitive Smoot-Hawley tariff imposed in 1930), but did not use quantitative restrictions. In contrast, European countries employed highly restrictive trade and exchange rate policies, with a strong preference for quantitative and direct import controls as an antidote to currency devaluation, used to circumvent high protective tariffs ('beggar-thy-neighbour' policies) during the inter-war years. US foreign trade policy was reversed with the 1934 Reciprocal Trade Agreements Act, which called for less state intervention and the restoration of the free play of market forces in international trade. It authorized the President of the USA to negotiate tariff reductions and signalled the end of 60 years of unilateral tariff setting by congressional action (Low, 1975). From then on, under periodic extensions of the 1934 Act, the USA engaged in bilateral tariff bargaining on the basis of non-discrimination and the unconditional most-favoured nation clause, which automatically conferred any agreed tariff concessions to its trading partners.

However, it soon became apparent that tariff bargaining in the presence of discriminatory quantitative restrictions failed to secure fair import shares from its European trading partners. This convinced the USA early on that the elimination of quantitative restrictions was essential. But the damage had been done. The economic hardship and political discord generated by the practice of competitive currency devaluation, combined with tariff wars, count among the main causes of World War II.

By the early 1940s, work under the Atlantic Charter, on what was to become the Bretton Woods system, was led by Harry Dexter White from the US Treasury and Lord Maynard Keynes from the UK. They agreed on the need for a mutually reinforcing, rules-based international payments and trading system, but not on the modalities. Deliberations on bringing order into international financial, monetary, and exchange rate relations at first overshadowed trade concerns. Strong disagreement also prevailed on the principle of non-discrimination, which was dear to the USA, while the UK insisted on continuing preferential treatment for the Commonwealth countries, placing the latter and social policies before trade. But the more fundamental problem was a philosophical one: post-war plans and policy makers were strongly influenced by Keynesian economics, whereas for US proponents of freer trade the idea of government intervention in support of full employment policies was anathema.

In 1945, the US Congress renewed the reciprocal trade agreements legislation for three years, paving the way for a multilateral agreement on the mutual reduction of tariffs. Under the auspices of the USA and the newly created United Nations (UN), the charter for an international organization dealing with trade issues was drawn up. A draft produced in Geneva in 1947 dealt with three issues:

- the charter for the ITO;
- multilateral negotiations on the mutual reduction of tariffs;
- general clauses of obligations relating to the tariff commitments.

Only the latter two parts drafted by the USA survived, in the form of the GATT. There was a certain concern for the need to press ahead with some form of multilateral agreement on tariff deductions on a provisional basis before the US negotiating authority expired in 1948.

Opposition to the proposed ITO charter was rife. The charter included chapters on employment, development, antitrust, investment, agriculture and substantial exceptions to liberal trade rules. The International Chamber of Commerce (ICC), representing the liberal and business thinking of that time, was one of its most outspoken critics. It was considered that the charter encouraged the use of trade restrictions as a remedy for domestic policy mistakes and to accord precedence to national full employment policies at the expense of international cooperation (Curzon, 1965). Permission to use discriminatory quantitative restrictions for balance of payments purposes was seen to negate the very objectives the new organization was to fulfil. Ultimately, though approved at the UN Conference on Trade and Employment held in Havana, Cuba, between November 1947 and March 1948, the ITO failed to come into existence. The US Congress took the view that the 1945 Act under which tariff-negotiating authority was extended did not allow the President of the USA to enter into an agreement on the creation of an international organization. Consequently, the request for congressional ratification was withdrawn.

NATURE AND FUNCTIONS OF THE GATT[1]

The GATT was both a multilateral treaty and an instrument to ensure the functioning of the treaty by virtue of its secretariat in Geneva, Switzerland, which was the former interim commission for the ITO. It was a legal framework, a forum for negotiations aimed at reducing tariffs and quantitative restrictions, and a forum to settle trade-related disputes among members. Although the GATT was conceived as a stop-gap measure until the ITO became functional, its temporary status was made 'permanent' by the Provisional Protocol of Application. It entered into effect in January 1948, while the Havana Conference was still under way. Although it operated like an organization, legally the GATT never had that status. A renewed attempt in 1955 to turn it into a proper institution failed. The GATT's permanent uncertainty, indistinct identity and awkward acronym went a long way towards protecting it from public scrutiny, and allowed it to carry out its mandate of reducing border restrictions quietly and effectively. The GATT's existence can be split into three distinct phases:

- the tariff and quota cycle: between 1948 and 1968 under the continuous leadership of Windham White, when the GATT was a club of 'old hands' directly involved in its creation, who negotiated the agreement and knew it inside out;
- the Tokyo Round era (1973–1979) of non-tariff barriers under the guidance of Director General Olivier Long;
- the pre- and intra-Uruguay Round years (1984–1996) presided over by Arthur Dunkel from 1980–93, who steered the GATT through a sea change in the global trading system and prepared it for its new mission.

By and large, the GATT's structure did not stand in the way of fulfilling its basic mission and attracting new adherents.

One of the challenges of the GATT was to manage the contradiction inherent in its dual function as guardian of positive law and facilitator of diplomatic negotiations to reach compromise on trade agreements or disputes with the objective of establishing new procedures and new rules. The legal framework of the GATT consisted of rules and a patchwork of exceptions with enough formal or informal mechanisms to soften legal norms under

---

[1] The original contracting parties were: Australia, Belgium, Brazil, Burma, Canada, Ceylon, Chile, the Republic of China, Cuba, Czechoslovakia, France, India, Lebanon, Luxembourg, the Netherlands, New Zealand, Norway, Pakistan, Southern Rhodesia, Syria, South Africa, the UK and the USA.

certain circumstances (Jackson, 1969). Over time, new amendments of the rules and formal or informal (ie tacitly approved by the members) exceptions to the rules were introduced, creating a highly complex legal instrument and set of procedures. A degree of obfuscation suited some trade diplomats who hoped to find justification for a given measure their government may have had to introduce in contravention of GATT rules and disciplines. However, the increasingly diverse membership and growing economic interdependence left less room for diplomacy and demanded a more legalistic approach to GATT operations. As the old GATT hands were replaced, trade liberalization was beginning to impinge upon perceived prerogatives of national policy making, opening up a new era of negotiations.

BASIC RULES AND PRINCIPLES

The preamble of the GATT states as objectives:

- the raising of living standards;
- ensuring full employment;
- rising real income and effective demand;
- developing the full use of the world's resources;
- expanding the production and exchange of goods.

The contracting parties would contribute to achieving these goals, 'by entering into reciprocal and mutually advantageous arrangements directed to the substantial reduction of tariffs and other barriers to trade and to the elimination of discriminatory treatment in international commerce'.[2] This wording conveys the goal to have freer, not free, trade, while making non-discrimination the pillar of the multilateral trading system.

The principle of non-discrimination is further elaborated in Article I on most-favoured nation (MFN) treatment and Article III on national treatment. Through the MFN rule, the type and method of trade privileges granted to the products of one trading partner automatically and unconditionally apply to the like products of all contracting parties. The least that can be said is that, over time, the principle of unconditional MFN treatment suffered from erosion and in some instances gave way to the practice of conditional MFN. The national treatment clause says that imported products must be treated the same as domestic products in terms of taxation, marketing, distribution and

---

[2] The General Agreement on Tariffs and Trading (GATT 1947, as amended) GATT Secretariat, Geneva, Switzerland. Annexed to the legal texts 1994, p486.

transport. It implicitly ensures that domestic legislation and administrative measures do not constitute a form of protectionism against foreign products. The main exceptions to the principle of non-discrimination are customs unions and free trade areas (Article XXIV), general exceptions to protect public safety and national security (Articles XX and XXI), and an exemption of a historical nature, which allowed the continuance of preferences granted to former colonial territories when the GATT entered into force.

Some of the external changes that weakened the principle of non-discrimination were:

- the emergence of the European Economic Community and the grand-fathering of preferential arrangements of individual contracting parties;
- the emergence of developing countries as they gained independence, and their integration into the multilateral trading system;
- the accession of non-market economies in the late 1960s and early 1970s (Yugoslavia in 1966, Poland in 1967, Romania in 1971, and Hungary in 1973) for geopolitical reasons. This allowed contracting parties, for example, to use discriminatory quantitative restrictions against imports of the newly acceded countries.

The second most important principle of the GATT is enshrined in Article XI, which provides for the general elimination of quantitative restrictions (QRs). It specifically prescribes the exclusive use of duties, taxes or other charges, ie price-based measures, in restricting imports or exports. Although the trade-distorting effects of QRs, by interfering with the price mechanism and obscuring market signals, are well established, the prohibition of QRs was weakened by numerous exceptions, including:

- agricultural and fisheries products, to ensure stable domestic market conditions. Although the GATT does not distinguish between industrial and agricultural products, the exemptions to Article XI paved the way for hardcore agricultural protectionism from the mid-1950s onwards. Surpluses built up in the major exporting countries with governments heavily subsidizing agricultural production as war-torn Europe recovered and food shortages disappeared. The USA, for example, requested a waiver from its GATT obligations in 1951 to allow itself to impose discriminatory import restrictions on dairy products. In 1955 it obtained a general agricultural waiver to implement agricultural domestic price support measures. After 1957, with the Treaty of Rome and the establishment of the European Economic Community (EEC) and the European Free Trade Area (EFTA), agricultural protectionism enjoyed a practically free reign;

- protecting balance of payments equilibrium for a limited period of time subject to periodic consultation with the IMF under Article XII;
- quantitative restrictions imposed by developing countries to protect their balance of payments and vulnerable domestic industries for a given amount of time (the infant industry exception) under Article XVIII.B;
- safeguard provisions in Article XIX allowed for the use of non-discriminatory QRs to protect against sudden surges of imports that cause, or threaten to cause, serious injury to domestic industry. Such measures had to be compensated and limited in time. In view of the cumbersome procedures involved, countries tended to resort to other measures, such as extracting voluntary export restraints from trading partners. The lack of appropriate multilateral safeguard disciplines was considered to be a major weakness of the GATT.

The primary objective being that of reducing tariff barriers to trade, a central feature of the GATT is the commitment to limit tariff levels through bindings or concessions in schedules, as provided for in Article II. These voluminous schedules list detailed product descriptions and a specific or *ad valorem* tariff level, which constitutes the treaty obligation for that product or that country (Jackson, 1989). A bound tariff is a maximum ceiling that cannot be raised without compensating the affected contracting parties. Unbound tariffs can be set at any level, and many developing countries have short schedules, giving them ample discretion to raise or lower tariffs. Bindings have injected invaluable discipline into maintaining tariff schedules and helped secure a predictable trading environment. Together, Articles I and II form Part I of the GATT, amendments of which require unanimity.

Part II (Articles III–XVII) comprise most of the substantive obligations and instruct governments as to how to regulate their international trade (Jackson, 1989). The disciplines apply to both imports and exports, although the rules are mostly relevant for imports. They include anti-dumping and countervailing duties (Article VI), customs valuation (Article VII), procedures of customs administration (Articles VIII and X), subsidies (XVI), state trading monopolies (Article XVII).

Part III, besides provisions for regional arrangements (Article XXIV), deals mostly with administrative provisions, such as waivers of obligations (XXV) including voting requirements, the modification of tariff schedules (XXVIII), periodic negotiations to achieve progressive substantial reduction of tariffs (Article XXVIIIbis), accession (XXXIII), and the non-application of the Agreement (XXXV).

Part IV, added in 1964, addresses the problem facing developing countries.

Dispute settlement procedures of the GATT were essentially dealt with in Articles XXII on Consultation and XXIII on the Nullification and Impairment of Benefits. Emphasis was placed on conciliation efforts. Failing those, the complaint could be submitted for consideration by the contracting parties acting jointly. The latter was the highest decision-making body of the GATT, charged with the operation and promotion of the objectives of the Agreement. Although it was governed by majority vote, there was a preference for consensus decisions. Formal voting was reserved for waivers, membership and treaty amendments. The consensus approach was a problem in disputes when Council approval was sought and the country at fault could block consensus. Dispute settlement came to be considered as a major weakness of the GATT, and was substantially improved as a result of the Uruguay Round.

GATT business was carried out by an elaborate group of committees, working parties, panels and other bodies. The most important body was the Council, set up in 1960 to take care of day-to-day GATT business. This increasingly became a process of managing relations between national capitals and the Geneva-based secretariat and representatives or government delegates.

ACHIEVEMENTS OF THE GATT

The early GATT negotiating rounds (five) focused on tariff reductions and were concluded within one year. Participants rose from the original 23 contracting parties to 48 at the end of the Kennedy Round in 1967. The value of trade involved rose from US$10 billion to US$40 billion. However, this progress in lowering tariffs was countered by domestic producers increasingly taking recourse to non-tariff barriers to replace the protection high tariffs had offered. The Tokyo Round placed priority on tackling non-tariff barriers. Membership had risen to 99 countries and the value of trade covered was US$155 billion (Jackson, 1990). In contrast, the value of trade covered in the Uruguay Round amounted to US$3,700 billion (Jackson, 1998).

By the 1970s, the GATT was not just one treaty instrument but a collection of treaties, including agreements to amend the GATT. Most of the substantive treaties were added during the Tokyo Round, which for the first time addressed the problem of non-tariff measures, partly by clarifying and strengthening existing rules and disciplines, and extended the scope of GATT coverage. In addition to tariff reduction protocols, the Tokyo Round yielded three Arrangements on Bovine Meat, Dairy, and Trade in Civil Aircraft; six special agreements or Codes, covering technical barriers to trade (TBTs), anti-dumping, import licensing procedures, customs valuation, subsidies, and government procurement; and four Understandings (or 'Framework' agreements) were agreed upon.

The Codes attracted much criticism and controversy because on the one hand they were stand-alone treaties with signature clauses and their own dispute settlement mechanism (binding only those nations that signed and ratified them and creating confusion as to whether GATT dispute mechanism procedures or that of the Codes applied). On the other hand, some of them were directly related to GATT Articles (eg Agreement on Implementation of Article VI – Anti-dumping) with contracting parties who had not signed on to the Codes arguing that they do not bind them.

The Tokyo Round also achieved some solid results for developing countries with the Decision on Differential and More Favourable Treatment, Reciprocity and Fuller Participation of Developing Countries, known as the Enabling Clause. It provided a legal basis for those industrialized countries that wished to give preferential market access to products from developing countries through a national General System of Preferences (GSP). As such, the enabling clause provided legal cover for what amounted to a violation of the MFN principle. Developing countries had become more vocal with the establishment of the United Nations Conference on Trade and Development and the addition of Part IV in the GATT in 1964. The latter was largely symbolic in encouraging industrialized countries to take into account the special problems and needs of developing countries and to refrain from creating additional barriers to their trade. A novel addition was wording that released developing countries from the principle of reciprocity in trade negotiations.

As successful as the GATT was in bringing average tariff levels on industrial products to about 4.7 per cent in the Tokyo Round, it was a total failure in two important sectors (agriculture and textiles and clothing). Although, in principle, GATT rules covered all products, agriculture was dominated by government intervention. From the early 1950s onwards, with the blessing of GATT waivers, the USA and later the European Community (EC) heavily subsidized domestic production and protected high internal prices through both tariffs and import quotas. The problem was exacerbated in the early 1970s when the former Soviet Union entered world grain markets as a food importer and raised the spectre of world food shortages and dramatic price rises. The USA blundered by placing an embargo on soya beans and, a few years later, on grain sales to the Soviet Union. As a result, agricultural trade became highly distorted. The EC later compounded the damage with its extensive use of export subsidies under the Common Agricultural Policy.

By the early 1980s, however, the USA had revamped its agricultural sector and was desperately looking to find export markets. It was therefore not surprising that the first call for a new multilateral trade round came from the USA in 1982 at the GATT Ministerial meeting in Geneva – barely three years after the conclusion of the Tokyo Round. In the event, the US proposal, which had agricultural reform as a centrepiece, was rebuffed, its major trading partners showing little interest breaking a cycle that for once was in their favour. To halt this corrosive process, the USA led a movement to combat unfair trade practices by other countries, especially Japan, which was to dominate the 1980s and which is still in practice at the beginning of 21st century (Yeutter, 1998).

Rules and disciplines leading to the reform and liberalization of the agricultural sector were finally put in place as a result of the Uruguay Round. But that process is far from completed, and the role of agriculture inside the multilateral trading system continues to divide major trading partners, such as for example, the USA and the Cairns Group[3] of agricultural exporters, on the one hand, and the European Community, Switzerland and Japan, on the other, and both of those groups and the developing countries.

Trade in textiles and clothing was central to discussions begun in 1981 regarding the crisis of the GATT and how to deal with outstanding problems. Agreements on special rules for textiles and apparel preceded the Kennedy Round and the Tokyo Round, the last being the Multifibre Arrangement (MFA). The MFA was a derogation from the GATT, and open to both contracting parties and outsiders. With the exception of Japan, all the countries subject to MFA restrictions were developing and Eastern European countries.

The Uruguay Round succeeded in bringing textiles and clothing under the WTO umbrella, by providing for a structured phase-out of the discriminatory quota system by end-2004. It remains to be seen whether or not textile importers will be ready and willing to submit this sector to WTO rules by that deadline.

---

[3] The Cairns Group, consisting of 18 agricultural developed and developing country exporters, was created in August 1986 under Australian leadership to promote agricultural trade reform.

THE END OF AN ERA

The GATT's narrow mandate, the rapidly growing membership and the exposure of public and private protective measures at the domestic level with the decline in tariff barriers, ultimately rendered the GATT constitution and structure inadequate. It can be and has been argued that the GATT was a mere smokescreen behind which countries played out real protectionist scenarios. The strict emphasis on lowering tariffs and eliminating quantitative restrictions, or border measures, in fact gave governments a strong, but possibly wrong, feeling of control over national policies. In fact, the continuous growth of international trade to the mutual benefit of all trading partners required increasing coordination of national policies, production methods and standards. In that sense, the opponents of the stillborn ITO were right in their criticism that the Havana Charter gave free licence to protectionist measures in the face of macroeconomic mismanagement and imbalances. Be that as it may, the GATT has played a monumental role in liberalizing trade despite the ever-present threat of protectionism hovering over the trading system.

The history of the GATT is testimony to the fickle role of trade policy and the fine line governments have had to tread in ensuring prosperity and satisfying the demands of domestic constituents. This may go some way towards explaining the insistence by contracting parties on discretion, secrecy and privacy in conducting GATT work and negotiations. Guarding the secrecy of tariff offers and requests was considered an essential negotiating tactic, a requirement anchored in GATT rules. Until the Tokyo Round, the GATT operated in relative obscurity. However, as trade obstacles shifted from the border to the domestic policy arena and market access, a level playing field and transparency became the new battle cries. The institution and the process were subject to growing public scrutiny and criticism. Indeed, the requirement for transparency in government regulations and procedures on all matters regarding trade became a basic principle enshrined in WTO agreements.

Aside from dealing with the two renegade sectors, the need for a new round, negotiating voiced soon after the Tokyo Round, included the following reasons, notably:

- the appearance of new subjects, eg services, intellectual property and trade-related investment measures;
- concern about the relationship between the Tokyo Codes and the GATT;
- dissatisfaction with the GATT's dispute settlement procedure;

- the quasi-acceptance of the circumvention of GATT rules through grey area measures, such as voluntary export restraints, prior import deposit schemes etc;
- 'fair' trade practices in the form of stepped-up anti-dumping and counter-vailing action that accompanied liberalization;
- rapid changes in the world economy and growing interdependence due to technological innovation and breakthroughs in wireless and digital communications;
- renewed recognition of the value of international rules for keeping domestic excesses in check;
- burgeoning membership;
- the need for a new and stronger GATT constitution.

After four years of intense and strenuous preparation, the Uruguay Round was launched in Punta del Este in 1986 under the leadership of Arthur Dunkel. It was apparent from the outset that this round would be like no other. It would go beyond border measures deep into the realm of domestic regulatory policy and be driven by new negotiating dynamics. Developing countries would play a major role and new alliances would cut across North–South divides, such as the Cairns Group of agricultural exporters, including Canada and Australia, and several developing countries. It would be a long haul.

REFERENCES

Curzon, G (1965) *Multilateral Commercial Diplomacy*, Michael Joseph, London, p34

Jackson, JH (1989) *The World Trading System* MIT Press, Cambridge, Mass, p118, ibid., p40

Jackson, JH (1969) *World Trade and the Law of GATT*, Bobbs-Merrill, Indianapolis, pp35–46 and 535–536

Jackson, JH (1990) *Restructuring the GATT System* Chatham House Papers, The Royal Institute of International Affairs, London, p37

Jackson, JH (1998) *The World Trade Organization – Constitution and Juris-prudence* Chatham House Papers, The Royal Institute of International Affairs, London, p21

Low, P (1975) *Trading Free – The GATT and US Trade Policy* Twentieth Century Fund Press, New York, p37

Yeutter, C (1998) 'Bringing agriculture into the multilateral trading system' *The Uruguay Round and Beyond: Essays in Honour of Arthur Dunkel* Springer Verlag, Berlin, p63

Before, During and After the Uruguay Round

Michaela Eglin, formerly ICC, Geneva

BUILDING UP MOMENTUM

The 1980s was a momentous decade for the world economy. In the aftermath of two oil shocks, a worldwide recession was marked by double-digit interest, unemployment and inflation rates in the USA and elsewhere. At the same time, macroeconomic imbalances were evident in misalignments of exchange rates, while foreign investment continued to grow and economies became increasingly open, as shown by high trade to gross domestic product (GDP) ratios. Meanwhile, US farmers were on the brink of revolt, as high prices and farm support systems, especially under the European Community Common Agricultural Policy (CAP), had led to huge surplus production in grains and other farm produce. In addition, a strong US dollar lowered competitiveness of US exports on world markets and caused unprecedented trade deficits. It allowed newcomers, in particular Japan, to challenge the USA's position as the number one economy in the world.

HARASSMENT IN BETWEEN ROUNDS

Dissatisfied with the way the General Agreement on Tariffs and Trade (GATT) did or did not represent their trading interests, the USA embarked on a path of unilateral activism in trade matters, backed up by tough domestic trade legislation. In order to deal with perceived unfair trading practices of its trading partners it resorted to two main forms of action: one consisted of extracting unilateral trade concession from others in the form of voluntary export restraints (VERs), orderly marketing arrangements (OMAs), and similar arrangements collectively known as grey area measures. The second sought to pursue countries that unfairly subsidized their exports or dumped goods in the imports market at below-cost prices.

Traditionally, the concept of unfair trade did not play a role in economics, because unilateral trade liberalization is considered to benefit a country, regardless of the actions of the trading partner. The GATT being founded on the mercantilist principles of reciprocity and mutual concessions, however, has a built-in fair trade mechanism by allowing contracting parties to impose countervailing duties against foreign subsidization of exports and anti-dumping duties against presumed predatory effects of dumping. To face off the threat of Japanese competitors in some high technology industries thought to benefit from government support, a concerted battle against import competition was waged by extending fair trade mechanisms to export markets and third markets. At the same time, new areas were targeted as they were thought to impede market access, such as differences in retail distribution systems, savings rates and workers' rights. Although the USA was not alone in resorting to anti-dumping and countervailing procedures on a regular basis during the 1980s, it did so more frequently than Canada, Australia and the European Community (EC). In addition, although in most of the US cases there were positive findings of subsidization or dumping, the proof of determination of injury to domestic industry was less often the case (Low, 1993).

The new protectionism, and threat to the multilateral trading system that characterized the 1980s, was enshrined in sectoral trading arrangements to protect domestic industry against successful competitors. It mainly involved the three major players, the USA, Japan and the EC, agreeing on trading restraints under threat of more severe action. The most famous arrangements concerned the sectors of steel, textiles and clothing, and automobiles and semiconductors, where a combination of cultural, social and political factors made Japan vulnerable to accusations of unfair trading by US and EC industries that felt threatened or were just plain inefficient. Over time, fair trade rhetoric and crowbar politics became favoured tools for achieving market access. Aggressive unilateralism was about demanding access to foreign markets while shielding domestic industry from having to adjust to competition from world markets.

Pressure for a new trade round built up as the reduction of average tariffs in industrialized countries to very low levels during successive GATT rounds and the accelerating changes in economic activity and international inter-dependence required regulatory, institutional and structural adaptation. In particular, the industrialized countries considered that, with the cycle of shallow integration completed, that of deep integration had to be embarked on by dismantling hidden discriminatory domestic practices that were inimical to trade. The relevance of the GATT and the survival of the multilateral trading system were at stake. The necessary dynamism and growth was seen to come from devising multilateral rules for new activities, like services with which the USA had built up a comparative advantage, and from integrating developing countries at a time when some of them had made great economic strides through a strong export performance. For example, certain Asian Tiger economies, so called because of the fast-growing economies in the 1970s and 1980s based on aggressive export policies, came to be regarded as free riders that no longer deserved exemptions from GATT rules, and special and differential treatment.

Worldwide mobility of different production phases and processes, as a result of increased foreign investment, called for more uniformity in international standards. The activities of multinational companies drew attention to the need for harnessing globalization and adapting the rules to further trade in this new global environment. Many of the developing countries were not yet prepared to follow the style and pace of development imposed by industrialized countries. It was not until the early to mid-1990s that they acknowledged that the open market model yielded more benefits for them than protection. Such recalcitrance inspired a group of like-minded countries, led by the USA, into thinking that the multilateral trading system should be open only to those willing and capable to abide by the rules of the system.

The GATT seemed to have lost its grip on the multilateral trading system, unable to discipline its greatest guarantor, the USA, which behaved like a pariah of the system. Some blamed the GATT approach or 'old hands' diplomacy, which went a long way towards accommodating individual nations' trade interests and adjustment requests. Agriculture and textiles and apparel, which were effectively shielded from the reach of multilateral disciplines, are evidence of that (Baldwin, 1998). Equally, the proliferation of regional arrangements was blamed in part on lax GATT enforcement of Article XXIV in not checking the conformity of regional trade rules with multilateral rules. Their discriminatory elements are well documented both in theory and in practice, not only in terms of trade diversion but also in terms of the use of rules of origin for protectionist ends.

While the acceleration of economic, financial and technological changes in the 1980s led to surprising shifts in competitive advantages, they were perceived to be unfair and to merit aggressive unilateral trade action. Luckily, help for the multilateral trading system came from unexpected quarters. One was the Plaza Agreement on exchange rate alignment in 1985, which aimed to bring about macroconomic policy coordination. This strengthened the resolve to get the Uruguay Round (UR) negotiations started in 1986 – and with a very ambitious agenda. The other was the fall of the Berlin wall in 1989 and the dissolution of the Soviet Union in 1992. These gave renewed impetus to the negotiations after an unsuccessful mid-term review held in Montreal in 1988, and again when negotiations and the GATT seemed moribund after a disastrous meeting in Brussels in 1990, which was intended to end the round but failed to do so. In fact, at the 1988 World Economic Forum in Davos, Lester Thurow (an academic and public policy advocate) proclaimed prematurely, 'the GATT is dead'.[1] The prospect of a unified world devoid of the disruptive and destructive bipolar ideologies of communism versus capitalism (and undoubtedly the prospects of new markets and trading opportunities) lent a new shine and credibility to capitalism and the market-based multilateral trading system. The demise of communism furnished proof that planned economies stifle development and trade.

RISING TO THE CHALLENGE

The challenges for trade ministers of the GATT contracting parties at the launch of the UR in Punta del Este in September 1986 were to:

- mend the multilateral trading system, which had suffered fragmentation as a result of the Tokyo Round;
- stop and reverse protectionism, aggressive unilateralism, and remove distortions to trade caused by recourse to grey area measures;
- extend GATT disciplines to agriculture and new areas, eg services;
- improve old sectors, eg textiles, and old issues, eg safeguards;
- embrace new issues such as intellectual property rights and foreign investment;
- improve the dispute settlement mechanism and the functioning of the GATT altogether.

At the outset, there was a tangible difference between the views of the industrialized and the developing countries. Tariff reductions focused on

---

[1] To which the renowned economist, Jagdish Bhagwati responded, 'The GATT is dead, long live the GATT' (Bhagwati, 1991).

industrial tariffs, which were of more benefit to the former, while the sectors of importance to developing countries, namely textiles, clothing and agriculture, had so far been skilfully excluded. Many others sectors in which developing countries enjoyed a comparative advantage, eg footwear and leather goods, and agricultural produce, had high tariffs or tariffs escalating with the degree of processing and added value. For these and other reasons discussed above, the developing countries did not support the addition of new sectors in the early years of the UR negotiations, pointing to the backlog of issues, lending a North–South dimension to the negotiations (Ricupero, 1998).

The UR was supposed to last for four years. In the event, it was not concluded until the end of 1993, with the Final Act Embodying the Results of the Uruguay Round of Multilateral Trade Negotiations signed at Marrakesh on 15 April 1994. The UR was a remarkable achievement by which 120 countries agreed on a myriad of rules and disciplines covering old and new sectors and issues. It was called a single undertaking, which meant that nothing was agreed until everything was agreed. Although many developing countries later faulted the formula of the single undertaking for making them take on commitments and obligations that they did not understand and that far exceeded their implementation capacity, they gained much strength and experience in the process. Their substantial contribution to negotiating the various multilateral trade agreements ensured a better balance of the outcome.

THE WORLD TRADE ORGANIZATION – NATURE AND FUNCTION

The World Trade Organization (WTO), which entered into force on 1 January 1995, provided a stronger and clearer framework in comparison with the GATT, including a more effective and reliable dispute settlement mechanism with the creation of an appellate body. Apart from the global reduction by 40 per cent of tariffs, the establishment of a multilateral framework of disciplines for trade in services, the protection of trade-related intellectual property rights, and the reinforced multilateral trade provisions in agriculture and in textiles and clothing, one of the most surprising outcomes of the UR was the Marrakesh Agreement establishing the WTO. It filled a void in international policy making that had existed since 1948 when the creation of the International Trade Organization (ITO) had failed so dramatically. Harking back to its intended role, that of the third pillar of the Bretton Woods system, the WTO resolved to strive for greater global coherence of policies in the fields of trade, money and finance, including cooperation with the International Monetary Fund (IMF) and the World Bank for that purpose (WTO, 1995). Ironically, whereas the ITO was given short shrift in the post-war climate (see Chapter 1.1 pp4–5), it emerged the stronger as the WTO, towering over the Bretton Wood twins in terms of its importance in and influence over the global economy.

For the first time, developing countries participated to a considerable degree in multilateral trade negotiations. Many of them implemented autonomous economic reforms and trade liberalization measures, as did formerly centrally planned economies after the Iron Curtain meltdown. As a consequence, the needs of developing, and the least developed, countries are explicitly addressed in the preamble of the WTO Agreement, with longer transition periods for implementing the various multilateral WTO agreements (2000 for the former and 2002 for the latter ie 5 and 7 respectively from the date of WTO effectiveness (1995)).

The objectives of the WTO remain the same as those of the GATT as well as:

> expanding the production of and trade in goods and services, while allowing for the optimal use of the world's resources in accordance with the objective of sustainable development, seeking both to protect and preserve the environment and to enhance the means for doing so in a manner consistent with their respective needs and concerns at different levels of economic development.[2]

The five basic functions of the WTO are to:

- implement and administer the WTO Agreement and the multilateral and plurilateral agreements that form an integral part thereof;
- serve as a negotiating forum;
- administer the Dispute Settlement Understanding (DSU);
- administer the Trade Policy Review Mechanism (TPRM);
- achieve greater coherence in global economic policy making through cooperation with the IMF and the International Bank for Reconstruction and Development (also known as World Bank).

The entirety of the representatives of WTO members (currently 148) has authority over all matters concerning the WTO. In the guise of the Ministerial Conference, it is the highest organ of the WTO with ultimate decision-making

---

[2] Source: preamble of the WTO Agreement.

authority over multilateral trade agreements. As the General Council, it oversees the management of the organization and the supervision of all its work in regular meetings, and constitutes the dispute settlement body and the trade policy review body. Equally it is the General Council that oversees the work of the three main Councils (trade-related intellectual property rights, trade in goods, trade in services) in their exercise of functions assigned them in the respective agreements. The Councils can, and have, set up subsidiary bodies under the terms of the various UR agreements – be they for agriculture, subsidies, market access or under the mandated negotiations of the General Agreement on Trade in Services (GATS) or related ministerial decisions.

Contracting parties to the old GATT became original members of the WTO. Thereafter, membership is gained through an accession process of negotiating terms to be agreed by the existing members and the acceding country. Although formal voting rules exist, they only apply when the preferred decision making by consensus breaks down.

KEEPING UP THE MOMENTUM

Over the past 50 years, the multilateral trading system has triumphed over protectionist regimes but failed to prevent the concomitant proliferation of regional pacts and regional trade agreements (RTAs).[3] Alternatively considered to be building blocks towards multilateral integration or discriminatory arrangements that fragment the multilateral trading system, the jury is still out on the real value and contribution of most regional arrangements in terms of trade creation or trade diversion. However, one thing that is known, is that compliance with multilateral rules is of the utmost importance for regionalism to have the least discriminatory impact.

For these reasons, and to prevent a return to protectionism, the bicycle theory of multilateral trade liberalization is important. Some of the WTO agreements have built in the momentum for further trade liberalization. In particular, the Agreement on Agriculture (AoA), which *inter alia* provides for the submission of this renegade sector to multilateral disciplines through the elimination of quota systems and variable import levies through a process called tariffication, is far from compliant with basic WTO rules. Export subsidies, which are prohibited under the Agreement on Subsidies and

---

[3] More than 60 per cent of world trade is regional and almost all major countries belong to at least one regional trade agreement.

Countervailing Measures but permitted under the AoA, are only one example. In order to ensure the continued reform and liberalization of trade in agriculture, the AoA contains a mandate for negotiations in the year 2000. Similarly, the GATS, which established a multilateral framework of principles and rules aimed at progressive liberalization of trade in services, does not meet the high standards and universal coverage of WTO rules and disciplines. To improve services commitments, expand the coverage of sectors and negotiate rules for unfinished business, such as safeguards and subsidies, negotiations were mandated to start in January 2000. Both of these mandated negotiations on agriculture and services are under way. Moreover, negotiations on the liberalization of trade in financial services, basic telecommunications and on the movement of natural persons were authorized to be held after the completion of the UR. Those on financial services and telecommunications ended in 1997, and on the movement of natural persons in mid-1995, with modest results.

MINISTERIAL CONFERENCES AND THE FALLOUT FROM SEATTLE

Since the establishment of the WTO, five Ministerial Conferences have been held: the first in Singapore in 1996, the second in Geneva in the Spring of 1998, the third (and most infamous one) in 1999 in Seattle, Washington, USA, the fourth in 2001 in Doha, Qatar, and the fifth in 2003 in Cancun, Mexico. The first Ministerial Conference was notable for setting out future work in the areas of implementation of the UR agreements, which has turned out to be a serious problem for developing countries.

WTO membership requires, *inter alia*, that governments ensure the conformity of their laws, regulations and administrative procedures with their obligations under the WTO agreements. It has become painfully obvious that in order to meet these requirements, the institutional, legal and administrative infrastructure must be in place, as must be the trained officials and personnel and the Western traditions on which the requirements are modelled.

The Singapore Ministerial Declaration also commanded the analytical study of two areas that were addressed only partially in the UR: trade and competition, and trade and investment. Two working groups were set up for that purpose. The Singapore agenda also instructed the study of trade facilitation and of transparency in government procurement (one of the plurilateral agreements resulting from the UR).

The Geneva Ministerial Conference is largely remembered for focusing attention on the least-developed countries with the creation of the integrated framework, involving the WTO, the IMF, United Nations Conference on Trade and Development (UNCTAD), United Nations Development Programme (UNDP), the World Bank and the International Trade Centre (ITC) for the purpose of providing technical assistance and coordinated trade policy advice to ease their integration into the multilateral trading system.

By 1998, globalization and the role of the multilateral trading system and its proponents had attracted pointed and passionate criticism from civil society and non-governmental organizations (NGOs). Globalization had come to be seen as an evil force driven by international organizations in complicity with multinational companies in their quest for low-cost production using child labour and disrespecting workers' rights and environmental considerations. These arguments assumed a highly protectionist flavour with demands that the WTO sanction environmental and labour transgressions. A violent street demonstration took place during the Geneva Ministerial – however this paled in comparison to what awaited the 4,500 ministers and delegates in Seattle.

Calls for a new round became insistent soon after President Clinton announced that the USA wished to host the next Ministerial Conference in Seattle. The digital revolution, the Internet and e-commerce held out new promises and growth prospects. The Seattle Ministerial was billed as one that would launch the Millennium Round. In the event, the Seattle Ministerial will go down in history as one of the most spectacular failures at both the political and the diplomatic level. It was characterized by violent, globally televised demonstrations, replete with tear gas and police brutality. However, it would be wrong to say that the anti-globalization demonstrators, who availed themselves of the Internet (itself a promoter of globalization) to drum up worldwide NGO support, were responsible for preventing the more than 130 WTO member countries from launching a new round in Seattle.

The reasons for this failure lay in the confluence of unfortunate political circumstances and problems of a more substantive nature. In April 1999, the term of the second director general of the WTO, Renato Ruggiero, came to an end with no successor in sight.[4] The selection process of the new director

---

[4] The first director general of the WTO was Peter Sutherland. He was instrumental in bringing the UR to its conclusion in 1993, but then only continued in the position until July 1995, preferring to return to the private sector.

general proved difficult and revealed deep rifts among members along regional lines. In the end, a compromise solution was accepted with Mike Moore, a former New Zealand Prime Minister, sharing a six-year term with Supachai Panitchpakdi, then Deputy Prime Minister of Thailand. Moore began his term in September 1999, three months before the Seattle Ministerial. In the mean time, during the height of the preparatory period, the WTO was a vessel in unchartered waters. Matters could not have been worse when, in the middle of the year, the entire European Commission was replaced, and with it a highly experienced trade negotiating team. On the US side, Trade Representative Charlene Barshevsky, as the host of the Ministerial Conference, would also chair it. Her skills were known to be more on the bilateral than the multilateral side of trade negotiations. All in all, the Seattle Ministerial Conference was leaderless.

Efforts at drafting a Ministerial Declaration and proposals of negotiating positions were sustained in Geneva, but again only reflected a growing divergence of views among WTO members. Developing countries demanded extensions of the transitional periods, a review, possibly renegotiation, of certain agreements, eg on anti-dumping, textiles, dispute settlement, and the elimination of export subsidies in agriculture. Some countries, especially the USA, insisted on creating a trade link between WTO and labour and environmental issues. In Seattle, an ironic situation existed, whereby the demonstrators protesting against child labour, violation of workers' rights, and environmental degradation pretended to champion the cause of developing countries. However, developing countries firmly opposed the inclusion of these issues in the WTO, as they serve protectionist ends and would take away their comparative advantage. Another divisive issue was the demand by some countries, such as the EU, Japan and South Korea, for including trade and investment and trade and competition in a new round, which the USA and many developing countries opposed.

In the run up to the 4th Ministerial Conference in Qatar in November 2001, the situation was not much different in terms of basic positions, except that those involved had time to reflect on the mistakes that were made in Seattle.

REFERENCES

Baldwin, R (1998) 50 years looking back, looking forward, in *Pragmatism versus Principle in Gatt Decision Making: A Brief Historical Perspective*, University of Wisconsin-Madison (produced by the WTO, Geneva, Switzerland), pp1–14

Bhagwati, J (1991) *The World Trading System at Risk*, Harvester Wheatsheaf, Hemel Hempstead, p7

Low, P (1993) *Trading Free – The GATT and US Trade Policy*, Twentieth Century Fund Press, New York

Ricupero, R (1998) Integration of developing countries into the multilateral trading system *The Uruguay Round and Beyond: Essays in Honour of Arthur Dunkel* Springer Verlag, Berlin, pp9–36

WTO (1995) *The Results of the Uruguay Round of Multilateral Trade Negotiations* The Legal Texts, WTO, piv, Geneva, Switzerland. First published by the GATT Secretariat, June 1994

1.3

The Doha Agenda and Beyond

Stephen Orava, King & Spalding International LLP, London[1]

THE DOHA MINISTERIAL CONFERENCE AND THE NEW NEGOTIATION ROUND

The 4th WTO Ministerial Conference was held in Doha, Qatar from 9 to 14 November 2001. It was preceded by early efforts beginning in January 2000 to rebuild confidence and get the organization back on its feet after the failure in Seattle. These efforts included specific initiatives to assist least-developed countries (LDCs); a special mechanism for discussing and negotiating implementation issues; a comprehensive examination of technical cooperation and capacity building activities; and a system of frequent open-ended and informal heads of delegation meetings, complemented with consultations in other formats for ensuring more active and effective participation of Member governments in the WTO.

In addition, General Council Chairman Stuart Harbinson and Director-General Moore worked closely with Member governments with a view to uncovering bottom-line or at least more compatible positions. WTO Member governments also held a series of meetings among themselves outside the formal General Council process to test levels of support on a range of issues, which included non-agricultural market access, investment, competition, environment, fisheries subsidies, and reform of the Dispute Settlement Understanding.

The major outcomes of the Doha Ministerial included the Ministerial Declaration, the Declaration on the TRIPS Agreement and public health, and the Decision on implementation-related issues and concerns. The Ministerial Declaration, also known as the Doha Development Agenda (DDA), mandates

---

[1] The author wishes to thank Xiaolu Zhu at King & Spalding International LLP for her assistance in the preparation of this chapter.

a negotiating agenda under which an explicit consensus on modalities for negotiations shall be reached at the 5th Ministerial with regard to several issues. It also incorporates other important decisions and activities necessary to address the challenges facing the multilateral trading system, including negotiations on services; clarifications and improvements of various WTO rules[2] and of the Dispute Settlement Understanding; the relationships between trade and environment, trade and debt and finance, trade and technology transfer, and issues concerning developing countries, such as technical cooperation and capacity building, and special and differential treatment.

The Declaration set 1 January 2005 as the date for completing all but two of the negotiations. Negotiations on the Dispute Settlement Understanding were to end in May 2003, and those on a multilateral register of geographical indications for wines and spirits by the 5th Ministerial Conference in 2003. Progress was to be reviewed at the 5th Ministerial Conference in Cancun, Mexico, 10–14 September 2003. Below is a summary of the negotiating agenda mandated by the DDA in some of the key areas.

Agriculture

The negotiations on agriculture began in early 2000, under Article 20 of the WTO Agreement on Agriculture, and were incorporated into the DDA in November 2001. Under the DDA, governments committed themselves to comprehensive negotiations aimed at substantial reductions of trade barriers for agriculture products; reductions of all forms of exports subsidies with a view to phasing out these subsidies; and substantial reductions for trade-distorting domestic supports.

The Declaration makes special and differential treatment for developing countries integral throughout the negotiations, both in countries' new commitments and in any relevant new or revised rules and disciplines. It also takes note of the non-trade concerns (such as environmental protection, food security, rural development, etc) reflected in the negotiating proposals already submitted. The Ministers confirmed that the negotiations would take these into account, as provided for in the Agriculture Agreement. Members agreed to the following key dates: formulas and other 'modalities' for Members' commitments by 31 March 2003; Members' comprehensive draft commit-

---

[2] They include: disciplines and procedures under the Anti-dumping Agreement, the Agreement on Subsidies and Countervailing Measures, and the existing WTO provisions applicable to regional trade agreements.

ments by the 5th Ministerial Conference in 2003; 'stock-taking' (ie, assessing the status) at the 5th Ministerial Conference in 2003; and the deadline for the conclusion of negotiations in the form of a single undertaking by 1 January 2005.

TRIPS and public health

Under Article 31(f) of the Agreement on Aspects of Trade-Related Intellectual Property Rights (TRIPS), production under compulsory licensing must be predominantly for the domestic market. This effectively limits the ability of countries that cannot make pharmaceutical products from importing cheaper generics produced by way of compulsory licensing from countries where pharmaceuticals are patented. In the Doha Declaration, Ministers stressed that it was important to implement and interpret the TRIPS Agreement in a way that supported public health. They referred to their separate declaration on this subject, which was designed to respond to concerns about the possible implications of the TRIPS Agreement for access to medicines. The Declaration clarified some of the forms of flexibility available, in particular compulsory licensing and parallel importing, which would enable Members without pharmaceutical manufacturing capacity to import, in times of national emergency, generic forms of patented pharmaceutical products under compulsory licensing.

As far as the DDA is concerned, this separate declaration set two specific objectives. First, the TRIPS Council was instructed to find a solution to the problems countries may face in making use of compulsory licensing if they have too little or no pharmaceutical manufacturing capacity. Second, the declaration extended the deadline for least-developed countries to apply provisions on pharmaceutical patents until 1 January 2016.

Non-agriculture market access

The Ministers agreed to launch tariff-cutting negotiations on all non-agricultural products. The aim was 'to reduce or, as appropriate, eliminate tariffs, including the reduction or elimination of tariff peaks, high tariffs, and tariff escalation, as well as non-tariff barriers, in particular on products of export interest to developing countries'. These negotiations were intended to take fully into account the special needs and interests of developing and least-developed countries, and recognize that these countries do not need to match or fully reciprocate tariff-reduction commitments by other participants.

At the start, negotiators were required to reach agreement on how ('modalities') to conduct the tariff-cutting exercise (in the Tokyo Round, the participants used an agreed mathematical formula to cut tariffs across the board; in the Uruguay Round, participants negotiated cuts product by product). The agreed procedures were to include studies and capacity-building measures that would help least-developed countries participate effectively in the negotiations.

While average customs duties are now at their lowest levels after eight GATT Rounds, certain tariffs continue to restrict trade, especially on exports of developing countries – for instance, 'tariff peaks' (ie relatively high tariffs) remain in force in developed countries against 'sensitive' products such as agricultural products. For developed countries, tariffs of 15 per cent and above are generally considered 'tariff peaks'.

Another example is 'tariff escalation', in which higher import duties are applied on semi-processed products than on raw materials, and higher still on finished products. This practice protects domestic processing industries and discourages the development of processing activity in the countries where raw materials originate.

Members agreed to the following key dates: start of negotiations by January 2002; 'stock taking' at the 5th Ministerial Conference in 2003; and deadline for the conclusion of negotiations in the form of a single undertaking by 1 January 2005.

Services

Pursuant to Article XIX on 'progressive liberalization' under the General Agreement on Trade in Services (GATS), Members started a new round of services negotiations in 2000, which was incorporated into the DDA in November 2001. The services negotiations generally rely on the traditional 'request-offer' approach as the main method of negotiation. Within the timeframe of the overall negotiating deadline of 1 January 2005, the DDA established that 'participants shall submit initial requests for specific commitments by 30 June 2002 and initial offers by 31 March 2003'. A general stock taking was planned for the 5th Ministerial in September 2003.

'Singapore Issues'

During the 1996 Ministerial in Singapore, Members agreed that the relationships between trade and competition and between trade and investment required further examination. Trade facilitation and transparency in government procurement were also set apart for further study. Three working groups were organized within the WTO to address these areas, but a decision on whether or not to formally integrate these four issues, commonly referred to as the 'Singapore issues,' into the WTO framework was delayed until Doha in 2001. It was there that the WTO recognized a 'case for multilateral rules' in these areas, and mandated that decisions at the 5th Ministerial be reached as to whether negotiations on these issues could begin.

China's accession to the WTO

Apart from the Doha Declaration and the accompanying documents, another important outcome of the Doha Ministerial Conference was China's accession to the WTO. After nearly 15 years of arduous negotiations, China finally became a Member of the WTO on 11 December 2001. China's accession was a landmark event with far-reaching ramifications for China, her trading partners, and the WTO.

China's commitments to further open its economy in order to gain membership in the WTO are sweeping. They include significant reductions in tariffs that will bring the average level to under 10 per cent by 2005; the introduction of a tariff-rate quota system that brings the tariff rate for key agricultural commodities, such as wheat, almost to zero for a significant volume of imports; the gradual elimination of all quotas and licences that have restricted the flow of some imports; a substantial reduction in the use of state trading as an instrument to control the volume of imports of agricultural and other key commodities; and the opening of critical services sectors such as telecommunications, distribution, banking, insurance, asset management, and securities to foreign direct investment.

In addition, the protocol governing its accession sets forth China's commitment to abide by international standards for the protection of intellectual property and to accept the application by WTO Members of a number of unusual trade remedy mechanisms that could be used to reduce the flow of Chinese goods into foreign markets.[3]

Clearly, implementation is, and will continue to be, a major challenge for China and its reformers. They must find ways to ensure that recalcitrant

---

[3] *See* Lardy, N R, *Issues in China's WTO Accession,* the U.S.-China Security Review Commission, May 9 2001

ministries, State-owned enterprises and provincial and municipal authorities all act in conformity with China's WTO commitments. Despite numerous challenges, China has made significant efforts to implement its WTO commitments with good faith, and has achieved success during the 18 months following accession.

China has begun to take concrete steps to remove non-tariff trade barriers in virtually every product sector.[4] For certain products, China has lowered tariffs ahead of the WTO schedule.[5] It has begun to implement far-reaching services commitments, and has also repealed hundreds of trade-related laws, regulations and other measures and modified or adopted numerous other ones in an effort to become WTO-compliant in areas such as import and export administration, standards, and intellectual property rights, among many others.[6] Difficulties regarding compliance remain in some areas, in particular the complicated import licensing procedures, the implementation of agricultural tariff rate quotas, and inadequate adherence to commitments benefiting foreign insurers.[7] Nevertheless, China's leadership remains fully committed to China's integration with the world trading system, and appears prepared to undertake the challenges in the process.

The integration of such a huge yet only partially reformed economy is expected to have massive impact on the world trading system. The greatly increased market access for goods and services offers enormous potential commercial opportunities for firms outside China, while Chinese firms also enjoy the benefits of lower trade barriers abroad as a result of China's WTO membership. Meanwhile, the increased competition among Chinese and foreign firms will result in more trade frictions and probably trade disputes between China and her trading partners. Furthermore, as a major developing country Member, China will bring new dynamics in the current and future trade negotiations, which may lead to a more balanced trading system that gives greater considerations to the common interests of developing countries.

---

[4] *See* Deputy U.S. Trade Representative Jon M. Huntsman, Jr., Statement To the Congressional-Executive Commission on China, June 6, 2002, available at: http://usinfo.state.gov/topical/econ/wto/02060643.htm

[5] *See* The U.S.-China Business Council, 'China's WTO Implementation: A Mid-Year Assessment', available at: http://www.uschina.org/public/documents/2003/06/17-wto analysispaper.pdf

[6] *Supra* fn.3

[7] *Supra* fn.4

THE CANCÚN MINISTERIAL CONFERENCE AND THE NEGOTIATIONS UNDER THE DOHA DEVELOPMENT AGENDA

The 5th WTO Ministerial Conference took place in Cancún, Mexico from 10 to 14 September 2003. The main task was to take stock of (ie to assess progress that has been made in) negotiations mandated by the DDA. However, the significant gap between developing and developed countries' negotiating positions and the uncertain political will to achieve an agreement caused the Ministerial to collapse with no consensus on key issues.

With negotiations dragging on after Doha with few major breakthroughs, the outlook for the Cancún Ministerial was gloomy up until late August 2003 when WTO Member governments broke their deadlock over TRIPS and public health.

Negotiations on TRIPS and public health reached a standstill when the United States rejected a proposal for an agreement in late December 2002, due to a dispute about which diseases would be covered by the agreement. The United States favoured a relatively limited definition of which diseases would apply under the agreement (HIV/AIDS, malaria, tuberculosis, and other similar infectious diseases), because they were afraid a broader definition may give rise to disincentives to create new pharmaceutical products. Developing countries preferred not to specify diseases.

On 30 August 2002, Members finally reached a breakthrough and agreed to a 'Decision on implementation of paragraph 6 of the Doha Declaration on the TRIPS Agreement and public health' (the 'Decision'). The Decision waived countries' obligations under Article 31(f) of the TRIPS Agreement and allowed countries producing generic copies of patented products under compulsory licences to export the products to eligible importing countries. All WTO Member countries are eligible to import under this decision, but 23 mostly developed countries are listed in the decision as announcing voluntarily that they will not use the system to import. The waiver applies to the diseases specified in Article 1 of the Doha Declaration on the TRIPS Agreement and public health, namely HIV/AIDS, tuberculosis, malaria and other epidemics, and it would last until the TRIPS Agreement is amended.

A separate statement by General Council chairperson Carlos Pérez del Castillo, Uruguay's ambassador, was designed to provide comfort to those who feared that the decision might be abused and undermine patent protection. The statement described Members' 'shared understanding' on how the decision should be interpreted and implemented. It stated that the decision would be used in good faith in order to deal with public health problems and not for industrial or commercial policy objectives, and that issues such as preventing the medicines getting into the wrong hands were important.

While the negotiations on TRIPS and public health finally moved forward, agriculture remained one of the most sensitive and contentious areas of the negotiations. Much of the success of the DDA hinged upon whether or not satisfactory agreement on modalities for agriculture negotiations could be reached. The deadline for the agreement on modalities, which was originally set for 31 March 2003, was missed when the proposed modalities, drafted by Chairman Harbinson, were rejected.

The original deadlock over negotiating modalities was primarily caused by the EU's failure to agree on a Common Agricultural Policy (CAP) reform to reduce supports for agriculture, and complicated by the US post-Doha implementation of the Farm Bill, which dramatically increased federal support for agriculture. (This step shocked developing countries, as the United States had previously been pushing for agriculture liberalization along with the developing world.) An added frustration to the negotiations was Japan's refusal to compromise in the area of its exceptionally high tariffs on certain agriculture products, especially rice.

The policies of these developed country Members were devastating to farmers in developing countries. At home, they are unable to compete with heavily subsidized imports, such as cotton from the USA and sugar from Europe; abroad, they lack market access for their agriculture products due to the high barriers in developed countries. Thus, increasing agriculture market access and substantially reducing farm subsidies were the priority issues for many developing countries, especially for the poorest Members whose economies are entirely dependent on agriculture and for those high population countries like India and China that are home to hundreds of millions of farmers.

Progress had been made in certain areas, albeit far from satisfactory for the success of the DDA. The EU agreed on an internal CAP reform policy that most notably attempted to sever the tie between subsidies and production, ie the so-called 'decoupling'. However, while the reform may have been a big step for the EU, it represented only a small step toward the success of the wider negotiations. For example, the decoupling is partial and will only take place after 2006 for some countries, including France. Certain key products, such as sugar, are largely spared from reform, and key issues such as the reduction of export subsidies and increased market access are not addressed at all.

Another pre-Ministerial development was the proposal by the European Union and the United States on a framework for a joint approach to agriculture with limited cuts to the most trade-distorting subsidies and some reductions in the high tariffs that apply to developing country farm exports. However, the proposal was rejected by the developing countries, which argued that it did not address developing countries' key concerns adequately, and that the agreement was too vague to provide a useful starting point for negotiations. Instead, they insisted on product-specific reductions of domestic support, and the total elimination of export subsidies.

Despite being the most contentious topic, agriculture was not the 'official' cause for the collapse of the Cancun Ministerial, although the lack of progress on agriculture was certainly the largest factor contributing to the failure. Rather, it was reportedly Members' entrenched disagreement on the Singapore issues that seemingly precipitated the failure at Cancún. Developed countries considered that these issues were the necessary next step for the WTO. Developing countries remained skeptical as to whether the WTO was the right forum to address these issues, particularly trade and investment. These countries also feared that any agreement on these issues may adversely interfere with their development opportunities in the long run. In addition, debate arose as to whether these four issues should be 'unbundled' and pursued separately, as unanimity may have been easier to achieve for some of the issues but not the others.

On the fifth day of the Cancún Ministerial, after four days devoted almost exclusively to agriculture and after releasing a revised draft declaration, the Chairman of the negotiating body decided to address the Singapore issues first on the agenda. The EU immediately proposed to unbundle the Singapore issues by removing trade and competition from the table, limiting trade and investment to further study, and proceeding with negotiations on trade facilitation and transparency in government procurement. Japan and Korea rejected the EU's (arguably belated) proposal and instead insisted on simultaneous progress on all four issues. Angered by such relentless pursuit of what was unacceptable to the poor countries, African ministers insisted that none of these four issues could proceed. Chairman Derbez of Mexico then concluded that there was no basis to think that an agreement could be reached and ended the Ministerial in mid-afternoon.

Certain Members contended that the Chairman ended the meeting prematurely, because Members were still in a position to compromise and many of the strident positions could be characterized as hard negotiating. However, the general feeling was that certain countries were prepared to leave the Ministerial without an agreement, largely for political reasons. Ministers may have been looking to elections in the near future or to other political pressure that would prevent a deal that gave too much on agriculture, for example, without counter-balancing commitments in other areas like investment. In any event, the Chairman of the negotiations, in consultation with others, may have simply recognized this reality and decided that further negotiating conflicts at the Ministerial would do more harm than sending the negotiations back to Geneva for further work.

The collapse was undoubtedly a major disappointment for the global trading system and the DDA, with the 1 January 2005 deadline to conclude DDA negotiations likely to be extended. Another cause for pessimism is the upcoming elections in the United States, India, and certain EU Member States, including France, which means that it will be more difficult to obtain any shift in negotiating positions from these Members. However, although the failure to reach consensus is disheartening to some, this failure is by no means a fatal blow to the WTO or the DDA, as evidenced by the positive response to similar 'failures' during the Uruguay Round.

As described earlier, the DDA was launched to rebuild confidence after the Seattle Ministerial. It was characterized by a very ambitious negotiating agenda that incorporated the reduction of the world's poverty alongside the goals of trade liberalization. Nevertheless, the failure at Cancún highlighted the limitations of the current rule-making or 'legislative' procedures of the WTO, particularly the reliance on consensus. It also demonstrated that instead of overburdening the WTO with multifarious tasks, Members should rid the negotiations of unnecessary hurdles and focus on the areas that are critical to the DDA's objectives. A greater flexibility for Members to legislate on a continuous basis, rather than in contentious 'rounds', may facilitate a more focused negotiating agenda.

Another important development from Cancún was that the developing countries, for the first time, rallied in support of their interests and formed alliances that significantly changed the negotiating dynamics. The question remains whether the Members in these alliances, with a multitude of shared as well as divergent interests, will continue to exert influence over the negotiations and whether such influence will ultimately have positive or negative effects. The developing countries, however, must use the new dynamics constructively to ensure the eventual success of the DDA, especially as the collapse of multilateral WTO negotiations increases the risk of further bilateral and regional negotiations that leave many developing and least developed countries behind. If the DDA were to fail, all Members would lose, with the most harm again falling on the world's poorest.

SUMMARY

A close look at the evolution of multilateral trade agreements reveals that they have been growing in fits and spurts with interludes of inactivity and even regression. Tariff reductions have exposed the nature of trade barriers to be far more complex than imagined. Pragmatism and diplomacy characterized the evolution of the GATT; and ingenuity on the part of its leaders turned it from a flawed document and a makeshift organizational set-up into a highly effective market-opening tool. The WTO, which has its own official identity, operating budget, clear mandate, and binding dispute settlement, is now being held up as the saviour for, and villain causing, almost all of the world's complex social and economic ills.

A striking feature of the WTO in comparison to the GATT is that the former has had three director generals in nine years, the same number as the latter in 45 years. This points up the highly political and visible nature of the WTO as opposed to the quiet and diplomatic institution that was the old GATT. Civil society groups, NGOs and even UN organizations are attempting to make the WTO responsive to, and hence responsible for, all global concerns, including low-wage and abusive labour practices, environmental degradation, development and the digital divide, human rights, and gender and animal welfare. By doing so, they risk detracting the organization from its main job – the promotion and management of the multilateral trading system.

The future challenge for the WTO and its 148 Members lies in preserving the universality of the multilateral trading system that the Uruguay Round of multilateral trade negotiations managed to achieve. What must be avoided is the renewed fragmentation of the system and the weakening of the fundamental principles of transparency and non-discrimination on which the system is based.

REFERENCES

Center for International Development at Harvard University, *Cancun Ministerial Page*, http://www.cid.harvard.edu/cidtrade/cancun/cancun.html
Lardy, N R (2001) *Issues in China's WTO Accession*, the U.S.-China Security Review Commission, May 9 2001

Legal Elements of the WTO

Michaela Eglin, formerly ICC, Geneva

The achievements of the Uruguay Round, especially those enshrining the multilateral trading system in a solid legal framework, were heavily reliant on the invaluable experience and jurisprudence built up under 46 years of GATT operations. Differences of opinion persist as to whether the system should be driven by peer pressure, consultations and diplomacy or whether disputes should be settled primarily through the new dispute settlement mechanism. WTO experience being relatively short, discussion of its legal elements necessarily involves the GATT.

THE LEGACY OF THE GATT

The GATT provided a legal foundation upon which international trade could be reconstructed in an orderly fashion after World War II. Trade diplomacy, flexibility in applying the rules, and mediation to defuse confrontation and outright disputes between governments characterized the GATT's handling of legal claims, at least until the end of the 1970s. However, growing membership brought with it a diversity of economic systems, commercial interests, views and philosophies concerning the evolution of the multilateral trading system. The GATT was ill-equipped to deal with both the expansion of membership and the economic and technological innovations and attendant integration, with its profound effects on intergovernmental relations in matters of politics and trade. It was difficult for the GATT to keep pace with these external developments because of its 'permanently' provisional status, doubts as to its position vis-à-vis both international and national law, its club-like operation, and its rigid formal amendment procedures. Amendments to GATT rules entailed changes in the domestic law of the contracting parties, a prospect that held governments captive to prudence and reticence. Amendments required unanimity for Articles I, II and XXX; for others mostly a two-thirds majority. Neither were easily achieved, but the GATT contracting parties were disinclined to vote and preferred consensus.

In addition to its provisional nature, the inhibiting amendment formalities made the GATT a static instrument for trade liberalization. Apart from amendments to existing articles, practically the only way to bring about change in the form of new rules was to conclude new agreements, usually in the context of a negotiating round. As an example, the Enabling Clause adopted in the Tokyo Round in 1979 has its antecedents in the 1966 adoption of Part IV of the GATT, which included the liberation of developing countries from the reciprocity obligation in international trade negotiations with industrialized countries. It took 15 years for governments to agree to convince their parliaments to make the necessary legal changes at the national level (Long, 1984). Similarly, a code for anti-dumping was agreed in the Kennedy Round, which largely languished due to conflicts with US law until the side agreement on anti-dumping concluded in the Tokyo Round replaced it, and even then it was an optional agreement for governments to sign on to.

What cannot be agreed unanimously or by vote by the entire membership can still be agreed on by a subgroup of governments. In some ways, the rigid GATT legal framework, and the absence of a will to enforce the rules, may have restrained multilateralism, especially when it came to tackling trade barriers other than tariffs and quantitative restrictions. The Tokyo Round brought on a fragmentation of the system due to the addition of the codes or side agreements on non-tariff barriers. Not only were they optional but they also contained dispute settlement features separate from those of the GATT, which caused confusion. Very soon after the conclusion of the Tokyo Round it became apparent that a more dynamic instrument and method of trade liberalization was needed, and one which was unifying rather than divisive.

With the creation of the WTO, both dynamism and unification were achieved. The WTO is the instrument of change to which all countries can subscribe because objective procedures and disciplines are in place whereby a Member violating the rules can be challenged and obliged to honour its commitments under the WTO. Moreover, the built-in agenda for continued negotiations and the review mechanisms that are written into the Uruguay Round agreements add a dynamic element to trade liberalization. Contracting parties to the GATT were loathe to apply retaliatory measures, such as suspending concessions and rebalancing of benefits, even when authorized to do so by majority vote. In point of fact, up to mid-1988 this happened only once as a result of a complaint brought by the Netherlands against the USA, which applied GATT illegal import restraints on dairy products from the Netherlands. Despite the authorization to apply restraints against imports of US grain for seven consecutive years, the Netherlands never followed through, mainly because it was known that such retaliation would not influence the US position (Jackson, 1989). This type of experience, and the associated sense of failure to get satisfaction from a country that violated GATT rules or nullified the benefits a country (especially small and developing countries) could legitimately expect from a trading partner, added to the growing disenchantment with the old GATT. The WTO resolves the functioning of the organization and the measures of redress of which countries can avail themselves, owing to the reformed Dispute Settlement Mechanism and the innovative addition of an Appellate Body.

The Dispute Settlement Understanding (DSU) of the WTO for the first time established a treaty text implementing procedure for the result of panel reports, including measures for compensation or retaliation. Although GATT panel reports were considered legally binding, their weakness lay in the ability of contracting parties (usually the guilty party) to block consensus on adoption, leaving the panel report in legal limbo. Under the WTO, panel report recommendations represent international law obligations upon the Member at whom the findings are directed, to make its practice consistent with the treaty text obligations of the WTO and annexed agreements.

THE RESULTS OF THE URUGUAY ROUND (THE LEGAL TEXTS)[1]

The Results of the Uruguay Round negotiations were far reaching and profoundly important for the multilateral trading system. Apart from the creation of a legitimate international institution with its own budget, secretariat, decision-making mechanism and detailed amendment provisions, the Marrakesh Agreement establishing the WTO (also referred to as the WTO Agreement) states that:

> the WTO shall be guided by the decisions, procedures and customary practices followed by the contracting parties to GATT 1947 and the bodies established in the framework of GATT 1947 (Article XVI.1).

---

[1] 'The Results of the Uruguay Round of Multilateral Trade Negotiations; the Legal Texts.' First published in June 1994 by the GATT Secretariat, reprinted in 1995 by the WTO, Geneva, Switzerland.

Moreover, Article XVI.4 states that:

> each Member shall ensure the conformity of its laws, regulations and administrative procedures with its obligations as provided in the annexed Agreements.

It goes on to say that:

> no reservations may be made in respect of any provision of the WTO Agreement (Article XVI.5).

These provisions leave no doubt as to the applicability of WTO law at the domestic level, and the nature and extent of commitments entered into by Members.

The functions of the WTO are to:

- administer the WTO multilateral and plurilateral agreements, the Understanding on Rules and Procedures Governing the Settlement of Disputes and the Trade Policy Review Mechanism (TPRM);
- serve as a negotiating forum and framework for implementing results of negotiations; and
- increase coherence in global economic policy making by cooperating with the International Monetary Fund (IMF) and the International Bank for Reconstruction and Development and its affiliated agencies (the World Bank).

In providing an umbrella for the GATT with all its amendments, annexes and schedules of concessions, in addition to the Side Agreements of the Tokyo Round and the new multilateral and plurilateral agreements, two important handicaps in the evolution of the multilateral trading system were removed. One was the sheer impossibility of introducing new rules to the GATT due to its provisional character. The second was the unification of an increasingly fragmented trading system that had evolved because of it, by removing the optional character of the Tokyo Round Codes and applying for the first time the concept of a Single Undertaking.

In legal terms, the new WTO provides a clean institutional structure and tasks through the WTO Agreement. The concept of the Single Undertaking (nothing is agreed until everything is agreed) obliged all Members to accept as binding international law obligations, the GATT as amended over time, the Tokyo Round Side Agreements, Understandings, Decisions and the new agreements on services, trade-related intellectual property rights, and trade-related investment measures, as annexed:

- *Annex 1* contains the multilateral agreements on trade in goods covering GATT 1994 and a number of Understandings on Interpretations of certain articles and provisions in addition to 12 Agreements, many of which improved Tokyo Round Codes. These are the Agreements on agriculture, textiles and clothing, (to be terminated on 1 January 2005) sanitary and phytosanitary measures, technical barriers to trade, anti-dumping, trade-related investment measures, customs valuation, preshipment inspection, rules of origin, import licensing procedures, subsidies and countervailing measures and safeguards.
- *Annex 1B* is the General Agreement on Trade in Services (GATS).
- *Annex 1C* is the Agreement on Trade-Related Aspects of Intellectual Property Rights (TRIPS). Both of these constitute new sectors, which were supported by the industrialized countries, initially with strong opposition from the developing countries.
- *Annex 2* is the Understanding on Rules and Procedures Governing the Settlement of Disputes.
- *Annex 3* is the Trade Policy Review Mechanism.
- *Annex 4* contains the Plurilateral Trade Agreements. Currently, only two of them are still in force. They are the Agreement on Trade in Civil Aircraft and the Agreement on Government Procurement. Both the International Dairy Agreement and the Bovine Meat Agreement were terminated at the end of 1997.

RATIFICATION OF THE WTO AGREEMENT

After the signing of the Final Act of the Uruguay Round at Marrakesh on 15 April 1994, all governments that were signatories to the WTO had to ratify the WTO Agreement to ensure implementation of the WTO agreements at the national level. In the case of the USA, international treaty approvals follow a statutory procedure whereby Congress confers upon the Executive the authority to enter into such agreements. Since the Trade Agreements Act of 1974, this has been done under the so-called fast track procedure, which prevents amendment of a bill and imposes strict time and debate limits for its consideration.[2] The implementing legislation of the treaty is part of domestic law and often includes language drawn from the treaty itself.

---

[2] The conclusion of the Uruguay Round was hastened by the fact that US negotiating authority expired at the end of 1993.

Similarly, the European Community approval process was complicated because the approval of an international agreement by the Council of Ministers of the European Community applies merely to commercial policy, a term not further defined in the Treaty of Rome. Therefore, it is considered not to apply to certain parts of the Uruguay Round text, as for example, the General Agreement on Trade in Services and the Agreement on Trade-related Investment Measures (TRIMS), over which areas individual European Union members were found to retain competence. Ultimately, the Uruguay Round Results were approved as a single package by unanimous vote of the Council upon the consent of the EU Parliament, and then ratified individually by each Member State just in time for the December 1994 deadline. After considerable debate and controversy, the Council's approach was explicitly based on the non-applicability of the Uruguay Round texts themselves, which is similar to the way the USA handled the ratification of the UR Results.

Japan, a parliamentary democracy, approved the WTO Agreement in time, although the conformity of Japanese law with the WTO Agreement may not stand up to challenge in courts, especially in view of the USA's and possibly the EU's denial of direct applicability (Jackson, 1998).

THE BLURRING OF SOVEREIGNTY

A frequent complaint about the latter-day GATT was that the institution robs nations of their sovereign right to take policy decisions affecting their citizens, especially as it began to tackle non-tariff barriers to trade that lurked in national administrative regulations and public and private business practices. These complaints became more adamant as trade liberalization and the push for market access were seen to require a level playing field, and with the creation of the WTO. The debate on the loss of sovereignty concerns essentially the allocation of power between nation states and the international regulatory system. The diminution of decision-making power goes hand in hand with the adherence to international agreements, as governments accept product standards and harmonization of certain practices and policies and even a competent body charged with settling disputes in case of disagreement. Undeniably, economic integration and globalization require governments to be circumspect about adopting policies that might unfavourably affect their neighbours or even countries far away. For example, policies that affect the environment and traded products which might be harmful in their use or consumption call for concerted action and international agreement on acceptable standards. In that sense, the loss of sovereignty is for the common good. Equally, policies that facilitate trade for the benefit of all adherents to an international treaty or regulatory body can not, at the same time, be faulted for reducing freedom of decision making.

An interesting case is the GATS, under which Members agree to progressively liberalize trade in services through successive rounds of multilateral negotiations. With most obstacles to trade in services consisting of government regulations, a loss of sovereignty is implicit in those sectors and areas where Members have made specific commitments under the agreement. That notwithstanding, the GATS explicitly recognizes the rights of Members to regulate and to introduce new regulations on the supply of services within their territories to meet national policy objectives. The GATS has come under attack for undermining national sovereignty particularly in the areas of education and health services, so it is worth stressing that governments are at liberty to refrain from scheduling commitments in any sector. Still, domestic regulation affecting services is subject to international scrutiny through provisions on transparency and the requirement that measures relating to professional qualifications and procedures, technical standards and licensing do not constitute unnecessary barriers to trade in services. The rules and disciplines under the GATS need further refinement, a task that is under way as part of the built-in agenda.

An area that clearly diminishes national sovereignty is macroeconomic policy coordination among nations. This has become necessary to some degree at the international level, but especially at a regional level. A case in point is almost 30 years of monetary policy coordination and exchange rate targeting ultimately leading to the European Union and a single currency.

Loss of sovereignty at the limit occurs when a country loses its freedom to choose its policies, which occurs in the absence of democratic structures. In the end, countries are free to accept and implement international treaty norm, or to dismiss it altogether. If a treaty is self-executing or directly applicable in a domestic legal system, the loss of sovereignty again is self-induced. Even when it is not directly applicable, it still would tend to influence domestic policy debate and domestic interpretation by domestic courts. A nation can always decide how to respond to a complaint that it breached international law, including living with the breach.

FALLBACK POSITIONS

As regards the multilateral trading system, in signing on to the myriad of agreements, understandings and decisions that comprise the WTO, governments confirmed their willingness to cede sovereignty on policies and practices they consider of benefit for their countries. This is not surprising in light of the option to revoke the WTO Agreement at a six-month notice (Article XV) – an option that has never been exercised but clearly represents an important safety valve. Moreover, the agreements themselves, including the GATT, contain escape clauses or safeguards to provide for a variety of situations where a sudden rise in imports and other WTO obligations harm or threaten economic or industrial interests of the importing country. The WTO Agreement on Safeguards, which establishes detailed rules for the application of safeguard measures provided for in GATT Article XIX, is considered to be a major achievement of the Uruguay Round. The provisions in the Agreement set out the conditions under which safeguard measures may be applied to prevent or remedy serious injury and to facilitate adjustment of the concerned sector or industry, as well as the duration and review of the measures.

PROVISIONS STRENGTHENING THE FUNCTIONS OF THE WTO

The practice of consensus was never defined in the GATT but evolved over time because of vague wording on decision-making power, which did not entice governments into strict voting. The WTO explicitly describes consensus as the absence of a formal objection by a Member present at the meeting when the decision is taken. Decisions of the Ministerial Conference and the General Council are taken by majority vote, unless otherwise provided in the agreements. Interpretation of multilateral agreements are adopted by the General Council upon recommendation from the Council overseeing the relevant agreement and voted on by a three-fourths majority of the Members. A voting mechanism of three-fourths of the membership, in a situation where consensus fails, also applies for certain waiver requests. Amendments to provisions of the WTO agreements must be submitted to the Ministerial Conference, which decides by consensus, and failing that by a two-thirds majority, whether or not to submit the proposal to the Members. Voting on acceptance of amendments depends on whether or not the latter alter the rights and obligations of Members. In case a proposed amendment is not of such a nature, it must be accepted by two-thirds of the Members. Procedures are more complicated in cases where the rights and obligations of Members are affected. Moreover, amendments to the provisions of certain articles require unanimity (Article IX of the WTO Agreement on decision making, Articles I and III of GATT 1994 most-favoured nation (MFN) and National Treatment, ie non-discrimination, Article II:1 of the GATS, and Article 4 of the Agreement on TRIPS).

Accession to the WTO (Article XII) is largely guided by the same conditions as under the GATT. It requires the acceding country to accept the WTO agreements, including GATT1994 with all its tariff concessions equivalent to reciprocal reductions achieved over time as an 'entry ticket'. The terms and conditions of membership are decided by the existing Members based on bilateral negotiations, the results of which are then extended to all Members on the basis of the MFN principle. A Member may choose not to apply the WTO to a newcomer at the time of accession only. This is the opt-out clause contained in Article XIII.

THE DISPUTE SETTLEMENT UNDERSTANDING (DSU)

The centrepiece of the WTO is the DSU with much improved procedures. Third-party adjudication to enforce obligations contained in trade agreements was first considered under the stillborn ITO Charter. The GATT, which was to be an interim agreement on tariff reductions until the ITO entered into force, but which ended up being applied in its provisional form for 46 years, never adopted a three-tiered adjudication procedure. The underlying notion was that the objective of trade liberalization and the mutual benefits gained were enough of an incentive for governments to meet their contractual obligations. In the early GATT years, legal claims were referred to working parties consisting of a cross section of contracting parties. In the 1950s, a panel on complaints rendered objective decisions based on expertise rather than political representation of individual governments. This system worked well as long as old GATT hands and experienced and senior people directly involved in negotiating the GATT itself were available. With their disappearance, GATT secretariat staff were increasingly relied on for providing neutral working party rulings. Still, the GATT had a vested interest in stepping lightly with respect to rendering verdicts on violation of the rules. GATT legal obligations were not always received favourably by capitals, so throwing its full weight behind rulings that governments might be unable to comply with threatened the viability of the GATT itself. Diplomatic obfuscation, in a way, protected the GATT from hostile forces in national capitals.

During most of the 1960s, there was no adjudication of legal claims in the GATT owing largely to the emergence of the European Economic Community. While meeting most GATT legal requirements for a customs union, the EEC was in gross violation on two accounts: the Common Agricultural Policy (CAP) and preferential arrangements with former colonies. Community officials successfully argued for a less legalistic GATT approach to traded problems under threats of leaving the GATT. The other decisive factor in placing adjudication on hold was the threefold increase in the number of developing countries that acceded to the GATT during this period as they gained independence from former colonial powers. Their accession was quasi-automatic and, given the state of their economic development, they were technically in violation of most GATT rules. Using their majority position, these countries in turn began to call for the enforcement of legal obligations of the developed countries, many of which indeed maintained discriminatory trade barriers against exports of developing countries, especially in agricultural products and textiles and apparel.

With the rise of protectionism in the 1970s in the form of non-tariff barriers, the USA once again took on a leading role, this time in pressing for legal reform with a measure of success. The dispute settlement procedure was strengthened in the Tokyo Round by a restatement of GATT customary practice. In codifying and legitimating main elements of established procedures, governments felt entitled to make more use of them. The formation of trading blocs such as the USA, the EC, Japan and developing countries coupled with a more aggressive defence of national interests, coincidental with fair trade pursuits of that era, contributed to heightened tensions. Consequently, lawyers were attracted to the GATT adjudication procedure and began to replace trade diplomats and their courteous and artful approach to solving trade conflicts.

However, a larger GATT with a bigger business agenda, limited resources and a rising volume of GATT litigation meant that panels received less expert attention from the GATT secretariat. The result was an increase in problematic rulings and erroneous decisions. By the early 1980s, it was clear that the GATT had to abandon its no-lawyer approach and furnish panels with expert legal advice from the inside. Even though the EEC continued to support the customary diplomatic approach to legal claims, a one-man legal office was established for the first time in the GATT, ostensibly on a temporary basis, and by 1983, it had a three-member staff. From then on, lawyers were assigned a more prominent role in the GATT secretariat. The GATT dispute settlement process improved considerably and with it the confidence of governments to present sensitive and difficult cases. (Hudec, 1998 pp114–116)

In 1984, the EC strengthened the common commercial policy by adopting a regulation on illicit commercial practices. Partly modelled on the US Section 301 procedure of the 1974 Trade Agreements Act, the EC regulation enables individuals or firms to petition the EC Commission to begin an investigation of foreign government practices inimical to EC trade. More importantly, and reflecting different motivations arising from the special governmental context of the EEC, it strengthened the position of Member States to influence the adoption of trade restrictive measures, depending on their influence in the Council, and made it easier for the Commission to launch a GATT dispute settlement procedure. It also provides for an international proceeding to be followed through to its conclusion before retaliatory measures may be applied (Jackson, 1989, pp107–109). The USA and the EU can be regarded as the genetic parents of the GATT/WTO dispute settlement mechanism, and shaped both its structure and the procedures. At the same time, their different domestic political and legal history is reflected in their trade legislation, and brought to light in the numerous trade disputes and the way they are resolved by the Dispute Settlement Mechanism (DSM) in the WTO.

A major problem with GATT panel reports was that their adoption of rulings required consensus, whence some governments' outright refusal to accept decisions. The growing confidence in the quality of GATT dispute settlement rulings in the 1980s, and growing willingness to use the dispute procedures, were reflected in the highest volume of litigation ever in the history of the GATT by the end of the 1980s. As of September 1988, 233 cases were initiated, of which 9 were under the Tokyo Round Code provisions, 42 were withdrawn before constitution of a panel, and about 73 cases were completed by panel or working party reports. Most of the panel reports were adopted and although none were explicitly rejected some were merely noted or lingered as the losing party blocked consensus by refusing to join in the decision to accept. Most of the cases were brought by developed countries against developed countries. However, developing countries increasingly made use of dispute settlement procedures, including among themselves, where they were complainants and respondents in 20 per cent of the cases (Jackson, 1989, p 99).

MAIN FEATURES OF THE WTO DISPUTE SETTLEMENT UNDERSTANDING

The acceptance of a strengthened DSM in the WTO was partly due to that confidence and experience acquired over time and conditional on the furnishing of protection against legal error in the form of an independent Appellate Body with its own legal staff. The honing of dispute settlement procedures and growing emphasis on a juridical or legalistic approach to complaints in place of consultation and trade diplomacy draws the Members' attention to the rules of the multilateral trading system and enhances the certainty and predictability in economic affairs, especially for traders and entrepreneurs. The requirement specified in the WTO Agreement that the WTO shall be guided by GATT history – a provision intended to safeguard the jurisprudence of GATT contained in dispute settlement reports – enriches this process.

Some of the GATT dispute procedures as developed over time are continued by the DSU in addition to some new features and an elaborate treaty text to govern this practice. If a request for consultations by a complainant does not yield settlement, a panel procedure automatically follows according to strict time limits. The panel issues a report, based on testimony and oral and written arguments, which then goes to the Dispute Settlement Body (DSB). A report is adopted unless a consensus exists to reject it. This reverse consensus makes adoption virtually automatic.

This innovation with respect to the automaticity of panel procedures and the removal of Members' ability to block adoption is balanced by the right to appeal, which did not exist under GATT procedures. If a Member appeals, the Appellate Body produces a report, which is again sent to the DSB for consideration and adoption under the reverse consensus procedure. The DSU also details rules for enforcement of rulings in cases where the losing party fails to implement the recommendation of the reports, such as compensation through trade measures or retaliation.

Some of the most drawn-out and spectacular trade disputes have involved the USA and the EU on beef hormones and bananas, to mention only two recent ones, or the USA and developing countries involving environmental complaints in the high profile shrimp/turtle and gasoline cases.

Many critics of the legalistic approach of the WTO to trading disputes are worried about the making of rules through the Dispute Settlement Mechanism and interpretations by the Appellate Body rather than negotiating on rules in the context of multilateral trade negotiations. However, this may merely reflect nostalgia for a bygone era of trade relations. For an idea of how Members appreciate the new DSU, and which sectors need attention in future trade negotiations, suffice it to mention that as of 26 June 2003, a total of 295 complaints had been brought to the WTO. Of these, mutually agreed solutions were reached in 44 cases, and complaints became settled or inactive in 24 cases. In addition, 18 were under panel or appellate review proceedings, and 83 resulted in adoption of panel or Appellate Body recommendations. Among the 83 cases, only 7 resulted in authorizations of suspension of concessions. The remaining 126 complaints were still under consultations. The USA has been the complainant in the majority of cases, followed by the EU, Canada, and Brazil. The majority of the respondents by far were developed countries. TRIMS, TRIPS and GATS.[3] Even a cursory look at this picture, provides a fairly clear picture of where the problems in international trade lie and what the priorities for a new round of multilateral trade negotiations should be.

REFERENCES

Hudec, RE (1998) 'The role of the GATT secretariat in the evolution of the WTO dispute settlement procedure' *The Uruguay Round and Beyond: Essays in Honour of Arthur Dunkel* Springer Verlag, Berlin, p116

Jackson, JH (1989) *The World Trading System – Law and Policy of International Economic Relations* MIT Press, Cambridge Massachusetts, p96

Jackson, JH (1998) *The WTO – Constitution and Jurisprudence* Chatham House Papers, The Royal Institute of International Affairs, London, England, pp30–33

Long, O (1984) *La Place du Droit et ses Limits dans le Systeme Multilateral du GATT*, Receuil des Cours, Collected Courses of the Hague Academy of International Law, 1983. Martinus Nijhoff Publishers, The Hague, p33

---

[3] Source: WTO Secretariat, Media Relations.

Forging the Tools of Trade – Core Tasks of the International Chamber of Commerce

Richard Bate, Director, ICC, UK

INTRODUCTION

The International Chamber of Commerce (ICC) has a central role in international trade. ICC issues rules, mechanisms and standards for international business that are accepted globally and whose authority stems from a reputation built over more than 80 years of service to world business. Knowledge of ICC's work is of fundamental importance for traders.

While companies worldwide accept ICC rules voluntarily, those same rules can often be incorporated in binding contracts. This contractual function is often forgotten by those critics of business self-regulation who complain that self-regulation has no teeth and mistakenly believe that government intervention is always the answer.

The best known ICC rules are the standard trade terms known as Incoterms, and the Uniform Customs and Practice for Documentary Credits (UCP 500). Like all ICC rules and voluntary codes, they are the product of extensive consultation with business users on every continent.

Incoterms are a basic reference for sales contracts and are in constant daily use wherever business deals are struck. Banks throughout the world use UCP 500 (incorporating eUCP) to finance billions of dollars of international trade every year.

There is much more. Arbitration under the rules of the ICC International Court of Arbitration is on a rising curve in today's global economy. Since 1999, new cases have been coming in to the Court at a rate of more than 550 a year, more than half involving multi-million dollar sums.

ICC model contracts give parties a neutral framework for their contractual relationship. They are drafted to ensure consistency with the parties' legal systems without expressing a bias for any one legal system. The model contracts are flexible and user friendly.

ICC voluntary codes cover marketing and advertising, the suppression of extortion and bribery, sound environmental management practices, and, more recently, Corporate Social Responsibility. ICC codes are often applied as a reference point for solving national or cross-border disputes. They can be enacted in national legislation, applied directly by companies or they can be adapted to local or specific professional requirements.

In the changing legal and business environment confronting companies at the beginning of the new millennium, the business experts who draw up ICC rules review them frequently to make sure that they remain relevant and effective. Whenever necessary, the rules are extended into new areas, like that of electronic commerce.

THE ORIGINS AND FUNCTIONS OF THE ICC

This chapter provides a brief introduction to how ICC contributes to the smooth conduct of international trade through business self-regulation. More information is available on the ICC website (iccwbo.org) and from ICC publications,[1] many of them written by the experts who draft ICC rules.

But first, let us take a look at the ICC itself. Founded in 1919, it is the only business organization that covers the entire world, represents all business sectors, and includes companies and business associations of every size. Companies judged to be committed to private enterprise are eligible to join one of ICC's national committees. In those countries where there is no national committee, companies or business associations can become direct members.

National committees form the supreme governing body, the World Council. Meeting twice a year, it is the equivalent of the general assembly of a major intergovernmental organization. The World Council elects the Chairman and Vice-Chairman for two-year terms and also elects the Executive Board, which

---

[1] ICC's publications list can be consulted at the Business Bookstore at www.iccbooks.com. The books may be ordered online through the Bookstore from ICC Publishing SA or from ICC UK and other ICC national committees throughout the world.

has between 15 and 20 members and is responsible for setting strategy and implementing ICC policy.

ICC commissions draft the rules and standards that are the bedrock of ICC. They total some 2,000 experts drawn from member companies in every business field. Commissions cover anti-corruption, arbitration, banking, biosociety, business in society, commercial law and practice, competition, customs and trade regulations, e-business, IT and telecoms, environment and energy, financial services and insurance, intellectual property, marketing and advertising, taxation, trade and investment policy and transport and logistics. Increasingly, ICC commissions pool their expertise in cross-disciplinary initiatives, for example ICC's electronic commerce project or its work on climate change.

THE ICC INTERNATIONAL COURT OF ARBITRATION

ICC arbitration is perhaps the organization's most widely known activity, deserving pride of place in this brief account of ICC work. Established in 1923, the ICC International Court of Arbitration has pioneered international commercial arbitration as it is known today.

Over the decades, the Court has led the way in securing worldwide acceptance of arbitration as the most effective means of resolving international commercial disputes and in demonstrating the advantages of institutional as compared with *ad hoc* arbitration. ICC led the movement that resulted in the adoption in 1958 of the New York Convention on Recognition and Enforcement of Foreign Arbitral Awards – the most important multilateral treaty in international arbitration.

Court members are mostly lawyers or specialists in international business. The Court itself does not resolve disputes, but names independent arbitrators to carry out this task. It organizes and supervises arbitration, helps in overcoming obstacles and makes sure that ICC Arbitration Rules are followed faithfully. The Court ensures that as far as possible, awards are enforceable.

Support staff assist parties, counsel and arbitrators in Arabic, Cantonese, English, French, German, Italian, Polish, Portuguese, Russian, Spanish and Swedish. One of seven secretariat teams headed by a counsel follows each case. To reduce processing time, the Court secretariat relies on state-of-the-art computerized case management and information retrieval systems.

Parties are free to submit disputes to arbitrators of their choice and to fix the place and language of the arbitration, as well as the applicable law. The arbitral tribunal is usually composed of one or three members. When there is only one arbitrator, he or she is appointed by the parties. Failing agreement, the Court appoints the arbitrator.

The decision to refer to ICC arbitration should ideally be made when parties are still negotiating terms of an international contract – long before there is any hint of a dispute. The precaution may never be needed, but if it is much anguish may be avoided by thinking ahead with as much precision as possible.At the very least, parties should include in their contract the recommended standard ICC Arbitration clause: 'All disputes arising out of or in connection with the present contract shall be finally settled under the Rules of Arbitration of the International Chamber of Commerce by one or more arbitrators appointed in accordance with the said Rules.'[2]

In addition, parties may find it useful to stipulate in the arbitration clause the law governing the contract, the number of arbitrators and the place and language of arbitration. They should also consider the possible need for special provisions in the event that arbitration is contemplated among more than two parties.

Trading partners should bear in mind that alternatives to arbitration are also at their disposal in the event of dispute. The ICC Commission on Arbitration has also recently published the 'ICC ADR Rules and suggested clauses' which offers a full range of possibilities for amicable dispute solution, including mediation and other techniques. ICC's International Centre for Expertise is a further means of resolving disputes. At the request of the parties, the Centre can call on hundreds of experts in a broad range of technical areas to pronounce on factual issues. The Centre also administers a specific procedure, known as DOCDEX, for resolving disputes involving documentary credits.

DOCDEX AND INCOTERMS

DOCDEX was created to resolve misunderstandings and delays on the part of certain traders and banks in dealing with documentary credits, a problem that increasingly plagues international trade. When the documentary credit system breaks down, international trade as a whole suffers. DOCDEX is at

---

[2] PDF files of the standard clause and the full ICC Rules of Arbitration may be downloaded from the ICC website in Arabic, Chinese, English, French, German, Italian, Japanese, Portuguese, Russian and Spanish.

the heart of ICC's global effort to maintain the integrity of the immensely valuable documentary credit system.

Prevention, of course, is better than cure. While Incoterms cannot provide protection against every type of dispute, when used correctly they can reduce the risk of a broad range of disputes over the terms of international sales contracts. In the interest of precision and legal certainty, Incoterms should be incorporated into contracts under the specific reference 'Incoterms 2000'.

Since ICC first published Incoterms in 1936, they have been updated six times, and the latest version came into force in 2000. Incoterms precisely define the responsibilities of buyer and seller. Endorsed by the United Nations Commission on International Trade Law (UNCITRAL), they are recognized as the international standard by customs authorities and courts in all the main trading nations.

The 2000 version takes account of international traders' growing reliance on intermodal transport. Increased use of FCA (Free Carrier). . . named place, has prompted ICC to simplify delivery obligations under this term. While mode of transport is no longer the key criterion for the transfer of costs and risks from seller to buyer, FCA Incoterms 2000 focuses on place of delivery alone.

Among the best known Incoterms are EXW (Ex works). . . named place, FOB (Free on board). . . named port of shipment , CIF (Cost, Insurance and Freight). . . named port of destination, DDU (Delivered Duty Unpaid). . . named place of destination, CPT (Carriage Paid To). . . named place of destination, DAF (Delivered at frontier). . . named place.

Here are three examples of correct use of Incoterms:

- CPT Kuala Lumpur Incoterms 2000;
- FOB Liverpool Incoterms 2000;
- DDU Frankfurt Schmidt GmbH Warehouse 4 Incoterms 2000.

Many false, inaccurate or incomplete versions of Incoterms and their definitions are available on the Internet. These can cause problems for the unwary since only the full definitions published by ICC are authentic. Traders risk legal disputes if they use summaries or shortened versions because important aspects of the rules are almost invariably left out.

OTHER ICC INSTRUMENTS AND GUIDELINES

Banks, as well as the traders they serve, make extensive use of ICC instruments. Prominent among them are Uniform Customs and Practice for Documentary Credits (UCP 500, revised 1993), Uniform Rules for Demand Guarantees (URDG 458, 1992) and Uniform Rules for Collections (URC 522) all of which have been endorsed by UNCITRAL.

UCP 500, now also incorporating eUCP, are the most widely used, with banks from more than 100 countries signed up to the UCP 500 adherence list on the ICC website.

International Standby Practices (ISP 98, adopted 1999) – while the impact of ISP 98 is still to be assessed, it is already estimated that 15–20 per cent of Standby Letters of Credit use ISP 98. The most recent ICC Banking instrument is International Standard Banking Practice (ISBP645, 2002) and is used alongside UCP 500.

Under the heading of insurance, ICC Uniform Rules for Contract Bonds (URCB, 1994) regulate the provisions of conditional guarantees. Their use is increasingly widespread.

Excellent examples of how the private sector successfully cooperates with intergovernmental organizations in trade facilitation is provided by ICC International Customs Guidelines and the UNCTAD/ICC Rules for Multimodal Transport Documents.

The Customs Guidelines were developed with the assistance of the World Customs Organization as a set of business principles that modern and efficient customs administrations are urged to follow.

The UNCTAD/ICC Rules for Multimodal Transport Documents set the only globally accepted standard in their field. They represent a reasonable compromise between shipper and carrier interests and work through incorporation into private transport contracts.

ICC MODEL CONTRACTS

No summary of ICC's contribution to international trade would be complete without mention of ICC model contracts. They are particularly valuable to small companies that cannot afford big legal departments.

A major advantage of the model contracts is that they avoid the need to draft an international contract from scratch. They can be used either as complete sets of clauses (with parties filling in the blanks and choosing the relevant alternative when asked to do so) or as check lists.

The following model contracts are available:

- ICC Model Commercial Agency Contract;

- ICC Model Distributorship Contract (sole Importer-Distributor);
- ICC Model Sale Contract (Manufactured goods intended for resale);
- ICC Model Occasional Intermediary Contract (non-circumvention and non-disclosure agreement);
- ICC Model International Franchising Contract;
- ICC Short Form Model Contracts: Agency & Distributorship;
- ICC Force Majeure Clause 2003; ICC Hardship Clause 2003.

E-COMMERCE

Finally, we take a look at cyberspace, where there are no frontiers and no physical divisions. Basic rules of the road will be crucial to the commercial success of open networks such as the Internet.

ICC's task is to provide those rules. As in the realm of paper-based trade, it does not compete with other business or professional bodies, but provides universal standards that all can use.

One of the first ICC instruments specially designed for e-commerce is a set of guidelines for ensuring trustworthy digital transactions over the Internet, known as GUIDEC. ICC experts are now building on these rules by creating a harmonized certification mechanism that will allow contracting parties to securely verify their partners' identities over a network.

ICC's World Chambers Federation has established World Chambers Network (WCN), a global hub on the Internet where chambers and individual companies exchange information about themselves, their products and business opportunities.

An online application has been launched that enables businesses to conclude contracts with the help of secure interactive software. The new business-to-business facility is based on the ICC Model Sale Contract mentioned above, which has been in worldwide use since 1997.

Other projects in the pipeline are:

- guidelines for marketing on the Internet, catering for the varied sensitivities of a global audience;
- new tailor-made contract clauses that can be applied by business partners to avoid complications arising from differing data protection regimes;
- measures to avoid abuse of domain names and copyright on the Internet;
- a self-regulatory framework for electronic documentation, governing import and export transactions, transport and trade finance;

- for companies drawing up contracts, links to an E-TERMS database service providing full definitions of the legal terms they intend to use;
- facilitation of dispute resolution mechanisms in cyberspace, to overcome associated problems of jurisdiction and applicable law.

THE ATA CARNET

The picture would not be complete without a mention of the 'Passport for Goods', the ATA Carnet. This is an international customs document that permits duty-free temporary import of goods for up to one year for such purposes as commercial samples, professional use or exhibition at trade fairs.

ATA Carnets are issued exclusively through chambers of commerce and similar organizations affiliated to the ATA international guarantee chain. The chain is administered by the World Chambers Federation (WCF), the part of ICC that acts as a hub for chambers of commerce worldwide.

All the activities described here have to do with the fabric of international business, the day-to-day conduct of trade and relations between business partners. They are at the core of ICC's work, but are far from the whole story.

This overview has made no mention of ICC's other main task – to be the advocate of business at the highest level, whenever governments make decisions that crucially affect corporate strategies and the bottom line. That is a subject for another article.

The Pattern and Trends in World Trade

Jonathan Reuvid

TWENTIETH CENTURY TRADE IN RETROSPECT

The focus of this first part of the *Handbook of World Trade* is on trade development since 1945. However, the historical context of the growth in trade throughout the 20th century puts into perspective the efforts that have been made globally in the past 40 years to stimulate international trade to the benefit of participating nations within a broadly Free Trade environment.

In Table 1.6.1 the rate of growth in the volume of merchandise exports for 11 countries and the world is summarized for the period from 1870 to 1998. In global terms, the annual average compound growth rate between 1913 and 1950 was less than one per cent, compared to pre-1913 growth of 3.4 per cent. The following 23-year period was one of strong international trade expansion with annual compound growth averaging 7.9 per cent, which then eased off to 5.1 per cent over the 25-year period 1973–98.

Comparing the two most recent periods, among developed economies annual average growth fell back with the exception of the UK where the growth rate increased from 3.9 to 4.4 per cent. The growth rate of merchandise exports from Germany fell back from 12.4 to 4.4 per cent as the post-war reconstruction period of German industry came to a close, while the annual growth in exports from the USA remained at the 6.0 per cent level. However, the fall in merchandise export growth has been most marked in the case of Japan, where the annual rate fell by almost two-thirds from 15.4 per cent over 1950–73 to almost European levels (5.3 per cent) during the 1973–98 period.

By contrast, the volume of merchandise exports from developing countries in Asia and Latin America soared. China's annual growth rate more than quadrupled from 2.7 to 11.8 per cent, while Mexican export growth rose from 4.3 per cent to 10.9 per cent.

Table 1.6.1 Rate of growth (%) in volume of merchandise exports, 11 countries and world, 1890–1988 (annual average compound growth rates)

	1870–1913	*1913–50*	*1950–73*	*1973–98*
France	2.8	1.1	8.2	4.7
Germany	4.1	−2.8	12.4	4.4
Netherlands	2.3	1.5	10.4	4.1
United Kingdom	2.8	0.0	3.9	4.4
Spain	3.5	−1.6	9.2	9.0
United States	4.9	2.2	6.3	6.0
Mexico	5.4	−0.5	4.3	10.9
Brazil	1.9	1.7	4.7	6.6
China	2.6	1.1	2.7	11.8
India	2.4	−1.5	2.5	5.9
Japan	8.5	2.0	15.4	5.3
World	3.4	0.9	7.9	5.1

Source: Derived from Appendix 1.6.2, 1950–98 IMF International Financial Statistics, supplemented by UN Yearbook of International Trade Statistics, various issues.

The growing significance of merchandise exports to the economies of individual countries is illustrated in Table 1.6.2, which charts over six selected years in the same span of the past 130 years how exports as a percentage of GDP at 1990 prices fluctuated. Globally, exports fell back from 9.0 per cent of GDP in 1929 to 5.5 per cent in 1950 before recovering to 10.5 per cent in 1973 and moving forward to 17.2 per cent in 1998.

Broadly, the developed countries conformed to this pattern with much higher rates of growth export ratios in Europe and lower rates in the USA and Japan. By 1998 the exports/GDP ratio had reached 25.0 per cent in the UK and 38.9 per cent in Germany. For the USA and Japan the ratios were 10.1 and 13.4 per cent respectively. The highest export/GDP ratio for 1998 among developed countries was recorded in the Netherlands at 61.2 per cent.

Among developing countries, in spite of their superior rates of export growth since 1973, export/GDP ratios are comparatively modest. In 1998 Mexico's merchandise exports represented 10.7 per cent of GDP, while China's export/GDP ratio was only 4.9 per cent, giving a chilling reminder

Table 1.6.2 Merchandise exports as a percentage of GDP in 1990 prices, 11 countries and world, 1870–1998

	1870	*1913*	*1929*	*1950*	*1973*	*1998*
France	4.9	7.8	8.6	7.6	15.2	28.7
Germany	9.5	16.1	12.8	6.2	23.8	38.9
Netherlands	17.4	17.3	17.2	12.2	40.7	61.2
United Kingdom	12.2	17.5	13.3	11.3	14.0	25.0
Spain	3.8	8.1	5.0	3.0	5.0	23.5
United States	2.5	3.7	3.6	3.0	4.9	10.1
Mexico	3.9	9.1	12.5	3.0	1.9	10.7
Brazil	12.2	9.8	6.9	3.9	2.5	5.4
China	0.7	1.7	1.8	2.6	1.5	4.9
India	2.6	4.6	3.7	2.9	2.0	2.4
Japan	0.2	2.4	3.5	2.2	7.7	13.4
World	4.6	7.9	9.0	5.5	10.5	17.2

Source: Appendix 1.6.1, sources for Fig. 1.6.1, Maddison (1997), Table 13

of the likely impact of Chinese exports on world trade as its per capita industrial output approaches more closely the developed economy levels.

For readers requiring more detail on the progression of exports round the world, the value of merchandise exports at constant 1990 prices for 35 countries is tracked for the same six years over the 1870–1998 period in Appendix 1.6.12 to this chapter.

TRENDS IN MERCHANDISE TRADE AND COMMERCIAL SERVICES BY REGION

The growth by region in the value of world merchandise trade and world trade in commercial services between 1990 and 2001 in terms of annual percentage change are charted in Tables 1.6.3 and 1.6.4.

In terms of merchandise trade, the EU (within Western Europe) is the biggest grouping in both exports ($2,291 billion) and imports ($2,334 billion) with imports marginally exceeding exports. The rate of growth of imports fell from 6 per cent in 2000 to a decline of 1 per cent in 1999, while exports declined in 2001 by 1 per cent against 3 per cent growth the previous year.

Table 1.6.3 Growth in the value of world merchandise trade by region, 2001 (billion dollars and percentage)

	Exports				Imports			
	Value	Annual percentage change			Value	Annual percentage change		
	2001	1990–01	2000	2001	2001	1990–01	2000	2001
World	5984	5	13	–4	6270	5	13	–4
North America[a]	991	6	14	–6	1408	7	18	–6
Latin America	347	8	20	–3	380	11	16	–2
Western Europe	2485	4	4	–1	2524	4	6	–3
European Union (15)	2291	4	3	–1	2334	4	6	–3
C./E. Europe/Baltic States/CIS	286	7	26	5	267	6	14	11
Central and Eastern Europe	129	8	14	12	159	10	12	9
Russian Federation	103	–	39	–2	54	–	13	20
Africa	141.2	3	27	–5	136	3	4	2
Middle East	237	5	42	–9	180	5	13	4
Asia	1497	7	18	–9	1375	6	23	–7
Japan	403	3	14	–16	349	4	22	–8
China	266	14	28	7	244	15	36	8
Six East Asian traders	568	7	19	–12	532	6	26	–13

[a] Excluding Mexico throughout this report.

Note: It should be mentioned at the outset that there are breaks in the continuity of the figures at the country and regional levels.

Source: WTO (www.wto.org)

Asia is the second largest exporting region ($1,497 billion) with exports exceeding imports by $122 billion in 2001. Following the 1997/8 Asian financial crisis, the annual growth in exports recovered from 6 per cent negative to 18 per cent positive in 2000 before falling back 9 per cent in 2001. Likewise, imports revived from 1998's decline of 13 per cent and peaked at 23 per cent growth in 2000 before declining 7 per cent in 2001.

Conversely, North America (excluding Mexico) was the world's second largest importing region in 2001 ($1,408 billion), although only third in exports ($991 billion). However, export growth recovered by 4 per cent in 1999 (1998 – 1 per cent negative) and peaked at 14 per cent growth in 2000 before declining 6 per cent in 2001. Imports achieved 18 per cent growth in 2000 against 5 per cent in 1998 before declining 6 per cent in 2001.

Although exports from Central and Eastern Europe increased only marginally in 1999 by 1 per cent against a 10-year average growth rate of 7 per cent, growth was more robust in 2000 and 2001 (11 per cent) to a total of $129 billion. Imports declined by 1 per cent in 1999 against 10 per cent average for the decade, but grew strongly in 2000 and 2001 to a total $159 billion. Thus, the annual trade deficit for the region was maintained at the level of $30 billion from 1999. The Baltic States and CIS countries together achieved an export surplus of $31 billion in 1999 with exports slowing by 2 per cent and imports by 24 per cent and in 2001 the trade surplus had widened to $49 billion.

African imports were at a similar level ($128 billion) to the CEE in 1999 but grew more modestly in 2000 and 2001 to $136 billion. Exports from Africa grew more rapidly from $117 billion (1999) to $141 billion (2001) thereby achieving a small trade surplus.

The pattern of 2001 world trade in commercial services was rather different. Although the world average annual growth rate in the value of exports over the 10-year period to 2000 at 6.5 per cent was the same as for merchandise trade, the decline in the export of commercial services in 2001 was only 0.5 per cent compared to 4.5 per cent in the case of merchandise. Both Western Europe and North America (again, excluding Mexico), the first and third exporting regions, were net exporters of commercial services to the values of $32 billion and $70 billion respectively. By contrast in 2001, Asia, now the second-ranking region in commercial services, was a net importer to the value of $52 billion. Neither Central and Eastern Europe nor the Baltic States and the CIS registered as significant in commercial services world trade.

Table 1.6.4 Growth in the value of world trade in commercial services by region

	Exports					Imports			
	Value	Annual percentage change				Value	Annual percentage change		
	2001	1990–01	2000	2001		2001	1990–01	2000	2001
World	1460	6	6	0		1445	5	7	–1
North America[a]	299	6	9	–3		229	6	14	–6
Latin America	58	6	11	–3		71	7	12	0
Western Europe	679	5	2	1		647	5	2	1
European Union (15)	612	5	1	1		605	5	2	2
C./E. Europe/Baltic States/CIS	56	...	11	11		59	...	19	13
Africa	31	5	0	0		37	3	7	–3
Middle East	33	...	16	–7		45	...	8	–7
Asia	303	8	12	–1		355	6	8	–3
Japan	64	4	13	–7		107	2	1	–7
China	33	17	15	9		39	23	16	9
Six East Asian traders	146	9	12	0		133	8	13	–3

* Excluding Mexico throughout this report.

Note: It should be mentioned at the outset that there are numerous breaks in the continuity of the figures at the country and regional levels due to frequent revisions to the trade in services data.

Source: WTO (www.wto.org)

More detailed analyses of the shares of world foreign trade accounted for by region and principal trading nation are reproduced in Tables 1.6.6 to 1.6.8. In terms of merchandise trade, the value of exports and imports of developing economies grew by 9.0 per cent and 8.5 per cent respectively between 1990 and 2000, compared to world trade growth of 6.5 per cent (see Appendix 1.6.4). However, developing economies' imports declined 4.0 per cent in 2001 while their exports fell by 6.5 per cent.

FOREIGN TRADE BETWEEN TRADING BLOCS AND THEIR MEMBERS

An alternative approach to the analysis of regional merchandise trade is in terms of intra- and extra-exports and imports between the principal trading groups[1] and their members: APEC, EU, NAFTA, ASEAN, CEFTA, MERCOSUR and ANDEAN. This data for 1990, 1995 and 2001 is analysed in Table 1.6.5 in respect of percentage share of exports/imports and annual percentage change, and in value for 2001.

In the case of APEC, exports between the 21 country membership in 2001 exceeded exports to other regions in the ratio 71.8 to 28.2. Similarly, the ratio of intra-imports to extra imports was 69.9 to 30.1.

Exports between the 15 members of the EU in 1999 exceeded exports to other regions in the ratio 61.85 to 38.15 while intra- and extra-imports followed a closely similar pattern.

Given the comparatively recent formation of the NAFTA, it is encouraging to find that in 2001 intra-exports and intra-imports represented 55.5 per cent and 39.5 per cent respectively of total exports and imports.

Among the four other trade groups the incidence of intra-exports and imports is less dominant. The proportion of intra-exports between the 10 ASEAN and 4 MERCOSUR members was 23.5 per cent and 17.3 per cent and, similarly, 22.8 per cent and 18.9 per cent respectively for intra-imports.

Intra-trade between the 7 members of CEFTA (exports: 12.4; imports: 9.9 per cent) and 5 members of the ANDEAN group (exports: 11.2 per cent; imports: 13.3 per cent) were less significant but were growing quite strongly in the case of the ANDEAN 5. The potential foreign trade benefits for all trading blocs from enhanced free trade through the further evolution of the WTO are manifest if the Doha round can be revived and pursued to a positive conclusion.

---

[1] See Appendix I for membership of trading blocs.

Table 1.6.5 Merchandise trade of selected regional integration arrangements, 2001(billion dollars and percentage)

	Value	Share in total exports/imports			Annual percentage change		
	2001	1990	1995	2001	1990–01	2000	2001
APEC (21)							
Total exports	2700	100.0	100.00	100.00	7	17	−8
Intra-exports	1938	67.5	73.06	71.78	7	20	−9
Extra-exports	762	32.5	26.94	28.22	5	11	−4
Total imports[a]	2969	100.0	100.00	100.00	7	21	−7
Intra-imports	2076	65.4	71.74	69.92	8	20	−8
Extra-imports	893	34.6	28.26	30.08	6	24	−2
EU (15)							
Total exports	2291	100.0	100.00	100.00	4	3	−1
Intra-exports	1417	64.9	64.01	61.85	3	1	−2
Extra-exports	874	35.1	35.99	38.15	5	7	0
Total imports	2334	100.0	100.00	100.00	4	6	−3
Intra-imports	1421	63.0	65.23	60.89	3	1	−2
Extra-imports	913	37.0	34.77	39.11	4	15	−4
NAFTA (3)							
Total exports	1149	100.0	100.00	100.00	7	15	−6
Intra-exports	637	42.6	46.06	55.46	9	18	−6
Extra-exports	512	57.4	53.94	44.54	4	11	−6
Total imports[b]	1578	100.0	100.00	100.00	8	18	−6
Intra-imports	624	34.4	37.72	39.55	9	17	−7
Extra-imports	954	65.6	62.28	60.45	7	19	−6
ASEAN (10)							
Total exports	385	100.0	100.00	100.00	9	19	−10
Intra-exports	90	20.1	25.52	23.46	11	28	−12
Extra-exports	295	79.9	74.48	76.54	9	16	−9
Total imports	336	100.0	100.00	100.00	7	22	−8
Intra-imports	77	16.2	18.89	22.77	10	28	−12
Extra-imports	260	83.8	81.11	77.23	6	21	−7

Table 1.6.5 *(continued)*

	Value	Share in total exports/imports			Annual percentage change		
	2001	*1990*	*1995*	*2001*	*1990–01*	*2000*	*2001*
CEFTA (7)							
Total exports	138	–	100.00	100.00	–	13	11
Intra-exports	17	–	14.54	12.37	–	14	14
Extra-exports	121	–	85.46	87.63	–	13	11
Total imports	168	–	100.00	100.00	–	12	8
Intra-imports	17	–	11.23	9.91	–	13	12
Extra-imports	151	–	88.72	90.09	–	11	8
MERCOSUR (4)							
Total exports	88	100.0	100.00	100.00	6	14	4
Intra-exports	15	8.9	20.51	17.26	13	17	–14
Extra-exports	73	91.1	79.49	82.74	5	13	9
Total imports	84	100.0	100.00	100.00	10	8	–6
Intra-imports	16	14.5	18.07	18.88	13	12	–11
Extra-imports	68	85.5	81.93	81.12	9	8	–5
ANDEAN (5)							
Total exports	53	100.0	100.00	100.00	5	34	–9
Intra-exports	6	4.2	12.16	11.19	15	30	14
Extra-exports	47	95.8	87.84	88.81	4	34	–12
Total imports[c]	44	100.0	100.00	100.00	9	9	12
Intra-imports	6	7.7	12.83	13.32	14	29	8
Extra-imports	38	92.3	87.12	86.68	8	7	12

[a] Imports of Canada, Mexico (1990–99), Peru. and Australia are valued f.o.b.

[b] Imports of Canada and Mexico (1990–99) are valued f.o.b.

[c] Imports of Peru and Venezuela are valued f.o.b.

Note: The figures are not fully adjusted for differences in the way members of the arrangements in this table record their merchandise trade.

Source: WTO (www.wto.org)

INTRA- AND INTER-REGIONAL MERCHANDISE TRADE

North America's biggest regional export markets are Asia and Western Europe, accounting respectively for 19.0 per cent and 20.9 per cent of total exports in 2001. Asia accounted for 32.7 per cent of total US imports of which 9.9 per cent were sourced from China. A further 19.5 per cent originated from Western Europe.

For Western Europe, intra-trade accounted for 67.5 per cent of exports and 66.4 per cent of imports in 2001. The 32.5 per cent of exports shipped in 2001 from Western European countries to external markets were diffused more evenly between North America (10.2 per cent) and Asia (7.9 per cent) with the remainder distributed between Latin America, Africa and the Middle East in almost equal proportions. Of the 33.6 per cent of imports sourced outside Western Europe, 11.3 per cent were imported from Asia, 8.0 per cent from North America, 6.7 per cent from Central and Eastern Europe and CIS countries and 3.0 per cent from Africa.

The exports of Central and Eastern European countries, the Baltic and CIS states outside the region are sold primarily into Western European markets. The two other significant regional markets are Asia and North America. By contrast, more than 60 per cent of Latin America's exports are sold to North American markets, with Western Europe and Asia its more important secondary regional markets.

North America is also the primary extra-export market for Asian goods with Western Europe the dominant secondary market. Asia is the primary export region for Middle Eastern merchandise with Western Europe and North America its major secondary markets. Finally, Africa follows a similar pattern to Central and Eastern Europe, the Baltic and CIS states with more than half of export goods shipped to Western Europe and the bulk of remaining extra-exports to North America and Asia.

A more succinct account of recent trends in the value and volume of overall regional trade in merchandise and commercial services is displayed in Appendices 1.6.5 to 1.6.11. In all cases, other than the transition economies of Central and Eastern Europe where foreign trade continued to flourish, the impact of the world economic slowdown in 2001 is evident.

The league table of leading exporters and importers

The top 50 exporting and importing countries in world merchandise trade, excluding intra-EU trade, are identified in Table 1.6.6. The EU and US head both league tables, the EU as a net importer (2001 – $39 billion deficit) and the US with the world's largest trade deficit (2001 – $449 billion). Japan ranks third both in merchandise exports and imports with the largest trade surplus (2001 – $54 billion) followed by mainland China in fourth place with a surplus of £23 billion.

Canada holds fifth place with a surplus of $32 billion and Hong Kong is listed sixth with a net deficit of $11 billion after accounting for re-exports and retained imports. Mexico ranks seventh with a deficit of $18 billion and the trio of former Asian tigers, Korea, Taiwan and Singapore, make up the remaining top ten. Germany, France and the UK were previously listed individually in the WTO top ten but are now grouped within the EU.

The top 10 lists of exporters and importers of commercial services, before the exclusion of EU intra-trade, (see Table 1.6.7) are somewhat different to those for merchandise trade.

The US ranks first both as an exporter and importer of commercial services with a net surplus in 2001 of $76 billion. The UK ranks second as an exporter but fourth in imported services with a surplus of $17 billion. Conversely, Germany, second as an importer and fourth in exports, reported a deficit of $53 billion. France, ranking third in exports and fifth in imports, achieved a similar net result to the UK with a surplus of $18 billion. Japan, lying third in imported services and fifth in exports echoed Germany's performance with a net deficit of $43 billion.

Of the remaining top ten in exported commercial services, Spain (6th) and Italy (7th) delivered surpluses of $24 billion and $1 billion respectively. The Netherlands (8th) was just in deficit and Belgium-Luxembourg (9th) recorded a surplus of $3 billion. As last of the top ten, Hong Kong China achieved an equivalent surplus to France and the UK of $17 billion.

Of the remaining 29 countries listed, among the Western European economies Austria, Denmark and Portugal showed small surpluses and Switzerland a larger surplus of $10 billion in commercial services for 2001. The three largest transition economies, Poland, Hungary and the Czech Republic, were also in surplus. Most other countries, except for Norway, Turkey, Greece, Singapore and Egypt, were in deficit. One of the largest deficits ($25 billion) was recorded by Ireland.

Table 1.6.6 Leading exporters and importers in world merchandise trade (excluding intra-EU trade), 2001 (billion dollars and percentage)

Rank	Exporters	Value	Share	Annual percentage change
1	Extra-EU exports	874.1	18.4	0
2	United States	730.8	15.4	–6
3	Japan	403.5	8.5	–16
4	China	266.2	5.6	7
5	Canada	259.9	5.5	–6
6	Hong Kong, China	191.1	4.0	–6
	domestic exports	20.3	0.4	–14
	re-exports	170.8	3.6	–5
7	Mexico	158.5	3.3	–5
8	Korea, Rep. of	150.4	3.2	–13
9	Taipei, Chinese	122.5	2.6	–17
10	Singapore	121.8	2.6	–12
	domestic exports	66.1	1.4	–16
	re-exports	55.6	1.2	–6
11	Russian Fed.	103.1	2.2	–2
12	Malaysia	87.9	1.9	–10
13	Switzerland	82.1	1.7	1
14	Saudi Arabia	68.2	1.4	–12
15	Thailand	65.1	1.4	–6
16	Australia	63.4	1.3	–1
17	Brazil	58.2	1.2	6
18	Norway	57.9	1.2	–3
19	Indonesia	56.3	1.2	–9

Rank	Importers	Value	Share	Annual percentage change
1	United States	1180.2	23.5	–6
2	Extra-EU imports	912.8	18.2	–4
3	Japan	349.1	7.0	–8
4	China	243.6	4.9	8
5	Canada	227.2	4.5	–7
6	Hong Kong, China[a]	202.0	4.0	–6
	retained imports[a]	31.2	0.6	–11
7	Mexico	176.2	3.5	–4
8	Korea, Rep. of	141.1	2.8	–12
9	Singapore	116.0	2.3	–14
	retained imports[a]	60.4	1.2	–20
10	Taipei, Chinese	107.3	2.1	–23
11	Switzerland	84.1	1.7	1
12	Malaysia	74.1	1.5	–10
13	Australia	63.9	1.3	–11
14	Thailand	62.1	1.2	0
15	Brazil	58.3	1.2	0
16	Russian Fed.	53.9	1.1	20
17	Poland	50.3	1.0	3
18	India	49.6	1.0	–3
19	United Arab Emirates	41.7	0.8	9

Table 1.6.6 (continued)

Rank	Exporters	Value	Share	Annual percentage change	Rank	Importers	Value	Share	Annual percentage change
20	India	43.6	0.9	3	20	Turkey	40.6	0.8	-26
21	United Arab Emirates[b]	42.9	0.9	-2	21	Czech Rep.[c]	36.5	0.7	14
22	Poland	36.1	0.8	14	22	Israel	35.1	0.7	-7
23	Czech Rep.	33.4	0.7	15	23	Hungary	33.7	0.7	5
24	Philippines	32.1	0.7	-19	24	Norway	32.4	0.6	-6
25	Turkey	31.2	0.7	12	25	Philippines	31.4	0.6	-7
26	Hungary	30.5	0.6	9	26	Saudi Arabia[b]	31.2	0.6	3
27	South Africa	29.3	0.6	-2	27	Indonesia	31.0	0.6	-8
28	Israel	29.0	0.6	-8	28	South Africa	28.4	0.6	-4
29	Venezuela	27.4	0.6	-14	29	Argentina	20.3	0.4	-20
30	Argentina	26.7	0.6	1	30	Venezuela	18.0	0.4	11
31	Iran, Islamic Rep. of[b]	25.3	0.5	-11	31	Iran, Islamic Rep. of[b]	17.5	0.3	22
32	Algeria	20.1	0.4	-9	32	Chile	17.2	0.3	-5
33	Nigeria[b]	19.2	0.4	-9	33	Ukraine	15.8	0.3	13
34	Chile	17.4	0.4	-4	34	Vietnam	15.6	0.3	2
35	Ukraine	16.3	0.3	12	35	Romania	15.6	0.3	19
36	Kuwait	16.1	0.3	-17	36	Slovak Rep.[c]	14.8	0.3	16
37	Iraq[b]	15.9	0.3	-23	37	New Zealand	13.3	0.3	-4
38	Vietnam	15.1	0.3	4	38	Colombia	12.8	0.3	11
39	New Zealand	13.7	0.3	3	39	Egypt	12.8	0.3	-9

Table 1.6.6 (continued)

Rank	Exporters	Value	Share	Annual percentage change	Rank	Importers	Value	Share	Annual percentage change
40	Slovak Rep.	12.6	0.3	6	40	Nigeria[b]	11.2	0.2	28
41	Colombia	12.3	0.3	−6	41	Iraq[b]	11.0	0.2	−1
42	Libyan Arab Jamahiriya[b]	11.7	0.2	−13	42	Morocco	11.0	0.2	−5
43	Romania	11.4	0.2	10	43	Pakistan	10.6	0.2	−6
44	Oman	11.1	0.2	2	44	Slovenia	10.1	0.2	0
45	Qatar	10.9	0.2	−6	45	Algeria	9.7	0.2	6
46	Slovenia	9.3	0.2	6	46	Tunisia	9.6	0.2	11
47	Pakistan	9.2	0.2	2	47	Dominican Republic[b]	8.8	0.2	−7
48	Kazakhstan	8.6	0.2	−5	48	Peru	8.6	0.2	−2
49	Morocco	7.1	0.2	−4	49	Bangladesh	8.4	0.2	0
50	Angola	6.7	0.1	−15	50	Belarus	8.0	0.2	−7
	Total of above[d]	4553.0	96.1	–		Total of above[d]	4603.0	91.7	–
	World (excl. intra-EU trade)[d]	4738.0	100.0	−5		World (excl. intra-EU trade)[d]	5020.0	100.0	−5

a Retained imports are defined as imports less re-exports.
b Secretariat estimate
c Imports are valued f.o.b.
d Includes significant re-exports or imports for re-export.

Source: WTO (www.wto.org)

Table 1.6.7 Leading exporters and importers in world trade in commercial services, 2001(billion dollars and percentage)

Rank	Exporters	Value	Share	Annual percentage change	Rank	Importers	Value	Share	Annual percentage change
1	United States	263.4	18.1	-3	1	United States	187.7	13.0	-7
2	United Kingdom	108.4	7.4	-6	2	Germany	132.6	9.2	0
3	France	79.8	5.5	-2	3	Japan	107.0	7.4	-7
4	Germany	79.7	5.5	-1	4	United Kingdom	91.6	6.3	-4
5	Japan	63.7	4.4	-7	5	France	61.6	4.3	0
6	Spain	57.4	3.9	8	6	Italy	55.7	3.9	2
7	Italy	57.0	3.9	2	7	Netherlands	52.9	3.7	2
8	Netherlands	51.7	3.5	0	8	Canada	41.5	2.9	-3
9	Belgium-Luxembourg	42.6	2.9	-1	9	Belgium-Luxembourg	39.3	2.7	2
10	Hong Kong, China	42.4	2.9	2	10	China	39.0	2.7	9
11	Canada	35.6	2.4	-5	11	Ireland	34.8	2.4	21
12	China	32.9	2.3	9	12	Spain	33.2	2.3	7
13	Austria	32.5	2.2	5	13	Korea, Rep. of	33.1	2.3	0
14	Korea, Rep. of	29.6	2.0	0	14	Austria	31.5	2.2	6
15	Denmark	26.9	1.8	10	15	Hong Kong, China	25.1	1.7	-2
16	Singapore	26.4	1.8	-2	16	Taipei, Chinese	23.7	1.6	-8
17	Switzerland	25.2	1.7	-4	17	Denmark	23.5	1.6	6
18	Sweden	21.8	1.5	9	18	India	23.4	1.6	19
19	India	20.4	1.4	15	19	Sweden	22.9	1.6	-2
20	Taipei, Chinese	20.3	1.4	2	20	Russian Fed.	21.1	1.5	20
21	Ireland	20.0	1.4	20	21	Singapore	20.0	1.4	-6
22	Greece	19.4	1.3	1	22	Malaysia	16.5	1.1	0
23	Norway	16.7	1.1	12	23	Mexico	16.5	1.1	-1
24	Turkey	15.9	1.1	-17	24	Australia	16.4	1.1	-8

Table 1.6.7 (continued)

Rank	Exporters	Value	Share	Annual percentage change	Rank	Importers	Value	Share	Annual percentage change
25	Australia	15.7	1.1	-12	25	Brazil	15.8	1.1	0
26	Malaysia	14.0	1.0	3	26	Norway	15.3	1.1	6
27	Thailand	12.9	0.9	-6	27	Switzerland	14.9	1.0	-3
28	Mexico	12.5	0.9	-7	28	Thailand	14.5	1.0	-6
29	Poland	11.9	0.8	14	29	Indonesia[a]	14.5	1.0	...
30	Israel	11.3	0.8	-21	30	Israel	12.3	0.9	1
31	Russian Fed.	10.9	0.7	9	31	Greece	11.2	0.8	2
32	Egypt	8.8	0.6	-9	32	United Arab Emirates[a]	10.5	0.7	...
33	Brazil	8.7	0.6	-1	33	Poland	8.7	0.6	-2
34	Portugal	8.7	0.6	4	34	Finland	8.1	0.6	-3
35	Hungary	7.6	0.5	23	35	Argentina	7.9	0.5	-8
36	Czech Rep.	6.9	0.5	4	36	Saudi Arabia	7.2	0.5	-35
37	Finland	5.7	0.4	-6	37	Egypt	6.5	0.4	-10
38	Saudi Arabia	5.2	0.4	8	38	Turkey	6.4	0.4	-16
39	Indonesia[a]	5.2	0.4	...	39	Portugal	6.0	0.4	-5
40	Croatia	4.8	0.3	18	40	Czech Rep.	5.5	0.4	3
	Total of above	1340.0	91.9	-1		Total of above	1315.0	91.1	-1
	World	1460.0	100.0	0		World	1445.0	100.0	-1

[a] Secretariat estimate.

Note: Figures for a number of countries and territories have been estimated by the Secretariat. Annual percentage changes and rankings are affected by continuity breaks in the series for a large number of economies, and by limitations in cross-country comparability.

Source: WTO (www.wto.org)

MERCHANDISE TRADE BY PRODUCT GROUP

Selected long-term trends

Merchandise trade is classified into three primary groups: agricultural products, mining products (including petroleum) and manufactures. Average annual percentage changes in volume terms of trade and world output for each group and total merchandise trade are detailed in Figure 1.6.1 over four periods between 1950 and 2001. The same data for trade is condensed, graphically and in histogram form, covering the same timespan, in Figure 1.6.2.

Together the charts show that the increases in volumes of trade for each product group have consistently outpaced increases in output, except for mining products between 1973 and 1990, the period of the world oil crises. The strongest period of growth for mining products and manufactures was 1963 to 1973 and for agriculture 1950 to 1963. The weakest period of growth overall was 1973 to 1990 and growth in all sectors of world merchandise trade during the final decade of the 20th century did not return to 1950–1963 or 1963–1973 levels.

The growth of trade in manufactures consistently outpaced mining and agricultural products over the second half of the 20th century. The growth in volume of world merchandise exports against volume production and GDP is detailed in Appendix 1.6.1 for the period 1990 to 2001. Over the whole period trade in both agricultural and mining products grew by an average of 3.5 per cent and manufacturing by 6.0 per cent annually. After growing 13.5 per cent in 2000, trade in manufactures fell back by 2.5 per cent in 2001. As well as outpacing production, export growth has consistently exceeded the growth of world GDP throughout the period.

Merchandise trade with the developed countries

In Appendix 1.6.4 and 1.6.8, the growth in exports from and imports to developing countries and transition economies are charted for the period 1995 to 2000.

The growth by volume and value of merchandise exports from and imports to developing countries, as well as GDP exceeded the world average by two or more percentage points in the decade 1990 to 2000. However, both export and import values declined by 6.5 per cent and 4.0 per cent respectively in 2001 reflecting the global downturn.

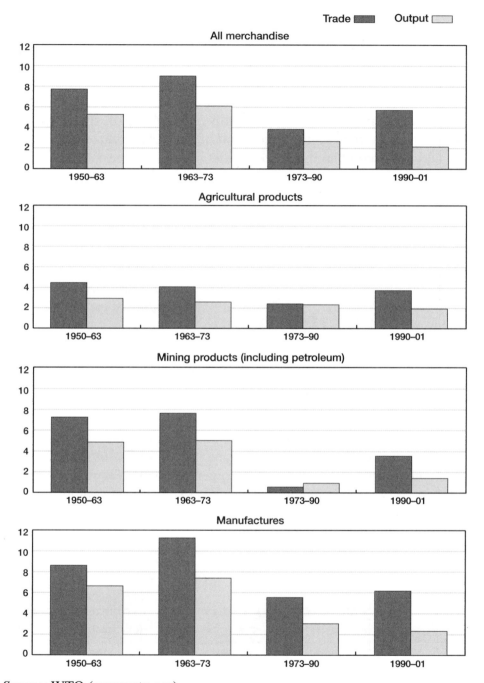

Source: WTO (www.wto.org)

Figure 1.6.1 World merchandise trade and output by major product group, 1950–01 (average annual percentage change in volume terms)

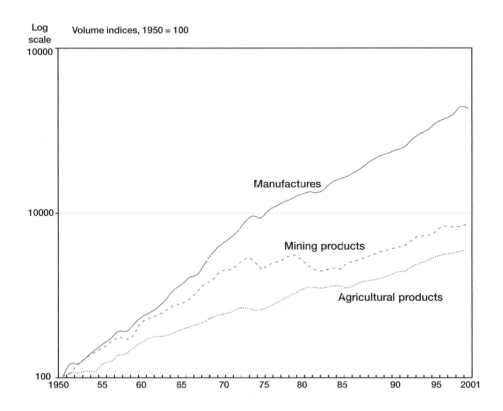

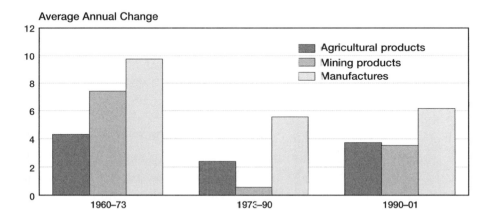

Source: WTO (www.wto.org)

Figure 1.6.2 World merchandise trade by major product group, 1950–01 (average annual percentage change in volume terms)

In the case of the transition economies of Central and Eastern Europe, which are scheduled for integration within the EU from May 2004, the growth rates in the value of imports of merchandise and commercial services surpassed those of Central and Eastern Europe generally in 2000 and 2001. However, growth in the value of exports of both merchandise and services from the overall CEE region exceeded those of the transition economies in both years. Oil exports from Russia and other oil-rich states were a significant factor.

WORLD TRADE SINCE 2001

The full WTO statistical report for 2002 is not yet at hand as this chapter is written. Fortunately, however, the OECD produces statistics for those countries and its estimates of world trade on a more frequent basis so that it is possible to develop an overview of trade in goods and services for OECD members individually during 2002 and for the OECD and world trade overall for the first two quarters of 2003.

In 2002 world exports of goods and services combined topped $8,131 billion, of which OECD countries accounted for $5,723 billion. Of the OECD total, goods accounted for $4,441 billion. In the first half of 2003 OECD exports of goods at $2,253 billion were 3.7 per cent ahead of the comparable period of 2002, signalling a revival in trade as the world economy began its recovery. World exports of goods and services in the first six months of 2003 were 3.5 per cent ahead year over year, although exports from OECD countries were only 1.9 per cent up at $2,872.4. It follows that the trade in services of OECD members remained depressed.

Looking in more detail at the top 10 trading nations in 2002 and 2003, the OECD data (including the value of intra-trade) in goods records a deficit of $507 billion for the US in 2002. The 12-month deficit to the end of August 2003 has been reported as rising further to $538 billion. Germany achieved a trade surplus of $122 billion in 2002 and healthy exports in 2003 have maintained a $136 million surplus for the 12 months to end-August 2003 in spite of the stagnant economy. France has almost maintained its small trade surplus of $7.6 billion for 2002 in the year ended August 2003 at $5.5 billion, while the UK's trade deficit in merchandise at $61 billion for 2002 had risen over the same period to $72 billion, although the UK is the only major economy in the EU showing current year growth. Other EU economies have experienced mixed fortunes. The Netherlands has increased its 2002 trade surplus of more than $25 billion to $30 billion for the year ended August 2003, while Italy's surplus shrank from $8 billion to $2 billion; Spain's 12-month deficit of almost $40 billion for 2002 had risen to just short of $47 billion by mid-year 2003. Overall, the Eurozone area's 2002 trade surplus of $92 billion was reduced to $83 billion for the 12 months to the end of July 2003.

In terms of foreign trade, Japan has weathered its economic crisis well by increasing the trade surplus for 2002 of $79 billion to $96 billion in the August to August period. One element in Japan's strong export performance has been the growth of exports to China, mainly of raw materials and semi-finished goods to Japanese factories on the Chinese mainland. For example, exports of electrical components to China increased 43 per cent year-on-year in July 2003, compared with a global increase of 6.3 per cent.

Indeed, any overview of the changing patterns of world trade over the past two years would be incomplete without reference to the impact of growing Chinese exports and imports since China's entry to the WTO in December 2001. In the year to September 2003 exports rose 31 per cent but were outpaced by imports, which increased nearly 40 per cent compared with just 3.4 per cent two years previously. As a result, the 12-month trade balance to that date was held at just under $20 billion.

The main beneficiaries of the current Chinese economic phenomenon have been the suppliers of machinery and electronics, in South-East Asia (Japan, Korea and Taiwan) and in the EU, which have accounted for much of the past year's $300 billion plus Chinese imports. However, as well as providing the major contribution to export recovery in Asia, Chinese imports and exports are also impacting parts of Latin America. On the one hand, market access has allowed Chinese manufacturers to deploy their cheap labour to undercut Latin-American competitors in sectors such as textiles, shoes and toys – Mexico has proved particularly vulnerable. On the other hand, countries such as Argentina and Brazil, whose mining and agri-business companies are world-class cost leaders, have been the main recipients of China's escalating demand for copper, iron ore and soya beans. The enhanced demand for commodity exports has strengthened their recovery from the financial crises of 2002. Although starting from a low base, compared with established Latin-American trade with Europe and the US, China was Argentina's biggest export market in June and July 2003, and Brazil shipped 136 per cent more to China (almost $3 billion) in the first eight months of 2003 than in 2002. If this trend persists it is not too fanciful to envisage a paradigm shift in which efforts to diversify economically in Latin America are reversed

Table 1.6.8 Share of goods and commercial services in the total trade of selected regions and economies, 2001 (billion dollars and percentage, based on balance of payments data)

	Exports			Imports		
	Value	Share		Value	Share	
	Total	Goods	Commercial services	Total	Goods	Commercial services
World	7520	80.6	19.4	7500	80.7	19.3
North America	1291	76.8	23.2	1603	85.7	14.3
Canada	304	88.3	11.7	268	84.5	15.5
United States	987	73.3	26.7	1335	85.9	14.1
Latin America	413	85.9	14.1	436	83.7	16.3
Argentina	31	87.2	12.8	27	70.8	29.2
Brazil	67	87.0	13.0	71	77.9	22.1
Chile	21	81.6	18.4	21	78.0	22.0
Colombia	15	85.7	14.3	16	77.9	22.1
Mexico	171	92.7	7.3	185	91.1	8.9
Venezuela	28	96.2	3.8	22	80.0	20.0
Western Europe	3106	78.2	21.8	2983	78.3	21.7
Austria	99	67.3	32.7	100	68.4	31.6
Belgium-Luxembourg	204	79.1	20.9	197	80.1	19.9
Denmark	78	65.4	34.6	67	65.2	34.8
Finland	49	88.2	11.8	38	78.9	21.1
France	371	78.5	21.5	350	82.4	17.6
Germany	650	87.8	12.2	620	78.6	21.4
Greece	30	35.4	64.6	41	72.6	27.4
Ireland	98	79.6	20.4	83	58.2	41.8
Italy	299	81.0	19.0	282	80.3	19.7
Netherlands	259	80.0	20.0	236	77.6	22.4
Norway	75	77.8	22.2	49	68.8	31.2

Portugal	34	74.8	25.2	45	86.6	13.4
Spain	175	67.2	32.8	182	81.8	18.2
Sweden	98	77.8	22.2	85	73.1	26.9
Switzerland	121	79.2	20.8	110	86.4	13.6
Turkey	50	68.4	31.6	45	85.8	14.2
United Kingdom	384	71.8	28.2	416	78.0	22.0
Africa	179	82.7	17.3	160	76.6	23.4
Egypt	16	44.4	55.6	20	68.2	31.8
Morocco	11	65.2	34.8	12	85.6	14.4
Nigeria	22	95.8	4.2	14	72.1	27.9
South Africa	35	87.1	12.9	31	83.5	16.5
Tunisia	9	70.4	29.6	10	87.7	12.3
Asia	1917	84.5	15.5	1813	80.4	19.6
Australia	79	80.2	19.8	78	79.0	21.0
China	299	89.0	11.0	271	85.6	14.4
Hong Kong, China[a]	233	81.8	18.2	224	88.8	11.2
India	65	68.6	31.4	74	68.3	31.7
Indonesia	65	92.0	8.0	52	72.0	28.0
Japan	447	85.8	14.2	420	74.5	25.5
Korea, Rep. of	181	83.6	16.4	171	80.6	19.4
Malaysia	102	86.2	13.8	86	80.8	19.2
New Zealand	18	77.0	23.0	17	74.8	25.2
Philippines	34	90.9	9.1	34	84.8	15.2
Singapore[a]	149	82.3	17.7	130	84.6	15.4
Taipei, Chinese	142	85.7	14.3	126	81.1	18.9
Thailand	76	83.0	17.0	69	79.0	21.0
Memorandum item:						
European Union (15)	2830	78.4	21.6	2744	78.0	22.0

a Trade in goods includes significant re-exports or imports for re-exports.

Note: Trade in goods is derived from balance of payments statistics and does not correspond to the merchandise trade statistics given elsewhere in this report.

It is likely that for most economies trade in commercial services is understated.

Source: WTO (www.wto.org)

and the focus is transferred back to agricultural and industrial commodities, the sectors of traditional comparative advantage.

The geo-political implications of a return to the past in a region habitually dominated by the US are deeply worrying for the US government. Of more immediate concern to the US is China's growing trade surplus, which rose at an annualized rate of $28 billion in the first half of 2003. Although this increase was offset by a fall in the combined surpluses of Japan, Taiwan, South Korea, Indonesia, Malaysia, the Philippines and Thailand of $26 billion over the same period, the crunch comes in the pegging of China's yuan against the US dollar. US manufacturers suffering from the competition of imports from China would like to persuade the WTO that China has violated its trading obligations by pegging its currency but the US government is unlikely to force a confrontation on these grounds. For China, removal of the fixed peg and market-driven revaluation of the yuan would pose unacceptable risks to economic growth and, more particularly, the Chinese banking system where solutions are being sought to the major problem of non-performing loans. The most hopeful solution to the currency issue in the medium-term may be the introduction of a floating peg within prescribed limits to be negotiated between China and its main trading partners.

Appendices to Chapter 1.6:
statistical information

Appendix 1.6.1 Growth in the volume of world merchandise exports and production by major product group, 1990–01 (annual percentage change)

	1990–01	*1998*	*1999*	*2000*	*2001*
World merchandise exports	5.5	4.5	4.5	11.0	−1.5
Agricultural products	3.5	2.0	1.0	4.5	1.5
Mining products	3.5	5.5	−2.0	3.0	1.5
Manufactures	6.0	4.5	5.0	13.5	−2.5
World merchandise production	2.0	2.0	3.0	4.5	−1.0
Agriculture	2.0	1.5	3.0	1.0	0.5
Mining	1.5	1.0	−1.0	3.5	0.0
Manufacturing	2.5	2.5	3.5	6.0	−1.5
World GDP	2.0	2.5	3.0	4.0	1.5

Note: World merchandise production differs from world GDP in that it excludes services and construction.

Source: WTO (www.wto.org)

Appendix 1.6.2 Growth in the volume of world merchandise trade by selected region, 1990–01 (annual percentage change)

Exports				*Imports*		
1990–01	*2000*	*2001*		*1990–01*	*2000*	*2001*
5.5	11.0	1.5	World	6.0	11.5	−1.5
6.0	9.5	−5.0	North America[a]	7.5	11.5	−3.5
8.0	8.5	2.0	Latin America	10.0	12.5	−1.0
4.5	9.0	−1.0	Western Europe	4.0	8.0	−3.0
4.5	9.5	−1.5	European Union (15)	4.0	8.0	−2.5
5.5	17.0	8.0	C./E. Europe/Baltic States/CIS	5.0	16.0	14.0
7.0	16.0	−3.5	Asia	7.0	16.0	−1.5
1.5	9.5	−10.0	Japan	4.5	11.0	−1.5
9.0	16.5	−5.5	Six East Asian traders	6.5	16.5	−9.0

a Excluding Mexico.

Source: WTO (www.wtp.org)

Appendix 1.6.3 World exports of merchandise and commercial services, 1990–2001 (billion dollars and percentage)

	Value	*Annual percentage change*				
	2001	*1990–00*	*1999*	*2000*	*2001*	*2002 (first half)*
Merchandise	5984	6.5	4.0	13.0	–4.5	–4.0
Commercial services	1458	6.5	3.0	6.0	–0.5	...

Source: WTO (www.wto.org)

Appendix 1.6.4 Trade and output growth of developing economies, 1990–2001 (annual percentage change)

	Developing economies				*World*
	1999	*2000*	*2001*	*1990–00*	*1990–00*
GDP	3.5	5.5	2.0	5.0	3.0
Merchandise export volume	7.0	14.5	0.0	9.0	6.5
Merchandise import volume	6.0	16.0	–0.5	8.5	6.5
Merchandise export value	10.0	24.0	–6.5	9.0	6.5
Merchandise import value	5.0	20.5	–4.0	8.5	6.5

Source: WTO (www.wto.org)

Appendix 1.6.5 GDP and trade developments in North America, 1990–2001 (annual percentage change)

	North America				United States				Canada			
	1990–00	1999	2000	2001	1990–00	1999	2000	2001	1990–00	1999	2000	2001
GDP	3.2	4.2	3.9	0.4	3.2	4.1	3.8	0.3	2.8	5.5	4.6	1.5
Merchandise												
Exports (value)	7	4	14	–6	7	2	13	–6	8	11	16	–6
Imports (value)	9	11	18	–6	9	12	19	–6	7	7	11	–7
Exports (volume)	7	6	9	–5	7	4	9	–6	9	11	9	–4
Imports (volume)	9	11	12	–3	9	11	11	–3	9	11	13	–6
Commercial services												
Exports (value)	7	5	9	–3	7	5	9	–3	7	5	8	–5
Imports (value)	7	4	14	–6	7	3	16	–7	5	6	7	–3

Source: WTO (www.wto.org)

Appendix 1.6.6 GDP and trade developments in Latin America, 1990–2001 (annual percentage change)

	Latin America				Mexico				Other Latin America			
	1990–00	1999	2000	2001	1990–00	1999	2000	2001	1990–00	1999	2000	2001
GDP	3.3	0.1	3.5	0.3	3.5	3.6	6.6	–0.3	3.2	–0.6	2.9	0.5
Merchandise												
Exports (value)	9	7	20	–3	15	16	22	–5	6	0	19	–2
Imports (value)	12	–3	16	–2	15	14	23	–4	9	–14	11	–1
Exports (volume)	9	5	8	2	14	12	13	–2	6	–1	4	7
Imports (volume)	11	0	13	–1	13	15	19	–4	9	–10	7	1
Commercial services												
Exports (value)	7	1	11	–3	7	1	17	–7	7	1	9	–1
Imports (value)	7	–4	12	0	5	12	19	–1	8	–8	10	0

Source: WTO (www.wto.org)

Appendix 1.6.7 GDP and trade developments in Western Europe, 1990–2001 (annual percentage change)

	Western Europe				European Union (15)				EU (15) excl. intra-trade			
	1990–00	1999	2000	2001	1990–00	1999	2000	2001	1990–00	1999	2000	2001
GDP	2.1	2.4	3.5	1.3	2.1	2.6	3.4	1.5	...	...	...	...
Merchandise												
Exports (value)	4	0	4	–1	4	0	3	–1	5	–1	7	0
Imports (value)	4	2	6	–3	4	2	6	–3	5	4	15	–4
Exports (volume)	5	3	9	–1	5	3	9	–1	4	1	13	0
Imports (volume)	5	4	8	–3	5	5	8	–3	5	6	9	–2
Commercial services												
Exports (value)	5	2	2	1	5	4	1	1	...	...	...	...
Imports (value)	5	3	2	1	5	3	2	2	...	...	...	...

Source: WTO (www.wto.org)

Appendix 1.6.8 GDP and trade developments in transition economies, 1995–2001 (annual percentage change)

	Transition economies				C./E. Europe				Russian Federation			
	1995–00	1999	2000	2001	1995–00	1999	2000	2001	1995–00	1999	2000	2001
GDP	2.2	3.7	6.5	4.4	3.1	2.4	3.7	2.8	1.3	5.4	9.0	5.0
Merchandise												
Exports (value)	8	0	26	5	8	1	14	12	…	1	39	–2
Imports (value)	6	–12	14	11	9	–1	12	9	…	–33	13	20
Exports (volume)	7	–2	17	8	…	…	…	…	…	…	…	…
Imports (volume)	8	–9	16	14	…	…	…	…	…	…	…	…
Commercial services												
Exports (value)	2	–14	11	11	1	–12	14	13	–1	–27	10	9
Imports (value)	3	–8	19	13	4	1	11	7	–3	–19	32	20

Source: WTO (www.wto.org)

Appendix 1.6.9 GDP and trade developments in Africa, 1990–2001 (annual percentage change)

	Africa				South Africa				Other Africa			
	1990–00	*1999*	*2000*	*2001*	*1990–00*	*1999*	*2000*	*2001*	*1990–00*	*1999*	*2000*	*2001*
GDP	2.3	2.6	3.3	3.1	1.7	2.1	3.4	2.2	2.5	2.8	3.3	3.4
Merchandise												
Exports (value)	4	11	27	–5	2	1	12	–2	4	12	32	–6
Imports (value)	3	–3	4	2	5	–9	11	–4	2	–2	2	4
Commercial services												
Exports (value)	5	10	0	0	4	–4	–3	–4	5	13	1	1
Imports (value)	4	–2	7	–3	4	2	0	–8	4	–3	8	–2

Source: WTO (www.wto.org)

Appendix 1.6.10 Trade developments in the Middle East, 1990–2001 (annual percentage change)

	1990–95	1995–00	1990–00	1998	1999	2000	2001
Merchandise							
Exports (value)	2	12	6	–22	30	42	–9
Imports (value)	5	5	5	0	3	13	4
Commercial services							
Exports (value)	8	9	8	5	9	16	–7
Imports (value)	3	5	4	–11	1	8	–7

Source: WTO (www.wto.org)

Appendix 1.6.11 GDP and trade developments in Asia, 1990–2001 (annual percentage change)

	Asia				Japan				Asia (5)[a]			
	1990–00	1999	2000	2001	1990–00	1999	2000	2001	1990–00	1999	2000	2001
GDP	3.3	2.8	3.9	0.9	1.4	0.7	2.4	−0.6	5.3	6.9	7.2	2.7
Merchandise												
Exports (value)	8	7	18	−9	5	8	14	−16	11	10	19	−11
Imports (value)	8	10	23	−7	5	11	22	−8	8	15	28	−9
Exports (volume)	8	7	16	−3	3	2	9	−10	14	13	20	−2
Imports (volume)	8	10	16	−2	5	10	11	−1	9	17	22	−5
Commercial services												
Exports (value)	9	4	12	−1	5	−2	13	−7	10	0	8	−2
Imports (value)	7	5	8	−3	3	3	1	−7	11	4	16	−2

[a] Asia (5) comprises the five countries most affected by the financial crisis in 1997/98: Indonesia, The Republic of Korea, Malaysia, Philippines and Thailand.

Source: WTO (www.wto.org)

Appendix 1.6.12 Value of merchandise exports at constant prices (35 countries), 1870–1998 (Million 1990 dollars)

	1870	1913	1929	1950	1973	1998
Austria	467	2,024	1,746	1,348	13,899	69,519
Belgium	1,237	7,318	7,845	8,182	61,764	175,503
Denmark	314	1,494	2,705	3,579	16,568	49,121
Finland	310	1,597	2,578	3,186	15,641	48,697
France	3,512	11,292	16,600	16,848	104,161	329,597
Germany	6,761	38,200	35,068	13,179	194,171	567,372
Italy	1,788	4,621	5,670	5,846	72,749	267,378
Netherlands	1,727	4,329	7,411	7,411	71,522	194,430
Norway	223	854	1,427	2,301	11,687	58,141
Sweden	713	2,670	4,167	7,366	34,431	103,341
Switzerland	1,107	5,735	5,776	6,493	38,972	78,863
United Kingdom	12,237	39,348	31,990	39,348	94,670	277,243
Total	30,396	119,482	122,983	115,087	730,235	2,219,205
Australia	455	3,392	3,636	5,383	18,869	69,324
Canada	724	4,044	7,812	12,576	60,214	243,015
United States	2,495	19,196	30,368	43,114	174,548	745,330
Total	3,674	26,632	41,816	61,073	253,631	1,057,669
Spain	850	3,697	3,394	2,018	15,295	131,621
USSR	n.a.	6,666	3,420	6,472	58,015	119,978
Argentina	222	1,963	3,096	2,079	4,181	23,439
Brazil	854	1,888	2,592	3,489	9,998	49,874
Chile	166	702	1,352	1,166	2,030	18,228
Colombia	114	267	811	1,112	2,629	11,117
Mexico	242	2,363	3,714	1,999	5,238	70,261
Peru	202	409	1,142	1,172	4,323	6,205
Venezuela	n.a.	1,374	2,593	9,722	23,779	29,411
Total	2,126	8,966	15,300	20,739	52,178	208,535
Bangladesh	–	–	–	284	445	4,146
Burma	–	–	–	269	235	1,075
China	1,398	4,197	6,262	6,339	11,679	190,177
India	3,466	9,480	8,209	5,489	9,679	40,972
Indonesia	172	989	2,609	2,254	9,605	56,232
Japan	51	1,684	4,343	3,538	95,105	346,007
Pakistan	–	–	–	720	1,626	9,868
Phillippines	55	180	678	697	2,608	22,712
South Korea	0	171	1,292	112	7,894	204,542
Taiwan	–	70	261	180	5,761	100,639
Thailand	88	495	640	1,148	3,081	48,752
Total	5,230	17,266	24,294	21,030	147,733	1,025,122

Source: Volume movement in Western Europe, Western Offshoots and Japan from A. Maddison, *Dynamic Forces in Capitalist Development,* OUP, 1991, Appendix F, updated from OECD, *Economic Outlook,* December 1999. Spain 1826–1980 from A. Carreras, ed., *Estadisticas Historicas de España· Siglos XIX–XX,* Fundacion Banco Exterior, Madrid, 1989, pp. 346–7. USSR, Latin America and Asia from sources cited in A. Maddison, *The World Economy in the Twentieth Century,* OECD Development Centre, 1989, p. 140, updated with volume movements derivable from IMF, *international Financial Statistics,* various issues. Brazil 1870–1913 from R.W. Goldsmith, *Brasil 1850–1984. Desenvolvimento Financeiro Sob um Secolo de Inflacâo,* Harper and Row, Sao Paulo, 1986, pp. 54–5 and 110–111: Peru 1870–1950 from S.J. Hunt, "Price and Quantum Estimates of Peruvian Exports, 1830–1962", Discussion Paper 33, Research Program in Economic Development, Princeton University, January 1973, (1929 weights for 1900–50, 1900 weights for 1870–1900): Venezuela 1913–29 from A. Bapista, *Bases Cuantitativas de la Economica Venezolana 1830–1989,* C. Corporativas, Caracas, 1991, and 1929–92 from ECLAC sources. 1990–8 movements from ADB, OECD, ECLAC, IMF.

Part 2

Regulatory Issues and Disputes in International Trade

Customs Duties and Tax

Kevin Newbold, Deloitte & Touche Customs and International Trade Group

INTRODUCTION

Companies involved in international trade, whether as importers or exporters, soon realize the impact that customs and tax issues can have on overall profitability. Although contracts with suppliers and customers may be driven by purely commercial considerations, failure to address the customs and tax implications of those contracts at an early stage can have significantly adverse consequences. These consequences can include increased costs, in terms of customs duties and taxes; delays at the ports in getting goods cleared through customs controls; and, ultimately, seizure of goods and the imposition of financial penalties.

Customs authorities throughout the world take the view that it is the individual company's responsibility to be aware of the customs legislation applicable to its business. Consequently, even when a company employs third party customs clearance agents, it cannot usually avoid the adverse consequences of failing to satisfy customs requirements.

It remains the case that the movement of goods across international boundaries is subject to the control of customs authorities. All such movements have to be reported to the customs authorities by way of a legal declaration, with Customs having the power to take criminal action against any company which makes an incorrect declaration.

Certain goods are subject to import and/or export restrictions. In some cases the restriction applies to the type of goods involved. In other cases it applies to the country to or from which the goods are consigned.

THE CHANGING NATURE OF CUSTOMS CONTROLS

Historically, it has been the case that European Union (EU) Customs exercised their controls at international borders. The required documentation would be presented to Customs and they would allow clearance and removal of the goods only once they were satisfied that all formalities were in order and the correct amount of duty had been accounted for. This led to goods being held up at the ports while Customs' queries were resolved.

The situation today is very different. In most cases, Customs undertake only minimal checks when the goods and documentation are presented to them. Instead, they now have in place a system of post-clearance audits, under which documentation relating to individual consignments is subject to verification by Customs periodically, at the company's premises.

Unfortunately, suppliers to countries outside the EU, particularly emerging markets, can find that their Customs authorities continue to rely on the tried and tested method of retaining goods at the port while they clarify any queries they may have.

E-COMMERCE

The advent of e-commerce has undoubtedly opened up new markets and opportunities for business. However, in many cases it has also exposed companies to overseas customs regimes in a new and potentially difficult way.

Many customers ordering goods over the Internet want nothing to do with the customs clearance procedures. Instead, they want to pay an agreed price for the goods to have them delivered to their door. Attractive though it may be for a company to receive orders over the Internet, possibly in new territories, selling goods in this way means that they expose themselves to the Customs legislation in the customer's country. Unless sufficient research into Customs' requirements is undertaken prior to such supplies taking place, companies can quickly find that they face higher duty costs than anticipated and even risk being liable for value added tax (VAT)/GST or corporate tax liabilities in the customer's country. Sensible companies are now exploring the customs and tax implications of e-commerce before going 'live' in any particular territory.

THE STATUS OF THE IMPORTING ENTITY

When deciding to operate in a new territory, a multinational group has various options. It can utilize an unrelated entity or it can utilize another group company. If an unrelated company is used, there is the question of whether it will act as a selling agent or as a principal. If another group company is used, there is then the question of whether to use a branch office, a subsidiary in a commissionaire or selling agent capacity, or a subsidiary in a buy–sell arrangement. This decision can have a significant impact on the direct and indirect tax costs of trading in that territory.

If the importing company acts as a selling agent or commissionaire, or is a branch office of the company which supplies the goods, then the customs value is frequently based on the price at which the importing company sells the goods rather than the price at which it acquires the goods. This is higher than would usually be the case if the importing company acted as a principal, which buys and sells goods in its own right and at its own risk. Unfortunately, this higher duty liability is often not realized until Customs examine the transactions during a post-importation audit and subsequently issue an assessment for additional duty.

HOW CUSTOMS DUTY LIABILITY IS DETERMINED

In the majority of countries in the world, including the EU, the amount of customs duty levied on the importation of goods depends on three factors:

- the percentage rate of duty is dependent on the classification of the goods under that country's tariff;
- the percentage is then applied to the 'customs value' of those goods, which is determined in accordance with the country's valuation legislation;
- the country from which the goods originate can be a factor as many countries are now granted preferential trade status under bilateral or multilateral agreements.

International trade agreements now usually adopt the principle of 'most favoured nation' (MFN) treatment. This principle was incorporated in the General Agreement on Tariffs and Trade in 1948 and lays down that any advantage, favour, privilege or immunity granted by any contracting party to any product originating in, or destined for, any other country shall also be granted to like products originating in, or destined for, the territories of all other contracting parties. This means that, under the MFN principle, an importing country may not single out an individual country for protectionist measures.

CLASSIFICATION OF THE GOODS

The detail in a country's tariff regime can be staggering. For example, there are over 80,000 commodity codes in the EU tariff. Failure to use the correct commodity code can result in too much, or too little, duty being paid. Unfortunately, many companies leave it up to their customs clearance agent to determine which commodity code is most appropriate. It is not appreciated that the agent often has insufficient technical information on the product to enable him to determine with total accuracy which commodity code is correct. Often, all he can do is make a 'best guess', and leave it to the company to suffer the consequences if it turns out to be incorrect.

THE CUSTOMS VALUE OF THE GOODS

The majority of countries now base their customs valuation legislation on the valuation code agreed under the 1979 General Agreement on Tariffs and Trade, which was continued under the World Trade Organization (WTO). The valuation code lays down specific rules under which the customs value is determined. Unfortunately, there still exist inconsistencies between individual countries on how to interpret the provisions of the valuation code.

Under the code, the starting point for determining the customs value is the price paid for the goods by the buyer in the country of import. However, this price is subject to certain adjustments for customs valuation purposes, so that additional royalties, research and development (R&D) contributions, some commissions and other payments can be liable to customs duty. Many companies fail to appreciate this point and, consequently, incur a duty liability significantly higher than they had originally built into their cost of sale calculations.

Under customs valuation legislation there is also scope to exclude certain costs from the customs value, such as some post-importation charges (eg assembly, maintenance costs), certain warranty costs and interest charges by suppliers for deferred payment terms. However, many companies are unaware of the relevant legislative provisions and, consequently, fail to take advantage of the opportunity to exclude such costs from customs values.

DUTY RATES AND PREFERENTIAL TRADE ARRANGEMENTS

It is fair to say that the percentage rates of duty levied by most developed countries have been falling over the last decade or so. One obvious factor influencing the downward trend is the success, albeit stuttering, of the argument in favour of global free trade and against overt protectionism. The EU, for example, was happy to sign up to 'across the board' duty rate reductions which were agreed at the WTO Uruguay Round. As well as these 'across the board' reductions, certain industry sectors have seen additional cuts in duty rates. For example, as a consequence of multilateral agreements, certain pharmaceutical products and information technology products now attract zero duty rates on import into most developed countries, irrespective of their country of origin.

The last decade has also seen a number of preferential trade agreements being implemented or expanded in all trading regions. North America has the North American Free Trade Agreement (NAFTA), South America has Mercosur, Asia has the Association of South-East Asian Nations (ASEAN) and the South African Development Community has announced plans for a free trade agreement. Closer to home, the EU now has preferential trade agreements with Eastern European countries, under which products originating in these countries can gain entry into the EU free of duty, and vice versa.

Of course, the EU has controls in place to verify that claims to duty free import under preferential trade arrangements are made only in respect of goods which do 'originate' in the consignor's country. Historically, across all industry sectors, many such checks have shown claims to preference to be invalid and, unfair or not, it is the EU importer who is liable to pay the duty, not the overseas supplier.

RELATED PARTY TRANSACTIONS

Transactions between related parties have always attracted the attention of Customs authorities because of their concern that prices for goods sold between them can be manipulated to minimize the group's customs duty burden. In response to this concern, customs legislation provides for a price between related parties to be acceptable as a customs value only if it can be shown that the relationship between the buyer and seller did not influence the price.

The valuation code refers to several 'test' methods by which a buyer can demonstrate that the relationship with their seller does not influence prices of goods. For example, does the supplier sell to unrelated and related buyers at the same price? Is the supplier's price sufficient to cover all of the costs plus a profit that is representative of its profit in sales of goods of the same class or kind? Is the price determined in a manner consistent with the normal pricing practices of that industry? The valuation code leaves it up to the buyer to decide how best to demonstrate that prices are not influenced by their relationship with the seller.

Historically, many importers have failed to give sufficient consideration to the customs duty implications of transfer prices. Consequently, some companies have struggled to satisfy Customs that transfer prices represent acceptable values for duty purposes. Fortunately, companies are becoming more aware of the importance of this issue.

RELATED PARTY TRANSACTIONS – FROM A TAX PERSPECTIVE

Cross-border related party transactions have also attracted the attention of tax authorities around the world, who are concerned that multinational firms are shifting profits from one tax jurisdiction to another. This can be done, for example, by selling goods or services to group companies at less or more than current market prices in order to minimize the group's tax burden. From a tax perspective, if a firm manipulates its transfer prices, it may shift the group's profits to avoid tax. In response to potential manipulation of prices by multinational firms, tax legislators in many countries now require firms to demonstrate that the relationship between the related buyer and seller has not influenced the trading terms of a related party transaction. To address its concern that transfer prices may be used to manipulate taxable income, the UK tax authority has enacted transfer pricing legislation, requiring multi-national firms to demonstrate that reasonable steps have been taken to apply the internationally accepted 'arm's length' standard.

The purpose of the transfer pricing legislation and the requirement of multinational firms by tax authorities worldwide to satisfy the arm's length standard is to ensure that the group's transfer prices have not been manipulated to avoid tax in the UK. The burden of satisfying the arm's length standard can be complex and time-consuming. Although multinational firms may rely on several transfer pricing methods specified in the Organization for Economic Cooperation and Development (OECD) Transfer Pricing Guidelines, most methods require firms to benchmark cross-border related party transactions against those of unrelated parties. However, since publicly available transactional information on unrelated parties is limited, firms are often restricted to using profitability data to apply profit-based methods. Under these methods, firms target a range of operating returns that is acceptable to tax authorities. If actual returns are outside the arm's length range, then they have to make year-end adjustments, either upwards or downwards, in order to bring them within the range.

It is a fact of commercial life that multinational companies have to put considerable effort into satisfying tax and customs authorities that transfer prices are arm's length. As a consequence of tax pressures in particular, it is becoming more common for companies to set a provisional transfer price for transactions which take place during a tax year and then agree an adjustment to the price, upwards or downwards, at the year end. The aim of this is to ensure that the adjustment can be calculated to convert the provisional transfer price into a price that will definitely satisfy the arm's length criteria.

As a basic principle, any year-end adjustment to transfer prices that relates to imported goods will have an impact on the importer's customs duty liability. However, some transfer prices must be adjusted downwards, so that the importer receives some form of rebate from the supplier. Some Customs authorities are reluctant to repay duty unless there has been prior disclosure to them of the arrangements and they have accepted that the initial transfer prices were, indeed, provisional.

DUTY RELIEFS

As the global economy has become more integrated, it is more common to find that a finished product includes components or sub-assemblies originating in a number of countries. Raw materials or components from one or more countries are used by a processor in another country, with the end product being sold to markets worldwide. For example, companies may import components from the USA or Asia for use in EU manufacturing operations. Similarly, some EU companies send materials or components to Eastern Europe for processing and subsequent return to the EU.

Such movement of raw materials, components, sub-assemblies and finished goods clearly makes commercial sense to many companies. However, it also increases the exposure to customs import and export formalities in the various countries and the associated risks, should there be any failure to comply with all the relevant legislation. Also, unless the various parties in the chain of manufacture take steps to utilize all available relief schemes, then unnecessary customs duty costs are incurred in the movement from one country to the next.

FUTURE DEVELOPMENTS

Over the last few years, it has become increasingly common for overseas suppliers to service the EU market through regional distribution centres. Under such an arrangement, goods are imported into one or two EU countries, for ultimate distribution to the other member states. Such trading arrangements have allowed the importing company to maximize the cash flow benefit of using a customs warehouse, which allows goods to be stored without payment of duty until they are released on to the EU market.

However, customs procedures in the EU are being revised to assist companies that import into more than one member state. Traditionally, it has been necessary to report imports to Customs in each member state into which goods are imported. Unfortunately, some importers have found that Customs in the various countries have issued to them conflicting rulings in respect of commodity codes or valuations. Traditionally, it has also been necessary to submit applications to each Customs authority to obtain approval to use relief schemes in that particular member state.

Customs legislation now allows a company to obtain a single authorization from one Customs authority, which will allow the company to utilize relief schemes throughout the EU. Under such an arrangement the company can also deal with one Customs authority to obtain rulings on commodity codes or customs values for imports into all member states.

Deloitte & Touche is the UK's fastest growing professional services firm, the UK practice of the global leader Deloitte Touche Tohmatsu. For further information contact knewbold@ deloitte.co.uk

Anti-dumping Regulations and Practices (with particular reference to EU law)

Philippe Ruttley, EC and WTO Group,
Clyde & Co., London[1]

INTRODUCTION

This chapter gives a brief outline of anti-dumping law from an EU perspective, but set in the context of the World Trade Organization's rules on anti-dumping.

Article VI of the 1994 General Agreement on Tariffs and Trade sets out broad principles on the overall shape and content of anti-dumping policies and laws. These are then expanded by the Agreement on Implementation of Article VI which sets out detailed rules on various issues of anti-dumping law such as the determination of injury, the manner in which investigations are to be conducted, evidence, undertakings and the imposition of anti-dumping duties.

While these WTO rules are applicable and binding on all 142 WTO Members, each Member is left with a considerable amount of discretion as to the shape and content of its own domestic anti-dumping legislation. This chapter will therefore only survey the anti-dumping laws of one WTO Member, namely the European Communities, which together with their 15 Member States,[2] are a full Member of the WTO.

---

[1] The author wishes to thank Elizabeth Park and Joanna Ludwig (both of Clyde & Co.) for their assistance in the preparation of this and the following chapter.

[2] The 15 Member States are: Austria, Belgium, Denmark, Finland, France, Germany, Greece, Ireland, Italy, Luxembourg, the Netherlands, Portugal, Spain, Sweden and the United Kingdom.

THE EC'S EXTERNAL TRADE POLICY

The EU's anti-dumping rules are contained in EC Council Regulation 384/96,[3] an instrument of the EC's common commercial policy (CCP) as regards trade with the outside world. The CCP is created by Articles 131 to 135 of the EC Treaty[4].

As a result of the constitutional structure of the EC Treaty, the 15 Member States have generally transferred their individual sovereignty in international trade matters to the EC. In EC law terms, the EC now has 'exclusive competence' in external relations matters for those issues covered by the CCP. In those areas not covered by the CCP, Member States retain their competence. Occasionally, a treaty will contain areas covered by both Community and Member State areas of competence, in which case there will be 'mixed agreements'.

The CCP is administered by the European Commission's Directorate-General for External Relations (DG Trade). Anti-dumping investigations are carried out by special teams within DG Trade.[5] The organization of these teams is designed to ensure that there is a separation between the investigation of dumping and the investigation of injury. Nevertheless, although the Commission formulates proposals for EC action against dumping, the Member States continue to exercise ultimate control over the implementation of the common commercial policy, since it is the Council of Ministers of the EC which enacts the EC's external trading laws and adopts the regulations necessary to impose anti-dumping duties and similar measures.

This chapter provides an outline of the EC's practice and procedure in applying Regulation 384/96. All references in the footnotes are to Regulation 384/96 unless otherwise indicated.

---

[3] Regulation 384/96 in OJ 1996 L56/1 as amended (most recently by Regulation 2238/2000 in OJ 2000 L257/2).

[4] Formerly Articles 110–16 until renumbered by the 1997 Treaty of Amsterdam.

[5] Useful information and an organigram can be accessed at the Commission DG Trade's website: http://europa.eu.int/comm/trade/index_en.htm

ESSENTIAL FEATURES OF THE EC ANTI-DUMPING REGULATION

General scheme of the Regulation

Anti-dumping duties may be imposed if an exporter into the EC has sold products at prices such as to cause injury to European Community industry. The existence of dumping will therefore be established by the Commission, going through the following four steps:

1. calculating the ordinary price of a product in the exporter's country (known as the 'normal value');
2. calculating the ordinary price for the product in the EC (known as the 'export price');
3. comparing the normal value with the export price;
4. calculating injury to EC industry. (This will be determined if it can be established that the dumping practice decreases the market share of EC producers as a result of abusive price undercutting, or has the effect of preventing the growth of EC industry, etc.)

The methodology used by DG Trade for determining what is the normal value and the export price will have a crucial bearing on the calculation of the dumping margin and the level of duties imposed.

These concepts will now be analysed in more detail.

The concept of dumping

A product is considered to be dumped if its price on the EC market is less than the price of the 'like product' when sold on its home market.[6]

Where the Commission investigation determines that a product has been dumped on the EC market, anti-dumping measures will be imposed by the Council if the dumping is causing injury to Community industry, and if it is in the interest of the Community to impose such measures.[7]

---

[6] Regulation 384/96, Article 1(2).
[7] Article 9(4) and Article 21.

The concept of normal value

There are different rules for calculating the normal value of a product for market economy countries and non-market economy countries.

The following are classified by Regulation 519/94[8] (as amended by Regulation 905/98[9]) as non-market economy countries: Albania, Armenia, Azerbaijan, Belarus, Georgia, Kazakhstan, North Korea, Kyrgyzstan, Moldavia, Mongolia, Tajikistan, Turkmenistan, Ukraine, Uzbekistan and Vietnam.

Where it can be demonstrated that 'market economy conditions prevail for [the] producer or producers in respect of the manufacture and sale of the like product concerned,'[10] exports from the People's Republic of China and the Russian Federation are analysed as if they originated from market economies: otherwise their exports are treated as if they originated from non-market economies pursuant to Regulation 519/94.

(i) Calculating the normal value in market economy countries

Article 2, Part A of Regulation 384/96 sets out the rules for calculating normal value. The normal value will generally be the price paid (or payable) in the ordinary course of business by independent customers in the exporting country: an independent customer will not include customers related to the producing company by a structural link, such as being part of the same industrial group. In certain circumstances, it will not be possible to use prices in the exporting country to determine the normal value of a product. It may occur, for example, where:

- the relevant transaction involves companies which are not independent of each other;
- there is no sale of a 'like product' in the exporting country;
- the sale of a 'like product' in the exporting country amounts to less than 5 per cent of the volume of exports of the product to the EC; or
- the sale of the 'like product' in the exporting country may have occurred at prices below costs over an extended period of time.[11]

In cases where the normal value cannot be determined in the ordinary course of trade, EC law provides alternative means for determining it:

---

[8] OJ 1994 L67/89.

[9] OJ 1998 L 128/18.

[10] Article 1(b) of Regulation 905/98.

[11] There are special rules for start-up costs.

- Where an exporter does not sell a 'like product' in the exporting country, the normal value can be based on the prices of other sellers or producers.
- In other cases, the normal value can be 'constructed', ie estimated on the basis of the costs of production, the product, adding a reasonable amount for sale, general and administrative costs, as well as a reasonable profit margin. The Commission may also disregard sales below costs.

(ii) Calculating the normal value in non-market economy countries
In non-market economy countries, the normal value of a product will be determined on the basis of a price or the 'constructed value' of the like product in a market economy country which is not a Member of the EC. This country is known as the 'Reference Country' or the 'Analogue Country'.[12]

The choice of the most appropriate reference country is often a matter of extensive discussion with the Commission, which allows parties involved in the proceedings to make their own suggestions as to the appropriate Reference Country. The final decision on the choice of the appropriate Reference Country is the Commission's.

Determination of the export price

The export price is the price actually paid (or payable) for the product when sold from the exporting country to the EC.[13] However, there may be cases where there is no export price or where any calculation of the export price is unreliable. This will occur where the export price of a product sold between the exporter and the EC importer is distorted because of the trading or structural relationship that exists between these two parties, so that the sale is not 'at arm's length'. In such cases, the Commission will 'construct' the export price on the basis of the prices which the imported products were first resold to an independent buyer. The Commission will make deductions for costs incurred between the import and the resale, including a reasonable amount for sales, general and administrative costs, as well as a reasonable profit margin.

---

[12] Article 2(7).
[13] Article 2(8).

Calculation of the dumping margin

The 'dumping margin' is the amount by which the normal value exceeds the export price.[14] The size of the dumping margin is calculated by comparing the export price and the normal value. This comparison will be made in the same level of trade and there will be adjustments made by the Commission for factors affecting the comparability of prices. These factors will include differences in physical characteristics of the product being investigated (indirect taxes, discounts, rebates, transport costs, miscellaneous insurance, handling and loading costs, as well as consideration of packing costs, after sales expenses, commissions and currency conversation costs).

The dumping margin may be established either:

- by comparing a weighted average of the normal value with a weighted average of the export prices; or
- by individual comparison of normal value with export prices on a case by case basis; or
- where those prices vary significantly, by a weighted average normal value compared with individual export prices.[15]

The determination of injury

(i) General issues

The Council can only impose anti-dumping duties where the alleged dumping causes injury to the Community industry or where it threatens to cause material injury, or where it threatens to cause material retardation of the establishment of Community industry. The allegation of threat to Community industry must be based on a reasonable level of probability. In other words, it must be shown that the dumping either causes or will forcibly cause injury.

In determining whether there is a threat to EC industry, the DG Trade investigation team will consider the volume of dumped imports, the effect of these dumped imports on the EC market for the 'like product' and the consequent impact on EC industry of these practices.[16] The DG Trade team will examine, in particular, whether there has been any increase in the volume

---

[14] Article 2(12).

[15] Article 3(2).

[16] Article 3(2).

of dumped imports in the EC, whether there has been any significant price undercutting caused by the dumped imports, or whether the effect of the dumped imports has been to drive down prices in the EC or prevent 'normal' price increases. In addition, the Commission will consider other relevant economic factors relating to the state of the EC industry, but it will ignore other factors which may have caused injury to the Community industry: such factors will include the volume of 'like product' at non-dumped prices in the Community, changes in the patents of demand, anti-competitive practices, technological advances and the export performance of the EC industry, as well as its productivity.

(ii) The concept of 'Community industry'

The imposition of anti-dumping duties can only occur to protect 'Community industry'. The concept of 'Community industry' means EC producers as a whole of 'like product' or any Community producer whose output constitutes a major proportion of total EC production of this product.[17] However, DG Trade may exclude in consideration any EC producers who are linked to the exporters of the product under investigation. A complainant on behalf of EC industry must be supported by those Community producers whose collective output constitutes more than 50 per cent of the total production of the 'like product'. If the complaint is only supported by less than 25 per cent of the Community producers, it will be rejected by the Commission.[18]

(iii) The concept of 'Community interest'

Anti-dumping duties can only be imposed to protect the interests of Community industry. Determining what is or what is not in the Community's interest will be the result of the consideration of the interests of EC industry, users of the product and consumers of the product.[19]

---

[17] Article 4(1).
[18] Article 5(4).
[19] Article 21(1).

PROCEDURE IN ANTI-DUMPING CASES

Introduction

EC procedure in anti-dumping cases is characterized by a wide degree of discretion on the part of the Commission. This is particularly evident in the Commission's response to complaints and the determination of the extent (if any) of injury to EC industry as a result of alleged dumping practices.

The procedure in anti-dumping cases is broadly similar to competition cases. The Commission usually reacts to a complaint and investigates it by means of questionnaire and investigations. It then formulates a proposal for a Community measure to deal with a dumping duty, after due consultation with the 15 Member States of the EC. Finally, the Council adopts a Decision, imposing duties at the appropriate level to offset the injury caused by the dumping practice.

Complaints

Complaints must be brought by individuals or legal entities (ie companies or trade associations) acting on behalf of more than 50 per cent of producers in the relevant Community Industry.[20] As stated above, the Commission will not consider complaints brought by producers accounting for less than 25 per cent of EC production.[21] In addition, the complaints have to contain enough evidence to demonstrate a *prima facie* case of dumping, of the injury caused to EC industry and the causal link between the dumping and the injury.[22] Complaints may also be presented by Member States.[23]

The Commission examines the complaint

The Commission will examine the complaint brought by the complainant to determine whether there is enough evidence to justify the initiation of anti-dumping proceedings. Often, because of the political considerations in the EC's international trade relations, it will first seek to find a political solution. It will also consult with the Advisory Committee of Member States, which

---

[20] Article 5(4).
[21] Article 5(4).
[22] Article 5(2).
[23] Article 5(1), second paragraph.

is composed of one representative for each of the 15 Member States of the EC from the relevant ministry dealing with international trade issues. In the UK, a representative will be sent from the Department of Trade and Industry. The Commission also sends a representative to the Advisory Committee, who acts as Chairman.[24]

Procedure if the complaint is accepted

When the Commission accepts the complaint, it publishes a notice in the EC Official Journal, announcing the initiation of proceedings.[25] The Commission notifies the parties known to it as being involved in the dumping practice, as well as the government of the exporting country against whom a dumping allegation has been made. All these parties receive a copy of the written complaint which may be in a 'non-confidential version' where the Commission has been asked to protect confidential business information.

In practical terms, it is not possible to challenge the Commission's Decision to begin an investigation.

Procedure when the complaint is rejected

The Commission will make a decision to reject the complaint after consultation with the Advisory Committee within 45 days of the lodging of the complaint.[26] It will reject the complaint where there is not sufficient evidence to establish either dumping or injury on the basis of reasonably objective evidence. It is possible to challenge the Commission's decision not to begin an investigation.

The investigation by the DG Trade team

The procedure for investigations is set out in Article 6 of Regulation 384/96. Once the Commission has advised to initiate proceedings, its investigation team will analyse both the alleged existence of dumping and will try to estimate the degree of injury to EC industry. The Commission will select an investigation period for the purposes of investigating dumping, which will

---

[24] Article 15(1).
[25] Article 5(9).
[26] Article 5(9).

be at least six months, but normally one year immediately preceding the date when the Commission decided to initiate proceedings. It is common for the Commission to investigate the existence of injury to EC industry over a longer period, in order to establish a pattern of market evolution.

The exporters and importers of a product named in a complaint will receive a questionnaire from the Commission. It is important to respond to questionnaires as accurately and fully as possible. Frequently, questionnaires are not answered correctly, or are even ignored. Parties who fail to cooperate with the Commission will inevitably find themselves disadvantaged when the Commission concludes its investigation since the Commission will have no choice but to base its decisions on estimates of facts which may not be accurate in the opinion of the company against which the dumping duties have been imposed.

The questionnaire requests detailed information from the exporters and importers concerning costs of the product, the prices and volumes of products sold in the domestic market of the exporter and in the EC. It is standard practice for the Commission to allow only 30 days for an answer to the questionnaire, but extensions can be obtained in appropriate cases.

The DG Trade team will also visit the exporters, the importers and the factories of the Community producers to check on the information given in the questionnaire. Naturally, where there are a great number of producers or exporters, the Commission will only investigate and visit a significant sample.

Parties to the investigation (ie the addressees of the questionnaire, including the complainants) may request a Hearing before the Commission. The Hearing will be before the Commission and the EC Member States' representatives and the parties will have the right to present their views.

If proceedings are not terminated because a complaint is either withdrawn or where the DG Trade investigation concludes that there is no need for anti-dumping measures, the Commission will formulate a proposal for the Council to impose the necessary anti-dumping duties at the appropriate levels.

ANTI-DUMPING DUTIES

General

The EC has a range of options to deal with anti-dumping. Broadly speaking, EC law makes a distinction between provisional and definitive anti-dumping measures. As their name suggests, provisional duties are imposed where the situation requires immediate action. Provisional duties are imposed by way of a Commission Decision, subject to confirmation by the Council. Once the investigation has come to a final conclusion, definitive measures will be imposed by way of a Regulation adopted by the Council. In addition, as will be explained below, EC law has appropriate provisions to deal with anti-absorption and anti-circumvention.

Provisional anti-dumping measures

After the Commission team has reported that its initial conclusion is that dumping exists and injury has resulted to the EC industry, and that this requires action to protect the Community's interests, the Commission must consult with the Advisory Committee before it can impose provisional anti-dumping measures.

The Commission may impose provisional measures normally 60 days after the initiation of proceedings (but in less time in case of urgency) but no later than nine months after the initiation of the investigation.[27] The amount of provisional anti-dumping duty cannot be more than the provisionally determined dumping margin and, after they have been imposed, importers of the product subject to the provisional duty must lodge security for payment of the duties when importing the product in question. This guarantees the effectiveness of the provisional duties.

Provisional duties are being imposed for a nine-month period, alternatively for six months extended by a further three.

It is possible to challenge the imposition of provisional anti-dumping before the EC Court of First Instance (see Chapter 2.3).

Definitive anti-dumping duty

At the end of the Commission's investigation, the DG Trade team may conclude that there is definitive evidence of dumping and injury which requires Community action. In such an event, the Commission must first consult with the Advisory Committee of Member States, and then formulate a proposal for a Council Regulation. The Council of Ministers will then vote by way of a simple majority of the 15 Member States whether or not to impose definitive anti-dumping duties.[28] The amount of the definitive anti-

---

[27] Article 7.

[28] Article 9(4).

dumping duties cannot be more than the dumping margin, and must be proportionate to the injury and the need to protect EC industry. Thus if the Community's interest would be protected by dumping duties lower than the dumping margin, the Council is obliged to set them at such a level.

Normally, the Council will set anti-dumping duties as a percentage of the CIF price at the place of import into the EC. It may also set the anti-dumping duties at a level corresponding to a fixed amount per unit, or per measure or according to the difference between a declared price and a 'floor' price or any other appropriate criteria in the particular circumstances of the case.

When the Council decides to impose definitive anti-dumping measures, it will also decide what proportion of the provisional anti-dumping duties (if any) should be collected. Naturally, if the definitive duties are set at a lower level than the provisional duties, only the lower amount of (provisional) duties will need to be collected.[29] However, if the definitive duties are set at a higher level than the provisional duties were set, the Commission will not collect the difference between the two.

Finally, anti-dumping duties are normally prospective.[30] Exceptionally they are only set retrospectively, usually to deal with breaches of past undertaking or where there has been an attempt to undermine the effectiveness of the dumping duties.

Anti-dumping duties are collected at the EC border by the customs authorities of the Member States.

Undertakings

It is possible to negotiate with the Commission to avoid the imposition of dumping duties: this is done by providing price and/or volume of undertakings.

The offer of undertakings must come from the exporters and the Commission now has power to oblige exporters to provide undertakings.[31] The Commission will only accept undertakings where the exporter agrees to provide information on a periodic basis and where it will allow verification of compliance with the undertaking by appropriate procedures.

---

[29] Article 10(3).
[30] Article 10(1).
[31] Article 8(2).

It should be borne in mind that the Commission has a wide discretion whether or not to accept undertakings.[32]

Anti-avoidance rules

EC law contains appropriate means to deal with attempts to circumvent or to avoid anti-dumping measures. There are occasions where measures have been rendered ineffective by exporters succeeding in some way to absorb and not pass on the anti-dumping duties in their sale price. In these cases, the Commission may re-open the investigation, but it must conclude its review in six months and recommend to the Council appropriate amendments to the original anti-dumping duties.

Another method of avoidance is circumvention. EC law allows anti-dumping duties to be extended to apply to third country imports of 'like products' where there is evidence of circumvention. Equally, EC law allows the imposition of dumping duties to be extended to component parts of the like product.

There are three major categories where Community law will consider circumvention to have occurred in so-called 'assembly operations':

- where the assembly operations started after the opening of the anti-dumping investigation and the component parts involved are from a country subject to anti-dumping measures. The same will occur where the assembly operation was started immediately prior to the investigation or was substantially increased immediately after the start of the investigation; and
- the component parts concerned in the assembly operation constitute 60 per cent or more of the total value of the component parts of the assembled product. (There is an important exception that circumvention will not be deemed to have occurred where the value added to the parts brought in during the assembly process exceeds 25 per cent of the manufacturing costs of the products); and
- where the remedial effect of the anti-dumping duties is being undermined by the exporter and there is evidence that dumping is continuing to occur, by reference to the normal value previously established.[33]

---

[32] Article 8(3).
[33] Article 13(2)(a) to (c).

The Commission will initiate investigations of alleged circumventions after receiving a complaint to that effect with appropriate evidence. The Commission must first consult the Advisory Committee, after which it will initiate its investigation of the circumvention and will instruct the customs authorities of the Member States to make imports of the relevant products subject to registration. The investigation of circumvention must be concluded within nine months.

As with definitive anti-dumping duties, the Council will vote by a simple majority whether or not to extend the duties to cover the like product or the component parts.

The duration of the anti-dumping duties

Definitive anti-dumping duties last for five years after their enactment by the Council.[34] They are reviewable, subject to the review procedure described below.

REVIEW OF THE DUTIES

Introduction

Duties may be reviewed either during the course of their life by convincing the Commission that the circumstances have so changed that they are no longer appropriate. Alternatively, when the duties come to the end of the five-year period, the Commission will either decide to continue the duties after investigation or may be requested to review the continued appropriateness of their maintenance. Finally, it is also possible, in certain circumstances, to challenge the legality of the duties by an action before the EC Court of First Instance.

Interim reviews

At least 12 months from the date of the imposition of the definitive anti-dumping duties, exporters, importers or EC producers may request the Commission to review the continued appropriateness of the anti-dumping

---

[34] Article 11(2).

duties. In addition, such a request may come from a Member State of the EC and, finally, a review may be initiated by the Commission on its own motion.[35]

For an interim review to be opened, sufficient evidence must be presented to the Commission that the continued imposition of the anti-dumping duties is no longer necessary to offset the dumping and the injury that are alleged to occur from the dumping. Alternatively, it must be established that dumping practices will not re-occur, or, even if they did, that the existing measure is not sufficient to counteract the dumping which is causing injury.

If the Commission is convinced that there are sufficient grounds to review the duties, it will publish an announcement in the EC Official Journal and contact the parties to the original investigation (ie the complainant, the exporter and the importers). The review will take no more than 12 months, at the conclusion of which the Commission will recommend that the anti-dumping duties be either repelled, maintained at their present level, or amended pursuant to such a review. It should be borne in mind that the Commission is entitled to recommend an increase of the anti-dumping duties as a result of a review and that such reviews are not always successful.

New producers of a product may also request the review of the applicability of the dumping duties to them. A 'new exporter' from the relevant exporting country is entitled to ask for such a review provided it has not exported the product during the period of investigation on which the measures were based[36] and provided the new exporter can demonstrate that it is not related to any of the exporters or producers in the exporting country subject to anti-dumping measures.

'Sunset' or expiry reviews

At an 'appropriate time' in the final year of the duties' life (usually six months from expiry), the Commission publishes a Notice in the EC Official Journal announcing the impending expiry of the duties.[37] Three months before the end of the five-year period of the dumping duties, the parties to the original investigation which had led to the imposition of anti-dumping duties may request their review. This request may come from either the complainants,

---

[35] Articles 11(2) and 11(3).

[36] Article 11(4).

[37] Article 11(2), final paragraph.

the exporters who have been subject to dumping duties, or the importers. The 'sunset' review investigation will determine whether the continued imposition of anti-dumping duties is warranted.

If the Commission determines that it is necessary to continue the anti-dumping duties in order to prevent a recurrence of dumping or a continuation of dumping, the anti-dumping measures will be continued for a further five-year period. The continuation of the anti-dumping duties can only be done by the Council, following a recommendation from the Commission having consulted the Advisory Committee. If there are no grounds for the continuing imposition of duties, the duties merely elapse at the date of expiry of the original Regulation which imposed the duties.

The availability of refunds for importers

Importers who have imported goods subject to anti-dumping duties may, in certain circumstances, request a refund of the duties.[38]

A refund can only be obtained where the dumping margin has been eliminated or reduced to a level which is below the level of the anti-dumping duties in force. Normally, the exporter will have to cooperate with the importer, since the importer will have to present evidence in his application for a refund as to the normal value and the export price of this relevant product.

The Commission, after consultation with the Advisory Committee, will then decide whether or not to grant a refund. Alternatively, it may investigate the claim for a refund by means of an interim review, in which case the refund will only be determined on the basis of the review's findings.

It is important to bear in mind that it is the importer who has the initiative in such cases, and he will claim his refund from the Customs Authorities of the relevant Member States that have levied the duties.

Suspension of duties

It is possible in certain circumstances to obtain a suspension of anti-dumping duties.[39] To obtain suspension, the applicant must demonstrate that market conditions have temporarily changed to such an extent that any injury to EC

---

[38] Article 11(8).
[39] Article 14(4).

industry will be unlikely to continue as a result of the suspension being granted. To date, the Commission has only granted suspension in the case of expanding markets, where any injury to Community industry as a result of the dumping activities would be 'diluted' as the market expands (including EC producers).

The Commission must consult the Advisory Committee before agreeing to the suspension of measures which will normally last nine months (up to a maximum of one year).

A suspension application is often linked to a review application (both 'sunset' review or interim review).

Challenging Anti-dumping Duties Before the EC Courts

Philippe Ruttley, EC and WTO Group,
Clyde & Co., London

INTRODUCTION

There are two basic ways of challenging community duties before the EC Court of First Instance (CFI) and the European Court of Justice (ECJ). The first is by way of direct action before the CFI challenging a Community Decision. The second is a more round about way, which involves challenging the legality of the administrative acts of the customs authorities of Member States in national courts on the grounds that these acts infringe EC law, and then asking the national court to make a 'reference' for a ruling of interpretation of EC law to the ECJ.

Direct actions before the CFI (Article 230 EC)

The CFI has jurisdiction to hear appeals against the imposition of anti-dumping duties or against decisions made by the Commission in the context of anti-dumping duties, where such decisions alter the legal status of the parties involved.[1]

The procedure for direct actions before the CFI is set out in Article 230 EC. An application for the annulment of a Council Regulation imposing an anti-dumping duty must be made within two months of the decision being addressed to the applicant. This means either publication of the EC Official Journal, or, alternatively, it means that an application must be made within

---

[1] Before 15th March 1994, the European Court of Justice had jurisdiction. This was then transferred to the CFI by the Council's Decision of 7th March 1994, OJ 1994 L66/29.

two months of the existence of the Council Regulation being brought to the knowledge of the applicant. The same time limit applies where the applicant challenges the legality of a Commission Decision (ie refusing to accept undertakings, etc).

The applicant can only challenge a Community Act before the CFI on limited grounds, namely lack of competence, infringement of the EC Treaty, misuse of powers, breach of an essential procedural requirement and breach of a rule relating to the implementation of the Treaty. The EC courts have ruled that this last category includes a requirement that EC anti-dumping measures comply with the GATT 1994 Anti-dumping Code. It should also be borne in mind that the CFI has shown itself to be much more vigilant in recent years concerning breaches of essential procedural requirements by the Commission (such as allowing the defence adequate opportunity to contest the methodology used by the DG Trade team in determining the existence of dumping or injury to EC industry).

An appeal on pure points of law lies against the judgments of the CFI to the ECJ.

National challenges leading to a reference to the ECJ (Article 234 EC)

The anti-dumping duties imposed by the Council's Regulations will be levied by the national customs authorities of Member States. An importer will therefore be able to challenge the legality of the act of the customs authorities before national courts. In appropriate cases, the importer may be able to challenge the legality of the original community measure in the context of the reference for an interpretative ruling of EC law sent by the national Courts seized of the dispute. The procedure for References is set out in Article 234 EC. Thus, the national courts, faced with the plea that the Council Regulation imposing the duty was unlawful (eg because of a basic procedural error or a misuse of the Council's powers) will refer the matter to the ECJ for an interpretative ruling. In the context of the plea before the ECJ determining the issue of EC law to be interpreted, Article 241 of the EC Treaty allows the legality of the Regulation to be brought into question notwithstanding the fact that the two months' time limit imposed by Article 230 for challenging community measures directly has expired. The time limits for bringing such an action before national courts will depend on the administrative law of the Member State in question. In English law, actions for judicial review of the administrative acts of HM Customs and Excise must be brought within three months.

It is important to remember that where a party had an opportunity to bring a direct challenge for the CFI under Article 230, but failed to do so, then he cannot have a second opportunity to challenge the validity of the same measure under the reference procedure of Article 234.

The ECJ's ruling of interpretation on the reference is binding and cannot be appealed.

RELIANCE OF WTO RULES IN EC LITIGATION

The WTO Agreements are now part of EC law. However, it is now settled EC law that the WTO agreements do not have direct effect, namely that they do not create individual rights within the Community legal system which individuals can enforce through the Community courts or those of Member States. The European Court of Justice has ruled that:

> [H]aving regard to their nature and structure, the WTO agreements are not in principle among the rules in the light of which the Court is to review the legality of measures adopted by the Community institutions.[2]

While that ruling was made in the context of a direct action involving an EC Member State, it seems clear that this principle must *a fortiori* also apply to direct actions by individuals. It is therefore not possible to rely on the WTO Anti-Dumping Agreement[3] nor on Article VI of the GATT 1994 directly within the Community courts.

However, there are other albeit indirect ways in which WTO rules can be invoked in Community courts. The first is a sort of 'compliance review' whereby the purported conformity of an item of EC legislation or act which claims to conform to or otherwise implement WTO rules can be gauged by the European Courts in the context of judicial review. Thus in *Nakajima*[4], the European Court of Justice held that it had jurisdiction to examine whether the EC Council had acted consistently with the GATT 1947 Anti-dumping Code in enacting the predecessor to the present Anti-dumping Regulation;[5]

---

[2] Case C-149/96 *Portugal v Council* [1999]ECR I-8395, para. 47.
[3] The Understanding on Article VI of the GATT 1994.
[4] Case C-69/89 *Nakajima All Precision Co Ltd v The Council of the European Communities* [1991] ECR I-2069.
[5] Regulation 2423/88 in OJ 1988 L 209/1 as amended by Regulation 522/94 in OJ 1994 L66/10.

that was not of course a means of attacking a particular anti-dumping measure adopted by the Community but a means of gauging the compliance of EC law to the international obligation it purported to implement as a matter of constitutional law. Again in *Fediol*,[6] it was held that, since Article 2(1) and the preamble of Regulation No. 2641/84 expressly referred to GATT 1947, individuals could rely on GATT 1947 provisions in order to obtain a ruling on whether conduct criticized in a complaint lodged under Article 3 of the Regulation constituted an illicit commercial practice within the meaning of that Regulation.

ACTIVATING THE WTO DISPUTE SETTLEMENT BODY

While the WTO agreements do not create directly effective rights, there is always the possibility of challenging EC anti-dumping measures before the WTO Dispute Settlement Body (DSB). However, access to the DSB is solely reserved to WTO Members and it is therefore necessary to obtain the support of the Member concerned.

Where the exporter originates from a WTO Member State (and it should be noted that most non-market economy countries are not yet WTO Member States[7]), the exporter's government may bring into motion the WTO dispute resolution procedure. This allows Member States aggrieved by an alleged breach of a WTO Agreement undertakings by the EC to challenge the lack of compliance by the EC before the Dispute Settlement Body of the WTO. In the event of a failure to achieve an amicable resolution of the dispute, the WTO Appellate Body has binding and final jurisdiction over trade disputes of this nature. A recent example of such a procedure was India's successful challenge to EC zero-rating procedures when establishing the dumping margin in anti-dumping procedures.[8]

---

[6] Case 70/87 *Fédération de l'industrie de l'huilerie de la CEE (Fediol) v Commission of the European Communities* [1989] ECR 1781.

[7] The People's Republic of China is close to WTO Accession at the time of writing (July 2001) while Albania, Georgia, the Kyrgyz Republic and Mongolia (countries within the list of Regulation 519/94) are now WTO Members.

[8] European Communities – Anti-Dumping Duties on Imports of Cotton-Type Bed-Linen from India. Complaint by India (WT/DS141/1), report of the WTO Appellate Body adopted 21st March 2001.

Conversely, there also exist means by which an EC exporter faced by WTO-inconsistent anti-dumping rules can activate the WTO's dispute settlement procedures: again, given the lack of direct access for private parties in the WTO, such means are indirect and such complainants are obliged to use the complaints mechanism provided by the so-called EC Trade Barriers Regulation (Regulation 3286/94[9]) described in Chapter 2.7 of this volume.

---

[9] Regulation 3286/94 in OJ 1994 L349/71 as amended by Regulation 356/95 in OJ 1995 L41/3.

Mechanisms for Regulating Environmental Barriers to Trade within the WTO

Philippe Ruttley, Marc Weisberger and Fiona Mucklow,
EC and WTO Group, Clyde & Co., London

INTRODUCTION

This chapter focuses on the mechanisms for regulating environmental trade barriers in the context of GATT 1994 and WTO/GATT jurisprudence. It does not deal with the mechanics of enforcing the WTO agreements in the context of health or environmental measures, which are dealt with elsewhere in this part of the book.[1]

The WTO Agreement cites, as one of the principles which guided the WTO Members, the aim of conducting international economic relations *inter alia* 'seeking both to protect and preserve the environment and to enhance the means of doing so in a manner consistent with their respective needs and concerns at different levels of economic development.'[2] However, the WTO Agreements do not cover environmental issues specifically, in the sense of there being a WTO Agreement on environmental protection. Instead, the inter-relationship between environmental protection measures and barriers to international trade is covered by the WTO provisions permitting derogations from WTO rules for the sake of protecting the environment or natural resources. Furthermore, many WTO agreements[3] have environmental impacts

---

[1] See chapters 2.6 and 2.7.

[2] WTO Framework Agreement, first Preamble.

[3] Such as the Agreement on Agriculture, General Agreement on Trade in Services, Agreement on Government Procurement, the Agreement on Trade-related Investment Measures, Agreement on Trade Related Intellectual Property Rights (TRIPS).

and environmental provisions,[4] the main three of which are the General Agreement on Tariffs and Trade (GATT 1994) and the Agreement on Sanitary and Phytosanitary Measures (SPS).

However, to date, there has only been one instance of a Member successfully invoking the GATT 1994 environmental exceptions.[5]

THE 1994 GENERAL AGREEMENT ON TARIFFS AND TRADE

GATT 1994 is directed at 'the substantial reduction of tariffs and other barriers to trade and [at] the elimination of discriminatory treatment in international commerce' in order to raise global living standards, ensure full employment, ensure large and steadily growing real income and effective demand, develop the full use of the resources of the world, and expand the production of and trade in goods and services.[6]

The core WTO/GATT principles are embodied in Articles I, III and XI and apply to 'like products'.[7] Article I sets out the most-favoured nation principle which requires that if special treatment is given to the goods of one country, they must be given to the like goods of all other WTO Members. Article III sets out the principle of 'national treatment' which requires that goods of other WTO Members be treated in the same way as like domestic goods. Article XI imposes another type of limit on trade barriers, namely Members' use of quantitative (and other non-tariff) restrictions on imports, including the prohibition of the use of quotas, import or export licences, or similar measures relating to the import or export of goods.

Thus, the core principles of GATT 1994 support free trade. However, in certain cases a country may perceive the needs of the environment as superior to those of free trade. It could then enact legislation which apparently furthered

---

[4] UNEP, *Environment and Trade: A Handbook* (2000), at chapters 5 and 6.

[5] *European Communities – Measures Affecting the Prohibition of Asbestos and Asbestos Products*, Panel Report, WT/DS135/R (18 September 2000), Appellate Body report, WT/DS135/AB/R (12 March 2001), adopted on 5 April 2001. (*EC – Asbestos*).

[6] Preamble, GATT 1994.

[7] *United States – Restrictions on Imports of Tuna*, (*Tuna-Dolphin I*), DS21/R (3 September 1991), unadopted; *United States – Restrictions on Imports of Tuna*, (*Tuna-Dolphin II*), DS29/R, circulated on 16 June 1994, not adopted; *United States – Import Prohibition of Certain Shrimp and Shrimp Products*, (*Shrimp-Turtle*), Panel report, WT/DS58/R (15 May 1998); Appellate Body report, WT/DS58/AB/R (12 October 1998), adopted on 6 November 1998.

its environmental policy, but also breached either the core principles referred to above or other WTO rules. How can such a country justify its actions?

ENVIRONMENTAL EXCEPTIONS

Under GATT 1994, environmental measures are justifiable if they fall within the environmental exceptions under Article XX. The two key exceptions under which WTO Members can justify environmental measures are contained in Article XX (b) and (g) of the 1994 GATT, which read as follows:

> *Subject to the requirements that such measures are not applied in a manner which would constitute a means of arbitrary or unjustifiable discrimination between countries where the same conditions prevail, or a disguised restriction on international trade, nothing in this Agreement shall be construed to prevent the adoption or enforcement by any contracting party of measures:*
>
> *. . .*
>
> *(b) necessary to protect human, animal or plant life or health;*
>
> *. . .*
>
> *(g) relating to the conservation of exhaustible natural resources if such measures are made effective in conjunction with restrictions on domestic production or consumption.*

WTO case-law has drawn a distinction within Article XX between sub paragraphs (b) and (g) on the one hand, and the introductory paragraph or *'chapeau'* on the other. WTO Members must meet a two stage test. First, they must bring the substance of the contested measure within the 'tests' of subparagraph (b) or (g). Secondly, they must also show that it has in fact been applied consistently with the *chapeau*. Thus, a measure which apparently meets the requirements of either subparagraph (b) or (g) on the face of it may still be declared unlawful if its application 'on the ground' breaches the *chapeau*.[8]

---

[8] *Shrimp-Turtle* (1998), Appellate Body, paragraph 160.

ARTICLE XX IS AN EXCEPTION

Article XX is an exception to the general rules and obligations contained in the GATT; it must therefore be construed narrowly or restrictively,[9] although that interpretative attitude does not add anything to the Article's 'ordinary meaning.'[10]

The onus of proof is on the WTO Member claiming legitimate use of the Article XX exception.

The burden of proving the compliance of a measure with the conditions of Article XX lies on the party claiming it.[11] Thus, a WTO Member relying on Article XX(g) must show that the relevant law relates to the conservation of natural resources; and secondly, that the law was accompanied by domestic-level restrictions on management, production, or consumption of the resource to be conserved.

THE INTERPRETATION OF ARTICLE XX (B) AND (G) IN GATT/ WTO JURISPRUDENCE

Article XX(b) requires WTO Members to show that:

- The policy of the measure is in fact a policy to protect humans, animals or plants. Policies that have been held to come within Article XX(b) include: the reduction of cigarette consumption,[12] the protection of dolphins,[13] the reduction of air pollution resulting from gasoline consumption[14] and protection from the risks of chrysotile-cement products.[15]

---

[9] Panel Report: *United States – Section 337 of the Tariff Act of 1930*, BISD 36S/345, adopted on 7 November 1989, paragraphs 5.26-27; *Canada – Administration of the Foreign Investment Review Act*, L/5504-30S/140, adopted on 7 February 1984, paragraph 5.20; *Tuna II*, paragraph 5.26.

[10] See Appellate Body in *Hormones*, paragraph 104.

[11] eg *Canada – Administration of the Foreign Instrument Review Act* (1984), see note 9 above, paragraph 5.20, or the Appellate Body's Report in *United States – Measure Affecting Imports of Woven Wool Shirts and Blouses from India*, WT/DS33/AB/R (24 April 1997), adopted on 23 May 1997, Section IV.

[12] *Thailand – Restrictions on Importation of and Internal Taxes on Cigarettes*, BISD 37S/200, adopted on 7 November 1990 (*Thailand – Cigarettes*).

[13] *Shrimp-Turtle*.

[14] *United States – Standard for Reformulated and Conventional Gasoline*, Appellate Body Report and Panel Report, adopted 20 May 1996, WT/DS2/9 (*US – Gasoline*).

[15] *EC – Asbestos*.

- The measure is 'necessary' for the protection of humans, animals or plants. This means that if there is a less trade-restrictive measure reasonably available to the relevant WTO Member, the impugned measure will not come within Article XX(b). For example, Thailand banned the import of cigarettes on health policy grounds. A GATT panel held that the ban was not 'necessary' for the purposes of Article XX(b) because Thailand could implement other measures, consistent with GATT, to achieve the objective of discouraging smoking. For example, Thailand could regulate the quality of cigarettes through labelling, ingredient disclosures, and ingredient standards. Thailand could also reduce the quantity of cigarettes consumed via a ban on cigarette advertising.[16]

In the *Asbestos* case, France banned the import and domestic production of certain asbestos products to prevent their health risks. It was held that controlled use of these products was not a reasonable alternative to the ban, as this would allow a continuation of the very risk which the French ban aimed to eliminate.[17]

Article XX(g) requires WTO Members to show that:

- The policy of the measure is in fact related to the conservation of exhaustible natural resources. Surprisingly, there has been some dispute in the past as to whether the species or resource covered by the measure comes within the scope of Article XX(g). However, panels and the Appellate Body have generally taken a wide view of the matter. Policies held to come within the scope of Article XX(g) have included the conservation of fish stocks,[18] dolphins,[19] gasoline resources,[20] clean air[21] and sea turtles;[22]
- The measure is 'related to' the conservation of exhaustible natural resources. This means that the measure does not have to be 'necessary' for conservation (in the sense of Article XX(b)), but it does have to be

---

[16] *Thailand – Cigarettes.*
[17] *EC – Asbestos.*
[18] *Tuna-Dolphin I*; *Tuna-Dolphin II*; Canada – *Measures Affecting Exports of Unprocessed Herring and Salmon*, adopted on 22 March 1998, BISD 35S/98 (*Salmon-Herring*).
[19] *Tuna-Dolphin I*; *Tuna-Dolphin II*.
[20] *US – Gasoline.*
[21] *US – Gasoline.*
[22] *Shrimp-Turtle.*

primarily aimed at conservation.[23] The WTO will therefore look at the relationship between the general structure and design of the measure and the policy of conservation it purports to serve. In *Shrimp-Turtle*, the Appellate Body held that a US law forcing other countries to adopt laws requiring 'turtle-friendly' fishing methods was directly connected with the policy of conservation of sea turtles.

- The measure was made effective 'in conjunction' with restrictions on domestic production or consumption. This requires WTO Members to be even-handed in the imposition of conservation restrictions. The WTO will not embark on a detailed inquiry into the measure's economic effects on imported and domestic goods respectively. It simply requires the WTO Member to show that the measure generally affects imported and domestic goods in the same way. For example, in *Reformulated Gasoline*, the regulation of domestic production of 'dirty' gasoline was established jointly with corresponding restrictions on imported gasoline. This was held to satisfy the third requirement of Article XX(g).

THE *CHAPEAU* OF ARTICLE XX

As was mentioned above, the *chapeau* requires the WTO to look at the application of the measure in question. The three prohibitions in the *chapeau*, 'arbitary discrimination', 'unjustifiable discrimination' and 'disguised restriction' on international trade all prohibit the abuse or illegitimate use of the exceptions in Article XX.[24]

Behaviour which has been prohibited under the *chapeau* includes:

- not exploring means of allowing foreign producers to benefit from the same treatment as domestic producers;[25]
- ignoring the costs resulting for foreign producers from the imposition of a stringent standard, while avoiding such costs for domestic producers;[26]
- attempting to coerce the policies of other WTO Members into line with domestic policies;[27]

---

[23] *Herring-Salmon.*
[24] *US – Gasoline.*
[25] Ibid.
[26] Ibid.
[27] *Shrimp-Turtle.*

- failing to negotiate agreements on conservation before implementing import bans;[28]
- treating WTO Members differently under the measure, eg different phase in periods and technology transfers for certification purposes;[29]
- rigidity and inflexibility in applying the measure;[30]
- denying basic fairness and due process to foreign certification applicants.[31]

SPS AGREEMENT

The SPS Agreement aims to elaborate on the general provisions of GATT and in particular the provisions of Article XX(b).[32] It covers all measures that protect animals and plants from pests and diseases, protect humans and animals from risks in food or feedstuffs, or protect humans from animal-borne diseases (SPS Measures).

Governments can implement such measures, but they must:

- be applied only to the extent necessary to protect life and health;
- be based on scientific principles;
- not be maintained if scientific evidence is lacking.

Governments can still impose precautionary SPS measures where sufficient scientific evidence is not yet available, but they must continue to seek out such evidence in the interim.

A WTO Member can fulfil its SPS Agreement obligations by either basing their SPS measures on international standards[33] or by imposing a higher level of protection in accordance with the SPS Agreement. In essence, for such a higher level of protection to be imposed, a scientific justification must be established and a valid risk assessment carried out before the measure can be imposed.

---

[28] Ibid.

[29] Ibid.

[30] Ibid.

[31] Ibid.

[32] Preamble, Article 3, SPS Agreement.

[33] Set by the FAO/WHO Codex Alimentarius Commission. the International Office of Epizootics, and organizations operating within the framework of the International Plant Convention.

The EC ban on imports of hormone-treated beef from the US was declared unlawful under the SPS Agreement because the EC had not carried out a proper risk assessment before imposing the ban (which went beyond international standards).[34]

CONCLUSION

Prior to the recent *Asbestos* case, Article XX (b) and (g) had never been successfully invoked in any WTO/GATT trade disputes. However, this recent ruling will reassure WTO Members that they can legitimately put health and environment concerns above pure trade concerns. Nevertheless, many issues still remain to be resolved in the challenge to strike a balance between trade and environment objectives.

---

[34] *European Communities – Measures Concerning Meat and Meat Products (Hormones)*, WT/DS26/AB/R, WT/DS46/AB/R, adopted 13 February 1998.

Unilateral and Multilateral Political Embargoes and their Impact

Stephen Tricks, Partner, Clyde & Co., London

Exporters and traders have to face many obstacles in doing business. In previous chapters in this section we have looked at controls imposed for the primary purpose of regulating international trade. In this chapter we look at controls imposed on trading activities for political or military purposes. In short, economic sanctions.

Sanctions can be imposed either on a unilateral basis, ie by a single state against another state, or on a multilateral basis, ie by collective organizations such as the United Nations or the European Union, with support from individual states, against a single state or group of states. The use of sanctions as an alternative or in addition to military action has increased over the past two decades. The states affected in recent years include Afghanistan, Angola, Cuba, Eritrea, Ethiopia, India, Indonesia, Iran, Iraq, Libya,[1] Myanmar, North Korea, Pakistan, Sierra Leone, Sudan, Syria and Yugoslavia. This is not an exhaustive list. Between 1993 and 1996 the US Congress and Administration enacted 61 laws and executive actions aimed at 35 countries.

Not only does the list of countries affected change from day to day, but there is also a wide diversity in the scope of sanctions. In some cases the sanctions seek to impose almost total control over the target state's imports and exports. In other cases the sanctions relate only to certain types of transactions, such as arms trading.

It is therefore not possible to give specific advice in this publication on particular sanctions against a particular state. But in order to help exporters, traders and their advisers to assess the likely impact of sanctions, we shall

---

[1] As at 1 September 2003 Libya had agreed to pay compensation to the families of the victims of the Lockerbie bombing, and the UN was debating a lifting of sanctions.

look at how sanctions are imposed and how they are operated. In particular we shall look at the following topics:

- multilateral sanctions;
- unilateral sanctions;
- persons/companies affected by sanctions;
- prohibited transactions and penalties;
- compensation.

MULTILATERAL SANCTIONS

Most multilateral action is initiated by the UN or by other collective entities, such as the EU. However, it is possible for other groups of states, notably the G8, to agree to take collective action. The right of the UN to impose sanctions in the face of a threat to peace or an act of aggression is embodied in Article 41 of the UN Charter. Under Articles 39 and 40 the Security Council has the responsibility for monitoring any threat to the peace and may call upon the parties concerned to comply with such provisional measures as seem necessary or desirable. If that does not produce an immediate solution, the Security Council shall decide what measures are to be taken to maintain or restore international peace and security. The Security Council's first step will normally be to invoke Article 41, which provides:

The Security Council may decide what measures not involving the use of armed forces are to be employed to give effect to its decisions, and it may call upon the Members of the United Nations to apply such measures. These may include complete or partial interruption of economic relations and of rail, sea, air, postal, telegraphic, radio and other means of communication, and the severance of diplomatic relations.

If the Security Council considers that such sanctions will not be adequate, it may arrange military intervention, such as a UN peace-keeping force under Article 42. Any situation which requires UN military intervention will be sufficiently serious to be reported in detail by the media, and so is unlikely to be missed by the exporter and trader. The greater difficulty arises from the long-simmering disputes which may give rise to economic sanctions under Article 41 but are not sufficiently newsworthy to hit the headlines. In these situations, one may need the assistance of government departments, chambers of commerce and professional advisers to monitor developments on the imposition, amendment and relaxation of sanctions.

Sanctions imposed by the UN will normally be adopted by the EU and may be incorporated into the legislation of individual states. The EU may also take the initiative in imposing sanctions where it considers there is a particular risk to European security, as it did at various stages of the crisis in Yugoslavia. Occasionally, EU initiatives may apply outside Europe, as was the case with restrictions on dealings with Myanmar.

UNILATERAL SANCTIONS

While many states will place restrictions on the rights of their own nationals to deal with enemy states in times of hostilities, the major user of unilateral sanctions for political purposes is the USA. As mentioned in the introduction to this chapter, the number of countries against whom the USA has taken some action in recent years is considerable.

Not all unilateral sanctions are accepted by third party states. Indeed, it is possible that other states or groups of states may directly oppose such sanctions. For example, in 1996 the EU objected to both the Helms-Burton Act (an attempt by the USA to strengthen economic sanctions against Cuba by allowing US nationals to sue companies and individuals, wherever located, who 'traffic in property confiscated by the Castro regime'), and the Iran and Libya Sanctions Act (ILSA), which purported to impose sanctions on foreign companies engaging in specified economic transactions with Iran and Libya. In both cases the EU introduced blocking legislation prohibiting EU residents, nationals and EU-incorporated companies complying with the respective US enactments. In May 1998, the EU and the USA reached an understanding on the operation of the Helms-Burton Act and the ILSA, but there are still potential questions over the legal status of that understanding.

This type of dispute over the operation of unilateral sanctions presents the exporter or trader with a serious problem, particularly if he is potentially subject to the jurisdiction of the states on both sides of the blocking dispute, because he may face a penalty whatever he does.

PERSONS/ENTITIES AFFECTED BY SANCTIONS

The dispute between the EU and the USA over the Helms-Burton Act and the ILSA, described above, demonstrates the necessity of establishing precisely who is and who is not subject to sanctions regulations. In the case of multilateral sanctions imposed by the UN, those sanctions will usually be adopted by the EU and by individual states; so it is to the latter orders or legislation one must first look. The normal position is that any nationals of an adopting state, and any companies incorporated in an adopting state, will be subject to the sanctions and must comply with the terms of those sanctions in doing any business with the target state.

Similarly, unilateral sanctions will normally be binding only on nationals of the implementing state, or companies incorporated in the implementing state. The problems arising on the Helms-Burton Act and the ILSA did so because the USA tried to give extra-territorial effect to those enactments. However, even if there is no attempt to give extra-territorial effect to an enactment, nationals or companies in third party states should be careful before taking any action which would potentially be in breach of the sanctions. For instance, an EU-incorporated company doing business in the USA may find it is subject to US jurisdiction for the purposes of any US unilateral sanctions against a target state with which that company also does business.

PROHIBITED TRANSACTIONS AND PENALTIES

The prohibited transactions under either multilateral or unilateral sanctions may extend far beyond the sale and purchase of goods. There will often be a ban on transport links, which means that any commercial sea, land or air carrier will be prevented from carrying goods in or out of the target state. Furthermore, there will often be a ban on financial assistance and other services to persons dealing with the target state. Therefore bankers and insurers may unwittingly find themselves in breach of sanctions if they are providing finance or insurance backing for prohibited transactions.

As mentioned in the introduction, the sanctions may range from a total ban on all transactions through to a limited ban on certain categories of goods. Different provisions may apply to arms, technological know-how, strategic commodities such as oil, foodstuffs, medicines and humanitarian aid. Again it is necessary to look at the detail of the regulations to check precisely what is and what is not allowed. Sometimes the prohibited categories of goods may be determined by the scale of the dispute, but sometimes it is also driven by self-interest of the state implementing sanctions. For example, when the US Government imposed unilateral sanctions on India and Pakistan under the 'Glenn Amendment' following the detonation by those countries of nuclear devices, it was discovered that US farmers would lose hundreds of millions of dollars in grain exports to India and Pakistan if their farm credits were cut off. Congress promptly introduced legislation to exempt farm credits from the 'Glenn Amendment'.

The penalties for breach of sanctions may range from loss of government contracts through to fines and even imprisonment. Again, it is necessary to check the terms of the relevant legislation.

COMPENSATION

The normal position is that governments will not offer compensation to nationals affected by sanctions. It is deemed to be an ordinary risk of business and governments are not prepared to enter into a debate on what business a person or corporation might have done in the absence of sanctions. There are exceptions such as the United Nations Compensation Commission, set up to provide compensation to individuals, corporations and governments who suffered losses as a result of Iraq's illegal invasion and occupation of Kuwait in 1990/1991, but in order to be eligible for compensation, commercial claimants had to show that their losses were caused directly by the invasion and occupation. For instance, a loss of property was irrecoverable, as would be the loss of profit on a contract with an Iraqi or Kuwaiti entity which was under way at the time and was never completed. The United Nations has, however, made it clear that ordinary commercial losses caused by the sanctions against Iraq are not recoverable.

SUMMARY

Economic sanctions can present significant problems in that they are outside the control of the exporter or trader and may be implemented, amended or revoked with immediate effect and without any prior notice. It is therefore advisable for the exporter or trader dealing with a politically sensitive state to keep one eye on potential developments in this area. If in doubt, it is better to seek advice from the relevant government department, chamber of commerce or professional advisers before committing oneself to a deal, only to find that the deal is illegal.

Resolving Trade Disputes in the WTO

Philippe Ruttley and Marc Weisberger, EC and WTO Group, Clyde & Co., London

INTRODUCTION

The object of this chapter is to give an overview of the World Trade Organization (WTO) dispute settlement system, and to illustrate how private parties can play a role in its procedures. It will be seen that the system retains many of the features of a state-to-state dispute resolution mechanism with the emphasis on amicable settlement and conciliation. Nevertheless, the WTO's dispute settlement system represents a radical departure from the 'old' GATT 1947, creating a speedy and effective rules-based system for the resolution of trade disputes. The most fundamental and far-reaching change brought by the WTO over the 'old' GATT 1947 system is that a Report of a WTO Panel or of the Appellate Body is adopted, unless there is a consensus made up of *all* WTO Members not to adopt the Report. This is a near-impossibility since it would involve the 'winning' Member agreeing to veto the adoption of a Report. By contrast, under the pre-WTO GATT system, the 'losing' Member could veto an unfavourable Report, much reducing the level of effectiveness of dispute resolution under that system. The effectiveness of this new system is reflected in the very large number of cases brought since 1995 when the WTO dispute settlement system was established.

THE WTO DISPUTE SETTLEMENT SYSTEM

The obligations contained in the WTO agreements are legally binding on the WTO Members and can be enforced through the WTO's dispute settlement system.

Figure 2.6.1 Basic outline of DSU procedure

Time	Procedural Step	Ancillary Procedure
	Request for consultations	
Unless otherwise agreed, up to 10 days from receipt of request for consultations	Respondent replies to request for consultations	
Unless otherwise agreed, up to 30 days from receipt of request for consultations	Respondent enters into consultations	
After 60 days from receipt of request for consultations	Complainant may request establishment of panel	
By 1st DSB meeting following DSB meeting on whose agenda the request for a panel appears	Panel established	
Unless otherwise agreed, up to 10 days from establishment of panel	Panel composition	
Unless otherwise agreed, up to 20 days from establishment of panel	Panel terms of reference	
	Panel proceedings	Panel may request advisory report from expert review group on scientific/technical issues of fact. Panel issues factual and argument sections of draft report to parties. Parties may comment. Panel issues interim report. Parties may request panel to review aspects of interim report
Up to 6 months after composition and terms of reference agreed upon	Panel report issued to parties	
Up to 9 months after establishment of panel	Panel report circulated to DSB	
Within 60 days from circulation of panel report	Panel report adopted by DSB, unless losing party notifies decision to appeal	
		If decision to appeal notified by losing party, Appellate Body reviews panel report

Figure 2.6.1 (*continued*)

Time	Procedural Step	Ancillary Procedure
Usually up to 60 days from notification of appeal		Appellate Body circulates report
No more than 90 days from notification of appeal		
Within 30 days from circulation Up to 12 months from establishment of panel	Appellate Body report adopted by DSB	
Within 30 days of report adoption	Losing Respondent informs DSB of implementation plan	
Reasonable time	Compliance	Reasonable time: Period approved by DSB Period agreed by parties within 45 days of adoption of report Period determined by arbitration within 90 days of adoption of report (guideline for arbitrator; reasonable time = up to 15 months from adoption of report)
	Referral to Article 21.5 panel	
Within 90 days of referral	Article 21.5 panel circulates report	
No later than expiry of reasonable period of time	Compensation negotiations between parties	
20 days after expiry of reasonable period of time	Complainant may request authorization from DSB to suspend concessions or WTO obligations	
Within 30 days of expiry of reasonable period of time	DSB grants authorisation to suspend concessions or WTO obligations unless Respondent objects	
Within 60 days of expiry of reasonable period		If Respondent objects to suspension of concession or WTO obligations: Arbitration on level of retaliation
	DSB grants authorization to suspend concessions or WTO obligations	

The WTO dispute settlement system is governed by the WTO Understanding on Rules and Procedures Governing the Settlement of Disputes (DSU). The DSU is administered by the WTO General Council in its role as the Dispute Settlement Body (DSB). Only WTO Member governments can be official parties to DSU proceedings, but there are several ways for private parties to participate in and influence the outcome of WTO dispute settlement cases.

Figure 2.6.1 shows the basic procedural steps and time limits in a DSU case. At all stages, countries in the dispute are encouraged to consult each other in order to achieve a settlement. As can be seen, the process follows three distinct stages: consultation, panel/Appellate Body proceedings and implementation.

- **Consultations between the parties aimed at reaching a settlement**. To date,[1] the average length of consultations in dispute settlement has been 156 days, with some lasting as long as 300 days. This is clear evidence of the desire of WTO Members to arrive at an amicable settlement rather than to resort to litigation.
- **Panel and Appellate Body proceedings, leading to the adoption of the panel or Appellate Body reports by the DSB.** This stage involves the parties putting forward economic and legal arguments to WTO tribunals at first instance and appeal. Panels may call upon outside expertise to advise on scientific or technical issues.[2]
- The outcome of the Panel or Appellate Body phase is a ruling or recommendation to the 'losing' WTO Member to 'bring the [contested] measure into conformity with' the relevant WTO Agreement.[3]
- Once the Report of the Panel or of the Appellate Body has been issued, it is then formally adopted by the WTO Members acting collectively in the DSB.[4] An unadopted Report has no legal force, but to date all Reports have been adopted. Once adoption has taken place, WTO Members are

---

[1] This chapter was written in July 2001.
[2] As was done in European Communities – Measures Concerning Meat and Meat Products (Hormones), WT/DS26/AB/R, WT/DS46/AB/R, pursuant to Article 13 of the DSU.
[3] DSU Article 19.1.
[4] DSU Articles 16 and 17.14.

under an obligation both as a matter of general public international law[5] and WTO law[6] to comply.

Implementation raises complex legal and political questions. The losing party must implement the recommendations of the adopted reports within a reasonable period of time.[7] The parties can agree on what is to constitute a 'reasonable period of time' or the matter can be settled by arbitration.[8] While the DSU envisages a 15-month period,[9] statistically to date, the average reasonable period of time has been 11.5 months. If the losing party fails to implement the reports within a reasonable period of time, for example by enacting fresh laws which still breach WTO rules, the winning party can ask for a ruling that the losing party is still in breach of the WTO Agreement.[10] If the losing party still fails to comply, it can offer 'compensation' to the winning party.[11]

Compensation takes the form of trade concessions, whereby the 'losing' Member offers compensatory market access for goods or services of the 'winning' Member. Typically, that would involve the lowering of bound tariffs for another product to compensate for the failure to remove the trade obstacle that caused the original dispute. To date, compensation has never been accepted by a 'winning' Member. The alternative to offering compensation is 'retaliation': ie the DSB allows the winning party to suspend trade concessions it previously made to the losing party.[12] The level of retaliation can be determined by arbitration if the losing party believes it is too high.[13]

To date, the highest level of retaliation has been by Canada against Brazil in a dispute concerning aircraft subsidies. It totalled approximately US$ 227 million.[14] Another high profile case of retaliation has been by the US and Ecuador against the EC over the latter's banana import regime. Ecuador's

---

[5] Under the doctrine of *pacta sunt servanda*, see Vienna Convention on the Law of Treaties, Article 26.

[6] Article XVI:4 of the WTO Agreement provides that each Member must 'ensure the conformity of its laws, regulations and administrative procedures' with its obligations in the WTO Agreements.

[7] DSU Article 21.3.

[8] Ibid.

[9] See DSU Article 21.3(c).

[10] DSU Article 21.5.

[11] DSU Article 22.2.

[12] DSU Article 22.2 – 22.4.

[13] DSU Article 22.6-22.7.

[14] WT/DS46.

retaliation (worth approximately US$ 202 million) included the suspension of its commitments under the WTO Agreement on Trade Related Aspects of Intellectual Property Rights (TRIPS).[15] The USA's retaliation of 100 per cent duties (worth approximately US$ 191 million) affected such goods as hand-bags, wallets, batteries, bed linen, cardboard boxes and coffee makers from the EC.

The WTO dispute resolution process is very quick by international dispute resolution standards. The usual period between the establishment of a panel to the final adoption of the reports is up to 9 months if there has not been an appeal, or up to 12 months if the panel's decision is appealed.[16]

DSU STATISTICS[17]

As on 2 May 2001, there had been 231 requests for consultations under the DSU, of which 178 concerned distinct matters. Out of these, only 49 had been the subject of panels and/or Appellate Body reports. The emphasis is therefore very much on negotiated settlement between the parties to the dispute.

Moreover, the number of disputes which have involved clashes over implementation are even smaller, despite the disproportionate publicity they are given by the media and politicians. As at 2 May 2001, there had only been six adopted panel and/or Appellate Body reports on implementation, while the DSU had only authorized five suspensions of concessions against recalcitrant parties.

PRIVATE PARTY PARTICIPATION IN THE DSU

Although private companies or associations cannot participate as parties to WTO cases, they can contribute to proceedings by submitting *amicus curiae* (or 'friend of the court') briefs to panels and the Appellate Body. Panels and the Appellate Body are not bound to take such briefs into consideration. However, the Appellate Body has previously ruled that it and panels have the legal authority under the DSU to accept and consider *amicus curiae* briefs in cases in which the panel or Appellate Body members find it pertinent and

---

[15] Although Ecuador has chosen not to exercise that option to date. See generally WT/DS27.
[16] DSU Article 20.
[17] Source: WTO Secretariat, Overview of State-of-Play of WTO Disputes, 2 May 2001.

useful to do so. Timetables for the submission of *amicus curiae* briefs can be laid down and are strictly applied.

Private parties who have submitted *amicus curiae* briefs in the past have included such diverse groups as:

- The Consuming Industries Trade Action Coalition;
- The American Iron and Steel Institute;
- The Specialty Steel Industry of North America;
- The Center for Marine Conservation;
- The Center for International Environmental Law;
- The World Wide Fund for Nature.

Outside of formal dispute settlement proceedings, private parties can also have a great input into the collation of evidence and in the giving of technical advice to their 'home' governments. Very few WTO disputes are instigated without private party lobbying or use of national complaints mechanisms.[18] Moreover, very few governments will conduct a WTO case without closely consulting with the complaining industry. A well-documented example of such private party participation was the role of Chiquita Brands International Inc in instigating and driving through the USA's successful complaint against the EC banana import regime.[19]

---

[18] As to the EC complaints mechanisms, see Chapter 2.4.
[19] See *EC – Regime for the Importation, Sale and Distribution of Bananas* WT/DS27/AB/R.

Private Party Enforcement of WTO Law in the EC Legal Context

Philippe Ruttley and Marc Weisberger,
EC and WTO Group, Clyde & Co., London

INTRODUCTION

The object of this chapter is to show how European Community (EC) companies can complain about breaches of WTO rules by foreign countries, the EC, or the EC Member States. It considers three areas:

- the EC Trade Barrier Regulation;
- the Article 133 Committee;
- claims that EC or EC Member State measures are inconsistent with WTO rules.

PRIVATE PARTY PARTICIPATION IN THE EC

An important initial step in identifying trade barriers which may constitute infringements of WTO law is the Commission's Market Access Strategy programme. This consists of a database listing trade barriers experienced by Community industry in third countries. DG Trade's website[1] contains an interactive dialog box where the WTO Members' commitments in their national schedules can be compared with actual experiences, questions can be e-mailed to the Commission and specific complaints submitted.

Once a trade barrier has been identified, there are two routes by which companies can work with the institutions of the EC to challenge perceived

---

[1] The Market Access Database can be found at: www.mkaccdb.eu.int

breaches of WTO law by foreign countries. The first is the Trade Barrier Regulation[2] (TBR) and the second is the Article 133 Committee.

THE TBR[3]

Overview

The TBR gives the right to Community industries and enterprises to lodge complaints alleging breach of international trade agreements to which the EC is party: the TBR is primarily intended as a complaints mechanism relating to the WTO agreements but is also applicable to other international agreements to which the EC is a party, such as bilateral trade agreements.[4]

Once a complaint is lodged, the European Commission is obliged to investigate it and evaluate whether there is any evidence of a violation resulting in adverse trade effects or injury. The procedure will lead either to a mutually agreed solution between the EC and the third country or WTO dispute settlement procedures being launched.

Who can lodge a complaint?

A TBR complaint can be lodged by either:

- **Community industry**: ie a Community industry, or any association acting on its behalf.[5]
  - Community industries can complain about obstacles to trade that a) have an effect on the Community market and b) have caused them injury.
- **Community enterprises**: ie one or more individual companies or firms or any association acting on their behalf.[6]

---

[2] Council Regulation (EC) No 3286/94 (OJ 1994 L 349/71), as amended by Council Regulation 356/95 (OJ 1995 L41/3).
[3] For a more detailed treatment see P. Ruttley 'WTO dispute settlement and private sector interests: a slow, but gradual improvement?' in *'Due Process in WTO Dispute Settlement'* (eds. P. Ruttley, I. MacVay and M. Weisberger, Cameron May 2001) page 167 at 183 *et seq.*
[4] See Recital 5 to Regulation 3286/94.
[5] Article 3 of Regulation 3286/94.
[6] Article 4 of Regulation 3286/94.

– Community enterprises can complain about obstacles to trade that a) have an effect on the market of a foreign country and b) have caused them 'adverse trade effects'.

What needs to be shown?

The complainant needs to provide:[7]

- a definition of the goods or services affected by the trade barrier and a general identification of the complainant and its activities;
- *prima facie* evidence of the existence of the trade barrier;
- *prima facie* evidence of the existence of a right of action of the Community under international trade rules;
- *prima facie* evidence that the trade barrier results in adverse trade effects for Community enterprises or injury for Community industries.
  - To establish 'adverse trade effects', it must be shown that: a) the obstacle trade is having or threatens to have adverse effects on the product or service export market and b) the trade barrier has a material impact on the economy of the Community or of a region of the Community, or on a sector of Community economic activity. (It is not enough simply for the Community enterprises to show that they themselves are suffering from adverse trade effects on the export market: there must be a 'Community dimension' to the complaint.)
  - To establish 'injury', the Community industry must show that the obstacle to trade is causing or threatens to cause material injury, in respect of the service or product, to the industry on the Community market.

The Commission encourages potential complainants to make informal contact with it before lodging a formal complaint. The Commission's Directorate-General for Trade has a special TBR unit. The Commission can then advise the complainant on its case and suggest the best way to proceed. The Commission often provides guidelines for the submission of a complaint. This is particularly beneficial in reducing the complainant's costs.

Procedure post lodging of complaint

After a complaint is lodged:

---

[7] See the list in Article 10 of Regulation 3286/94.

- the Commission decides on its admissibility;
- if it decides the complaint is admissible, the Commission investigates and reports its findings to the EC Member States;
- finally, international action is taken by the Commission in respect of the trade barrier. This often involves consultations with the relevant government department(s) of the third country.[8]

Outcome of International Action

- If the third country takes satisfactory steps to eliminate the adverse trade effects or injury complained of, the TBR procedure is suspended[9] and the situation is monitored by the Commission; or
- if it appears that an international agreement is necessary, the TBR procedure is suspended to allow international agreement negotiations between the EC and the third country; or
- the EC initiates WTO dispute settlement procedures.[10]

Use of the TBR

Examples of the TBR complaints are:

- USA – Rules of Origin for Textile Products. The Italian Textile Federation (FEDERTESSILE) complained about changes in US origin rules for textile products, which adversely affected EC exports into the USA of dyed and printed fabrics and resulting flat products. After WTO consultations were initiated, the US changed its origin laws to the satisfaction of FEDER-TESSILE.[11]
- USA – Anti-dumping Act of 1916. This investigation at the request of the European Confederation of Iron and Steel Industries (EUROFER)

---

[8] Such as the recent round of consultations with Korea concerning shipbuilding subsidies which were the object of a TBR complaint by the Committee of European Shipbuilders Associations (OJ 2000 C 345/5).

[9] Pursuant to Article 11(2) (a) of Regulation 3286/94. A recent example was the suspension of the TBR complaint brought against Korea by the European Federation of Pharmaceutical Industries and Associations (notice of initiation in OJ 1999 C 218/3 and notice of suspension of the TBR procedure in OJ 2000 L 281/18).

[10] See chapter 2.6.

[11] See OJ 1996 C 351/03 for the notice of initiation, and Commission Press Release IP/97/744 of 7 August 1997 for a report on the successful outcome of the US-EC consultations.

alleged that the 1916 Act infringed the WTO Anti-dumping Agreement. The case eventually went all the way to the Appellate Body, which ruled in the EC's favour. The USA stated that it would implement the Appellate Body's findings.[12]

- Chile – Swordfish. Community fishing vessels were not allowed to trans-ship and/or land their catches of highly migratory species (such as swordfish) in Chilean ports, when these catches were made in contravention of conservation rules unilaterally imposed by Chile, regardless of the fact that they were caught in international waters. A TBR complaint by the Spanish National Association of Owners of deep-sea Longliners alleged that these measures were in breach of the GATT. After the EC requested WTO consultations, Chile agreed to grant controlled access to Community vessels. This agreement was supplemented by further co-operation on swordfish stock conservation.[13]

However, the TBR procedure is still comparatively cumbersome, and awards the Commission a great deal of discretion[14] in deciding how to deal with the complaint and whether to initiate investigations or WTO dispute settlement procedures. The exercise of this discretion by the Commission is only subject to judicial review by the European Courts[15] in exceptional cases where the Commission's exercise of its discretion can be demonstrated to amount to misuse of powers.[16]

The more effective means of bringing forward trade complaints is the Article 133 Committee procedure, which will now be considered.

---

[12] See notice of initiation in OJ 1997 C 58/14; the Commission Decision to initiate WTO proceedings in OJ 1998 L 126/36; the WTO Panel found the US measures to be in breach of WTO obligations, a finding confirmed on appeal by the WTO Appellate Body: see *United States – Anti-Dumping Act of 1916*, complaint by the European Communities (WT/DS136). The DSB adopted the Appellate Body report and the Panel report, on 26 September 2000.

[13] See Commission Press Release IP/01/116 of 25 January 2001.

[14] See Article 12 of Regulation 3286/94.

[15] Challenging the Commission for *not* deciding to initiate WTO proceedings would require an action for failure to act pursuant to Article 232 EC (formerly Article 175 EC).

[16] An example of an unsuccessful attempt to challenge the Commission's exercise of its discretion in the predecessor to the TBR can be found in Case 70/87 *FEDIOL v Commission* [1989] ECR 1781.

THE ARTICLE 133 COMMITTEE[17]

Article 133 EC[18] establishes:

[A] special Committee appointed by the Council to assist the Commission in the establishment of the Common Commercial Policy.

The Committee is composed of a representative of each EC Member State (known as 'Titulaires') with the Commission representative holding the Chair. It is an organ of the EC Council.

The Article 133 Committee provides an effective means for private industry interests to raise WTO compliance issues, without the need to face the considerable administrative and evidential burdens imposed by the Trade Barriers Regulation. It is the more popular vehicle for the presentation of private party complaints against WTO inconsistent measures than the Trade Barriers Regulation and, indeed, several such complaints which have led to successful EC actions in the WTO dispute settlement system originated from Article 133 Committee complaints rather than from Trade Barriers Regulation complaints.[19]

The Article 133 Committee is a key forum where authoritative officials meet to deal with the increasingly technical issues of international trade relations. Functionally, it is divided into the 'Titulaires' Committee, responsible for overall policy attended by the most senior Commission officials, meeting monthly. The Titulaires' work is assisted by a weekly meeting of the Deputies Committee, dealing with technically detailed issues and preparing the work of the Titulaires.

In addition, and within the framework of the Article 133 Committee, there is a weekly meeting of the Member States and Commission representatives in Geneva to discuss WTO matters, chaired by the EC Presidency. To reflect the increased specialization of trade issues, sub-groups focused on specific matters have been set up (eg the Article 133 Textiles Committee or the Article 133 Services Committee).

---

[17] For a more detailed account of the Committee's work, see Ruttley *op.cit.* note 3, at page 154.

[18] Formerly Article 113 of the EC Treaty.

[19] Eg the EC's WTO complaints against Japan (WT/DS8), Korea (WT/DS75) and Chile (WT/DS87) concerning trade barriers in the spirits industry were all started by Article 133 complaints rather than the TBR.

Although it has only a limited consultative role under Article 133, the Committee advises the Council of Ministers on all matters concerning the implementation of the Common Commercial Policy and participates in the formulation of trade policy.

While the Article 133 Committee does not itself vote, it has the practice of issuing opinions on Commission proposals for new trade-related legislation or on the handling of particular trade disputes. These opinions are not formal documents issued in its own name, but serve to express the consensus of the Member States' views.

ENFORCING WTO RULES BEFORE EC COURTS

Private industry may wish to challenge EC or EC Member States' laws as being inconsistent with the WTO Agreement. Alternatively, they may wish to recover non-contractual damages from the Community due to an alleged breach of WTO law. To do so, private parties must first show that the relevant WTO rule has 'direct effect' in Community law. That is to say, the relevant WTO rule gives the private party rights which it can rely on before the Community or national courts.

The European Court of Justice (ECJ) and European Court of First Instance (CFI) have recently decided that, as a general rule, the WTO Agreement does not have 'direct effect' in Community law. This means that private parties cannot generally obtain a judicial review of Community or national measures in the light of WTO rules, or claim that the Community has caused it loss as a result of its breach of the WTO Agreement.[20]

However, there are some limited exceptions to the above rulings. The WTO Agreement will be given direct effect where:

- the Community intends to implement a particular obligation of the WTO Agreement;
- the relevant Community measure expressly refers to a precise provision of the WTO Agreement.

---

[20] See Case C-149/96 *Portugal v Council* [1999] ECR I-8395 and Cases C-300/98 and 392/98 *Parfums Christian Dior SA and Tuk Consultancy –v- Assco Gerüste GmbH* (Judgment of 14 December 2000).

To date, no cases have been brought within these exceptions in relation to the WTO Agreement. The only two instances[21] where these exceptions have been applied were under the 1947 GATT, the predecessor to the WTO Agreement. However, in neither case was it found that the relevant GATT rules had been breached or misinterpreted. It therefore seems that the general rule against direct effect will apply to most cases, as the Community drafts-men will have made efforts to ensure that the wording of Community measures do not come within the exceptions.

---

[21] Case 70/87 *Fediol v Commission* [1989] ECR 1781: The ECJ decided it could review the Commission's interpretation of the GATT in a Trade Barrier Complaint because the complainants were alleging that GATT rules had been breached by Argentina. Case C-69/89 *Nakajima All Precision v Council* [1991] ECR I-2069: Because the challenged Community measure referred expressly to Article VI of the GATT Anti-dumping Code, it could be reviewed in the light of that agreement.

Dispute Resolution in International Trade

John Merrett, Arbitration Consultant to ICC, UK

INTRODUCTION

In broad terms, disputes arising under any type of business contract may be resolved either by direct negotiation, by one of the several forms of alternative dispute resolution (ADR), by arbitration, or by litigation before the courts of a country accepting jurisdiction over the dispute. Disputes arising under certain types of contract (eg employment contracts in some countries) may be barred by law from resolution by any means other than the local courts but, generally speaking, the full range of dispute resolution schemes is available to the parties in dispute. The vast majority of international business disputes which cannot be settled directly between the parties are resolved by arbitration.

In the case of domestic contracts (where for example, the parties are of the same nationality and there are no foreign aspects to the contract), the local national courts will have jurisdiction to resolve disputes, even in the absence of an express contract provision giving them jurisdiction. Parties to international contracts, however, need to agree in advance on what will happen if a dispute cannot be resolved by negotiation. This is best done at the time of negotiating the contract but it can be attempted at the time the dispute arises.

NATIONAL COURTS

Parties to international contracts occasionally designate a national court as the forum for resolving disputes; this is not uncommon in contracts concerned with financial and banking transactions. However, in most international trade and investment contracts, the parties are unlikely to agree on disputes being resolved by the national courts of either one of them; parties are unwilling to permit disputes to be determined in the home territory of the 'other side'. If both the parties have knowledge of, and confidence in, the courts of a third, neutral country, they may designate those courts. For example the English Commercial Court, the Swiss Federal Courts and the Southern District Court of New York have long enjoyed reputations for the just and reasonably efficient resolution of international trade disputes. Nevertheless, third country courts are unlikely to be appropriate for the majority of day to day transactions.

There are five main reasons why litigation in national courts may be unattractive:

- Judges may have different training and expectations from those of the businessmen and lawyers involved and their interpretation of the contract may produce unexpected results.
- The court may require that the contract and all the correspondence and documents relating to the dispute be translated into the working language of the court. The proceedings may also be in the language of the court, requiring the use of local lawyers who may be inclined to view the dispute in ways not foreseen or anticipated by the parties.
- Judges of national courts may not be fully committed to impartiality and may, by tradition in their courts, intervene in the dispute or conduct the case in ways not expected by parties. Equally, it may be that the court has no track record of handling international commercial disputes, sufficient to give confidence to both parties in the process and its outcome.
- Proceedings in many national courts encounter considerable delays and, consequently, unnecessary expense. In the worst instance, a case and its succeeding appeals against the initial judgments can take many years to resolve. However, some national courts have developed well-known procedures, capable of delivering expeditious and efficient resolution of disputes. For example, the Commercial Court in London, part of the English High Court, exists to specialize in domestic and international business disputes and, like all the English courts, now conducts cases under rules which have been radically reformed (known as the 'Woolf Reforms', embodied in the Civil Procedure Rules). Even then, many lawyers criticize such reforms for producing high initial costs resulting from the duty of the court and the lawyers to deal early with trial management as well as the substantive issues of the dispute.

- Court actions are open to public and competitor scrutiny. The ability to keep the fact of the dispute and the issues and amounts involved away from the eyes of competitors is regularly cited by businesses as the most important advantage of arbitration over litigation in national courts.

If, despite these disadvantages, the parties choose national court litigation as their preferred dispute resolution method, they will have to make one of three choices. They can:

- specify in the contract the courts of which country are to have jurisdiction over the dispute;
- wait until the dispute arises (in which case they run the risk that they may not agree);
- say nothing.

If nothing is said, any national court in which proceedings are started will have to decide according to its own 'conflicts' rules whether it or another national court is the most appropriate to resolve the dispute. This determination of who has jurisdiction is partly a matter of rules of the court and sometimes a matter of what is called *forum non conveniens* doctrine – a test of the practicality of trying a case in one court rather than another. The result of applying such tests to the dispute can be unpredictable; decisions about these matters of jurisdiction can often lead to proceedings being conducted in a place unexpected by the parties. For example, a respondent in proceedings started in the courts of country A may take out an injunction in the courts of country B, where it is resident, attempting to prevent the claimant from proceeding in country A. The claimant may respond with counter measures in the courts of country A or B. These difficulties can be largely avoided by a choice of arbitration in the contract.

ARBITRATION

Arbitration is the most common means of dispute resolution in international trade. Because its use is so widespread, the international businessman or woman must have a basic knowledge of where it can be obtained and how it is conducted. In contrast to litigation before national courts, arbitration is a private, contractual process (in the sense that it is derived from the parties' agreement to refer disputes to arbitration). It is nevertheless intended to result in a binding, enforceable award. Most standard arbitration clauses cover claims for breach of contract, specific performance of contract, misrepresentation and other claims 'arising out of or in connection with' the contract. Examples of two such standard clauses are included in Appendix 2.8.1.

Advantages of arbitration over litigation

The main advantages of international arbitration over litigation before national courts can be summarized as follows:

Neutrality
The arbitrator and the procedure for arbitration can be chosen so as to have a non-national character, acceptable to the parties, their representatives and the arbitrators who may be from different legal and cultural backgrounds. In 2002, for example, arbitrators in arbitrations conducted under the ICC Rules of Arbitration were drawn from 62 different nationalities, the parties came from 126 countries and the arbitrations were legally seated in some 43 countries (*Bulletin of the ICC International Court of Arbitration* Vol.14/No.1 – Spring 2003).

Confidentiality
Arbitration is a private process and the confidential nature of the dispute and the proceedings can generally be protected.

Procedural and legal flexibility
The parties are free to choose the procedure that suits them best. They are not bound by national court procedural rules. They may simply rely on the provisions of the local arbitration statute. For example, the English Arbitration Act 1996 provides a complete set of rules for the conduct of arbitrations that are legally seated in England. Other provisions specially chosen by the parties may also be applied, eg a 'fast track' timetable or special professional qualifications to be met by the arbitrator.

In certain countries, such as the UK, France, the USA and Switzerland, the national statute is supportive of dispute resolution by arbitration; in others less so. This is why the majority of international commercial arbitrations take place in those countries. It is advisable to stick to arbitration-friendly jurisdictions. Delays of many years can follow from an unwise choice of place of arbitration. Equally, the parties may rely on the rules issued and administered by an institution such as the International Chamber of Commerce, the

London Court of International Arbitration (LCIA) or the American Arbitration Association (see Appendix 2.8.3) or on a set of non-administered rules.

Expertise in arbitration
Arbitrators can be selected to fit the particular needs of a case, eg where specific technical knowledge, qualifications or experience are required. The number of arbitrators who constitute the tribunal is generally one or three. In 2002, 44 per cent of arbitrations conducted under the ICC Rules involved one arbitrator, the remainder three. Professional bodies generally maintain lists of approved arbitrators (see Appendix 2.8.3).

Speed and cost efficiency
The flexibility of the arbitration procedure can lead to savings of both time and money. The time and cost involved will depend on the procedure adopted, the degree of cooperation between the parties, the availability of the arbitrators and the fees charged by them. In some countries arbitrators have been given wide powers by statute to ensure efficiency, consistent with justice (eg sections 1, 33 and 40 of the English Arbitration Act 1996).

Arbitrators can, with the cooperation of the parties, produce efficient, cost- and time-saving procedures which may not be available to judges in national courts. For example, they may manage the preparation of expert witnesses' reports and evidence in such a way as to narrow down areas of disagreement. Again, they may insist on the identification of main issues and preliminary issues and the laying down of procedure and management at an early stage in the arbitration before too much cost has been incurred. (The ICC Rules encourage the parties to deal with practical matters and identification of the issues at an early stage in Article 18 – Terms of Reference and Procedural Time table. Many ICC arbitrations settle at this stage.)

Finality of awards
It is possible to exclude 'interference' by local courts in the form of their reviewing the findings of arbitrators through appeal and judicial review mechanisms. The courts may be either restricted or excluded entirely by local law or by agreement between the parties. For example Article 28.6 of the ICC Rules provides that the award is binding and has the effect of excluding appeals or judicial review insofar as exclusion is lawful in the countries concerned. National law in each relevant country must therefore be considered.

Enforcement of awards

Foreign arbitration awards are enforceable by a local court against assets in its jurisdiction largely without further review of the arbitrator's award. This is the case in more than 120 countries, which are parties to the 1958 New York Convention on the Recognition and Enforcement of Foreign Arbitral Awards. All the major trading nations are parties to the Convention but some have reserved enforcement only to awards which meet one or both of two conditions: they must be awards made in countries which have ratified the New York Convention or be awards concerning commercial disputes only. The Convention also allows the respondent to resist enforcement on technical grounds, such as that the original arbitration proceedings were not served on the respondent or enforcement is contrary to public policy, eg it is based on a transaction tainted by bribery. Information about the status of countries' ratifications of the Convention can be obtained from the major text books on arbitration (see Appendix 2.8.4), from the websites of arbitration institutions such as the ICC (www.iccarbitration.org) or by consulting appropriate foreign ministries.

In return for avoiding some of the problems involved in court proceedings described above, thought must be given to several matters at the time the contract is entered into. In more complex contract negotiations, several choices about the law governing the dispute and procedure can and may have to be made by the parties. As well as the law applicable to the substance of the dispute, they must consider the law that determines the validity of the arbitration agreement, the law governing the conduct of the arbitration itself and, if there is a conflict between two applicable substantive laws, the law under which that conflict is to be resolved. It may also be desirable to think about the law of the likely place of enforcement of the award in order to anticipate problems that may subsequently arise at the enforcement stage.

Disadvantages of arbitration over litigation

Despite these over-riding advantages of arbitration, there are some potential disadvantages in using arbitration as opposed to litigation in national courts.

Limited powers of arbitrators

Arbitrators cannot themselves enforce some of the orders they may make. For example, they cannot bring about the physical attendance of a witness in the way a judge can by threat of arrest. They cannot themselves force a party to preserve or sell an asset that is the subject of the dispute. In certain cases it may be necessary for the parties to apply to national courts, eg for injunctions or other forms of 'interim relief' which carry with them the threat of effective sanctions and can bind the parties wherever they may be. Many arbitration rules expressly provide that applications to the courts for such interim relief are not incompatible with the agreement to arbitrate.

Multiparty disputes

As the obligation to arbitrate the dispute is based on contract (ie on a clause in the contract or in an agreement made at the time the dispute arises), arbitrators have no power to join third parties (ie persons who are not parties to the agreement containing the arbitration clause) into arbitration proceedings against their will. In addition, they cannot order the consolidation of two or more arbitrations without the consent of all the parties involved, even when common questions of fact or law arise which affect all the parties.

Even when all parties agree to the consolidation of separate arbitration proceedings, practical difficulties can arise because workable procedures for multiparty arbitration (eg dealing with such matters as who is to be notified and how and when they are to be brought into the proceedings and availability of evidence to parties) are rarely provided for in existing arbitration rules. They are, however, often contained in arbitration rules designed for disputes between the members of a single industry or the several parties of complex development projects such as in the construction or downstream energy fields. Specialist legal advice is essential for the drafting of workable multiparty/multidispute arrangements. They may also embrace tiered levels of dispute resolution, eg negotiation within management, failing which assessment by a third party, failing which ADR, failing which arbitration.

Awards are not binding on third parties

An arbitration award cannot generally bind a third party who has not participated in the proceedings nor can it establish a binding legal precedent for future proceedings.

Is arbitration really a compromise solution?

There remains a perception in international business that the function of arbitration is to try to reach a compromise decision out of a reluctance to find unequivocally in favour of one party or the other. In reality however, this perception is unjustified. Unless expressly authorized to do otherwise (eg to resolve the dispute as *amiable compositeur* or *ex aequo et bono*), the arbitrator can be expected to decide the case in accordance with the rights of the parties under the contract and the applicable law.

Two types of arbitration

Arbitration may be conducted under the auspices of one of a number of international arbitral institutions (institutional arbitration) or may be handled simply by the parties and arbitrator (*ad hoc* arbitration), using rules tailored to the specific requirements of the parties and the circumstances of the case.

Institutional arbitration

The best-known and most frequently used international arbitral institutions are the International Court of Arbitration of the International Chamber of Commerce (ICC), the American Arbitration Association (AAA) and the London Court of International Arbitration (LCIA). Other prominent institutions include the International Centre for the Settlement of Investment Disputes (ICSID), the Stockholm Chamber of Commerce Arbitration Institute and a variety of regional institutions which have smaller case loads and are therefore less experienced. ICSID is based in Washington DC, for use in investment disputes between states or state agencies and nationals of other states, and trade agreements which are part of an investment. There is also a growing number of institutions catering for disputes arising in a particular trade area or industry such as the World Intellectual Property Organization (WIPO) and multilateral treaty-based systems such as in the European Energy Charter and the North American Free Trade Agreement (NAFTA). A list of the main international arbitral institutions given in Appendix 2.8.3.

Institutional arbitration is so called because the institution has developed and marketed its own tried and tested rules, sensitive to the needs of dispute resolution in international trade in general or in a special area. The institution, to a greater or lesser extent, supervises the conduct of the arbitration through to a final and binding award. The ICC is regarded as the most 'hands-on' institution with the result that arbitrations conducted under its supervision have a reputation for producing a very high level of effective and enforceable arbitration awards. Other institutions may supervise to a greater or lesser extent. Some, for instance, do no more than exchange the initial documentation between the parties and offer facilities such as arbitration rooms. Others, such as the LCIA, are willing to offer a service tailored to the applicant's needs in addition to their standard rules.

Ad hoc arbitration

Ad hoc, or unadministered, arbitration may be approached in two ways, with either specifically devised or general rules.

Specifically devised rules. Parties who are members of a particular industry may wish to use rules developed by that industry to take into account the nature of the particular disputes arising in it. For example, the rules of the London Maritime Arbitrators' Association have been specifically designed to deal with carriage by sea disputes. Utility sectors often have their own tailor-made arbitration rules.

General rules. The parties may devise *ad hoc* rules to fit their particular dispute. Equally, they may take as their starting point such rules as the United Nations Commission on International Trade Law (UNCITRAL) Arbitration Rules or the Rules for Non-administered Arbitration of International Disputes of the Center for Public Resources (CPR) based in New York.

The UNCITRAL rules were adopted in 1976 and have achieved wide international recognition. They are intended for use by parties who wish to avoid involving an arbitration institution but nevertheless wish to have a set of internationally accepted rules available to them. If the UNCITRAL rules are adopted, an appointing authority should be chosen, to select arbitrators if the parties fail to do so by agreement.

The conduct of arbitration

The place where the arbitration takes place or is legally located (its 'seat') is important to its success in avoiding unnecessary delay or cost. In the most progressive jurisdictions the underlying law of the country requires arbitrators and parties to have an objective in mind. For example, Section 1 of the English Arbitration Act 1996 says that it is a principle of arbitrations seated in England and Wales that '. . . the object of arbitration is to obtain the fair resolution of disputes by an impartial tribunal without unnecessary delay or expense'. Similarly, the better institutional rules of arbitration require targets, eg Articles 18.2 and 24 of the ICC Rules of Arbitration require the tribunal to deliver its award within eight months of receiving the file from the ICC Court and to work to a provisional timetable targeting a date for the award.

For these reasons, it is safer to provide for arbitration in well-known jurisdictions and according to well-known rules.

EXPERT DETERMINATION

It is common practice in international trade agreements to provide for disagreements of a technical, as opposed to contractual, nature to be determined by an expert either jointly appointed or appointed by an appointing authority. This is distinct from the use of expert evidence in litigation or arbitration; it is a dispute resolution mechanism of its own kind. It leads to a binding determination that is not subject to appeal.

There is little national law governing the behaviour of experts in how they resolve disputes. It is therefore wise to employ rules and engage an expert recognized by an appropriate professional body, eg The Academy of Experts based in the UK or the ICC International Centre for Expertise in Paris. The latter also provides simple rules for commercial and documentary credit (DOCDEX) questions.

Reference to expert determination is not an alternative to the judicial approach of litigation or arbitration or the compromise-seeking inherent in ADR. It should be used only for confined technical questions, eg the quality of goods or valuation of assets by relation to a formula.

Advantages of expert determination

Expert determination is best used for disputes where an expert knowledge of the subject is necessary. This is particularly the case when the parties have a continuing relationship which may give rise to specific issues needing resolution, such as the proper level of payment to be made by one party to another, taking into account prescribed factors; or how a technical, management or other decision is to be made.

Disadvantages of expert determination

Expert determination is least likely to be suitable when the dispute can be resolved by negotiation; when the expertise of the appointed person adds nothing to the process or criteria to be used; when a more formal, structured procedure is needed; when there is some benefit in hearing evidence given and cross-examined; or when the issue is of a subjective nature.

ALTERNATIVE DISPUTE RESOLUTION (ADR)

Although arbitration itself is an alternative to recourse to national courts, it should be distinguished from methods of dispute resolution conventionally designated as alternative dispute resolution or ADR.

Arbitration is intended to lead to a binding determination of the dispute, which is enforceable, if necessary, through execution by the appropriate court against the local or foreign assets of the losing party. By contrast, ADR is not usually intended to result in a binding determination of rights and obligations. ADR procedures may take many forms, from third party assisted negotiation to 'mini-trials'. They preserve confidentiality and may be more or less sophisticated and more or less formalized in structure. Much depends on the rules that have been chosen by the parties and their willingness to comply with them. The notion behind ADR is that the involvement of a perceptive, diplomatic and businesslike outsider may turn the disagreement towards compromise.

The most common ADR methods are negotiation, mediation, conciliation, mini-trial, non-binding arbitration, expert opinion (to be distinguished from legally binding expert determination) and early neutral evaluation. They may take the form of contractual obligations to have personnel of a certain level participate in discussions at the early stages of a dispute, or to seek an 'early neutral evaluation' of the merits of each party's case by an independent third party. In the 1980s, the international construction industry invented a mechanism called the Dispute Board. It has since spread into other fields of mid- or long-term contracts. Its basic purpose is to assist the parties right from the outset of a contract to avoid disputes 'snow-balling' into major disruptions to the business relationship. The Dispute Board is a body, co-terminous with the contract, which closely follows the contract performance and intervenes with binding decisions if difficulties arise.

Contracts often provide for a 'cooling off' period in which parties agree not to take any formal step, such as commencing arbitration, for a given period in order to allow an opportunity for the dispute to be resolved by other means. ADR is not a substitute for arbitration or litigation. Many parties to trade disputes, although happy to engage in negotiations or ADR, will ultimately wish to be able to rely on their contractual rights. Although use of ADR has rapidly increased, it cannot be relied on exclusively as a dispute resolution mechanism; arbitration clauses or jurisdiction clauses submitting disputes to national courts must remain a key part of international trade contracts. An ADR clause without a traditional binding disputes clause may leave the parties to a contract in a very unsure position when the dispute arises. Appendix 2.8.2 contains two examples of ADR clauses for insertion in contracts.

ADR organizations

The organizations providing assistance most suitable to trade disputes are the ICC International Court of Arbitration based in Paris (which despite its name and main business of the conduct of arbitrations runs an ADR scheme known as ICC Amicable Dispute Resolution), the Centre for Dispute Resolution (CEDR), the LCIA and the CPR Institute for Dispute Resolution based in the USA. Details and addresses appear in Appendix 2.8.3.

Advantages and disadvantages of ADR

The advantages and disadvantages of alternative dispute resolution are as follows:

Flexibility
The parties are free to adopt a wide range of solutions to the dispute. They may be far removed from the conventional outcome of arbitration or litigation, namely an award of damages, but may include a compromise or even a compensatory transaction in some area of business not directly related to the dispute.

Focus on the businesses
The involvement of neutral and senior management of the parties helps to avoid emotionalism, legal or jury-type approaches to the dispute.

Speed and cost efficiency
Disputes can be disposed of in days or weeks. This saves considerable management time and cost. No ADR is entirely free of cost but it is generally much cheaper than litigation or arbitration.

Success rates
Institutions conducting ADR such as the London-based Centre for Dispute Resolution report success rates in the region of 80–90 per cent. Also frequently claimed is that it is possible to maintain a good continuing business relationship after ADR.

Approach of the parties

The parties must have reached a point where they are genuinely interested in settlement of the dispute by compromise. Sometimes parties simply go through the motions of complying with a contractual ADR clause because they believe they will do better in the ensuing litigation or arbitration, or because they fear revealing their hand or showing weakness by a willingness to participate enthusiastically in ADR.

CONCLUSION

Whatever means of dispute resolution is employed, professional advice ought to be taken for the conduct of the process. Advice is also sensible at the time of drafting the contract clause whatever it may specify unless a well-known set of rules as indicated above is used. Although intended to replace the cost and delay often associated with litigation, the other mechanisms discussed in this chapter are not entirely free of legal complications, even though in most cases they may still be better than going to court.

APPENDICES

Appendix 2.8.1: Examples of recommended arbitration clauses

The ICC recommended arbitration clause and note is as follows:

All disputes arising out of or in connection with the present contract shall be finally settled under the Rules of Arbitration of the International Chamber of Commerce by one or more arbitrators appointed in accordance with the said Rules.

Parties are reminded that it may be desirable for them to stipulate in the arbitration clause itself the law governing the contract, the number of arbitrators and the place and language of the arbitration. The parties' free choice of the law governing the contract and of the place and language of the arbitration is not limited by the ICC Rules of Arbitration. Attention is called to the fact that the laws of certain countries require that parties to contracts expressly accept arbitration clauses, sometimes in a precise and particular manner.

The American Arbitration Association recommended arbitration clause and note is as follows:

> *Any controversy or claim arising out of or relating to this contract shall be determined by arbitration in accordance with the International Arbitration Rules of the American Arbitration Association. The parties may wish to consider adding:*
> *a) the number of arbitrators should be (one or three);*
> *b) the place of arbitration shall be (city or country);*
> *c) the language(s) of the arbitration shall be (specify).*

Appendix 2.8.2: Model clauses for conciliation or mediation

American Arbitration Association

The American Arbitration Association's model clause for conciliation or mediation is as follows:

> *If a dispute arises out of or relates to this contract, or the breach thereof, and if the said dispute cannot be settled through negotiation, the parties agree first to try in good faith to settle the dispute by mediation under the Commercial Mediation Rules of the American Arbitration Association, before resorting to arbitration, litigation, or some other dispute resolution procedure.*

Centre for Dispute Resolution

The Centre for Dispute Resolution's model clause for conciliation or mediation is as follows:

> 1. *If any dispute arises out of this agreement the parties will attempt to settle it by negotiation. [A party may not serve an ADR notice or commence court proceedings/an arbitration until [21] days after it has made a written offer to the other party[ies] to negotiate a settlement to the dispute.]*
> 2. *If the parties are unable to settle any dispute by negotiation [within [21] days], the parties will attempt to settle it by mediation in accordance with the Centre for Dispute Resolution (CEDR) Model Mediation Procedure.*
> 3. *To initiate a mediation a party [by its Managing Director/. . .] must give notice in writing (ADR notice) to the other party[ies] to the dispute [addressed to its/their respective Managing Director/. . .] requesting a mediation in accordance with Clause 2.*

In its Guidance Note on its Model ADR Contract Clauses, CEDR proposes certain optional/additional wording. Most importantly, the mediation clause should specify that if the parties have not settled the dispute within a given period of time from commencement of the mediation, the dispute shall be referred to arbitration or some other binding procedure.

Appendix 2.8.3: Useful addresses

Listed below are contact details of arbitral institutions and other useful organizations:

The Academy of Experts
2 South Square
London WC1R 5HP
United Kingdom
Tel: +44 20 7637 0333
Fax: +44 20 7637 1893
Website: www.Academy-experts.org/
E-mail: admin@academy-experts.org

American Arbitration Association
335 Madison Avenue
New York
NY 100174605
USA
Tel: +1 212 716 5800
Fax: +1 212 716 5905
Website: www.adr.org
E-mail: aaaheadquarters@adr.com

Centre for Dispute Resolution
Princes House
95 Gresham Street
London EC2V 7NA
United Kingdom
Tel: +44 20 7600 0500
Fax: +44 20 7600 0501
Website: www.cedr.co.uk
E-mail: mediate@cedr.co.uk

CPR Institute for Dispute Resolution
366 Madison Avenue
New York
NY 1–173122
USA
Tel: +1 212 9496490
Fax: +1 212 949 8859
Website: www.cpradr.org
E-mail: info@cpradr.org

Chartered Institute of Arbitrators
International Arbitration Centre
12 Bloomsbury Square
London WC1
Tel: +44 20 7421 7444
Fax: +44 20 7421 4023
Website: www.arbitrators.org
E-mail: 71411.2735@compuserve.com

China International Economic and Trade Arbitration Commission (CIETAC)
6/F Golden Land Building
32 Liang Ma Qiao Road
Chaoyang District
Beijing 100016
China
Tel: +86 10 6464 6688/3517
Fax: +86 10 6464 3500/3520
E-mail: cieta@public.bta.net.cn

Hong Kong International Arbitration Centre
38th Floor Two Exchange Square
8 Connaught Place
Hong Kong
China
Tel: +852 2525 2381
Fax: +852 2524 2171
Website: www.hkiac.org
E-mail: adr@khiac.org

Inter-American Commercial Arbitration Commission
OAS Administration Building, Room 211
19th and Constitution Avenue
Washington DC 20006
USA
Tel: +1 202 458 3249
Fax: +1 202 458 3293

International Arbitral Centre of the Austrian Federal Economic Chamber
Wiedner Haupstraat 63
PO Box 319
1045 Vienna
Austria
Tel: +43 1 501 05 3701
Fax: +43 1 502 06 3702
E-mail: iccat@wk.or.at

International Centre for Settlement of Investment Disputes
1818 H Street NW
Washington DC 20433
USA
Tel: +1 202 458 1534
Fax: +1 202 522 2615/2027

International Chamber of Commerce
International Court of Arbitration
38 Cours Albert 1er
75008 Paris
France
Tel: +33 1 49 53 28 28
Fax: +33 1 49 53 29 29
Website: www.iccwbo.org
E-mail: arb@iccwbo.org

International Commercial Arbitration Court at the Chamber of Commerce and Industry of the Russian Federation
6 Ilynka Street
Moscow 103012
Russian Federation
Tel: +7 095 929 0193
Fax: +7 095 929 0334

Jams Endispute
345 Park Avenue
8th Floor
New York
NY 10154
USA
Tel: +1 212 751 2700
Fax: +1 212 751 4099
Website: www.jams-endispute.com

Kuala Lumpur Regional Centre for Arbitration
12 Jalan Conlay
50450 Kuala Lumpur
Malaysia
Tel: +60 3 242 0103/0702
Fax: +60 3 242 4513
Website: www.klrc.org
E-mail: klrca@putra.net.my

London Court of International Arbitration
Hulton House
6th Floor
161–166 Fleet Street
London EC4A 2DY
United Kingdom
Tel: +44 20 7 936 3530
Fax: +44 20 7936 3533
Website: www.lcia-arbitration.com/lcia/
E-mail: lcia@lcia-arbitration.com

Netherlands Arbitration Institute
PO Box 190
3000 AD Rotterdam
Gebouw 'Plaza'
Weena 666
3012 CN Rotterdam
The Netherlands
Tel: +31 10 404 2200
Fax: +31 10 404 5140

Singapore International Arbitration Centre
1 Coleman Street #0508
The Adelphi
Singapore 179803
Singapore
Tel: +65 334 1277
Fax: +65 334 2942
Website: http://siac.tdb.gov.sg
E-mail: sinarb@singnet.com.sg

Stockholm Chamber of Commerce (Arbitration Institute)
PO Box 16050
103 21 Stockholm
Sweden
Tel: +46 8 555 100 50
Fax: +46 8 566 316 50
Website: www.chamber.se
E-mail: arbiration@chamber.se

United Nations Commission on International Trade Law
Vienna International Centre
PO Box 500
1400 Vienna
Austria
Tel: +43 1 26060 4060
Fax: +43 1 26060 5813
Website: www.un.or.at/uncitral
E-mail: uncitral@unvienna.un.or.at

WIPO Arbitration and Mediation Center
World Intellectual Property Organization
34 Chemin de Colombettes
1211 Geneva 20
Switzerland
Tel: +41 22 338 8247
Fax: +41 22 740 3700
Website: www.arbiter.wipo.int
E-mail: arbiter.mail@wipo.int

Appendix 2.8.4: Further reading on dispute resolution

Brown, H, Marriott QC, A (1999) *ADR Principles and Practice* 2nd edition, Sweet & Maxwell, London

Craig, L, Park, W, Paullson, J (2000) *International Chamber of Commerce Arbitration* 3rd edition, ICC Publications, Paris

Huleatt-James, M, Gould, N (1999) *International Commercial Arbitration: A Handbook*, LLP, London

Paullson, J, Rawding, N, Reed, L, Schwartz, E (1999) *The Freshfields Guide to Arbitration and ADR – Clauses in International Contracts*, Kluwer Law International, The Hague

Redfern, A, Hunter, M (1999) *Law and Practice of International Commercial Arbitration* 3rd edition, Sweet & Maxwell, London

Part 3

The Management of Foreign Currencies in International Trade

Introduction

Just for the want of a little training it has been estimated that in 1990 alone British exporters and importers lost extra profit/competitiveness in the region of £6 billion by selling and buying in the wrong currencies.

An export manager negotiating a £1 million contract in Egypt was confronted by a Japanese bid which was 7 per cent cheaper. He could not meet it and lost the business. By switching into yen he could have earned a forward premium of £178,620 (17.87 per cent). The chief buyer of another leading company negotiating a £3 million purchase contract in Portugal accepted a discount of £10,000 for payment in sterling when escudos could have been bought forward in London at a discount of £270,000.

The extra profit/competitiveness available to exporters in early 2000 for a sale of £10,000 invoiced in euros, Swiss francs and yen payable at three months was £63, £99 and £146 respectively; all for the cost of a telephone call. For major contracts of £2 million each in euros and yen on extended terms of payment over five years, the extra profit available was £117,105 and £352,997 respectively, again for the cost of a telephone call. In 1985, a similar contract in deutschmarks yielded an extra margin of 14.98 per cent and in December 1986 a £4 million contract in Swiss francs produced an extra margin of £868,071 (21.70 per cent).

A UK buyer with suppliers in France and Switzerland asked both to quote in their own currencies for a machine tool valued at about £1 million. Converted at the spot rates of exchange the quotes were very competitive in sterling terms and the order was placed with the Swiss. In arranging to buy the currencies forward, the Finance Department discovered that while the Swiss franc was at a premium against sterling of 7 per cent, the French franc was at a discount of 10.5 per cent. There was no difference between the prices of the products but a 17.5 per cent difference in the cost of purchasing the currencies forward.

All these profit margins mentioned above and in the text of this part of the book were available without an iota of speculation or gamble.

Foreign Exchange and the Euro-currency Markets

Derrick Edwards

THE EVOLUTION OF FOREIGN EXCHANGE

Money is like a sixth sense, without which you cannot make a complete use of the other five.

Of Human Bondage, Somerset Maugham

For most people, the term 'foreign exchange' conjures up a vision of a holiday spent abroad, crossing national frontiers, culminating in an accumulation of surplus assorted foreign coins and low value notes. In the context of the (European Union) EU, these might comprise national currency units, such as the franc, guilder, krone, mark, peseta and lira, interspersed with varying denominations of centime, cent, ore and pfennig. However, there is much more to foreign exchange – the conversion of one currency into another – with regard to international trading than travel and tourism, despite the expansion of the latter into a global industry involving the same two-way flow of currencies.

Trade began with a system of barter – the exchange of goods for goods. The products and tools of hunting doubtless figured in the earliest exchanges – skins, furs, spears, daggers, axeheads and arrows – in a ratio of perhaps one spear equals three axes equals twelve arrows. But before dismissing barter as an antiquated, outmoded form of trade engaged in by our primitive ancestors, we should not forget the modern barter deals in recent history of Eastern Europe involving the exchange of Russian watches, furs and oil for cereals, or Romanian foodstuffs for machine tools consequent on the non-convertibility of Council for Mutual Economic Assiatance (Comecon)

185

currencies. Nor indeed, the sophisticated barter transaction when the Italian car manufacturer, Fiat, successfully contracted to build, in the USSR, a complete automobile production plant. This was based on Fiat operational design, technology and expertise, and subsequently paid for in cars which rolled off the selfsame production line. Consider the implications of this 'barter' deal, denuded of a monetary role, safeguards or penalty clauses, in which Fiat secured a substantial order in the face of keen competition and the Russians the best of all possible guarantees as to quality and timely commissioning.

The increasing diversity and inequality of the goods exchanged by way of barter led to a growing demand for a common medium of exchange and eventually to the development of money. The pre-money era saw many strange objects used for this purpose; some useful, eg nails and fish-hooks, and others useless such as glass beads and the ubiquitous cowrie shell found along the shores of the Indian Ocean. Certain basic commodities, such as rock salt in north African Saharan territories and bricks of compressed tea in China were also traded in barter deals. Both commodities lasted well and, being capable of sub-division, could be adapted to a variety of purchases.

The Museum of Athens and the British Museum have many specimens of early coins, some dating back 2600 years. Certainly coins were struck, albeit crudely by today's electronic mass-minting standards, and were used as a medium of exchange long before Jesus Christ overthrew the tables of the money changers in the temple precincts of Jerusalem. Here the silver denarius, bearing Caesar's image, rubbed shoulders with the coins of Greece, Egypt, Asia Minor, Syria and further afield and quite possibly with the vast mintage bearing the effigy of Alexander the Great. This particular coin continued to be struck 150 years after his death, by which time the Greeks had elevated him to a place in the Pantheon.

Coins were initially struck in gold or silver with the metal content matching the face value, followed by copper or bronze coins for lower denominations. But as precious metals became scarce and money in short supply, emperors, monarchs and governments were not slow to spot and pursue a course of 'wealth creation' by reducing the precious metal content through clipping the edges and thereby debasing the coinage while retaining the face value of the coins. The Roman silver denarius of the early Christian era suffered this fate at the hands of Emperor Tiberius, with 'Divini Tiberie' inscribed on the coin, as the means of resolving the short funding of his widely scattered legions. Because of his imperious, extravagant lifestyle and expensive foreign policy, Henry VIII also found himself short of money and resorted to debasement of the Anglo-noble, the gold coin worth a third of a pound struck in the reign of Edward III. This was done by striking an inferior gold coin but retaining its former value which depicted Archangel Michael evicting 'the dragon' Satan on the obverse. Having lost some of its 'nobility', the new coin came to be known as the Angel.

Crœsus, King of Lydia (Asia Minor), 560–546 BC, was the first ruler to establish a coinage in gold and silver and for centuries in the Middle East and parts of Asia, gold has been the yardstick of individual wealth. There is nowhere more so than in India where, despite the abject poverty of millions, the custom of paying dowries in gold requires even the poorest to pursue its acquisition, however meagre, in the form of jewellery for bridal adornment. The total of privately held gold, in all forms, in India probably exceeds that held in any other country, including France, where many housewives used to have a small brick or two concealed among the groceries as a hedge against inflation. Despite the Indian government's legislation to stem or control the inflow of gold smuggled in sailing dhows from the Persian Gulf to one of the many small west coast ports, it continued apace.

The Royal Mint's gold sovereign, originally worth one pound, was first issued by Henry VII in 1849 and continued until the time of James I. It was revived by George III and has continued to be minted ever since. It weighs approximately eight grams and is made of 22-carat gold. Its free circulation in Saudi Arabia in the post-war years of the reign of King Ibn Saud stemmed from the Arabian American Company's (ARAMCO's) contractual obligation to pay all oil royalties in gold sovereigns. Monthly shipments were air-freighted to Jeddah where the government's clearing agent took delivery and transferred the sovereigns to the government's bankers, The Netherlands Trading Society. Here a number of 'tellers' brought in from the local *Sukh* would squat in a circle around the glittering pile of sovereigns on the spacious floor and, preparatory to counting, commence sorting those with Queen Victoria's head from those with King Edward VII's and George V's head in order to facilitate slight discounts for loss of weight through protracted usage. The fact that the entire operation in transferring the gold from the plane to the bank's strongroom was overtly conducted with little or no regard to security, only serves to reflect the draconian penalties of the law relating to theft – severing of the right hand for the first offence and beheading for the second.

Perhaps the best-known example of the converse of debasement is the old Saudi riyal, which was widely regarded in the early post-war years as the finest silver coin in the world. This fact soon rendered it attractive to the dual operators in hoarding and smuggling at the east coast Gulf ports, from where it followed the old gold route to India. This caused much discomfiture to the then Saudi government, which eschewed the notion of introducing paper currency because they feared the Nejdi tribesmen, passionately loyal to the ruling family, might rebel when it came to the monarch dispensing largesse. The silver riyal, now a collector's coin, has long since disappeared from circulation and been superseded by a range of paper currency, which enjoys worldwide confidence and, since 1986, a fixed exchange rate against the US dollar of 3.75 riyals. This arose as a consequence of oil price increases in 1974 and 1979 and the recognition of Saudi Arabia as the dominant member of the Organization of the Petroleum Exporting Countries (OPEC), the largest single producer of crude in the world and possessor of the largest known reserves.

With the establishment of money as a medium of exchange in interstate trade, the parity of one currency in terms of another became the stock in trade of the moneylenders, who first practised their profession in the market squares of major commercial towns of northern Italy. Indeed, it was the Lombards, a group of merchant moneylenders and traders from these independent cities (called the Lombard League) who left the Plain of Lombardy in the 12th century to settle in London, initially as the financial agents of the popes who had many dues to collect. They had their offices in the street which still bears their name and were responsible for many innovations to assist traders, one of which may be of particular interest. When a trader who was intending to make a purchase across a state boundary also wished to take advantage of a favourable exchange rate some time before making the purchase, they conceived the idea of lending him the money with which to buy the currency at the favourable exchange rate, then allowing him to put the bought currency on deposit with them at a fixed rate of interest until the time when he wished to make the purchase. As a result of this arrangement the purchaser was able to fix the exchange rate for the currency long before he needed to make the purchase and the cost of the transaction was the difference between the interest he had to pay on the borrowing and the interest he was going to earn on the deposit.

Following the expulsion of the Jews from England in 1290, the Lombards began to enjoy a special sphere of influence as lenders to the Crown as well as to those in arrears with the Pope's tithes. The royal patronage started with Henry III and continued through to Edward III, who borrowed so freely that the Lombard bankers began to look to their securities. However, their caution came too late and two of the three major firms were bankrupted with unpaid royal debts of 900,000 and 600,000 crowns. Up-and-coming English merchants stepped into the breach with the Lombards being finally expelled from the Kingdom by Queen Elizabeth who disapproved of their usurious activities.

It was not until the 17th century that the first European central banks were founded. Certain major commercial cities became the recognized centres of banking, notably London, Amsterdam, Paris, Brussels, Frankfurt, Zurich and Milan. The Bank of Amsterdam (1609) takes pride of place chronologically, followed by the more prestigious Bank of England (1694).

Post-World War I, Germany saw hyperinflation rampant, its currency virtually worthless and printing presses turning out postage stamps and currency notes bearing value figures of 'million' and 'milliard'. The most telling story was that of the German housewife who left her wicker basket crammed with the new paper currency on the laundry floor momentarily while she went next door. On her return she found the basket missing and the currency notes scattered on the floor.

Post-war situations invariably find the vanquished nation subjected to crushing reparations, annexation of territory, its industry in ruins, many towns and cities reduced to rubble and its currency system collapsed. Germany found itself in such a situation twice in the first half of the 20th century, and twice the nation succeeded, over a protracted period of struggle, discipline and self-sacrifice, to rebuild its shattered industry and restore its economy. This in spite of limitations, strictures and overall control imposed by the victors through an army of occupation.

On the economic side, the major banks found themselves largely owning what was left of industry in settlement of debts. And so it transpired that the German banks emerged holding the majority equity in industry in stark contrast with Britain, where other institutions are the principal shareholders.

Exchange control regulations were introduced in 1939 in order to conserve UK gold and foreign currency and to support the role of sterling as a major trading and reserve currency. They were also designed to restrict the outflow of sterling for purposes other than *bona fide* trade, and monitor through Customs and Excise the timely payment of trading debts. When exchange controls were abolished on 23 October 1979 the effect on the foreign exchange market, investment abroad, and forward dealing in particular, was momentous and it took both exporters and importers some time to appreciate their new-found freedom. No longer was it obligatory for the proceeds of export sales to be repatriated within six months from the date of shipment. Indeed, the dismantling of exchange controls meant greater freedom to companies and individuals for investment and movement of funds around the world. With North Sea oil revenues continuing to grow and an apparently healthy balance-of-trade surplus, the British government's funding of the economy, despite the outflow of capital, seemed set fair. However, that was before the subsequent sharp fall in the price of oil, rising value of imports, balance-of-trade deficits and weakening of sterling began to emerge. The consequent need to redress these adverse effects engendering inflationary pressures led once again to rising interest rates. Once again, however, British industry was not fully geared to take advantage of the techniques whereby they could mitigate the damage by making greater use of the euro-currency market.

THE EURO-CURRENCY MARKET

The euro-currency market, now referred to as the international money market, began after World War II when, by way of Marshall aid, the Americans poured billions of dollars into Western Europe to help reconstruct their economies. These dollars were not loans, but grants, and the UK Prime Minister, Winston Churchill, put it as the most generous act by any one nation to any other nation in the history of man. As those countries began to piece themselves together, sweep away the debris and build new factories, those factories began to make goods, profits, and thereby generate wealth.

Gradually, over the years, those dollars became surplus to their requirements; however, as they were grants and not loans which had to be repaid, no one quite knew at the time how they should best be managed. The City of London, therefore, decided to establish a market for them in London, which became known as the euro-dollar market, ie surplus dollars out of Europe. As other countries began to generate a surplus of their own currencies, these also found their way into the London market and the 'euro' part of the title was retained.

In establishing this market, however, London was up against a problem; no country is favourable to foreign banks because they will take a certain amount of business away from domestic banks. Nevertheless, London took the view that if it was going to have a market-place, the only one worth having was a big one. Therefore, instead of trying to keep foreign banks out, it decided to try and entice as many of the world's banks into the market-place to create as big a market as possible.

The first to join were the American banks. In the late 1940s and early 1950s many of them began to open branches in the City of London with the object of attracting the euro-dollars as deposits. By June 1967 the sterling value of all euro-dollars that had been placed on deposit, almost entirely with American banks in London, was £3145 million, of which no less than £3067 million (97 per cent) was fed back to the USA.

By June 1987 the number of foreign banks represented on the London money market had risen to approximately 500, and together with approximately 100 British banks made a total of approximately 600 banks. This constitutes the largest money market in the world by far. Similarly, the euro-currencies deposited in London with those banks had increased to a value of approximately £472 billion, out of which approximately £456 billion was fed back overseas.

These huge sums can be seen as the world's surplus liquidity and the market summarized as the world's banks dealing in the world's surplus liquidity. Over the years, however, it has been allowed to develop into a 'free' market, and in their dealing on the market, banks are establishing market interest rates for all the major currencies. These are distinct from the domestic interest rates which are imposed on those currencies by the politicians of the countries concerned. For example, in August 1989 while the US prime rate, which governs domestic interest rates in the USA, was 11 per cent per annum, the loan of Euro dollars for a fixed period of three months in London was being traded at 8.75 per cent per annum.

Although interest rates are governed by market forces, ie the law of supply and demand, they are nevertheless interrelated with their domestic interest rates. Moreover, politicians keep a watchful eye on the free market rates as a guide to their economic policies.

Exchange Rates and their Calculation

Derrick Edwards

SPOT RATES OF EXCHANGE

In the days of the British Empire, sterling was firmly fixed to the price of gold and, in turn, all the major currencies at that time were fixed to sterling. Before World War II, however, things had already started to change and, while sterling was having to relinquish its fixed price to gold, the US dollar was emerging as the leading international trading currency. At the Bretton Woods conference in 1944, the exchange rate between sterling and the dollar was fixed at US$4:£1 and, as the value of the dollar was already fixed to the price of gold, sterling was again fixed to the price of gold, albeit indirectly.

As Britain began to dismantle the Empire after World War II, the realignment of all the major currencies was precipitated and in 1949 sterling was devalued against the US dollar to US$2.80:£1, with a further devaluation in 1967 to US$2.40:£1. The politicians at that time were still striving to maintain fixed exchange rates but the pressures were mounting – in 1971, under the Smithsonian Agreement, the dollar was devalued against the price of gold and many major currencies were devalued against the dollar. A last stand was made to maintain a system of fixed exchange rates; this did not last however, and from then on there was a gradual breakdown of fixed exchange rates until finally they were allowed to float and find their own levels in a free market. This means that the 'floating' exchange rate goes up and down all day every day, reacting to political and economic events everywhere in the world, in exactly the same way as the price of shares on the stock exchanges. A 'spot' rate of exchange, therefore, is the rate of exchange at a precise moment in time. In actual deals, however, this will normally entail an interval of two working days.

The figures set out in Tables 3.2.1a and b against the US dollar and the pound have been extracted from the *Financial Times*, which provides the only

Table 3.2.1a Dollar spot forward against the dollar

Jan 27		Closing mid-point	Change on day	Bid/offer spread	Day's mid		One month		Three months		One year		JP Morgan index
					high	low	rate	%PA	rate	%PA	rate	%PA	
Europe													
Austria*	(Sch)	13.9225	+0.1786	190–280	13.9345	13.7260	13.8941	2.5	13.8365	2.5	13.5755	2.5	100.1
Belgium*	(BFr)	40.8154	+0.5238	051–257	40.8510	40.2390	40.7319	2.5	40.5634	2.5	39.7982	2.5	99.6
Denmark	(DKr)	7.5309	+0.0969	288–328	7.5375	7.4247	7.5164	2.3	7.4899	2.2	7.3714	2.1	100.7
Finland*	(FM)	6.0158	+0.772	143–173	6.0210	5.9309	6.0035	2.5	5.9787	2.5	5.8659	2.5	76.9
France*	(FFr)	6.6389	+0.0852	352–386	6.6426	6.5432	6.6233	2.4	6.5959	2.5	6.4715	2.5	101.5
Germany*	(DM)	1.9789	+0.0254	784–794	1.9806	1.9510	1.9748	2.5	1.9667	2.5	1.9296	2.5	99.0
Greece	(Dr)	335.510	+4.3900	310–710	335.710	330.760	336.325	-2.9	337.435	-2.3	336.86	-0.4	58.8
Ireland*	(IE)	1.2550	-0.0163	546–553	1.2729	1.2539	1.2576	-2.5	1.2628	-2.5	1.287	-2.6	–
Italy*	(L)	1959.09	+25.1400	860–959	1960.78	1931.44	1955.08	2.5	1946.99	2.5	1910.27	2.5	72.9
Luxembourg*	(LFr)	40.8154	+0.5238	051–257	40.8510	40.2390	40.7319	2.5	40.5634	2.5	39.7982	2.5	99.6
Netherlands*	(Fl)	2.2297	+0.0286	291–302	2.2316	2.1982	2.2251	2.4	2.2159	2.5	2.1742	2.5	98.5
Norway	(NKr)	8.1565	+0.0897	540–590	8.1725	8.0481	8.1555	0.1	8.1522	0.2	8.1137	0.5	93.3
Portugal*	(Es)	202.845	+2.6030	794–897	203.020	199.960	202.43	2.5	201.593	2.5	197.79	2.5	90.1
Spain*	(Pta)	168.347	+2.1600	305–390	168.490	165.970	168.003	2.5	167.308	2.5	164.152	2.5	73.8
Sweden	(Skr)	8.6330	+0.0990	280–380	8.6380	8.5159	8.6182	2.1	8.5888	2.0	8.4685	2.5	82.3
Switzerland	(SFr)	1.6327	+0.0220	322–332	1.6340	1.6073	1.6275	3.8	1.6168	3.9	1.5692	1.9	102.6
UK	(£)	1.6373	-0.0032	370–376	1.6403	1.6341	1.6372	0.1	1.6371	0.0	1.6367	0.0	108.7
Euro	(€)	0.9884	-0.0128	881–886	1.0027	0.9889	0.9904	-2.5	0.9945	-2.5	1.0138	-2.6	–
SDR†		0.73490	–	–	–	–	–		–		–		–

Americas

Country	Currency	Closing Mid-point	Change on day	Bid/offer spread	Day's High	Day's Low	One month	%PA	Three months	%PA	One year	%PA	J.P Morgan Index
Argentina	(Peso)	0.9998	—	998–998	0.9998	0.9998	—	—	—	—	—	—	—
Brazil	(R$)	1.7760	-0.0045	750–770	1.7800	1.7720	—	—	—	—	—	—	—
Canada	(C$)	1.4338	-0.0045	333–343	1.4396	1.4320	1.4326	0.8	1.4309	0.8	1.4232	0.7	81.5
Mexico	(New Peso)	9.5050	-0.0050	000–100	9.5220	9.5000	9.6085	-13.1	9.8085	-12.8	10.745	-13.0	106.9
USA	($)	—	—	—	—	—	—	—	—	—	—	—	—

Pacific/Middle East/Africa

Country	Currency	Closing Mid-point	Change on day	Bid/offer spread	Day's High	Day's Low	One month	%PA	Three months	%PA	One year	%PA	J.P Morgan Index
Australia	(A$)	1.5277	-0.0096	265–288	1.5340	1.5256	1.5273	0.3	1.5269	0.2	1.5262	0.1	82.4
Hong Kong	(HK$)	7.7800	—	795–805	7.7805	7.7784	7.7782	0.3	7.7769	0.2	7.7985	-0.2	—
India	(Rs)	43.5725	0.0063	700–750	43.6000	43.5700	43.6975	-3.4	43.9275	-3.3	45.0175	-3.3	—
Indonesia	(Rupiah)	7390.00	-60.00	500–500	7495.00	7330.00	7414.5	-4.0	7454	-3.5	7690	-4.1	—
Israel	(Shk)	4.0830	-0.0054	769–870	4.0919	4.0789	—	—	—	—	—	—	—
Japan	(Y)	104.995	-0.9300	990–000	105.910	104.700	104.51	5.5	103.495	5.7	98.515	6.2	152.7
Malaysia‡	(M$)	3.8000	—	000–000	3.8000	3.8000	—	—	—	—	—	—	—
New Zealand	(NZ$)	1.9716	-0.0014	701–732	1.9743	1.9589	1.9698	1.1	1.9681	0.7	1.9685	0.2	—
Phillippines	(Peso)	40.4000	-0.1000	500–500	40.4500	40.3500	40.508	-3.2	40.745	-3.4	42.2095	-4.5	—
Saudi Arabia	(SR)	3.7506	—	505–507	3.7507	3.7504	3.7504	0.0	3.7504	0.0	3.7505	0.0	—
Singapore	(S$)	1.6915	-0.0030	910–920	1.6944	1.6870	1.6876	2.8	1.6787	3.0	1.6415	3.0	—
South Africa	(R)	6.2110	+0.0435	060–160	6.2400	6.1645	6.2355	-4.7	6.2787	-4.4	6.4645	4.1	—
South Korea	(Won)	1125.50	-2.0000	500–600	1127.50	1125.00	—	—	—	—	—	—	—
Taiwan	(T$)	30.7780	-0.0145	760–800	30.7800	30.7760	30.663	4.5	30.513	3.4	30.228	1.8	—
Thailand	(Bt)	37.3550	-0.1200	300–800	37.5600	37.3300	37.29	2.1	37.165	2.0	36.95	1.1	—

† SDR rate per $ for Jan 26. ‡ Official rate set by Malaysian government. The WM/Reuters rate for the valuation of capital assets is 3.60 MYR/USD. Bid/offer spread in the Dollar Spot table show only the last three decimal places. UK, Ireland & Euro are quoted in US currency. JP, Morgan nominal indices Jan 26: Base average 1990 = 10 Bid, offer, mid spot rates and forward rates in both this and the pound table are derived from THE WM/REUTERS 4 pm (London time) CLOSING SPOT and FORWARD RATE services. Some values are rounded by the F.T. *EMU member. The exchange rates printed in this table are also available on the Internet at http:www.FT.com

Table 3.2.1b Pound spot forward against the pound

		Closing mid-point	Change on day	Bid/offer spread	Day's Mid high	low	One month rate	%PA	Three months rate	%PA	One year rate	%PA	Bank of England index
Europe													
Austria	(Sch)	22.7953	+0.2486	854 – 052	22.8052	22.4545	22.7477	2.5	22.6525	2.5	22.2198	2.5	100.5
Belgium*	(BFr)	66.8271	+0.7288	979 – 562	66.8570	65.8270	66.6874	2.5	66.4084	2.5	65.1398	2.5	99.2
Denmark	(DKr)	12.3303	+0.1348	246 – 359	12.3376	12.1513	12.306	2.4	12.262	2.2	12.065	2.2	101.4
Finland*	(FM)	9.8497	+0.1074	454 – 540	9.8540	9.7030	9.8292	2.5	9.788	2.5	9.6011	2.5	77.5
France*	(FFr)	10.8666	+0.1185	618 – 713	10.8713	10.7042	10.8438	2.5	10.7985	2.5	10.5922	2.5	102.1
Germany*	(DM)	3.2400	+0.0353	386 – 414	3.2424	3.1906	3.2332	2.5	3.2197	2.5	3.1582	2.5	99.0
Greece	(Dr)	549.331	+6.1280	903 – 759	549.759	541.269	550.64	-2.9	552.432	-2.3	551.356	-0.4	59.1
Ireland*	(I£)	1.3047	+0.0142	041 – 052	1.3052	1.2852	1.302	2.5	1.2965	2.5	1.2717	2.5	87.4
Italy*	(L)	3207.62	+34.9800	623 – 902	3209.02	3159.68	3200.91	2.5	3187.52	2.5	3126.63	2.5	72.9
Luxembourg*	(LFr)	66.8271	+0.7288	979 – 562	66.8570	65.8270	66.6874	2.5	66.4084	2.5	65.1398	2.5	99.2
Netherlands*	(Fl)	3.6507	+0.0398	491 – 523	3.6523	3.5961	3.6431	2.5	3.6279	2.5	3.5586	2.5	98.0
Norway	(NKr)	13.3547	+0.1212	481 – 612	13.3751	13.1727	13.3525	0.2	13.3465	0.2	13.2802	0.6	94.1
Portugal*	(Es)	332.118	+3.6210	974 – 263	332.263	327.151	331.424	2.5	330.037	2.5	323.733	2.5	89.3
Spain*	(Pta)	275.635	+3.0060	515 – 755	275.755	271.510	275.059	2.5	273.908	2.5	268.676	2.5	74.3
Sweden	(SKr)	14.1348	+0.1347	240 – 456	14.1456	13.9372	14.1099	2.1	14.0611	2.1	13.8608	1.9	82.5
Switzerland	(SFr)	2.6732	+0.0309	719 – 745	2.6745	2.6336	2.6646	3.9	2.6469	3.9	2.5683	3.9	102.4
UK	(£)	–					–		–		–		110.2
Euro	(€)	1.6566	+0.0180	559 – 573	1.6582	1.6318	1.6532	2.5	1.6462	2.5	1.6148	2.5	80.58
SDR†		1.203200	–				–		–		–		–

Americas

Argentina	(Peso)	1.6370	−0.0032	367 – 373	1.6400	1.6338	—	—	—	—	—
Brazil	(R$)	2.9079	−0.0130	057 – 100	2.9164	2.8997	—	—	—	—	—
Canada	(C$)	2.3476	−0.0120	463 – 488	2.3604	2.3450	2.3458	0.9	2.3428	0.8	2.3295	0.8	82.0
Mexico	(New Peso)	15.5626	−0.0386	515 – 736	15.5746	15.5349	15.7313	−13.0	16.0581	−12.7	17.587	−13.0	—
USA	($)	1.6373	−0.0032	370 – 376	1.6403	1.6341	1.6372	0.1	1.6371	0.0	1.6367	0.0	105.9

Pacific/Middle East/Africa

Australia	(A$)	2.5013	−0.0206	989 – 036	2.5158	2.4986	2.5002	0.6	2.499	0.4	2.4988	0.1	82.6
Hong Kong	(HK$)	12.7382	−0.0249	350 – 413	12.7607	12.7141	12.7346	0.3	12.7319	0.2	12.7642	−0.2	—
India	(Rs)	71.3413	−0.1497	241 – 584	71.4580	71.2140	71.5427	−3.4	71.916	−3.2	73.6825	−3.3	—
Indonesia	(Rupiah)	12099.65	−122.09	288 – 643	12267.80	12001.40	12139.21	−3.9	12203.32	−3.4	12586.62	−4.0	—
Israel	(Shk)	6.6851	−0.0219	772 – 929	6.6964	6.6772	—	—	—	—	—	—
Japan	(Y)	171.908	−1.8620	869 – 948	173.340	171.480	171.113	5.5	169.438	5.7	161.243	6.2	152.7
Malaysia‡	(M$)	6.2218	−0.0121	206 – 229	6.2330	6.2104	—	—	—	—	—	—
New Zealand	(NZ$)	3.2282	−0.0085	250 – 313	3.2316	3.2080	3.2267	0.6	3.2246	0.4	3.2273	0.0	85.5
Philippines	(Peso)	66.1470	−0.2933	530 – 409	66.2409	66.0530	66.3208	−3.2	66.7058	−3.4	69.0866	−4.4	—
Saudi Arabia	(SR)	6.1409	−0.0120	396 – 421	6.1519	6.1290	6.1404	0.1	6.1401	0.1	6.1387	0.0	—
Singapore	(S$)	2.7695	−0.0104	682 – 708	2.7792	2.7597	2.763	2.8	2.7483	3.1	2.6867	3.0	—
South Africa	(R)	10.1693	+0.0515	592 – 793	10.2130	10.0783	10.2089	4.7	10.2792	−4.3	10.5808	−4.0	—
South Korea	(Won)	1842.78	−6.8800	163 – 394	1848.95	1838.36	—	—	—	—	—	—
Taiwan	(T$)	50.3928	−0.1223	803 – 053	50.5065	50.2976	50.2022	4.5	49.9543	3.5	49.4757	1.8	—
Thailand	(Bt)	61.1614	−0.3164	092 – 135	62.9310	60.1190	61.0522	2.1	60.8447	2.1	60.478	1.1	—

*EMU member.

†Rates for Jan 26.

Bid/offer spreads in the Pound Spot table show only the last three decimal places. Sterling Index calculated by the Bank of England. Base average 1990 = 100. Index rebased 1/2/95.

Source: Financial Times (The exchange rates printed in this table are also available on the Internet at http://www.FT.com)

comprehensive daily cover of London's exchange and interest rates. These are obtained from a number of different sources and should only therefore be taken as an indication of the previous day's rates.

Up until 1993, the *Financial Times* only used to show the day's spread of spot rates of exchange and the amount of any premiums or discounts, thus leaving the reader to subtract any premium or discounts from the spot rate to calculate the forward rate and to add any discounts. They now publish every day the actual forward rates. Any spot rates shown in this book or used in any calculations are those shown under the columns headed 'closing mid-point' in Table 3.2.1a.

The figures shown in Table 3.2.4 (see page 209) were also extracted from the *Financial Times* on the same day as those shown in Tables 3.2.1a and 3.2.1b and have therefore been used in conjunction with Table 3.2.1a in any calculations shown in this part of the book.

All the spot exchange rates shown in both Tables 3.2.1a and 3.2.1b are equal to 1 US dollar and 1 pound sterling respectively. If the reader wishes to know the spot rate of, say, the Japanese yen against the Swiss franc the calculation is as follows. (While there is very little if no difference in working the calculations in sterling as opposed to dollars, they are invariably worked in dollars as this is now the world's leading currency.)

1 dollar = Swiss franc 1.6327 1 dollar = Japanese yen 104.995
therefore S/fr 1.6327 = ¥ 104.995

therefore 1 S/fr = ¥ $\dfrac{104.995}{1.6327}$ = ¥ 64.3075

This is known as a cross rate.

PREMIUMS AND DISCOUNTS

It is an extraordinary paradox that today one can hardly take a step unless armed with mobile phone, laptop computer and all the technical impediments of modern business, while having no knowledge of the technology of foreign exchange, and indeed, being terrified about even taking the very first steps to understand it. Perhaps the reason may be hidden in the fact that premiums and discounts resulting from the technique of selling and buying currencies forward was originally conceived by the Lombardies in the 12th century, and has served the bankers very well ever since. The first step for businessmen and women to take, therefore, is to allay their fear that it is all based on gamble and speculation. There is absolutely no gamble or speculation involved either by the banks or the users. Indeed, the only speculation or gamble is that taken by the exporter/importer himself who receives or places an order involving payment in foreign currency at some time in the future and then waits until he has to pay or receives the currency, thereby never knowing how much of his own currency he is going to earn or have to pay until the day of settlement.

Every time anyone sells or buys any product or service across any national frontier on terms other than immediate cash payment, there is a differential in the value of the two currencies and that differential does not go away. It can either be a plus quantity or a minus quantity, eg a UK/US exporter selling into Switzerland, invoicing his buyer in Swiss francs and expecting to receive payment in Swiss francs in three months time, could ring up any bank and sell them to the bank at a premium for conversion into sterling/dollars at a future date.

The exporter can now earn extra profit from the sale to the bank of his Swiss francs. That is over and above the profit which he is going to make from the sale of his product. What exporter can afford not to know what the additional profit is? In any event, it does not go away. He can either make himself more profit or, of course, he can reduce his Swiss franc price to the buyer and thereby make himself more competitive if necessary.

Conversely, if an exporter had been selling to Portugal in 1993 and was expecting to receive escudos in three months' time and rang up a bank in order to sell them to the bank and deliver them in three months' time for conversion to sterling, the bank would have bought them from him at a discount, which meant that every time he sold escudos to the bank for future delivery he was going to lose money. Some people might therefore be tempted to assume that if you are going to lose money every time you sell escudos to the bank for future delivery the obvious thing is not to invoice in escudos, but they would have been mistaken. The reason for this is explained in Chapter 3.4.

You will see in Table 3.2.2 a schedule of the 15 main trading currencies over the 19 years 1979–1997, and the three months average premiums and discounts against sterling. This schedule constitutes 257 currency years, and out of 257 currency years, British exporters selling in currencies would only have had to sell currencies at a loss on 80 occasions out of 257. On those 80 occasions however (shown in brackets in Table 3.2.2), and while the currencies were at a discount against sterling, sterling was at a premium against those currencies and could have yielded those countries more profit. British exporters however, selling in currencies, could have made additional

Table 3.2.2 Premiums and discounts

Year	US dollar	Canadian dollar	Dutch guilder	Belgian franc	Danish krone	German mark	Italian lira	Norwegian krone	French franc	Swedish krona	Austrian schilling	Swiss franc	Japanese yen	Portuguese escudo	Spanish peseta	Average London Base Rate
							Average 3 months premium/discount against sterling on forward sale of currencies. (Percentages per annum. ( ) = discount)								
1979	1.69	1.83	4.07	2.57	(1.52)	6.82	(0.84)	2.55	2.45	2.13	5.81	11.13	7.76			13.70
1980	2.45	3.43	5.34	2.16	(1.72)	6.86	(4.70)	3.96	3.83	1.40	5.26	9.93	4.86			16.30
1981	(3.06)	(4.51)	2.03	(4.38)	(1.97)	1.99	(9.63)	0.61	(4.19)	(1.64)	1.83	4.32	6.02			13.25
1982	(1.22)	(2.50)	3.69	(3.47)	(5.54)	3.56	(10.39)	(3.15)	(6.91)	(1.47)	3.83	6.91	5.06			11.99
1983	0.37	0.44	4.34	(1.15)	(2.42)	4.49	(8.46)	(3.35)	(6.39)	(1.41)	4.19	5.81	3.43			9.82
1984	(0.97)	(1.34)	3.67	(1.84)	(1.50)	4.01	(7.68)	(3.93)	(2.78)	(2.15)	2.95	5.42	3.50			9.54
1985	3.72	2.50	5.63	2.75	2.51	6.69	(1.85)	0.38	1.36	(2.12)	5.59	6.94	5.44			12.23
1986	4.00	1.61	5.13	2.45	1.62	6.18	(2.22)	(3.39)	1.40	0.63	5.07	6.46	5.72			10.94
1987	2.43	1.13	4.24	2.50	(0.79)	5.54	(1.49)	(4.96)	0.94	(0.12)	4.84	5.74	5.35			9.73
1988	2.25	0.61	5.39	3.45	1.48	5.83	(0.92)	(3.14)	2.00	0.01	5.24	7.02	5.60			10.10
1989	4.35	1.60	6.18	5.03	4.04	6.48	1.41	2.40	4.30	2.27	6.08	6.55	8.14			13.85
1990	6.24	1.66	5.87	4.79	3.64	6.06	2.79	3.19	4.22	1.12	5.70	5.56	6.85			14.76
1991	5.39	2.36	2.14	2.16	1.65	2.20	(0.16)	0.91	1.84	(0.04)	2.15	3.16	3.97			11.69
1992	6.05	3.10	0.28	0.39	(1.15)	0.20	(4.18)	(1.37)	(0.72)	(3.14)	0.34	1.70	5.29			9.55
1993	2.69	0.90	(1.01)	(2.29)	(4.81)	(1.38)	(4.29)	(1.32)	(2.69)	(2.56)	(1.06)	0.96	3.00	(7.09)	(6.21)	6.02
1994	0.90	0.14	0.17	(0.40)	(0.93)	0.03	(3.00)	(0.23)	(0.47)	(2.08)	0.19	1.26	3.15	(6.09)	(3.41)	5.46
1995	0.62	(0.57)	2.18	1.81	0.39	2.11	(3.67)	1.02	(0.06)	(0.43)	1.78	3.49	5.42	(3.63)	(3.08)	6.71
1996	0.50	1.23	2.92	2.64	1.85	2.67	(13.19)	1.07	1.87	0.04	2.51	3.97	5.53	(1.93)	(1.75)	5.96
1997	1.12	3.25	3.48	3.22	3.02	3.46	(0.20)	2.80	3.30	2.68	2.89	5.02	6.25	0.62	1.25	6.56

profit on 177 occasions. Table 3.2.1b shows that British exporters selling to Japan in yen at that time could have earned a premium on the one month forward sale of yen of 5.5 per cent per annum, 5.7 per cent per annum on the three months and 6.2 per cent on the 12 months. While the UK exporter could be earning additional margins of 5.5 per cent, 5.7 per cent or 6.2 per cent by selling his yen receivables for delivery to the bank 1, 3 or 12 months forward. Conversely, if he had been selling to Japan in sterling and, assuming that the Japanese buyer understood how the system works any better than the UK exporter, he could have bought the sterling forward at a discount of approximately 5.5 per cent, 5.7 per cent and 6.2 per cent. There is no evidence to show, however, that this assumption is correct. On the contrary, all the evidence points to the fact that overseas buyers understand trading in foreign currencies even less than the UK exporters; and this stems from the fact that there is only a limited forward market in most other major countries. Because neither seller nor buyer generates the premium/discount by using the forward market it simply goes by default and is lost.

Although the advent of the Euro has lessened the advantages when selling to EU countries, there are still good additional margins to be made in some other countries, especially Japan, which has very low interest rates.

As an example, Table 3.2.3 shows the premiums which accrued to British exports of £1 million to each of the nine countries scheduled over the three years from 1987 to 1989, translated into pounds sterling. Exporters should calculate from their own sales to these countries the amount of additional profit they would have made by selling in each of the currencies. For example, annual sales in US dollars to the value of £5 million in 1988 with an average period between date of order and date of payment of approximately three months would have yielded £28,125. Annual sales in deutschmarks to the value of £2 million in 1987 but with an average period between date of order and date of payment of six months would have yielded £13,850 × 2 = £27,700 (see note to Table 3.2.3) ×2 = £55,400. These figures should provide sufficient inducement to any exporter who is still selling in sterling to start selling in currencies.

For the cost of only a few telephone calls and with no exchange risk, UK exporters invoicing in the currencies shown below to the value of £1 million each, per year and with an average period of three months between date of order and date of payment, could have earned the approximate amounts shown below by way of forward premium.

Table 3.2.3 Extra profit/increased competitiveness from the use of foreign currencies, 1987–1989

Currency	1987	1988	1989	Totals
US dollar	6075	5625	10875	22575
Canadian dollar	2825	1525	4000	8350
Dutch guilder	10600	13475	15450	39525
Belgian franc	6250	8625	12575	27450
Deutschmark	13850	14575	16200	44625
French franc	2350	5000	10750	18100
Austrian schilling	12100	13100	15200	40400
Swiss franc	14350	17550	16375	48275
Japanese yen	13375	14000	20350	47725
Total	81775	93475	121775	297025

Note Where the period between date of order and date of payment is 6 months, the above figures should be multiplied by 2 and for 12 months multiplied by 4.

SELLING AND BUYING CURRENCIES FORWARD

Let us assume that a UK exporter has received an order from a Swiss buyer to the value of £10,000 and has converted that into Swiss francs (SF) at an exchange rate of SF2.6732:£1, as shown in Table 3.2.1b. That means that he now has an order for SF26,732 that he expects to receive in, for example, one month or three months. If he had the Swiss francs today and converted them back into sterling at SF2.6732:£1 he would have £10,000, but he is not going to receive them for one month or three months and he has no idea what they will be worth in sterling terms when he gets them.

In order to overcome this problem, therefore, the exporter rings up his bank and says that he will sell them the amount of SF26.732 on a particular day, and will undertake to deliver them on, or about day 30, 60, 90. He would not usually undertake to deliver them on a specific day because he is not sure when he is going to get them. He would invariably give himself some days' grace – a period during which he can deliver the Swiss francs. This period is called an 'option'. If the exporter was expecting to receive his Swiss francs in approximately three months, he might undertake to deliver them to the bank any day between day 90 and 120; in other words he is giving himself a month in which to deliver the Swiss francs. Nevertheless this is a firm undertaking by the exporter to deliver SF26,732 any working day between day 90 and day 120. If the currency is at a premium the exporter will earn the premium calculated to the earliest date, ie day 90 in the above example. If the currency is at a discount, the exporter will pay the discount calculated to the latest date, ie day 120. The situation is reversed in the case of imports; the importer will earn the discount calculated to the earliest date and pay the premium calculated to the latest date.

Up to this point it has not cost the exporter anything except the telephone call. He has merely made a commitment to deliver the Swiss francs. In exchange for the exporter's undertaking to deliver the SF26,732 any day between day 90 and day 120, the bank will fix the exchange rate at which it will convert those francs when the exporter delivers them any day between day 90 and day 120. This is called the 'forward rate' – a rate of exchange agreed on any given day at which a bank will convert currency either on a future date or between two future dates. Whatever the spot rate happens to be at the time, the bank is firmly committed to convert those Swiss francs back into sterling at the agreed forward rate. The 'one month' and 'three month' columns in Table 3.2.1b show the two forward rates, one month SF2.6646:£1 and three months SF2.6469:£1.

When giving the bank the order over the telephone it is important to state 'bank is buying' or 'bank is selling' as many people end up buying instead of selling or selling instead of buying. So, in order to avoid the confusion, think of them as importing and exporting. Obviously, if you are importing *you* are buying the currency in order to pay the supplier but the bank is selling. If you are exporting and receiving the currency, you are selling the currency to the bank to have it converted into sterling, but the bank is buying.

Assume that you are importing and you have placed an order for SF26,732 which you are going to have to pay in approximately one month. The same arguments apply insofar as no one knows how much sterling you will have to pay for those Swiss francs in one month. There is no law which says that you cannot buy them on that day at the spot rate of exchange and put them on deposit until you require them. They will earn a certain amount of interest but you might have better things to do with your money. So, you buy the Swiss francs forward and say to the bank, 'I will buy SF26,732 today and I will take up delivery of those Swiss francs on or about day 30, 60, 90 etc'. If you were undertaking to take up delivery of the francs on about day 30 then you would buy them at the rate of SF2.6646:£1. If you were taking up delivery of the francs in about three months then you would buy them at the rate of SF2.6469:£1 and in this case you would pay the premium of £99.

If you do not know exactly when during the next 30 or 90 days you will be requiring the currency, you can buy it forward with an open option. In this case you would pay the premium of £99 and be able to take delivery any day between days 1 and 90. If the currency was at a discount and you wanted to take up delivery between days 1 and 30 or 90, you would forfeit your discount and pay the spot rate current at the time you transacted the forward contract for the full period of the 30 or 90 days. To summarize: if you were exporting and delivering the Swiss francs on, approximately, day 30 you would earn a premium of £32; if you were delivering the francs on about day 90 you would earn a premium of £99. Conversely, if you were importing and taking up delivery of the Swiss francs on about day 30 you would pay £32 and if you were taking up delivery of the francs on about day 90 you would pay an extra £99.

Exporters and importers are very often asked, 'Do you want it fixed or option?' and they should be wary before replying. 'Do you want it fixed?' is easy enough – it means do you want to deliver currency to the bank or take up delivery of currency from the bank on a fixed date? But what does the bank mean by, 'Do you want it option?' It could mean, 'Do you want to deliver or take up delivery of currency between two future dates?' or it could mean, 'Do you want to deliver or take up delivery of the currency any day between days 1 and 30, 60, 90?' in which event you may forfeit any premium if exporting and discount if importing. The answer to the question is usually 'neither, we will deliver or take up delivery of the currency between that date and that date'.

CALCULATING PREMIUMS AND DISCOUNTS

Figures 3.2.1–3.2.9, calculated at rates shown in Tables 3.2.1a and b demonstrate the advantages to exporters of selling in various currencies, including the euro – and all for the cost of a telephone call. This is all that is required to fix the dollar/sterling prices of currency sales at the time the sales were transacted, which is what would have happened if the sales had been transacted in dollars or sterling. Now, however, they have produced more profit/competitiveness and the exporters do not have to try and guess how much the sales will bring in. The exchange rate is fixed and the sale is completed.

Spot rate at time of sale	DM 3,2400 = £1.	DM 32,400	= £10,000
1 month forward rate	DM 3.2332		= £10,021
3 month forward rate	DM 3.2197		= £10,063
12 month forward rate	DM 3.1582		= £10,259

Figure 3.2.1 Forward sale of the deutschmark

Spot rate at time of sale	€ 1,6566 = £1.	€ 16,566	= £10,000
1 month forward rate	€ 1.6532		= £10,021
3 month forward rate	€ 1.6462		= £10,063
12 month forward rate	€ 1.6148		= £10,259

Figure 3.2.2 Forward sale of the euro

Spot rate at time of sale	SF 2.6732 = £1.	SF 26,732	= £10,000
1 month forward rate	SF 2.6646		= £10,032
3 month forward rate	SF 2.6469		= £10,099
12 month forward rate	SF 2.5683		= £10,408

Figure 3.2.3 Forward sale of the Swiss franc

Spot rate at time of sale	¥ 171.9080 = £1.	¥ 1,719,080	= £10,000
1 month forward rate	¥ 171.113		= £10,046
3 month forward rate	¥ 169.438		= £10,146
12 month forward rate	¥ 161.243		= £10,661

Figure 3.2.4 Forward sale of the Japanese yen

Spot rate at time of sale	$ 1.6373 = £1.	$ 16,373	= £10,000
1 month forward rate	$ 1.6372		= £10,001
3 month forward rate	$ 1.6371		= £10,001
12 month forward rate	$ 1.6367		= £10,004

Figure 3.2.5 Forward sale of the US dollar

Spot rate at time of sale	KR 12.3303 = £1.	KR 123,303 = £10,000
1 month forward rate	KR 12.3060	= £10,020
3 month forward rate	KR 12.2620	= £10,055
12 month forward rate	KR 12.0650	= £10,220

Figure 3.2.6 Forward sale of the Danish krone

Spot rate at time of sale	FR 10.8666 = £1.	FR 108,666 = £10,000
1 month forward rate	FR 10.8438	= £10,021
3 month forward rate	FR 10.7985	= £10,063
12 month forward rate	FR 10.5922	= £10,259

Figure 3.2.7 Forward sale of the French franc

Spot rate at time of sale	Sp 275.635 = £1.	Sp 2,756,350 = £10,000
1 month forward rate	Sp 275.0590	= £10,021
3 month forward rate	Sp 273.9080	= £10,063
12 month forward rate	Sp 268.676	= £10,259

Figure 3.2.8 Forward sale of the Spanish peseta

$10,000 @ Spot yen	104.995 = 1,049,950	= $10,000
1 month forward rate	¥ 104.510	= $10,046
3 months forward rate	¥ 103.495	= $10,145
1 year forward rate	¥ 98.515	= $10,658

See Table 3.2.1a US dollars for rates

Figure 3.2.9 A US export to Japan in yen

Figures 3.2.10–3.2.12 show three further examples of exports in US dollars, euros and Japanese yen, covering major transactions with payments at six-monthly intervals over a five-year period. The US dollar is at a discount and the exporter will therefore have to make up the loss of £35,616 in his price or run the exchange risk on the whole amount by not selling the dollars forward. The forward sale of euros will produce an additional margin of £117,165 or 5.86 per cent on the face value of the contract, which may be useful in beating off any competition. The forward sale of Japanese yen,

Spot rate of exchange at time of contract, $1.5967 = £1
£3m = $4,790,100 payable in ten instalments of $479,010 = £300,000
Forward rates:-

6 months	$1.6004	=	£299,306	Discount	£694
12 "	1.6041	=	£298,616		384
18 "	1.6078	=	£297.929		2071
24 "	1.6115	=	£297,245		2755
30 "	1.6152	=	£296,564		3436
36 "	1.6189	=	£295,886		4114
42 "	1.6226	=	£295,211		4789
48 "	1.6263	=	£294,540		5460
54 "	1.6272	=	£294,377		5623
60 "	1.6309	=	£293,710		6290

Total discount   £35,616

NB: These rates are not shown in Tables 3.2.1a or b and were obtained from a bank.

Figure 3.2.10 A £3 million contract in US dollars

Spot rate of exchange at time of contract, € 1.6243 = £1
£2m = € 3,248,600 payable in ten instalments of € 324,860 = £200,000
Forward rates:

6 months	€1.6023	=	£202,746	Premium	£2,746
12 "	1.5804	=	205,556		5,556
18 "	1.5670	=	207,313		7,313
24 "	1.5536	=	209,101		9,101
30 "	1.5402	=	210,921		10,921
36 "	1.5268	=	212,772		12,772
42 "	1.5134	=	214,656		14,656
48 "	1.5000	=	216,573		16,573
54 "	1.4900	=	218,027		18,027
60 "	1.4800	=	219,500		19,500

Total premiums £117,165

Figure 3.2.11 A £2 million contract in euros

Spot rate of exchange at time of contract, YN 171.908 = £1
£2m = YN 343,816,000 payable in ten instalments of 34,381,600 = £200,000
Forward rates:

6 months	YN 167.2900	=	£205,514	Premium	£5,514
12 "	162.6840	=	211,340		11,340
18 "	158.1840	=	217,352		17,352
24 "	153.6840	=	223,716		23,716
30 "	149.0715	=	230,638		30,638
36 "	144.4590	=	238,002		38,002
42 "	140.0490	=	245,497		45,497
48 "	135.6400	=	253,477		53,477
54 "	132.1400	=	260,191		60,191
60 "	128.6400	=	267,270		67,270
			Total premiums		£352,997

Figure 3.2.12 A £2 million contract in Japanese yen

however, will produce a much larger premium of £352,997 or 17.65 per cent on the value of the contract.

WHAT IS A FORWARD RATE?

A forward rate in no way reflects what the bank thinks the spot rate is likely to be at some future time. No foreign exchange dealer is in the guessing game, and in order to understand the reason why this is the case one has to refer back to the days when the euro-currency market was being established in London, shortly after World War II. At that time no country had ever set out to establish a money market of this kind and, consequently, no one knew what the ground rules for running such a market should be. The banks in London therefore looked to the Bank of England in order to conceive a set of ground rules on which such a market should operate. After several months they came up with an appropriate set of rules within which the Bank of England insisted on the observance of the 'golden rule' principle that no bank should speculate in currencies.

In practical terms this means that banks in London have to close out their positions in currency at the end of each day within an agreed tolerance, and they do this by way of borrowing or lending the currency concerned against a lending or borrowing of the other currency involved. The premium or discount is therefore based on the difference in the international money rates. The figures set out in Table 3.2.4 have been extracted from the *Financial Times*. If a bank has bought or sold currency on a given day for delivery or receipt at some time in the future, it covers itself by setting up the deal on that given day.

Table 3.2.4 International money rates

	Short term	Seven days notice	One month	Three months	Six months	One year
Euro	$3^5/_{32}$–$3^3/_{32}$	$3^3/_{16}$–$3^3/_{32}$	$3^{11}/_{32}$–$3^7/_{32}$	$3^1/_2$–$2^3/_8$	$3^{23}/_{32}$–$3^5/_8$	$4^1/_{32}$–$3^{31}/_{32}$
Danish krone	$3^3/_8$–$2^7/_8$	$3^{11}/_{32}$–$3^1/_4$	$3^{15}/_{32}$–$3^5/_{16}$	$3^3/_4$–$3^{19}/_{32}$	4–$3^{27}/_{32}$	$4^7/_{16}$–$4^9/_{32}$
Pound sterling	$6^1/_4$–6	6–$5^3/_4$	6–$5^7/_8$	$6^1/_8$–$6^1/_{32}$	$6^{11}/_{32}$–$6^7/_{32}$	$6^3/_4$–$6^5/_8$
Swiss franc	$1^3/_4$–$1^1/_4$	$1^{27}/_{32}$–$1^{19}/_{32}$	$1^7/_8$–$1^{23}/_{32}$	$1^{31}/_{32}$–$1^{13}/_{16}$	$2^3/_{16}$–$2^1/_{16}$	$2^9/_{16}$–$2^7/_{16}$
Canadian dollar	$4^{25}/_{32}$–$4^{21}/_{32}$	$4^{15}/_{16}$–$4^{27}/_{32}$	$4^{15}/_{16}$–$4^{27}/_{32}$	$5^3/_{16}$–$5^3/_{32}$	$5^{13}/_{32}$–$5^5/_{16}$	$5^{29}/_{32}$–$5^{25}/_{32}$
US dollar	$5^{19}/_{32}$–$5^1/_2$	$5^{21}/_{32}$–$5^9/_{16}$	$5^{27}/_{32}$–$5^3/_4$	$6^1/_{16}$–$5^{15}/_{16}$	$6^1/_4$–$6^5/_{32}$	$6^{23}/_{32}$–6
Japanese yen	$^1/_{16}$–$^1/_{32}$	$^1/_8$–$^1/_{32}$	$^5/_{32}$–$^1/_{16}$	$^3/_{16}$–$^3/_{32}$	$^1/_4$–$^5/_{32}$	$^5/_{16}$–$^7/_{32}$
Asian Singaporean dollar	1–$^3/_4$	$2^7/_8$–$2^3/_8$	3–$2^3/_4$	3–$2^3/_4$	$3^1/_4$–3	$3^{11}/_{16}$–$3^7/_{16}$

Note: Short-term rates are all for the US dollar and Japanese yen, others: two days' notice. Three month Euribor Futures (MATIF) Paris Interbank offered rate.

Where the interest rate of any one of the International Money rates quoted in London is lower than another currency, the currency with the lower interest rate is at a premium against the other currency. Table 3.2.4 shows that at that time the Japanese yen was at a lower interest rate than any other, and the yen was therefore at a premium against them. If the interest rate is higher than that of the other currency, then the currency with the higher interest rate is at a discount against the other. The table above shows that the US dollar was at a discount against all but sterling.

In Figure 3.2.13 the exporter has sold Swiss francs to the bank for delivery in three months, and in order to close out its position on the same day the bank has borrowed the Swiss francs for a fixed period of three months at a fixed interest rate of 1 13/16 (1.81) per cent per annum, the lower of the two rates shown in Table 3.2.4. The bank will then convert the Swiss francs into sterling and lend the sterling for the same period at a fixed interest rate of 6 1/8 (6.1250) per cent per annum all on the same day. The bank is showing a profit of 4.3150 per cent per annum, and it is this profit which the bank passes on to the exporter by way of premium.

As we are looking at the three months forward rate we divide the difference of 4.3150 per cent per annum by four to get a flat rate of 1.0788 per cent, and then calculate 1.0788 per cent of the spot rate 2.6732, which works out as SF0.03, ie a premium of three cents. As it is a premium we subtract it from the spot rate, which gives a forward rate of SF2.6432:£1. Table 3.2.1 shows the three months forward rate as SF2.6469:£1 and the difference in interest rates as 3.9 per cent per annum, but these discrepancies only arise because the *Financial Times* gets its rates from a number of sources and takes an average so the sums rarely work out exactly alike. If the exporter were to get the premium and interest rates from the same bank, they would work out exactly because that, in effect, is how the bank itself has calculated the premium.

Bank lends 3 months sterling @ 6.1250% pa
Bank borrows 3 months SF   @ 1.8100% pa
Difference   4.3150% pa
÷ 4   = 1.0788% flat
1.0788% of spot rate SF2.6732 = SF0.03 premium
Subtract premium of 3 cents from spot 2.6732
three months forward rate of 2.6432 Premium £99

Figure 3.2.13 Swiss francs sold forward by exporter for conversion into sterling in three months

The bank's profit on the deal is calculated in the normal way by the difference in borrowing and lending the same currencies. Table 3.2.4 shows the lower borrowing rates and the higher lending rates against each of the currencies. The differences may seem surprisingly small but the volume of business within each bank is huge.

As a result of the way in which the forward deal is constructed, the bank has a balanced position with a liability by way of a borrowing of SF26,732 and an asset by way of a receivable from the exporter of SF26,732. Moreover, at the end of the three months the bank has already got the sterling which the exporter will want and has not indulged in any kind of speculation.

Bank borrows 3 months sterling @ 6.0313% pa
Bank lends 3 months krone   @ 3.7500% pa
Difference   2.2813% pa
÷ 4   = 0.5703% flat
0.5703% of spot DK 12.3303 = £1 = DK 0.0703 premium
Subtract premium from spot rate 13.3303
three months forward rate 12.2600
Cost of purchase at spot £10,000, at forward £10,057

Figure 3.2.14 Danish krone bought forward by importer for payment in three months

In the light of this example the reader might wish to reread the first section of Chapter 3.1 to see that what the bank did in Figure 3.2.14, the Lombardies were doing in the 12th century.

Bank lends 6 months sterling   @ 6.3438% pa
Bank borrows 6 months euros   @ 3.6250% pa
Difference   2.7188% pa
÷ 2   = 1.3594% flat
1.3594% of spot rate € 1.6566 = € 0.0225 premium
Subtract premium from spot rate = € 1.6341
6 months forward rate € 1.6341 = £1
€ 16,566 at spot rate = £10,000
at 6 month forward rate = £10,138 Premium on sale £138

Figure 3.2.15 Euros sold forward by exporter for conversion into sterling in six months (see Table 3.2.4)

Bank borrows 6 months sterling @ 6.2188% pa
Bank lends 6 months yen   @ 0.2500% pa
Difference   5.9688% pa
÷ 2   = 2.9844% flat
2.9844% of spot rate ¥ 171.908 = ¥ 5.1304 premium
Subtract premium from spot = ¥ 166.7776
6 months forward rate ¥ 166.7776 = £1
¥ 1,719,080 at spot rate = £10,000
at 6 month forward rate = £10,308 Premium on purchase £308

Figure 3.2.16 To cover import in Japanese yen

The bank's risk in a forward transaction arises when the exporter or importer cannot meet his obligation and has to close out the contract. In the event of a loss the bank's concern is 'can he afford to pay?' The bank is not at risk for the principal, unless it is funding the credit, but only for the difference in the forward and spot rates. It will usually protect itself against this risk by calculating up to 20 per cent of each forward transaction and arranging a cumulative limit up to which they will transact forward contracts.

We have assumed so far that the exporter and/or the importer is British and has to reconcile his debtors and creditors from a sterling base. The exporter who is selling in currency therefore wishes to fix the rate at which his currency receivables will be converted back into sterling at some time in the future. Similarly, the importer wishes to fix the rate at which his bank will convert sterling into currency at some time in the future.

This does not mean, however, that either cannot convert currencies into currencies other than sterling. A Swiss exporter, for example, sells forward in order to fix the rate at which his Japanese yen receivables will be converted back into Swiss francs. In this case the bank will close out its position by borrowing yen against lending Swiss francs and calculating the premium as shown below. Similarly, if the importer happens to be the UK subsidiary of an American parent, and is working from a US dollar base, he will buy lire at some time in the future. In this case the bank will close out its position by lending lire against borrowing dollars and calculate the discount or premium accordingly.

EXAMPLE

A Swiss export to Japan in yen payable in 6 months
Bank lends SFr for 6 months @ $^3/_{16}$ = 2.18758% per annum
Bank borrows ¥ for 6 months @ $^5/_{32}$ PA = 0.1562% per annum
Bank converts ¥ into SFr at spot 1 SFr = ¥ 64.3075
Difference 2.0313% per annum ÷ by 2 = 1.0156% Flat
1.0156% of spot ¥ 64.3075 = yen premium 0.6531
Subtract premium from spot and forward rate is yen 63.6544
£10,000 @ spot = ¥ 643,075. At forward = £10,103.
To calculate spot rate for ¥ against Swiss francs see page 196

Many exporters and importers express their concern about using the forward market because they always assume that they are irrevocably bound to deliver or take up delivery of currencies on a specific date and that failure to do so will offset any amount of premium or discount which may be available. This is definitely not the case. If the currency is due on day 90 but experience shows that it can be a few days early or a few days late, the exporter can simply undertake to deliver, or the importer undertake to take up delivery, any day between day 80 and day 100, for example. The bank will merely calculate the difference in the interest rates between those two dates and quote the lesser of the two premiums or the larger of the two discounts if it is an export or the lesser of the two discounts and the larger of the two premiums if it is an import. Reference to Table 3.2.4 shows that if the two dates were from day 30 to day 90 and the currency was US dollars, for example, the difference between the bank borrowing dollars at $5^3/_4$ and $5^{15}/_{16}$ and lending sterling at 6 and $6^1/_8$ would not be much. This type of contract is known as an 'option' contract whereas the other is a fixed contract, which prescribes a fixed date for delivery or for taking up delivery.

EUROPEAN CURRENCY UNITS (ECUS)

Prior to the launch of the euro, the European currency unit (ECU) consisted of numerous European Union (EU) currencies – formerly European Economic Community (EEC) currencies. The composition of the ECU was occasionally revised to allow new member countries entry. It was closely linked to the European Monetary System (EMS) and was designed as an initial step in providing greater stability from fluctuating exchange rates. The exchange rates of those countries which had become full members of the EMS were fixed within a narrow band to an ECU central rate, whereas the exchange rates for those countries which were not full members of the EMS floated against a theoretical or imputed ECU central rate. The exact weight of each currency as a percentage of the whole depended on its current exchange rate and changed continually. As an example, Table.3.2.5 shows the ECU central rate and corresponding percentage weights on a given date in late 1989.

In its ten years' existence, the ECU had grown very fast and its use in European commercial transactions continued to increase, not only by EEC countries. The USSR had announced, for example, that for major consortium contracts in future it would consider ECUs in order to minimize exchange rate movements. It had also been reported that airlines had announced that instead of using the US dollar for reconciliation purposes, then running at approximately US$15 billion, they were considering the ECU. A number of companies, and particularly those with wide European representation, were already dealing in ECUs. Moreover by 1992 it was expected that Europe

Table 3.2.5 Weighting of European Currencies against the ECU (September 1989)

Currency	ECU central rate (all=1 ECU)	Weight (%)
Deutschmark	2.05853	30.10
French franc	6.90403	19.00
Sterling	0.728627 (imputed rate)	13.00
Dutch guilder	2.31943	9.40
Belgian and Luxembourg francs	42.4582	7.90
Italian lira	1483.58	10.15
Danish krone	7.85212	2.45
Irish punt	0.768411	1.10
Greek drachma	150.792 (imputed rate)	0.80
Spanish peseta	133.804	5.30
Portuguese escudo	172.085 (imputed rate)	0.80

Table 3.2.6 Currency rates (11 September 1989)

Currency	Bank rate (%)	Special drawing rights	European Currency Unit
Sterling	–	1.25154	1.47882
US dollar	7	1.23648	1.04239
Canadian dollar	12.36	1.46857	1.23742
Austrian schilling	5	17.2613	14.6185
Belgian franc	7.75	51.2799	43.4415
Danish krone	9.50	9.52090	8.06652
Deutschmark	5.00	2.45219	2.07717
Dutch guilder	6.00	2.76415	2.34079
French franc	9.50	8.25969	6.99756
Italian lira	13.50	1757.59	1488.53
Japanese yen	3.25	181.268	153.721
Norwegian krone	8	8.91997	7.54794
Spanish peseta	–	152.951	129.517
Swedish krone	9.50	8.25721	6.98817
Swiss franc	5.50	2.11624	1.79426
Greek drachma	20.50	211.172	179.009
Irish punt	–	0.918560	0.778250

Sterling quoted in terms of SDR and ECU per £

would have become a single trading entity and the establishment of European prices in ECUs would then have become increasingly desirable in order to maintain a stable distribution network.

So far as the trader was concerned the ECU needed only to be seen as another currency whose spot rate was shown every day in the press. The figures shown in Table 3.2.6 showed a spot rate of ECU1.47882:£1. All the other currencies shown in the table were against the ECU, ie DM2.07717:ECU 1.

The Treasury Management Function

Derrick Edwards

THE TREASURY FUNCTION

There are two kinds of exposure to exchange risks which need to be managed:

- the translation exposure, ie translating the value of overseas assets from one currency into another;
- the transaction exposure, ie the exchange risks arising from sales and/or purchases.

The main object of this part of the book is to help exporters and importers to understand foreign exchange sufficiently to be able to obtain maximum benefit from using the available facilities. Therefore usage can only impinge on the treasury function in respect of the transaction exposure and the relationship between 'finance', 'sales' and 'purchasing'.

In larger companies there is often a central or group treasury department which will act as a bank for all UK-based subsidiaries and/or divisions. Provided that such a department is taking on the group's transaction exchange risks, by buying and selling forward at the current spot and forward rates as opposed to fictitious internal rates, this can only be of great assistance to the trading subsidiaries and divisions. By so doing, the group treasury department can go into the money market and trade in much larger sums than each division could on its own, and consequently provides the keenest rates. Moreover, it will have continuing up-to-date information on all currency transactions.

In many such treasury departments, however, there is reluctance to provide the subsidiaries and/or divisions with currency borrowing facilities, whereas they can freely use the forward market. In many cases there are substantial administrative advantages in using a currency overdraft as opposed to the forward market, and it should be perfectly feasible for the treasury function to provide this. Moreover, in many such groups, borrowing facilities are provided by the treasury department to the trading units at no cost, although each is considered its own profit centre. In such circumstances therefore there is little incentive for the trading units to reduce their cost of borrowing and they are reluctant to sell in foreign currencies. Consequently, the group as a whole is losing very substantial advantages.

Problems can arise when the treasury adopts a purely advisory role and advises the subsidiaries and/or divisions as to whether they should cover their exchange risk or not, in relation to what the treasury thinks the rate is likely to do. Trading divisions should not be expected to take any exchange risk. It is up to the treasury to manage the exposure, and having bought the group's exchange risk the treasury becomes its own profit centre. It should manage the total exposure as it sees fit using all the techniques available to it and with responsibility to the board of directors.

One of the main features of a successful treasury department is to establish good communications and working relationships between itself and sales and purchasing departments. This can provide up-to-date briefings for executives who are about to embark on overseas negotiations and a corresponding inflow of relevant market and buyer information which can be vital to the credit controller.

No company would normally approach any of its suppliers without having a very good idea as to what it requires from them and the competitive price. Banks are also suppliers and yet many companies sometimes approach them, particularly on matters of foreign exchange, with little or no idea of what they require, let alone the cost. As a result, mistakes and misunderstandings can arise. In order to avoid this, it is up to the treasury department to ensure that when contacting the bank with regard to a forward transaction, for example, it should have done the sums and have a good idea of what the premium or discount should be.

'I'm up to my eyes in the end-of-year accounts and annual budget. I simply don't have the time to think about additional profits'. This *cri de coeur* came from the finance director of a manufacturing company, 40 per cent of whose output is exported. 'We sell overseas in sterling whenever possible. Therefore we don't run any exchange risk. In any case our overheads are in sterling so we have to sell in sterling. Our job is to make valves, not to gamble in foreign exchange. Goodbye.' This short sharp telephone conversation came to an abrupt end. It did, however, encapsulate one of the basic problems confronting British manufacturing industry in its endeavours overseas. Is top management heaping too much responsibility on to the shoulders of its accountants simply because it does not understand the nature of the problem involved?

When the question of foreign currencies, almost entirely US dollars, began to emerge in the early 1950s, senior management assumed it was solely a question of finance and dumped the responsibility on the desk of the finance director. Although knowing very little about it, 'finance' found over the years that this newfangled magic called foreign exchange improved the status of the accountant no end and enhanced his position in the company. As a result, he was understandably reluctant to relinquish that responsibility and to redirect at least part of it towards those departments more immediately involved, ie sales/marketing and purchasing. The result is all too often the kind of situation described above with the additional problem of 'finance', 'marketing' and 'purchasing' tending to work in isolation and sometimes with unfortunate results.

Top management must also accept its share of the blame. While on the one hand it seems continually to be in hot pursuit of technical advances, mergers and acquisitions, with all the administrative restructuring involved, on the other hand it may have lost sight of some of the simple basic issues, such as the fact that the proper use of currencies in the sales and purchasing process can, in many cases, yield very substantial additional profit – rather more profit, in fact, than the introduction of some new technologies. For example, sales to Germany, the Netherlands, Switzerland and Japan transacted in local currencies instead of sterling in 1989 could have achieved approximate reductions in the cost of borrowing of no less than 6.48, 6.18, 6.55 and 8.14 per cent per annum respectively. These can be seen as savings in costs or increased profit/competitiveness on existing business. There are not many companies which can claim such additional margins from the introduction of new machines or new technology. Similarly, an exercise to cut the cost of production will entail much heart-searching, some redundancies and an eventual cost reduction of perhaps 1 per cent.

While the banks have a vested interest in providing money at the highest legitimate rates of interest, foreign exchange has been seen, in the past, almost entirely as a cause of risk. Consequently lectures and seminars on the subject have been based on the avoidance of risk and very little else. Very few have emphasized the positive aspects of understanding how the system works and of using the available facilities properly. Such action will not only avoid the risks but provide very substantial benefits. As with electricity, which can be extremely dangerous if not used properly, the use of foreign currencies in both exports and imports demands a disciplined approach in order to avoid risk. As with electricity, however, this does not mean 'leave well alone'.

MONITORING INTERNATIONAL MONEY RATES

The reason why it is so essential for both exporters and importers to understand how the forward market works is to ensure that they monitor the international money rates. Whereas the spot rate may well be fluctuating in an erratic fashion and the interest rates changing, international money rates do not move anything like as erratically as the spot rate. They therefore provide a much more stable factor, and it is the difference in these interest rates that needs to be monitored rather than the spot rate because these will show variations in the premiums and/or discounts, which in turn can be projected much more safely. For example, in order to brief a sales executive who may be setting out on an overseas trip lasting a month, it is of much greater practical help for him to know that however much the spot rate happens to move during that period he will still have an additional margin by way of forward premium with which to negotiate. To provide him with a fictitious rate based on someone's guess as to what the spot rate is likely to be might well have unfortunate results. (As an example, see Figure 3.3.1 for 1988 and 1989, bearing in mind that an interest rate that is higher than sterling constitutes a discount and one that is lower than sterling constitutes a premium.)

The figure shows quite distinctly that the Italian lira had gone from a discount to a small premium but the US dollar and the deutschmark were at a steady premium.

Figure 3.3.2 clearly shows the crisis in 1992 when the lira went up to 18 per cent, sterling plunged from 11 per cent to 7 per cent and the deutschmark went from a premium to a discount.

EXTENDING A FORWARD CONTRACT

One of the great problems in most people's minds about selling currency forward is what happens if, having undertaken to deliver the currency in approximately three months, for example, you cannot deliver it because the buyer is late in paying. This does not necessarily have to present a problem. Nevertheless you have to meet your commitment to deliver the currency and, as you are not going to receive the currency from the overseas buyer, you have

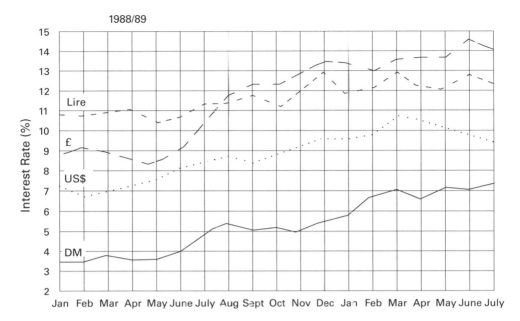

Figure 3.3.1 Interest rates denoting premiums/discounts against the pound

Note: Interest rates lower than sterling denote a premium against sterling; higher than sterling denote a discount.

to go into the open market and buy it at the spot rate in order to close out your contract with the bank. This may cost you money or you may make money, depending on how the spot rate has moved in relation to your original conversion rate and forward rate.

Figure 3.3.3 shows a case where an exporter received an order in March for $14,622 with payment due in June. Against a spot rate of $1.4622:£1 he sold the dollars forward for delivery and conversion in June at a rate of $1.4475:£1. There was a substantial delay in delivery and consequently payment. The exporter therefore had to close out his forward contract. He bought dollars at the current spot rate of $1.5072:£1 and they only cost him £9701, making him a profit of £299 against his original conversion rate. He did, however, still make his premium of £101 and his overall gain was therefore £400.

Having now closed out his contract with the bank he sold the dollar receivables forward again to the new anticipated date of receipt and the new forward rate of $1.4975:£1 was geared to the new spot rate of $1.5072:£1. When he subsequently delivered the dollars they were converted at $1.4975:£1 and only yielded £9764, thereby showing him a loss of £236.

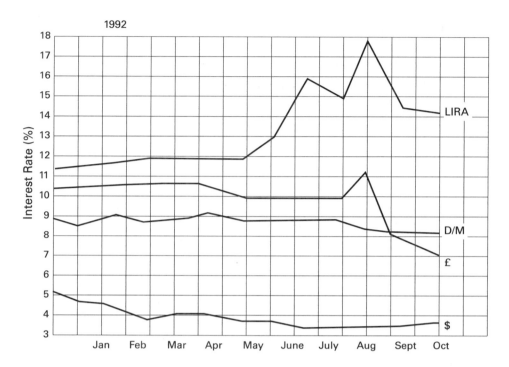

Figure 3.3.2 Interest rates denoting premiums/discounts against the pound

Note: Interest rates lower than sterling denote a premium against sterling; higher than sterling denote a discount.

Extending forward: contract £10,000

	March		June	
	Spot	3 months	Spot	3 months
	$1.4622	$1.4475	$1.5072	$1.4975
	$14,622	£10,101	£9.701	£9,764

		Gain	Loss
		£299	£236
	+Premium	£101	
	Total gain	£400	

Figure 3.3.3

222

Figure 3.3.4 illustrates a case in which the spot rate has gone against him when he comes to close out his contract and he has made a loss of £137 in buying the dollars spot. He still makes the premium of £101, however, and so his net loss is £36. On selling the receivables forward again to the new anticipated date of receipt he makes a gain of £243.

Extending forward: contract £10,000

	March		June	
Spot	3 months		Spot	3 months
$1.4622	$1.4475		$1.4425	$1.4275
$14,622	£10,101		£10,137	£10,243
			Loss	Gain
			£137	£243
	-Premium		£101	
	Net loss		£36	

Figure 3.3.4

In Figure 3.3.5 the exporter has sold the dollars forward at a discount of £102 and when he buys the dollars in June at the spot rate he makes a further loss of £137 as the spot rate has gone against him. Moreover, when he eventually delivers the dollars he will make another loss of £36 because the new forward rate is still at a discount.

Extending forward: contract £10,000

	March		June	
Spot	3 months		Spot	3 months
$1.4622	$1.4772		$1.4425	$1.4675
$14,622	£9,898		£10,137	£9,964
			Loss	Loss
			£137	£36
	+Discount		£102	
	Total loss		£239	

Figure 3.3.5

Figure 3.3.6 shows the reverse position, where a buyer has bought dollars forward for payment to an overseas supplier in three months. This will cost him a premium of $104. If he has to delay payment, however, and sell the dollars back to the bank at the spot rate of $1.5072:£1 in order to close out his contract he will only receive £9701 and thereby make a loss of £299. He will still have to pay the premium of £104, however, making a total loss of £403. On buying the dollars forward again for payment at the new anticipated date he will purchase them at $1.4970 which will cost him only £9768, thus providing a gain of £232.

Extending forward contract £10,000

	March		June	
	Spot	3 months	Spot	3 months
	$1.4622	$1.4471	$1.5072	$1.4970
	$14,622	£10,104	£9,701	£9,768
			Loss	Gain
			£299	£232
		+Premium	£104	
		Total loss	£403	

Figure 3.3.6

In Figure 3.3.7 the importer will gain £137 when closing out his contract but will have to pay the premium of £109, reducing his gain to £28. He will lose £250 when buying again at the new anticipated date.

In Figure 3.3.8 the buyer has bought the dollars forward at a discount of £102 but when he sells them back to the bank to close out his contract the spot rate has gone in his favour and he will make a further gain of £137, making a total gain of £239. Moreover, the new forward rate is also at a discount and he will make a further gain of £36.

If it is a question of having to close out the forward contract because you are never going to receive the currency due to the buyer's bankruptcy, then you have to buy the currency at the spot rate and you will either win or lose depending on the new spot rate compared with your original conversion and forward rates. The same will apply to the importer who has to close out his forward contract. If the exporter has credit insurance however, and incurs a

Extending forward contract £10,000

	March		June	
	March		**June**	
Spot	3 months	Spot	3 months
$1.4622	$1.4465	$1.4425	$1.4265
$14,622	£10,109	£10,137	£10,250
		Gain	Loss
		£137	£250
	Less Premium	£109	
	Net gain	£ 28	

Figure 3.3.7

Extending forward: contract £10,000

	March		June	
Spot	3 months	Spot	3 months
$1.4622	$1.4772	$1.4425	$1.4675
$14,622	£9,898	£10,137	£9,964
		Gain	Gain
		£137	£ 36
	+ Discount	£102	
	Total gain	£239	

Figure 3.3.8

loss covered by his policy, the additional loss which he may suffer by having to close out a forward contract may also be covered.

While this chapter discusses buying or selling the currency in order to close out a forward contract followed by selling or buying forward again to the new anticipated date of receipt or payment, in practice the two transactions are combined into one. They have been split to help the reader's understanding.

As Figures 3.3.3 to 3.3.8 have shown, the need to extend a forward contract does not necessarily spell disaster. While accepting that anything can happen, it is important to remember that premiums and discounts are only reflections of the differences in interest rates and that while they can and do move they do not usually do so catastrophically. Any alarmist who predicts that the deutschmark, for example, can go from a premium to a discount against sterling overnight is virtually saying that the deutschmark interest rates can go from 7 per cent per annum to 13 per cent per annum overnight, or that sterling can drop from 13 per cent per annum to 7 per cent per annum. This did happen in September/October 1992, but sterling interest rates only fell from 11 per cent to 7 per cent in a two-month period. However, it just goes to show that anything can happen! If that is a real deterrent, however, perhaps one should cease trading.

CURRENCY OPTIONS

This kind of option should not be confused with the option period contained in a forward contract, which provides days of grace for the delivery, or taking up delivery, of currency. It is a relatively new facility now available in the City of London. The benefit of a currency option against selling currency forward or buying currency forward is that it gives the purchaser of the option the right, but not the obligation, to buy or sell currency at a fixed rate of exchange at some time in the future (usually up to 12 months) and gives him the option of taking up that exchange rate if the current spot rate has gone against him. On the other hand, if the current spot rate has gone in his favour he does not have to meet any obligations as he would under a forward contract, but merely does not take up the option. Of course, he has had to pay the fee known as the premium, but again this should not be confused with the premium arising from a forward contract.

'Traded', 'exchange' or 'listed' options are those quoted on a recognized exchange, eg the London International Financial Futures Exchange (LIFFE) or the London Stock Exchange. These contracts are highly standardized, each having a fixed size and a range of specified strike prices and expiry dates. 'Over the counter' options are written by a number of leading banks and are available in most major currencies. They are more flexible and can be tailored to an individual customer's needs.

The factors which determine the premium (fee) are as follows:

- *maturity*: the tie to expiry of the option during which period the holder may wish to exercise the option;
- *the strike price*: the specified exchange rate at which the holder of the option can exercise this right to buy or sell a currency during the option period;

- spot and forward exchange rates prevailing for the currency of the option contract, at the date of taking out the option;
- whether the option is American or European (see Glossary at the end of Chapter 3.4);
- *volatility*: the expected fluctuation of the exchange rate of the option currency over the life of the option;
- the return on investing the premium.

Figure 3.3.9 illustrates a case where an exporter bought an option with a strike price of $1.40. When he came to exchange the $1m receivables the dollar had strengthened to $1.30, and so he let the option lapse and converted at the spot rate. After deducting the premium (fee) the net yield was £744,945. This yield shows a better result than was likely through a forward sale.

$1m receivable due in 3 months
Spot $1.40 = £1 – $ rises to 1.30 = £1
Let option lapse – deal at spot

Yield at 1.30	£769,231
– Fee @ 3.4% ($34,000)	24,286
Net yield	744,945
Yield @ forward: say 1.39	£719,424

Figure 3.3.9

Figure 3.3.10 shows an opposite situation where the dollar had weakened to US$1.50 and the exporter therefore took up the option and converted the dollars at $1.40. The net yield in this case was only £690,000, whereas a forward sale of the dollars may well have yielded more, eg £719,424.

Figure 3.3.11 illustrates the case of an importer with a payable figure of US$1m who buys an option with a strike price of US$1.40. When he came to pay the account the dollar had weakened to US$1.50. He therefore let the option lapse and dealt at the spot rate. After paying the premium the gross cost was £690,953, whereas if he had bought the dollars forward it could have cost him more.

Figure 3.3.12 shows the reverse situation when the dollar had strengthened to US$1.30 and so he exercised the option to buy at US$1.40. With the premium this cost him £738,572, whereas he might have been able to buy the dollars forward at a lower price.

$1m receivable due in 3 months
Spot $1.40 = £1 – $ falls to 1.35 = £1
Exercise option to buy £ at 1.40

Yield at 1.40	£714,286
– Fee @ 3.4% ($34,000)	24,286
Net yield	690,000
Yield @ forward: say 1.39	£719,424

Figure 3.3.10

$1m receivable due in 3 months
Spot $1.40 = £1 – $ falls to 1.50 = £1
Let option lapse – deal at spot

Cost at 1530	£666,667
– Fee @ 3.4% ($34,000)	24,286
Gross cost	690,953
Cost @ forward: say 1.39	£719,424

Figure 3.3.11

$1m receivable due in 3 months
Spot $1.40 = £1 – $ rises to 1.30 = £1
Exercise option to buy £ at 1.40

Cost at 1.40	£714,286
– Fee @ 3.4% ($34,000)	24,286
Gross cost	738,572
Cost @ forward: say 1.39	£719,424

Figure 3.3.12

Currency options represent one means of protection from exchange risks. They do not necessarily always represent the best method available and other means of covering currency exposure should also be considered. They can be very useful, however, particularly when there is a need to cover contingent liabilities such as when tendering for large export orders. They are also attractive to companies with an unquantifiable exposure, such as sales or expenses abroad, that are difficult to predict precisely or with a balance sheet exposure created by foreign subsidiaries.

Although the cases shown in Figures 3.3.9–3.3.12 explain the basic function of currency options, many variations and permutations have been developed by various banks and they are best suited to explain them in detail.

FINANCIAL FUTURES

Financial futures were introduced into Britain from the Chicago Mercantile Exchange in 1982, and the LIFFE started trading in September of that year. Unlike the forward market, where business is conducted by telephone or telex, financial futures are traded verbally in 'pits' on the floor of the exchange by brokers, although use of the Internet is now becoming more common practice.

A financial futures contract is a binding agreement between a seller to deliver, and a buyer to take up delivery of, a specific currency at an agreed exchange rate or funds at an agreed interest rate, on a stated date. Although such a contract is binding between both parties, unlike a forward contract, in practice those commitments can be, and usually are, easily cancelled out by offsetting arrangements.

The financial futures market is very different from the forward market in that it follows the practice of the commodity market treating money as any other commodity. While the forward market will handle virtually any reasonable amount for any reasonable period (up to five years for most of the major currencies) financial futures contracts are standardized contracts for specified amounts, with delivery on specified dates. For example the LIFFE dollar contract consists of US$1million for notional delivery on the third Wednesday of March, June, September and December of each year.

The method of pricing financial futures is also very different from the forward market. The prices of short-term interest rate contracts are determined by an index calculated by subtracting from 100 the interest rate on the instrument involved. For example, a price of 87.50 implies an interest rate of 12.5 per cent.

Whereas the forward market will fix exchange rates for the sale or purchase of currencies on or near a predetermined date in the future, financial futures will provide the corporate treasurer with the means of exercising his view of the future level of interest rates or exchange rates. As with currency options, however, many variations and permutations have been developed and the banks and institutions which specialize in this market are best suited to explain them in detail.

BORROWING CURRENCIES

There are, basically, two kinds of borrowing in foreign currency. There is a borrowing of foreign currency in order to fund the sale of goods or services and there is a borrowing of foreign currency for investment purposes. With regard to borrowing foreign currency in order to fund the sale of goods there are two kinds of sale: the 'one-off' sale in which the product is of considerable value, and the 'ongoing' sale of small units. There are in turn two types of borrowing to suit each type of sale. There is a term loan and an overdraft.

Figure 3.3.13 shows a sale to Germany concluded in January 2000, valued at 1.6566 million euros which will be payable in 12 months. There are two ways in which this deal can be transacted and the exporter's risk eliminated. First, he can sell the euros forward. As an alternative, however, he could borrow euros for a term of 12 months at a margin over $4^1/_{32}$ per cent fixed. On day one the bank would give him the euros which he would convert into sterling at the spot rate thus yielding £1 million. His liability to the bank would remain in euros, but if he is going to receive euros at the end of 12 months then these will merely be used when they come in to pay off the debt and the exporter does not have an exchange risk. On one side of the balance sheet he will have an asset, by way of a receivable, of 1,656,600 euros, and on the other side of the balance sheet he will have a liability by way of a borrowing of 1,656,600 euros.

As the forward premium is calculated on the difference in the interest rates in the first place, there is no basic difference in selling the euros forward and earning the premium or borrowing them at the lower interest rate. It may, however, be administratively more convenient for the exporter to borrow the currency as opposed to selling forward. Should the payment be delayed beyond the 12 months, the loan could either be extended for a further fixed term – albeit shorter than 12 months if necessary and at a different rate of interest – or it could be changed from a term basis to an overdraft as described

UK base rate 6% – 1 year euro $4^1/_{32}$%

Spot € 1.6566 = £1

One sale of € 1.6566 million single payment 1 year

Borrow € 1.6566 million for 1 year at margin over $4^1/_{32}$% fixed
and convert at € 1.6566 = £1 providing £1 million

Euro receivables will go to repay the loan

If used for a series of sales total has to be collected over year and repaid in one

Note: Borrowing rate for currency should usually be geared to same level above international money rate as above sterling base rate

Figure 3.3.13 Currency term loan

in the following paragraphs. Should the overseas buyer fail to pay, then the exporter would have to buy the currency at the spot rate and could win or lose depending on the movement of the spot rate since conversion from sterling into another currency. If, however, he uses credit insurance and incurs a loss covered by his policy, the additional loss which he may suffer by having to buy the currency may also be covered. If the exporter is selling on an ongoing basis, and therefore never knows when and for how much orders are going to come in, he may choose to fund these sales by way of a currency overdraft.

Based on a conservative estimate of the exporter's budgeted sales of £1 million over 12 months, say, he arranges an overdraft in euros (for example), draws it all down on day one and converts it all into sterling. Henceforth all quotes and prices, including price lists, are geared to that one rate of exchange until the total facility is committed. As euro payments are received they merely go to reduce the overdraft until it is extinguished and the exporter has no exchange risk. Although the overdraft renders the exporter vulnerable to changes in the currency's interest rate, this is no different to changes in his normal sterling overdraft's interest rate. While the advantages of the lower euro interest rate may not be substantial, euro prices are acceptable in all European Union (EU) countries and create a very beneficial marketing advantage, particularly to those exporters that employ local distributors in a number of EU countries.

The advantage of the currency overdraft is the flexibility that it provides. If the budgeted sales are exceeded, the overdraft will last a shorter period at the initial conversion rate; if sales have been over-estimated, the overdraft will last longer at the initial conversion rate. If the spot rate of exchange goes substantially in the exporter's favour during the course of the initial conversion, he can take any particular transaction outside the scope of the overdraft and use the forward market, thus obtaining the benefit of the better rate. This will merely have the effect of extending the overdraft over a longer period.

Borrowing currencies for investment purposes may have little to do with trading and is usually conducted purely as part of the overall treasury function. Nevertheless, it is important to guard against the exchange risk whenever possible.

OFFSETTING IMPORTS WITH EXPORTS

Where a company or group has export transactions, eg in guilders, and imports payable also in guilders, it is quite often tempting to try and balance receivables with payables, thus assuming there is no exchange risk. This practice can be very dangerous. It is not so much a question of balancing the import with the exports but the cash flow that matters. If a company has got to pay guilders on a given day but is not expecting to receive guilders for some months after that date, then it will merely have to buy the guilders at the spot rate of exchange and, of course, it has thus incurred the whole of the exchange risk. So, any function which tries to balance exports with imports in the same currency should look primarily at the cash flow position. Nevertheless, having said this, such a company is not getting the best possible result from its transactions.

If a company is exporting and importing in a currency which is at a premium against sterling, such as the Swiss franc, and is using its receivables in order to pay for its imports, then, of course, it can neither sell the currency forward and earn the premium nor borrow against it at a lower interest rate. However, the salesman may need to use that additional margin in order to reduce the price and make himself more competitive. This is denied to him now, and he may even lose the business. Therefore, in order to get the best of both worlds without running exchange risks, the company should sell in Swiss francs and earn the premium. Its buyers, however, should negotiate their purchases at fixed sterling prices as close to the spot rate as possible, thereby reducing the cost of the purchase by the amount of the premium.

Many buyers seem to think that such a negotiated purchase price is impossible to achieve, but this may well stem from the fact that few understand how to negotiate in currencies and merely refer it all to 'finance'.

Unfortunately, by the time it gets to the finance department it is usually too late. Many buyers, including some who spend large sums overseas, hide behind the fear that if they argue about currency their suppliers will refuse to supply them. It is difficult to image any exporter wantonly turning away good business from an important client simply because the buyer wants to pay in his own currency.

Export and Import Issues

Derrick Edwards

MARKETING AND SALES

In 1981 a half-page article appeared in *The Financial Guardian* newspaper of April 15th proclaiming in its headline that in the previous year Britain had lost £800 million arising from the inability of its exporters and importers to grasp this particular nettle, and, by making use of the facilities which the banks provide, to generate more profit, obtain better market penetration by improving their competitiveness and cut costs on their imports. By 1990 the overall situation was even worse. While surveys indicated that exports invoiced in local currencies to European Union (EU) countries may have risen to about 45 per cent and those to North America to 55 per cent, the total additional benefits which Britain's exporters and importers denied themselves was in the region of £6 billion. All for the sake of a little training. Moreover, Britain was mainly selling to overseas distributors in sterling, as a result of which they were adding up to 20 per cent when converting sterling prices into their local currency as a means of protecting themselves against the exchange risk.

From a marketing point of view, and because of the fierce competition in the world markets, Britain must strive continually to make it easier for buyers to purchase its products as opposed to someone else's. Certainly, one way in which this can be achieved is to sell to the buyer in his own currency or in a currency to which his is more closely allied, ie the US dollar. Those developing countries which are dependent on World Bank or International Monetary Fund (IMF) loans are more likely to wish to pay in US dollars. More-over, approximately 60 per cent of the world's trade is now conducted in dollars.

To underline the need to market overseas in foreign currencies one only has to look back to the mid-1970s in order to appreciate the extent to which Britain got it wrong at that time. Because approximately 90 per cent of all its exports were being invoiced in sterling, and because of inflation within the UK, British exporters were continually having to increase the sterling price. For example, if you take a three-year period in the mid-1970s Britain was having to increase sterling prices by at least 1–1.5 per cent every month simply because of inflation at home.

If you ask any buyer what he looks for more than anything else from a supplier, he will invariably tell you: 'at least stable prices for a reasonable period and reductions if possible' – that is precisely what Britain could not give its overseas buyers at that time. As a result of that one weakness the country lost a very large slice of its overseas mass markets.

If, for example, during the 70s and 80s we had been selling and invoicing our export sales in currencies we could have achieved an average reduction of 7.37 per cent per annum on US dollar sales during 1976, an average reduction of 8.44 per cent per annum on sales to Germany in deutschmarks during 1976, and an average reduction of 6.97 per cent per annum on sales to Japan in yen during 1976. The average reductions available throughout the 70s on these three currencies alone were 3 per cent per annum for sales in US dollars, 5.3 per cent per annum for sales in deutschmarks, and for sales to Japan in yen from 1976 to 1985 the average reduction available was 5.4 per cent per annum. All for the cost of a few telephone calls, with no hint of speculation, and with no loss of the profit built into the sale price. Throughout the 80s the average reductions available from sales in US dollars were 1.9 per cent per annum, from deutschmarks 5.1 per cent per annum and from yen 5.4 per cent per annum. Instead of which we were selling in sterling, increasing our sterling prices every month and losing a great many sales. And this is not with the benefit of hindsight. These facts and figures were known and were available at the time but unfortunately the technology of foreign exchange was even less understood then than it is today.

'Oh, the risk!' is the cry that often goes up from British exporters when it is suggested to them that they might be better off selling overseas in foreign currencies. 'If I invoice my buyer in sterling for £10,000 then I know I am going to receive £10,000 sterling and the risk of fluctuating exchange rates has gone away'. No part of any risk has gone away because the exporter has invoiced his buyer in sterling. All that he has done is transferred the risk to his buyer who may not have the facilities available to him, as those in London, with which to protect himself. That may be all right if the exporter is in a seller's market and can afford to adopt that attitude, but very few sellers are in such a position today. Everyone is virtually in a buyer's market and we should continually remind ourselves of that fact.

Any UK importer being offered a fixed competitive price in sterling as opposed to a foreign currency would confirm the attractiveness of such a deal, provided of course that it was also the 'correct' sterling price. As has already been shown, it is particularly important for those exporters selling to distributors overseas to be selling in local currency. If they are selling in sterling and passing on the exchange risk to the distributor, leaving him to fix the local currency price, he will invariably load it by a substantial margin to protect his profit. Consequently, that product may well be sold at much too high a price and certainly will be less competitive than it need be.

Moreover, a sale in sterling may very well be seen by the overseas distributor as an invitation to him to gamble on the exchange rate at the exporter's expense. If the rate goes in his favour he will most certainly not offer to pay a proportion of his gain to the exporter to make up part of the loss. Indeed, many exporters who do not understand the technology of foreign exchange enter into the most convoluted arrangements with their overseas distributors in order to try to even out such gains and losses, whereas they could easily offer their distributors fixed local currency prices, even at a reduction, and with no exchange risk.

If the spot rate of exchange at the time the deal with the distributor is struck is not particularly attractive, then the exporter need only cover the projected sales over a shorter period, eg 3 or 6 months as opposed to 12 months. This may entail a local price adjustment at 3 or 6 months, for example, but if it is downwards it will do no harm, and if it is upwards the forward premium or the lower interest rate at which the exporter is funding the sale may be able to absorb the increase.

Exporters selling to distributors in those countries whose exchange rates tend to be more volatile than perhaps the deutschmark, yen or Swiss franc are often rather more fearful to sell in local currencies, particularly if the currency concerned is at a discount against sterling. It should be remembered, however, that it is in fact the distributors in such countries who, when establishing their local currency prices, will tend to load their prices by a much higher margin in order to offset the more volatile movements in the exchange rate, thus making the British product even less competitive. Therefore, it is even more important in these countries to be selling in local currencies as, more often than not, the discount on the forward sale or the additional cost of borrowing the currency involved is much less than the additional margin with which the distributor will load his price, if asked to absorb the exchange risk.

Although it is generally agreed that the large majority of British exporters and importers, particularly at operational levels, have relatively little knowledge of how the foreign exchange market works in the UK and how best to apply the various techniques to commercial transactions, it is nevertheless assumed that the overseas buyers and suppliers are somehow endowed with all the knowledge about foreign exchange that British importers and exporters do not possess. There is absolutely no evidence to support such an assumption. Indeed, quite the reverse is the case: all the evidence points to the fact that, with very few exceptions, overseas buyers and suppliers understand it even less than British importers and exporters.

More often than not, however, overseas buyers and suppliers are good actors in that they give the impression of 'wheeling and dealing' in foreign exchange and knowing all about it. The best way to call the bluff of an overseas buyer or supplier in such circumstances is to ask what forward rate his bank quoted him that morning or whether you could use his phone to find out. He will then usually begin to prevaricate and say he never gambles. If he is that very rare bird, however, who does understand the forward market then no British export or import executive should ever be in the position of not knowing as much about it as his counterpart. He must always be negotiating, at least on level terms.

A good example of a major overseas buyer who did not understand the forward market, at least at operational level, is illustrated in Case Study 3.4.1.

Case Study 3.4.1

A British engineering company had been asked by a major buyer in Germany to quote for a £3 million contract. They also stipulated that they wished the quote to be in sterling. This fact prompted the impression that they might well be gambling on the devaluation of sterling against the deutschmark, in which event the sterling would cost them fewer deutschmarks when they came to pay.

Having prepared his sterling quotation the exporter decided to submit a deutschmark quotation as well. Should the buyer decide on the deutschmark quotation, the premium on the forward sale of the deutschmarks would represent an additional margin of approximately 15 per cent on the face value of the contract. This would not only provide the buyer with a very substantial cushion against any exchange risk during

---

the three-month quotation period, but also allow him to reduce the price in deutschmarks by 7 per cent.

On the receipt of the two quotations the buyer converted the sterling quotation into deutschmarks at the spot rate and discovered that that price was considerably cheaper than the sterling price. He sent a telex asking the exporter to confirm the two quotations as he thought that there had been a mistake, particularly because the UK exporter was now level pegging with a local German supplier. On receipt of the confirmation he accepted the deutschmark quotation against the local competition.

In some countries they have no forward market at all and in others only very limited facilities. Any UK exporter selling to them in sterling, therefore, is indeed making it very difficult for the buyer to buy his product simply because he may not be able to protect himself against the exchange risk even if he knew how. On the other hand, if sterling prices are converted into their currency, they can be given the benefit of the London money market. British exporters etc are not therefore asking overseas buyers to do them a favour by paying them foreign currencies but, instead, are doing overseas buyers a favour.

In addition to making it easier for the buyer to pay in his own currency, the biggest possible incentive for British exporters to sell in foreign currencies, as opposed to sterling, is reflected in the fact that in 177 currency years out of 257, British exporters could have sold currencies forward at a premium. This means that they could have earned more profit or been able to make themselves more competitive. Tables 3.2.1 and 3.2.2 show the amounts available during the 1979–1997 period.

Bearing in mind that premiums and discounts are merely a reflection of the difference in currency interest rates, the statistics show that in 177 currency years out of 257, UK interest rates were higher than its competitors. This means that, at the time of writing, against a UK base rate of 6 per cent per annum, German competitors, for example, are only paying approximately 3 per cent per annum for their money. In those terms it is not difficult to understand why they have been so successful. By invoicing in deutschmarks or euros, however, and either earning the premium by selling forward or funding the sale by way of a borrowing of deutschmarks or euros at approximately 3 per cent per annum, British exporters can bring their cost of money down to the competitors' level.

How often in the past has the cry been heard that with such high interest rates 'we can't compete in export markets!' In those circumstances the real answer must surely be, 'don't sell in sterling; sell in the other country's currency and plug yourself into the lower interest rate'. If, fully competitive when selling in sterling, it makes up the difference in the interest rates, keeping the extra profit is fully deserved.

As with everything else, an approach to an overseas buyer to pay in a different currency from that which he is accustomed has to be made with conviction. It has to be 'sold', particularly if that buyer does not understand the technology of foreign exchange and is used merely to taking a view on what he thinks the spot rate is likely to be at some future date. It is essential, therefore, that sales executives should at least be able to explain it to overseas buyers with skill and conviction.

QUOTING

Quoting in foreign currencies can give rise to exchange risks and care must therefore be taken to minimize or remove the risk altogether. There are several ways in which this can be achieved:

- Those exporters who have traditionally always sold in sterling can continue to quote and/or even publish price lists in sterling, but with the proviso that the sterling prices will be converted into the appropriate currency at the spot rate ruling in London on receipt of a firm order. This is tantamount to saying to the buyer that he will take the exchange risk up to the time he has decided to give the exporter an order, but on doing so the exporter will then take the risk right up to the time when the buyer is due to pay. This is still an infinitely better deal than saying to the buyer that he must take the whole of the risk for the full period.
- Quote in currency but subject to a validity period which should be kept as short as possible, and subject to a currency clause drafted by solicitors along the following lines:

  This quotation is calculated at an exchange rate of $x = £1$, but if the rate moves more than y per cent [whatever tolerance the exporter can carry and perhaps include in his price] during the validity period of this quotation then either party reserves the right to renegotiate the price.

If the exporter can be seen to be protecting the interest of the buyer as well as his own, the buyer is not likely to object. If the clause only takes care of the exporter's interest, the buyer may well object to the clause and insist on its removal leaving the exporter fully exposed to the exchange risk.

- In the case of ongoing sales on short terms of credit, the problem of quoting or publishing price lists in currencies may best be overcome by either selling forward an amount of currency based on a conservative estimate of the budgeted sales over a given period, eg 12 months, or by arranging an overdraft facility in the currency concerned for a similar amount and converting it at the current spot rate. Thereafter the one rate of exchange in each case will govern all quotations, price lists and sales until the forward contract or drawdown has been fully committed.

- As will be seen in the case studies which appear later in this chapter, the premiums involved, particularly those in some long-term contracts, can be very substantial, ie up to and over 15 per cent flat on the face value of the contract. In these circumstances the premium may well be sufficient, or even more than adequate, to offset any adverse movement in the exchange rate during the validity period of the quotation.

- A currency option may offer the necessary protection provided that the cost involved can be absorbed into the contract. Alternatively should the quote be successful, a premium would accrue on the forward sale of the currency.

- The Export Credit Guarantee Department's (ECGD's) Tender to Contract cover may also be used.

PRICING

An additional margin of 6 per cent per annum, or 1.5 per cent flat on goods being sold into Japan on an ongoing basis with an average period of three months between date of order and date of payment, must surely be included in the overall export strategy. It cannot be left as 'financial perks', because part of the marketing strategy might well require a reduction in price of 2 per cent, the failure of which might mean loss of orders. For the same reason the receivables concerned cannot be merely hived off to pay for imports, otherwise the 1.5 per cent is no longer available as the means of providing the reduction in price.

In the case of capital goods sold on extended terms of credit, the additional margins available from the forward sale of certain currencies can be very substantial, reaching up to 21 per cent on the face value of the contract. In such cases it is essential that the currency aspect be taken into account, not only from a pricing viewpoint but also with regard to quoting and the competition with which the exporter may be confronted.

With regard to imports direct from overseas payable in currencies, the buyer has to calculate the price of buying the currency forward in order to evaluate the whole cost of the import. Confronted by a sterling price offered to him by an overseas supplier, the buyer must be able to calculate the 'correct' sterling price, as opposed to what may merely appear to be a 'good' sterling price.

When buying imported goods in sterling from a UK importing agent the buyer must be careful to avoid an inflated sterling price into which the importing agent has loaded a bigger margin than the forward premium in order to protect himself against the exchange risk.

PURCHASING

In 1980 a survey was conducted jointly by Henley Management College and the British Institute of Management on purchasing methods as part of manufacturing industry's drive to cut costs. The researchers noted the disproportionate increase in company profits which can result from improvements in purchasing tactics. Their findings showed that a 2 per cent reduction in the cost of purchases could yield a 10 per cent addition to profit. They also claimed that a 5 per cent reduction in material costs would have a similar effect on profitability as a 10 per cent increase in sales.

These figures should be borne in mind when studying the cases shown on the following pages, and used to assess the additional profits which would have accrued to the companies concerned by virtue of the savings in cost. Moreover, the reader might benefit from assessing the situation in his own company.

Although the purchase of materials and components typically accounts for approximately 60 per cent of sales revenue in manufacturing industry, the departments involved have traditionally carried less status within companies compared with, say, production or marketing. It is not unknown, for example, for purchasing departments to consist of a few clerks who merely carry out the instructions of the engineers and, in these circumstances, it is not difficult to imagine how one company came to pay 17.5 per cent too much for its machine tool by buying it from Switzerland instead of France (see case studies).

Most senior buying executives would rightly claim to be expert at selecting the best product at the best price. When dealing across frontiers, however, it is essential to take account of the built-in price of the currency involved. It is not sufficient merely to look at the spot rate of exchange and consider the value in sterling terms converted at that rate, unless of course payment is going to be made at that time. If payment is to be made at some time in the future, then appropriate calculations have to be made to ascertain the cost at the forward rate of exchange. If the currency is at a discount, then it is in order to pay in that currency because the discount will reduce the cost of the product. If the currency is at a premium which will increase the cost of the product, then the buyer must know this so that he can offset as much of the premium as possible in his negotiations. In today's buyer's market no self-respecting buyer should expect to have to pay a substantial amount over and above the cost of the product for the doubtful privilege of paying the supplier in his own currency.

The most favourable deal for the buyer is to offer a fixed sterling price converted at the current spot rate, or as close to it as possible, but payable at the future date. If this offer is made at the time when the buyer is about to place a firm order it very often succeeds. If the buyer suspects, or at worst has assumed that his supplier knows more about the forward market than he does, he should stop and ask himself on what grounds he has based his assumption. The facts, backed by firm evidence, show that very few overseas suppliers ever use the forward market, let alone know anything about it. In many countries there is no forward market; in many others, even leading industrial countries, the forward market is so undeveloped that very few people use it. If the supplier is so knowledgeable and there is a forward market in his country, then he can just as easily sell to his UK buyer in sterling. He would merely have to load the sterling price by the amount of the discount he is going to lose on the forward sale of sterling (Case Study 3.4.2).

Case Study 3.4.2

A major British company intent on placing a large contract with an overseas supplier obtained its quotation in currency. After a good deal of negotiation, both parties agreed a currency price. Before placing the order however, the British importer requested a quotation in sterling – mainly in order to ascertain if the supplier understood the forward market. The subsequent quotation in sterling bore no relation either to the spot rate or the forward rate. It merely indicated that the supplier was not conversant with the forward market and consequently was loading the sterling price by a very large amount in order to offset the exchange risk. With this in mind, the buyer made sterling offers at various levels in excess of the spot rate but well below the ceiling of the forward rate. The final fixed sterling price which was agreed involved a premium of only £85,000 as opposed to the premium calculated at the forward rate of £200,000.

Before a buyer agrees an initial sterling price, either direct from an overseas supplier or from a UK importing agent, he should attempt to find out the currency price. Otherwise he will be unable to calculate the exchange rate at which the sterling price has been converted and compare this rate with the spot and forward rates. This may not always be easy but the buyer is at a very substantial disadvantage if he has to accept what merely appears to be a good sterling price.

As an alternative to offering a fixed sterling price based on the current spot rate, the buyer could offer a fixed sterling price based on a rate halfway between the spot and forward rates. He could then explain that they were each carrying half of the cost of the currency. In any event, and whatever the outcome, by understanding the technology and knowing how to apply it, the UK buyer has placed himself in the strongest possible negotiating position. He knows the facts and does not have to rely on guesswork or, even worse, waffle.

In cases where the buyer is considering a purchase from a country whose currency is at a premium against sterling, that premium indicates that the supplier's cost of money is lower than that in the UK. In these circumstances, and provided the deal has been struck in sterling, the buyer should not stifle his temptation to extract the maximum credit. Depending on his own company's cash position, he might even offer to pay for such credit at an interest rate slightly higher than that which the supplier is paying, but lower than that which his own company is paying.

Some buying executives tend to hide their lack of knowledge and understanding of this technology by stating that, unless they pay in the supplier's currency, the supplier will refuse to supply them. This has even been said by buyers responsible for purchases valued at many millions of pounds annually and can only be taken as a poor excuse. No exporter anywhere in the world with that kind of volume would turn business away simply because the buyer wanted to negotiate a price in his own currency as opposed to that of the supplier.

If the overseas supplier insists on payment in his own currency as opposed to sterling, and if that currency is at a premium, the UK buyer should equally insist on a penalty clause for delay or non-delivery. Having bought the currency forward he may be obliged to extend or even close out his forward contract and if the rate has gone against him this may cost him money.

The purchase of imported goods from UK agents needs to be looked at closely. In many cases, the importing agent does not use the forward market in order to cover his exchange risk with the overseas supplier and protects himself by loading the sterling price. This loading is invariably much higher than the cost of buying the currency forward and the UK buyer is therefore paying too high a price. A typical example is a UK agent buying from Italy and loading the sterling selling price by as much as 20 per cent to protect himself against the exchange risk. At the time he could have bought lire forward at a discount. Any buyer purchasing from UK import agents needs to understand the technology so as to ensure that he is not paying what appears to be a good price but which, in fact, is more expensive than it needs to be.

Case Study 3.4.3

A major British company had been quoted a fixed sterling price for a purchase from a Spanish supplier with payment in ten months. It was a very competitive sterling price and the buyer thought he had obtained for himself an excellent deal until it was pointed out that if the Spaniard was selling in sterling then he had an exchange risk. In order to protect himself over the ten-month period he would load the sterling price by, say, 10–15 per cent to give himself a cushion against any adverse fluctuations in the exchange rate over the ensuing ten months. As a result, the UK buyer was not getting as keen a price as he might have

---

obtained if he paid in pesetas, when the Spaniard would have no exchange risk and therefore no need to load the price. What is more, if the buyer had paid the supplier in pesetas he could have bought the pesetas forward at the time he placed the order at a discount of 8 per cent. So, although he had a seemingly favourable sterling price, he was in fact paying somewhere in the region of 18–23 per cent too much for his purchase.

Figure 3.4.1 shows the classic case of a currency at a substantial discount. The chief buyer of a major company negotiated a £3 million purchase contract from Portugal to be settled by a single payment at one year. The Portuguese preferred to be paid in sterling as opposed to escudos and so offered a discount of £10,000 for payment in sterling. This was accepted by the chief buyer.

Escudo spot rate 230.25 = £1 Esc: 690,750,000 = £3,000,000
1 year forward 253.275 = £1 Esc: 690,750,000 = £2,727,273
Discount: £272,727

Figure 3.4.1 Currency at a discount

There would have been no difficulty in payment in sterling provided the buyer had been able to calculate the right sterling price. The proper discount was not £10,000 but £272,000. He might not have been able to get away with the full amount but he should have known what it was in order to be able to negotiate successfully. Moreover, it is a sobering thought that if the Portuguese seller had understood the forward market he could have sold the sterling forward and earned himself a premium in escudos to the value of £272,000. (Perhaps he did!)

BUYING FROM UK IMPORTING AGENTS

If UK exporters sell to their distributing agents overseas in sterling, the distributors will invariably protect themselves against the exchange risk by 'loading' the local currency price. UK distributing agents for overseas suppliers will very often do exactly the same because, like many other British exporters and importers, they do not understand the forward market. As a result, the loading can sometimes be as high as 15 or 20 per cent, but in any event it is much more likely to be more than the amount of any premium involved in the forward purchase of the currency.

The amount of the loading will depend on the stability of the currency involved. If the importer is buying from those countries whose currencies tend to be volatile, he will tend to increase the loading because the risk of the exchange rates moving against him is considerably higher. If on the other hand he is importing from countries with very stable currencies the loading may be minimal.

Irrespective of where the goods originate, the ultimate UK buyer of those goods should understand the technology of foreign exchange sufficiently to know what the forward rate is and thereby ensure that he is not paying more than necessary. There is no reason why he should not ask the importing agent whether he is buying the currency forward or not.

CONCLUSION

In the past, too many sales and purchasing executives have been allowed to travel overseas, conducting business across national frontiers, with little or virtually no knowledge of how foreign exchange will affect their transactions. The evidence suggests that such knowledge should no longer belong exclusively to the finance department or treasury. It constitutes an essential part of any company's overseas marketing, pricing and purchasing strategy and has a direct bearing on the way in which overseas sales and purchases are transacted. It appears essential, therefore, that all executives concerned should be sufficiently trained to be able to conduct negotiations with the utmost skill and conviction, thereby at all times placing themselves in the strongest possible negotiating position. This is particularly important when having to combat stiff competition.

There can be little doubt that anyone involved in overseas sales or purchases who is not fully versed in this technology is at a considerable disadvantage and cannot, therefore, be expected to achieve the very best results for his company. However, unfortunately many still hold the view that such people cannot be fully trusted with complex matters such as foreign exchange. 'Let them just sell the product without giving them all this extra to think about' is all too often the common reaction by senior management.

In this age of high technology, such views can no longer be justified and can only lead to wasted opportunities. Moreover, experience has proved that once they have mastered the technology, such salesmen and buyers rapidly grow in confidence and stature, and soon reap the rewards of negotiating from strength. The realization that he knows more about foreign exchange than his counterpart acts as a spur to strike the best possible deal, and the knowledge that he has succeeded in doing this gives him the best possible satisfaction. He is much too valuable a member of any company team to be denied that reward.

CASE STUDIES

The spot and forward rates of exchange in all the case studies shown in this chapter were those ruling in London at the time of each case.

Exports

Figure 3.4.2 provides an excellent example of how the forward market works in a commercial way. A British chemical manufacturer had quoted a price of $772 per tonne to a Malaysian buyer for a type of fertilizer. Two weeks later one of the company's salesmen was in Malaysia in the hope of closing the sale. He was told, however, that a competitor was quoting a price of $704 per tonne, a reduction of 8.8 per cent, and so he rang his head office to enquire if he could meet it. If they were to get the order it would entail three shipments and consequently three payments at six, eight and ten months. At the current spot rate the contract would produce a price of £449 per tonne and their minimum price was $420 per ton. They enquired from their bank what the forward rates would be for delivery of dollars at the required intervals of six, eight and ten months at the reduced price of $704 and were given rates which would produce £422, £426 and £432 per tonne respectively.

In a matter of minutes they could advise the sales executive in the field and enable him to requote the price to meet the competition. Without the use of the forward market, however, and with all the imponderables involved they would have been hard-pressed to know whether they could meet the competition.

UK Exporter quoted US $772 per tonne
Spot rate $1.7170 = £1
@1.7170$772 = £449 min. price £420
$704 per tonne
Deliveries: SEPT-NOV-JAN
Forward rates 1.6670-1.6510-1.6300
$704 = £422-£426-£432

Figure 3.4.2

Figure 3.4.3 shows the details of a £5 million contract negotiated in US dollars with payments spread at six-monthly intervals over five years. Against a conversion rate of US$1.7735:£1, the forward rates range from $1.7528 down to $1.6885 and yield in total a premium of £199,916 or an additional margin of 4 per cent.

Spot $1.7735 = £1
£5m = $8,867,500 10 = $886,750

6 months	1.7528 =	£505,905
12 months	1.7340 =	511,390
18 months	1.7185 =	516,002
24 months	1.7045 =	520,241
30 months	1.6985 =	522,078
36 months	1.6935 =	523,620
42 months	1.6885 =	525,170
48 months	1.6885 =	525,170
54 months	1.6885 =	525,170
60 months	1.6885 =	525,170

Total premium £199,916 = 4%

Figure 3.4.3

This additional margin merely reflects the differences in the interest rates between borrowing US$886,750 for each of the ten six-monthly payments on the day on which they were all sold forward, against ten corresponding loans of sterling. Although the additional profit may be of some value in obtaining the order, it would hardly be sufficient to act as a cushion against the adverse movement of the spot rate during the quotation period.

Compared with Figure 3.4.4 showing details of a similar contract six months earlier, it is interesting to note that, whereas there had been a considerable movement in the spot rate from $1.5883:£1 to $1.7735:£1, the difference between the interest rates hardly moved and as a result the premium as a percentage of the value of the contracts remained virtually the same.

Previous contract spot $1.5883 = £1
£1m = $1,588,300 10 = $158,830

6 months	1.5703 =	£101,146
12 months	1.5544 =	102,181
18 months	1.5415 =	103,036
24 months	1.5286 =	103,906
30 months	1.5227 =	104,308
36 months	1.5167 =	104,721
42 months	1.5128 =	104,991
48 months	1.5088 =	105,269
54 months	1.5039 =	105,612
60 months	1.4989 =	105,964

Total premium £41,134 = 4.11%

Figure 3.4.4

Figure 3.4.5 shows that nearly two years later the interest rate differential had doubled owing to the rising rates in Britain over the period providing a premium of 8.77 per cent.

Figure 3.4.6 illustrates a £5 million contract denominated in yen with payments at six-monthly intervals over five years and shows an additional margin, by way of forward premium, of 12.81 per cent on the face value of the contract. This sum is surely sufficiently significant to alert any sales executive who is meeting Japanese competition in Saudi Arabia, for example, to switch out of sterling into yen, and thereby reduce his yen price to meet or even undercut the competition.

Spot $1.6245 = £1
£1m = $1,624,500 10 = $162,450

6 months	1.5879 =	£102,305
12 months	1.5513 =	104,719
18 months	1.5274 =	106,357
24 months	1.5035 =	108,048
30 months	1.4902 =	109,009
36 months	1.4770 =	109,986
42 months	1.4670 =	110,736
48 months	1.4570 =	111,496
54 months	1.4482 =	112,170
60 months	1.4395 =	112,852

Total premium £87,678 = 8.77%

Figure 3.4.5

Spot ¥ 227.5 = £1
£5m = ¥ 1,137.5m 10 = 113,750,000

6 months	221.95 =	£512,503
12 months	215.95 =	526,742
18 months	212.25 =	535,925
24 months	208.25 =	546,218
30 months	204.25 =	556,916
36 months	200.25 =	568,040
42 months	196.25 =	579,618
48 months	192.25 =	591,678
54 months	188.15 =	604,571
60 months	184.00 =	618,207

Total premium £640,418   = 12.81%

Figure 3.4.6

Figure 3.4.7 shows that a similar contract in yen negotiated 15 months later yielded a premium of 17.86 per cent. While the spot rate did not move, by virtue of the rising interest rates in Britain the premium increased by 39 per cent.

Spot ¥ 227.00 = £1
£1m = ¥ 227m 10 = 22,700,000

6 months	218.725 = £103,783
12 months	210.451 = 107,864
18 months	204.725 = 110,880
24 months	199.000 = 114,040
30 months	194.500 = 116,710
36 months	190.000 = 119,474
42 months	186.000 = 122,043
48 months	182.000 = 124,725
54 months	177.500 = 127,887
60 months	173.000 = 131,214

Total premium £178,620 = 17.86%

Figure 3.4.7

Figure 3.4.8 gives details of a £4 million contract, which a British construction company obtained in Egypt in the 1980s. Again, the payments were at regular intervals over five years. The company had quoted in sterling but during the course of the negotiations they were informed that a German competitor had undercut them by 6 per cent. The company could not reduce its sterling price by anything like 6 per cent and therefore switched out of sterling into deutschmarks and, as shown in Figure 3.4.8, were able to obtain a premium on the forward sale of the deutschmarks of no less than 14.98 per cent on the value of the contract. In those circumstances they had no difficulty in reducing their deutschmark price by 6 per cent and were subsequently awarded the contract.

Figure 3.4.9 shows that a similar contract in deutschmarks several years later yielded a premium of 13.07 per cent. It is worth noting in this case that while the spot rate had moved no less than 90 pfennigs in the interval, the premium only moved 1.91 per cent because the interest rates were relatively stable.

£4m @ spot DM3.8900 = £1
£4m = DM15,560,000 10 = 10 DM1,556,000

6 months	3.7650 =	£413,280
12 months	3.6625 =	424,846
18 months	3.5750 =	435,245
24 months	3.4900 =	445,845
30 months	3.4150 =	455,637
36 months	3.3450 =	465,172
42 months	3.2750 =	475,115
48 months	3.2100 =	484,735
54 months	3.1450 =	494,754
60 months	3.0850 =	505,376

Total premium £599,006 = 14.98%

Figure 3.4.8

Spot DM2.9955 = £1
£5m = DM14,977,500 10 = 1,497,750

6 months	2.9117 =	£514,390
12 months	2.8295 =	529,334
18 months	2.7630 =	542,074
24 months	2.6955 =	555,648
30 months	2.6505 =	565,082
36 months	2.6030 =	575,394
42 months	2.5755 =	581,538
48 months	2.5405 =	589,549
54 months	2.5105 =	596,594
60 months	2.4805 =	603,810

Total premium £653,413 = 13.07%

Figure 3.4.9

Figure 3.4.10 shows a similar negotiated contract which again, owing to the rising interest rates in the UK, yielded an additional margin by way of forward premium of 17.8 per cent.

Spot DM3.1988 = £1
£5m = DM15,994,000 10 = 1,599,400

6 months	3.0988 =	£516,135
12 months	2.9950 =	534,023
18 months	2.9175 =	548,209
24 months	2.8400 =	563,169
30 months	2.7650 =	578,445
36 months	2.6900 =	594,572
42 months	2.6150 =	611,625
48 months	2.5400 =	629,685
54 months	2.4650 =	648,844
60 months	2.3900 =	669,205

Total premium £893,912 = 17.8%

Figure 3.4.10

4m @ spot SF2.3620 = £1
£4m = SF9,448,000 ÷ 10 = 944,800

6 months	2.3246 =	£406,436
12 months	2.2034 =	428,792
18 months	2.1212 =	445,408
24 months	2.0438 =	462,276
30 months	1.9702 =	479,545
36 months	1.8978 =	497,840
42 months	1.8435 =	512,503
48 months	1.7899 =	527,851
54 months	1.7342 =	544,805
60 months	1.6793 =	562,615

Total premium £868,071 = 21.70%

Figure 3.4.11

In Figure 3.4.11 a contract with ten equal payments over five years negotiated in Swiss francs yielded a premium of no less than 21.7 per cent.

It is difficult to imagine that any export executive going overseas, either to negotiate a sale in Switzerland or having to combat Swiss competition in a third country, should have such an additional margin with which to compete if necessary, without knowing it is there.

When one ponders on the extent that we seem to exist at economic crisis level and yet have an entirely homespun technology, which can so easily produce additional profit margins or increased competitiveness purely at the cost of a telephone call, one has to question the effectiveness of our training facilities. It is a known fact that as a nation the UK spends less on management training than any of its major competitors. This example must surely bring home the need to rectify that situation. Where else in any company could one phone call produce a reduction in cost, increased profit or competitiveness of 21.7 per cent?

Bearing in mind that premiums are merely a reflection of the difference in interest rates, there are a number of companies manufacturing small units and funding their exports by way of currency overdrafts. One such company claimed that in the first six months of switching its sales to Germany from sterling to deutschmarks it reduced its cost of borrowing by over £100,000. Another was funding its sales to its six overseas distributing subsidiaries by way of six currency overdrafts and hoped to cut its cost of borrowing by at least £200,000 in 12 months.

Going back in time to January 1969 Ernest Scragg & Son Ltd, then one of the UK's leading textile machinery manufacturers, made a public statement carried by many national newspapers that it had forecast savings of £0.25 million during that current year by funding its exports in foreign currencies as opposed to sterling. The company did not have to employ any extra members of staff. What little additional administration was involved had easily been absorbed by existing staff. Even in the case of a company running six currency overdrafts, this can be managed by one financial accountant helped by a monitor, updating the exchange and interest rates.

The burden of additional staff and a high increase in cost was often given as the reason for staying in sterling. This was an entirely false assumption even before the introduction of today's IT systems and online information. Experience shows that existing staff, properly trained and enthusiastic, can quite easily absorb the work involved.

Imports

Figure 3.4.12 illustrates an almost classic situation in which no account was taken of the cost of buying the currency of the country from which the imported product was purchased.

Import order £100,000

Spot	12 months	
FF10.195 = £1	11.393 = £1	£89,486 – 10.51%
SwF3.10 = £1	2.898 = £1	£106,952 + 6.95%

Figure 3.4.12

The buyer in this case had two suppliers, one in France and one in Switzerland. He obtained quotations from each and they both quoted in their own currencies. On converting the quotations into sterling at the spot rate of exchange in order to evaluate them, the buyer found that they were very competitive with each other in sterling terms. As there was very little between the two prices he committed himself to the Swiss supplier and then passed the order up to the finance department for the payment process.

When the finance department came to buy the Swiss francs forward they discovered that it was at a premium against sterling of 6.95 per cent, whereas if the buyer had bought in France the French franc was at a discount against sterling of 10.51 per cent. Although there was virtually no difference in the cost of buying the two products, there was a difference of 17.46 per cent in the cost of buying the two currencies on a contract of £100,000.

Turning again to history, Figure 3.4.13 is a very good example of the situation that arose in the early 1980s. The world was in the doldrums, including the most powerful economy in the West: the new administration of the USA recognized the need to take the initiative and act as the locomotive to pull the Western world out of the recession. This would take a great deal of money, however, and they therefore set out to attract as much of the world's surplus liquid funds as possible. They achieved this by lifting the prime rate of interest to an almost record high thereby making the reward for investing in dollars very substantial. This policy had the desired effect: as the demand for dollars grew, the exchange rate began to come down and eventually came very close to parity with sterling, ie US$1:£1.

While the spot rate of the dollar was coming down, however, the forward rate was at a substantial discount against sterling simply because the dollar interest rate (domestic as well as euro) was considerably higher than sterling interest rates.

Figure 3.4.13 illustrates the advantage which a British buyer had at that time when buying from Japan. If he negotiated the purchase in yen and bought

14 August 1981: £100,000 purchase from Japan
Yen spot 456.90 = £1 ¥ 45,690,000
1 year 439.00 = £1 cost £104,077
US$ spot 2.0865 =£1 US$208,650
1 year 2.2035 = £ cost £94,690

Saving in cost £9,387 = 9.38%

Figure 3.4.13

the yen forward he would have paid a premium of 4.077 per cent, whereas if he had negotiated the purchase in US dollars, and the Japanese were happy to accept dollars, he would have bought the dollars forward at a discount of 5.31 per cent, thereby providing a total saving of 9.38 per cent.

Import from Taiwan, November 1983
Quoted: £0.49 or US$0.73
@Forward rate $1.509 = £1
US$0.73 = £0.484

Saving in year £50,000

Figure 3.4.14

Figure 3.4.14 shows that, although the dollar interest rates had come down considerably, they were still higher than sterling interest rates in 1983 and, as a result, the dollar was at a discount.

In the early 1980s a British company was importing small unit components from Taiwan and placing firm scheduled annual contracts. The supplier had always sold in sterling at a very competitive price. In November 1983, when the buyer was negotiating a new annual contract he asked his Taiwanese supplier to quote him a US dollar price as well as a sterling price. This he did by converting the sterling price into dollars at the spot rate and providing prices of 49 cents and 73 cents per unit. The buyer then bought the dollars at a forward rate of $1.5090:£1, resulting in a price of 48.4 pence per unit, and saving himself approximately £50,000 on his annual contract. This case is almost the perfect example of what technology is all about. Big additional profit margins of 21 per cent on forward exchange sales are impressive and

Import order
Buying forward DM£2,277,379
FF£2,185,833
Reductions against DM – 4.02%

Figure 3.4.15

underline the need for sales and purchasing executives to understand the technology and how to apply it to their commercial transactions.

Figure 3.4.15 tells the story, from the pre-Eurozone era, of a subsidiary of a large group of companies. This had a highly sophisticated treasury department at its head office, which was extremely well versed in all aspects of managing the group's currency exposure. The subsidiary, however, was far from sophisticated in its understanding of foreign exchange and, while importing all its basic raw material from France, the buyer had been paying the French supplier for many years in deutschmarks. When asked why he was paying in deutschmarks and not in French francs he had to admit he did not know, but asked if it really made a difference.

The company exported a high proportion of its output but as profit margins in the trade were very small (approximately 4 per cent) and, owing to the very keen competition, salesmen were constantly trying to shave the price. On having the French supplier's confirmation that he would happily accept payment in French francs, the buyer found that by paying in French francs instead of deutschmarks and buying them forward he could achieve a reduction in his cost of purchase of 4.04 per cent – as big a margin as the profit margin on the sale of the finished product.

The significance of this is best judged by the findings of Henley Management College and the British Institute of Management that, 'a 2 per cent reduction in the cost of purchases can yield a 10 per cent addition to profit'. Moreover, this group was no different from many others whose highly sophisticated treasury departments rarely have the time, the resources in manpower, or the practical experience to train the personnel in their subsidiaries.

Again, from the less recent past, Figures 3.4.16 and 3.4.17 illustrate the case of a company that did not protect itself against the exchange risk on its imports. It placed orders worth £10 million each with German and Japanese suppliers, but payable in deutschmarks and yen. If it had bought the currencies forward it would have paid premiums of approximately £300,000 for each currency. When it came to buy the currencies six months later, however, it paid an extra £1,924,398 for the deutschmarks and an extra £1,756,756 for the yen.

DM imports
Spot DM3.47 = £1 spot DM 6 months later 2.91 = £1
£10m order placed for DM34,700,000

Cost £11,924,398
6 months forward premium £300,000

Figure 3.4.16

Yen imports
Spot yen 261 = £1 spot yen 6 months later 222 = £1
£10m order placed for ¥ 2610 million

Cost £11,756,756
6 months forward premium £300,000

Figure 3.4.17

Some might argue that, 'you win some, you lose some' and if the exchange rates had gone the other way they would have been applauded. Not so. An exchange risk is not a commercial risk, and there is no way of assessing it.

The situation was well summarized by the chief foreign exchange dealer of a leading London bank when confronted by the chairman of a large engineering group who was in the habit of taking a view on how exchange rates were likely to fare in the future. He said, 'well, I make the rates, but I don't guess what they are going to be next week. What do you base your guess on?'

At an annual general meeting, a bad guess may be given the aura of respectability by such words as 'due to adverse currency movement,' whereas 'we gambled and lost' might be nearer the mark. Conversely, when a company has protected itself by using the forward market, and the rate has gone in its favour, thereby producing a situation where it would have made more money if it had not protected itself, this may again be reported as a loss due to adverse currency movements. It might be more accurately reported as, 'if we had gambled we would have made more money'.

GLOSSARY

American option: A currency option which can be exercised at any time up to the expiry date.

Arbitrage: Dealing between two trading centres in order to make a profit arising from a difference in rates at the two centres.

At par: When the international money rates are the same and hence there is no premium of discount on the forward sale or purchase of the currency. When the forward rate is the same as the spot rate.

At the money: A currency option with a strike price equal to the current exchange rate.

Bid: Normally the rate at which the market maker is willing to buy a currency.

Bretton Woods: The location in the USA where a conference was held in 1944 to establish the International Monetary Fund (IMF) and provide the means for the future economic reconstruction of the war-torn areas of the world.

Broker: The one who introduces business from one bank to another, either buyers and sellers or borrowers and lenders. He is paid a commission for so doing by both parties.

Call option: The right, but not the obligation, to buy the currency which is the subject of the option.

Certificates of deposit (CDs): A certificate issued by a bank with which a deposit has been made. It gives title of the deposited funds together with interest to the holder and can be traded accordingly.

Commission: Charge made by a bank to execute a foreign exchange contract. When Britain still had exchange controls, commissions were regulated at one per mille on the value of the transaction with a maximum of £10 or any one transaction. Since the lifting of exchange controls, commissions are a matter of negotiation between the bank and its clients in the same way as general bank charges.

Confirmation: After transacting a foreign exchange deal over the telephone or telex, the parties to the deal send to each other written confirmation giving full details of the transaction.

Convertible currency: Currency which can be freely exchanged for other currencies without special authorization from the appropriate central bank.

Cross rate: Exchange rate between two foreign currencies, eg when a dealer in London buys or sells deutschmarks against US dollars, as opposed to sterling.

Discount: When the interest rate of the home-based currency is lower than that of the foreign currency involved in a forward transaction.

Drawdown: Used in relation to a loan – term or overdraft denotes the actual payment to the borrower which may be at a later stage than when the loan was originally agreed.

Euro-currency: Currency held outside its own country, now referred to as international money.

European option: An option which can only be exercised on the expiry date.

Exchange contract: Verbal or written agreement between two parties to deliver one currency in exchange for another.

Expiry date: The final date on which a currency option can be exercised.

Export Credit Guarantee Department (ECGD): A government agency which insures exporters against loss arising from commercial and political risks.

Firm quotation: When a bank gives a firm selling and/or buying rate for immediate acceptance or with a time limit.

Floating exchange rate: When the value of a currency is decided by market forces.

Forward contract: Agreement between two parties to deliver one currency in exchange for another either on a future date or between two future dates.

Forward limit: Normally a cumulative limit up to which a bank will agree to transact forward sales and/or purchases.

Hedge: Action taken to reduce or eliminate a currency exposure.

Indication: When a bank gives a spot or forward rate of exchange for information only and does not intend it as a quotation. Similarly, if the client wants a rate purely for information purposes he should ask for an 'indication' only.

In the money: In a currency option when the strike price is better than the current exchange rate.

Intervention: When a central bank goes into the market to buy or sell a currency in order to influence the exchange rate.

London Interbank Offered Rate (Libor): The rate at which principal London banks offer to lend currency to one another. Often used as the basis for fixing the interest on bank loans.

LIFFE: The London International Financial Futures Exchange.

Mandate: Before a company can begin trading in the forward market, its bank will usually require a formal authority from the company stipulating *inter alia* the names(s) of the person(s) who are authorized to commit the company and the amounts up to which they are authorized to do so.

Maturity date: Date when settlement between the two contracting parties is due.

Option: (a) In a forward contract when it is agreed that the currency will be delivered or taken up between two fixed dates in the future. (b)An instrument whereby the buyer of the option has the right, but not the obligation, to buy or sell currency at the fixed rate of exchange for an agreed period, or borrow currency at an agreed interest rate.

Point: (a) One hundredth part of one cent, eg if the exchange rate moves from US$1.5822 to US$1.5825 it is often referred to as a move of three points. (b) It also denotes the movement of 1 per cent in interest rates, ie from 10 per cent to 11 per cent per annum.

Premium: (a) When the interest rate of the home-based currency is higher than that of the foreign currency involved in a forward transaction. (b) The fee involved in the purchase of a currency option.

Pu option: The right, but not the obligation, to sell the currency which is the subject of the option.

Rollover: Sometimes used to mean 'extending' a forward contract, but usually used when extending the maturity of a loan.

Settlement risk: The event of an exporter or importer failing to meet his obligation under a forward contract resulting in a loss at the time of settlement. It is this risk against which the bank covers itself by imposing a cumulative limit on the client's forward deals.

Smithsonian Agreement: Derives its name form the Smithsonian Institute building in Washington where an agreement was reached in 1971 by the world's ten leading industrialized countries to meet a proposed devaluation of the US dollar against gold and for many of the major currencies to return to fixed rates of exchange in line with the new devalued dollar.

Special Drawing Rights (SDRs): Conceived in the late 1960s by the International Monetary Fund as a means of offsetting imbalances between central banks. SDRs had a fixed gold value equivalent at the time to one US dollar.

Swap: A transaction involving the simultaneous buying and selling of a currency for different maturity dates, such as when a forward transaction is being extended.

Town cheque: A sterling cheque drawn on the City branch of a London clearing bank. For sums of £100,000 or over, it is possible for these to be cleared for value on the same day. For sums below £100,000 together with Country cheques (any sterling cheque drawn on a UK bank other than a Town cheque) the normal period for these to be cleared for value is three clear working days.

Transaction exposure: The exposure to exchange risk arising from a commercial transaction, ie the buying or selling of goods or services.

Translation exposure: The exposure to exchange risk arising from the translation of the value of an asset from one currency to another.

Value: Date on which a transaction has value, eg the drawing of a cheque does not give 'value' to the amount involved until the cheque has been cleared.

Part 4

International Trade Finance and Documentation

Methods of Settlement

George Curmi, Brocur Limited

INTRODUCTION

Before looking at methods of settlement in international trade, it is relevant to consider briefly the differences between domestic trade and international trade, and how they can affect the trader.

In domestic situations, the trader works in familiar surroundings with regard to language, transport systems, payment methods and timing, resulting in a well-controlled cash management situation. In international trade, however, the situation may be very different: lead times can be much longer; transit times in the carriage of goods or documents can be greater; there may be differences in language, time zones, local customs and laws, working week cycles and holiday periods, all of which may have an effect on methods of settlement and cash management.

Country risks arising out of political, economic and commercial situations may intervene; there may be inevitable delays in the settlement of insurance and other claims. Until such time as these claims are proven, problems with the payment mechanism selected, among other things, may occur. All these and other relevant factors will require an international trader to give careful consideration to the company's trading cycle in relation to its corresponding funding cycle, and whether it relates to a single transaction or a flow of transactions. This is important in order to ensure that, as far as is possible, the funding gap generated by the company's trading activity is not greater in magnitude, or longer in time, than may be desired.

As an example, consider a manufacturing company importing a given material for processing and eventual re-export. In the first instance, the raw material must be bought and paid for. There will be a delay for this raw material to reach the manufacturer, which could be weeks or months. When the material arrives, additional payments such as duties and storage charges may have to be made, a further time element will be required for the manufacture or conversion of the raw material and export of the finished product. Finally, yet more time will elapse before the manufacturer receives payment for the exported goods through the payment mechanism selected. Therefore, the time between the raw material being bought and paid for and when payment is finally received in respect of the finished goods could be considerable. A similar, but possibly simpler, situation could arise in the case of a merchant who would need to source and pay for particular goods prior to their eventual resale. Parallel situations could also occur in domestic trade, but the time element in each stage would be considerably shorter.

It is evident therefore that a clear understanding of the company's international trading cycle, the associated trade finance cycle and a judicious choice and structure of related payment mechanisms are all important factors in mitigating risks as well as ensuring effective international trade cash management.

ADVANCE PAYMENT

This method of settlement is self-explanatory and, from an exporter's point of view, an advance payment is ideal. Payment is secured in full, in advance of manufacturing or purchasing, the exporter's position is entirely secure and cash flow positive. There are no inherent risks, political or commercial, to the exporter who has, of course, the responsibility of performing correctly.

From the importer's perspective however, the situation is not so advantageous; the importer's cash flow and risk positions are the reverse of the exporter's. Consequently, the importer needs to make the fullest enquiries with regard to the exporter and must have full confidence in the exporter's ability to perform if goods are being imported on an advance payment basis.

OPEN ACCOUNT

In an open account situation both the goods and the documents would be despatched by the exporter directly to the importer. The importer would receive the goods and, in due course, remit the proceeds to the exporter in a manner agreed upon by both parties. It is evident that this procedure would be considered only in circumstances in which the importer is of the highest standing and is very well known to, and trusted by, the exporter, who would have made the fullest enquiries with regard to the importer's status.

Notwithstanding an excellent relationship between the two parties, however, the potential risks of this procedure are high. Unfavourable political developments, changes in exchange control regulations, embargoes, import restrictions and price fluctuations may affect the payment process adversely. There could be a real risk of a delay in the receipt of funds by the exporter or, more seriously, the funds not being received in full or at all.

DOCUMENTARY COLLECTIONS

Documentary collections would generally apply in cases where an open account situation may not be appropriate and where the exporter would wish to secure payment from lesser known but nonetheless reputable importers making use of the banking system to obtain payment or acceptance of a bill of exchange. The procedures governing the handling of documentary collections through the banking system are covered by the International Chamber of Commerce (ICC) Uniform Rules for Collection[1] which came into force in January 1996. Virtually all banks in the commercial world process documents which are submitted to them on a collection basis in accordance with the provisions of these ICC rules.

The Rules define collection as:

> the handling by banks of documents as defined in sub-Article 2 (b) in accordance with instructions received, in order to (i) obtain payment and/or acceptance; (ii) deliver the documents against payment and/or against acceptance; (iii) deliver the documents on other terms and conditions.

Typically, an exporter would, after shipping the goods, hand the shipping documents and other appropriate documents to its bank with instructions that they be transmitted to the buyer's bank and be released against payment by the importer or against acceptance of drafts drawn on the importer. Occasionally additional instructions, eg noting or protesting a bill of exchange or arranging for the storage and insurance of goods, may be given to the exporter's bank, but in all cases instructions given by the exporter to its bank must be full, clear and precise. As a result of this more structured and controlled environment, documentary collections generally offer a greater degree of protection to the exporter than open account trading.

---

[1] *ICC Publication No 522, 1995 revision.*

It must be borne in mind, however, that banks are not required to examine documents submitted to them for collection and that the onus is on the exporter to ensure that the documents handed to the bank are in accordance with the requirements of the particular contract, as agreed upon between the importer and exporter. Before shipping the goods, the exporter should ensure that the importer is in possession of the requisite import licence. This import licence must be valid for a period adequate for the goods to be cleared in the country of destination, allowing for any potential delays. Where applicable, the exporter should ascertain that current exchange control authorization has been granted to the importer to enable the importer to make payment immediately or at maturity of the usance drafts, in the currency of the collection and in accordance with the instructions contained therein. Documentary collections fall into two main categories:

- documents against acceptance;
- documents against payment.

Documents against acceptance (D/A)

In this situation, the exporter would hand the drafts and accompanying documents to its bank with instructions that the documents be released to the importer in exchange for the importer accepting the drafts for payment at maturity. The drafts would be drawn at a usance* agreed upon between the exporter and the importer. If the documents do not include documents of title (eg full sets of bills of lading), the position of the exporter is not very much better than in an open account situation, and there is no control over the goods. If the documents include documents of title, control of the goods can be retained by the bank until such time as the drafts have been accepted by the importer, after which time control of the goods is lost. There are risks in such situations, namely that:

- there may be possible delays in the importer accepting the drafts and the subsequent necessity to warehouse and insure the goods, thus incurring further costs;
- the importer does not accept the drafts and refuses to take up the documents;
- import controls or foreign exchange restrictions (political risks) introduced

---

* The Concise Oxford Dictionary defines usance as: 'the time allowed by commercial usage for the payment of foreign Bill of Exchange.'

after shipment of the goods affect the physical import of the goods, or the remittance of the proceeds of the collection upon payment of the drafts at maturity, or both;

- the importer defaults on payment of the accepted draft at maturity.

It would be prudent for the exporter to enquire about the legal position in the importer's country regarding the enforceability of claims against the importer in relation to the contractual obligations of the importer and, particularly in the case of default by the importer, either to accept the drafts accompanying the documents forwarded for collection, or to honour drafts accepted by the importer at the time payment is due. It is important therefore that the exporter give its bank full and clear instructions with regard to noting and protesting the drafts forming part of the collection, whether at the time acceptance is required or at maturity when payment is due. Instructions to warehouse and insure the goods should also be given to the bank in the case of non-acceptance.

The exporter may make arrangements with the importer whereby the importer's bank guarantees the payment of the accepted draft by adding its 'for aval' endorsement to the accepted draft. This may be resisted by the importer who will need to make arrangements with its bank.

Documents against payment (D/P)

The general principle and the process of this method of settlement are similar to the D/A situation, with the exception that the relevant documents are released to the drawee (the importer) against payment. Control of the goods is therefore retained by the exporter, provided that full sets of documents of title are included in the collection, until such time as payment is made by the importer. However, some of the risks mentioned under the D/A situation still remain. In the event that the importer is unwilling or unable to take up the goods, or that import controls or exchange control restrictions are introduced after shipment of the goods, the goods may have to be warehoused and insured pending a decision as to their disposal. As in the D/A situation, it is important that full and clear instructions are given to the banks with regard to the warehousing and insurance of the goods in the event that they are not taken up.

Generally, situations in which goods relating to documents forwarded under a documentary collection (whether D/P or D/A) are not taken up by the drawee could prove to be costly to the exporter. This is particularly the case if the goods are manufactured or purchased to special order, are commodities subject to potential large fluctuations in prices, or are perishable goods. In such cases it may not be possible to sell the goods elsewhere or at a loss; therefore the exporter may have to arrange for the goods to be auctioned at the place of discharge, if return of the goods to the exporter is considered to be uneconomic. In any of the above circumstances the exporter may be faced with a substantial loss.

Documentary credits

Documentary credits will be considered separately in the next chapter.

4.2

Documentary Credits

George Curmi, Brocur Limited

The documentary credit is potentially the most secure payment mechanism both for the exporter and the importer, when handled correctly by all parties. The exporter is assured of payment as stated in the credit and the importer is assured that the goods described therein have been shipped. The procedures governing the practice of documentary credits are covered by the International Chamber of Commerce's (ICC's) Uniform Customs and Practice for Documentary Credits[1] which came into force in January 1994. Almost all banks in the commercial world transact documentary credit business in accordance with these provisions, which will be referred to as UCP 500. All those involved in transactions in which documentary credits are used would be well advised to familiarize themselves with this publication.

The most recent developments relating to UCP 500 are the introduction, by the International Chamber of Commerce, of two new publications. The first is a supplement known as 'eUCP', which was introduced in January 2002 (ICC Publication No.500/2) and which provides for the electronic presentation of documents. The articles of eUCP are intended to work with UCP 500 where full, or part, electronic presentation of documents takes place. The second publication is the International Standard Banking Practice (ISBP) for the examination of documents under documentary credits (ICC Publication No 645) which was introduced in January 2003. This publication is intended to be a practical complement to UCP 500 and explains how the rules are to be applied. Both these publications can be considered as companions to UCP 500 and readers could find it advantageous to familiarize themselves with these publications as well as UCP 500.

A documentary credit is an undertaking in writing on the part of the issuing bank made at the request and on the instructions of a customer (the

---

[1] ICC *1993 Revision Publication No 500.*

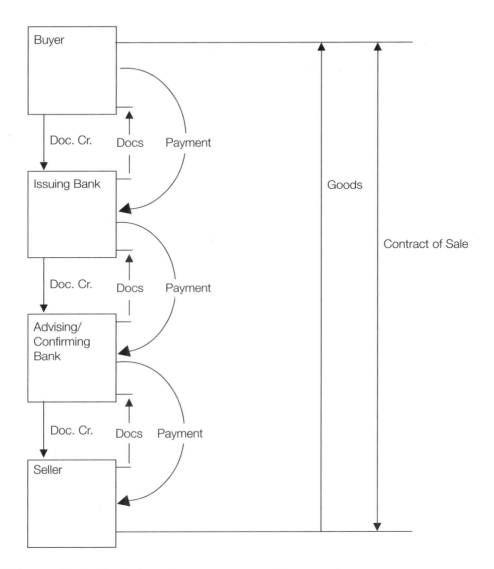

Figure 4.2.1 Cycle in a documentary credit operation

applicant) to make payment to a third party (the beneficiary) of a given sum of money at sight or at some determinable future date against presentation, within a specified time, of certain stipulated documents provided that the terms and conditions of the credit are complied with.

Figure 4.2.1 shows the different stages in the opening and utilization of a documentary credit and the operation of the 'cycle'. The first stage is for the exporter and importer to agree a commercial contract (contract No 1) and terms of payment, with these terms being reflected in the provisions of the documentary credit. This is followed by a sequence of three further sets of instructions, each one constituting a contract, as shown on the diagram. It is perhaps appropriate to note at this point that absolute clarity in instructions given, as well as in the description and nature of the documents required, is essential in order to avoid unnecessary problems.

It must be clearly understood that a documentary credit is autonomous and a separate transaction from any underlying contracts on which it may be based, even if reference to such contracts is included in the credit.

Article 4 of UCP 500 states that 'In credit operations all parties concerned deal with documents, and not with goods, services and/or other performances to which the documents may relate'. It is the responsibility of the beneficiary, therefore, to ensure that the documents presented for payment agree strictly with the terms and conditions of the credit, and with each other, and that they are presented to the bank, in order, on or before the expiry date stipulated in the credit.

Documentary credits may be issued in revocable or irrevocable form. UCP 500 Sub-Article 6c states that, 'in the absence of such indication the credit shall be deemed to be irrevocable'.

REVOCABLE CREDITS

Revocable credits may be amended or cancelled by the issuing bank at any moment and without prior notice to the beneficiary. As a result of this characteristic, revocable credits do not offer the beneficiary adequate security. They are rarely used in practice.

IRREVOCABLE CREDITS

Irrevocable credits, on the other hand, cannot be amended or cancelled without the express agreement of all parties to the credit, and thus constitute a definite undertaking on the part of the issuing bank, provided that the stipulated documents are presented to the nominated bank or to the issuing bank and that the terms and conditions of the credit are complied with.

When a credit is also confirmed by another bank (the confirming bank) usually at the beneficiary's location – such confirmation being at the request of, or with the authorization of, the issuing bank – it also bears the undertaking

Contract 1 – The buyer and seller negotiate the terms of the contract of sale and agree on the terms of the documentary credit to be opened by the buyer in favour of the seller.

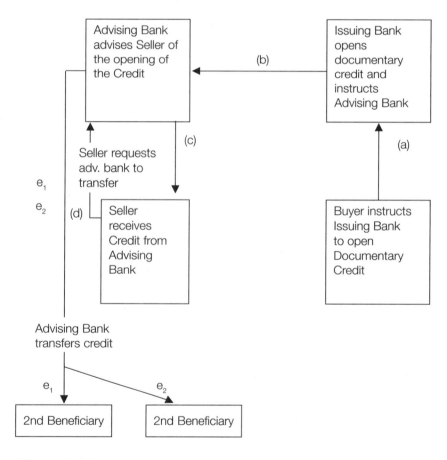

Figure 4.2.2 Cycle in a transferable credit operation

Contract 1 – The buyer and seller negotiate the terms of the contract of sale and agree on the terms of the documentary credit to be opened by the buyer in favour of the seller.

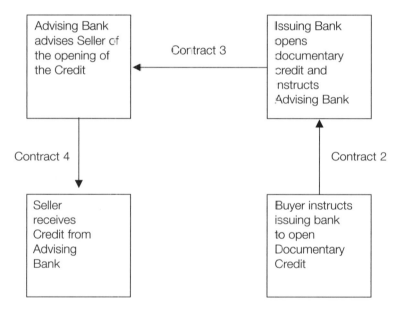

Figure 4.2.3 Contracts between the parties

of the confirming bank in addition to that of the issuing bank. This under-taking requires that the stipulated documents be presented to the confirming bank, or to any other nominated bank, and that the terms and conditions of the credit are complied with.

In accordance with Article 9 of UCP 500, irrevocable credits may provide for:

- *Sight payment*:   payment to be made at sight;
- *Deferred payment*: payment to be made on a maturity date determinable in accordance with the stipulations of the credit (eg 30 days after date of bills of lading);
- *Acceptance*:   (a) by the issuing bank to accept drafts drawn by the beneficiary on the issuing bank and pay them at maturity, or (b) by another drawee bank to accept and pay at maturity drafts drawn by the beneficiary on the issuing bank in the event that the drawee bank stipu-lated in the credit does not accept drafts drawn on it, or to pay drafts accepted but not paid by such drawee bank at maturity;
- *Negotiation*:   to pay without recourse to drawers and/or *bona fide* holders, drafts drawn by the beneficiary and/or docu-ments presented under the credit. *UCP 500* further stipulates that credits must not be issued calling for drafts to be drawn on the applicant. If however the credit does call for drafts to be drawn on the applicant, banks will consider such drafts as additional docu-ments.

THE UNCONFIRMED IRREVOCABLE CREDIT

An exporter receiving an irrevocable, but unconfirmed, credit is afforded a valid payment instrument, but the value of the undertaking lies in the standing of the issuing bank. The exporter is therefore reliant on the standing of the issuing bank as well as on the country risk of the country of issue. Both these factors should be considered by the exporter when deciding whether to accept an unconfirmed credit or whether to insist that the credit be confirmed by a bank acceptable to the beneficiary, at the beneficiary's location.

THE CONFIRMED IRREVOCABLE CREDIT

When a confirmed irrevocable credit is opened in favour of an exporter, the exporter further benefits from the undertaking of the confirming bank. The issuing bank risk and country risk are eliminated and the exporter is reliant only on the standing of the confirming bank. In such cases, documents would be presented to the confirming bank, or to any other nominated bank, and drafts would be drawn on the confirming bank or other nominated bank (UCP 500 Sub-Article 9b). This will be referred to again when dealing with risk mitigation.

Although it may seem obvious, the beneficiary of a credit is well advised to read the credit carefully as soon as it is received, ensure that the terms and conditions stated therein, as well as the documents stipulated, are clear and unambiguous, and that strict compliance with the terms stated is within the exporter's ability. This would be the time to request amendments, if necessary, and not to wait until shipment is imminent.

Inevitably in certain trades a deal is often put together in the face of extreme time pressure, and a documentary credit may be requested as being a generally recognized form of secure payment, without sufficient detailed thought being given to its terms. Although this is understandable in a trading context, it must be appreciated that the payment mechanism – in this case the documentary credit – is an essential part of the deal and to pay insufficient attention to it is to invite unnecessary risk, albeit unintentionally. It is certainly important to conclude the deal, but equally important to be paid.

RED CLAUSE CREDITS AND GREEN CLAUSE CREDITS

Both red clause credits and green clause credits allow for advances to be made to the beneficiary. As such they can be considered more as forms of finance rather than methods of settlement and will be considered in Chapter 4.4.

REVOLVING CREDIT

Documentary credits stated as being 'revolving' are reinstated automatically, without further notification after each 'revolution', according to the terms and conditions contained therein. They usually take two main forms – those that revolve automatically and those that revolve periodically.

A credit that revolves automatically is reinstated after each utilization, until either the maximum amount or the number of revolutions stated are reached. For example, a documentary credit for up to 100 units revolving automatically until a maximum amount of 1000 units are shipped will do just that, the limitation being the shipment of the full quantity stipulated. A final expiry date will be stated and care will have to be taken to allow for the presentation of documents within the prescribed limits.

A documentary credit for up to 100 units revolving automatically nine times will be reinstated every time the stipulated documents are presented and the credit utilized to the extent of up to 100 units, until nine revolutions are utilized at which time the credit will be considered fully utilized. A final expiry date would have been stated in the credit.

A credit revolving in time (or periodically) would be reinstated after each stipulated period of time had elapsed, again with a stated final expiry date that would take these revolutions into account. For example, a revolving credit for up to 100 units revolving every calendar month would be reinstated for this amount at the beginning of every successive calendar month until the final stipulated expiry date.

In view of the fact that UCP 500 states that documents must be presented within 21 days from date of shipment unless otherwise stated, care would have to be taken in defining whether the period of time stipulated relates to drawings or to shipment. For example, if shipment were to be effected on the 25th day of the month, presentation of documents could be made in the following month if this were permissible.

In the second and third examples given above, the credits would state whether the amounts are cumulative or non-cumulative, thereby stipulating whether any unutilized balance arising in any one 'revolution' may be carried forward to the next.

TRANSFERABLE CREDITS

All the above-mentioned forms of credit can be expressed as being 'transferable', and can be transferred only if expressly designated as transferable by the issuing bank. UCP 500 states that:

> . . . a transferable credit is a credit under which the beneficiary (first beneficiary) may request the bank authorised to pay, incur a deferred payment undertaking, accept or negotiate (the transferring bank), or in

the case of a freely negotiable credit, the bank specifically authorised in the credit as a transferring bank, to make the credit available in whole or in part to one or more other beneficiary (ies) (second beneficiary (ies)).

UCP 500 also determines that the bank requested to effect a transfer shall not be obliged to do so and thus the beneficiary of a transferable credit can request, but not demand, that the credit be transferred. A transferable credit can be transferred once only, and only on the same terms, ie CIF (Cost Insurance Freight), FOB (Free on Board) or other, as the original credit, the only permissible changes in the transferred credit are the amount of the credit; the unit price of the goods; the expiry date; the last date for presentation of documents; the shipping period; any or all of which may be reduced or curtailed.

The percentage for which insurance cover must be effected may be increased (usually *must* be increased) in such a way as to provide the amount of cover stipulated in the original credit. The name of the first beneficiary may be substituted for the name of the applicant, and the first beneficiary may request that payment or negotiation be effected to the second beneficiary at a place to which the credit has been transferred up to and including the expiry date of the credit. As such it is not possible to transfer separately the FOB, freight and insurance components of a transferable credit that stipulates CIF terms. Provided that part-shipments are permissible, parts of the credit may be transferred to different second beneficiaries, but this must be on CIF terms identical to the original credit. The first beneficiary's drafts and invoices may be substituted for those of the second beneficiary.

Particular care should be exercised in curtailing the amount of the transferred credit where a clean report of findings (CRF) – quality, weight and value – is called for under the original credit and the price shown on the CRF is to be reflected in the invoice. Pre-shipment inspection and the presentation of a CRF is an import requirement in some countries; this may restrict the first beneficiary's profit margin if the goods have to be sourced from other suppliers. The extent to which a restriction applies can be verified by discussing the matter with the relevant independent inspectorate and the buyers. Upward adjustment of the insured value in other cases may also give the second beneficiary a clear pointer to the first beneficiary's margin.

Although the use of a transferable credit apparently mitigates the first beneficiary's risk to some degree, the first beneficiary remains dependent on the second beneficiary to perform, and failure to do so may cost the first beneficiary the profit margin – at least. It must also be borne in mind that transfer commissions are paid by the first beneficiary, on the amount transferred, at the time of transfer.

BACK-TO-BACK CREDITS

It is important to understand that a 'back-to-back' is not actually a particular type of documentary credit. It is effectively a credit, opened on the instructions of a trader designed to match the terms and conditions of another separate and quite distinct original incoming credit in favour of the trader, in order to allow the trader to purchase the commodity and thus perform under the original incoming credit received. Thus, the trader receives a documentary credit covering the supply of a commodity and in turn, opens another documentary credit (the back-to-back credit) in favour of the end supplier in order to purchase the commodity. As the two transactions are quite separate, as far as the documentary credits are concerned, payment will have to be made under the documentary credit in favour of the supplier, even if the trader is unable to perform under the incoming original credit received. The risk to the trader and to the trader's bank are, therefore, much greater than with a transferable credit where the chain of transactions are covered by one credit only. The transferable credit has a much more rigid, although more secure, structure.

The administration of a 'back-to-back' credit situation is both complex and laborious, and in order to minimize the risks involved it is necessary to ensure that:

- The incoming credit in favour of the trader is received before the 'back-to-back' credit is opened. This may be difficult to achieve in practice but is the only way to ensure that the terms of both credits are 'matching' at the outset. If the incoming credit is not received before the 'back-to-back' is opened, it will not be possible to ascertain whether both credits will match, or if either of them can be amended; hence the risk to both the trader and the trader's bank.
- Both the incoming original credit and the 'back-to-back' outgoing credit are available at the counters of the same bank (the trader's bank), the first being confirmed by that bank and the second issued by it. Divergence from this procedure can cause problems of timing, control and presentation of documents.

Traders may sometimes need to buy on FOB terms and deal separately with freight and insurance, whereas the incoming credit in their favour is CIF. This would not be a real 'back-to-back' situation as they may need to open more than one credit to complete the 'back-to-back' cycle. Additional risks would therefore be introduced to the traders, as well as their bankers, in ensuring and controlling that documents received from different sources are assembled and matched to meet the incoming credit.

There are two features that traders in the oil industry would often wish to see incorporated. The first is that the shipping and timing parameters be as wide as possible with regard to shipping dates and cargo tolerances; this would avoid the need for amendments which would otherwise be necessary if logistics so dictate. Secondly, that if the pricing is based on a particular Platt[2] price scale, the credit incorporates an automatic adjustment to the total value and the unit price, upwards or downwards, in accordance with the Platt designated in the credit.

In commodity transactions, including oil, letters of indemnity (issued or countersigned by banks) are frequently used to facilitate payment, pending receipt of original documents which may not be available at the time they are required. Although this feature facilitates payment, the presentation of original documents conforming to the terms of the credit must be made in due course. If they turn out to be discrepant, release of the letter(s) of indemnity will be delayed until such time as the matter is resolved.

A further risk to bear in mind in 'back-to-back' operations is that the confirmation of the incoming credit in favour of the trader is necessary. If it is not, the bank will not become a 'party' to such a credit and consequently will not be able to reject amendments to the credit that the original issuing bank may make (UCP 500 Sub-Article 9d).

It is evident from the above that although 'back-to-back' credits are considerably more flexible than transferable credits and do not restrict document substitution, they do carry much greater risks, and exceptional vigilance is required both by banks and traders when dealing with them.

---

[2] Platt's is the commodities division of Standard & Poor's whose ultimate parent is the McGraw-Hill publishing group. Their activities cover, among others, monitoring price bases in the petroleum, natural gas and petrochemical industries. Platt's price indices as given in their various price reports are widely. if not universally, used as the bases for pricing in the respective industries.

SILENT CONFIRMATIONS

A confirmation commonly referred to as 'silent' is an undertaking given to the beneficiary of an unconfirmed credit by the advising bank, or by another party, without the request or authorization of the issuing bank. Some banks in certain countries traditionally issue documentary credits and ask the advising bank not to add its confirmation. If, notwithstanding this request, the advising bank adds a 'silent' confirmation, the issuing bank may consider such action unwarranted and the relationship between the two banks may suffer as a result.

In general, banks will tend to restrict this practice. As the mandate given by the issuing bank under UCP 500 has been exceeded, the situation is therefore not covered by UCP 500. The bank adding its silent confirmation may find therefore that it leads to difficulties.

4.3

Standby Letters of Credit

George Curmi, Brocur Limited

Standby letters of credit are covered both in Uniform Customs and Practice (UCP) 500, and in the more recently introduced International Standby Practices ISP 98[1] which came into force in January 1999. Developed in the USA, as a result of legal impediments there concerning the issuing of guarantees, standby letters of credit were originally included in the International Chamber of Commerce's (ICC's) UCP 400 (1983 revision). This inclusion was carried forward into UCP 500 (Article 1), which states that:

> The Uniform Customs and Practice for Documentary Credits 1993 Revision (ICC Publication No 500), shall apply to all documentary credits (including to the extent to which they may be applicable, standby letter(s) of credit where they are incorporated into the text of the credit). They are binding on all the parties thereto, unless expressly stipulated in the credit.

Essentially the standby letter of credit fulfils a function similar to that of a payment guarantee, and as such has the character of a 'default instrument' in that payment is triggered by default rather than by performance, as in the case of a documentary credit. The documentary credit is a payment undertaking and the standby letter of credit is effectively a security against default. It is pertinent therefore to consider briefly some of the main differences between standby letters of credit falling under UCP 500 and those under ISP 98. This is not intended to be a full comparison of the two ICC documents.

In both cases the standby letter of credit is an obligation on the issuing bank to pay. Under UCP 500 this may be a written revocable or irrevocable undertaking, and under ISP 98 this is a written irrevocable undertaking (Rule

---

[1] International Chamber of Commerce (ICC) Publication No 590.

1.06). Under UCP 500 it is a separate transaction from the sales or other contract on which the credit may be based; under ISP 98 it is an independent transaction from the sales or other contract. UCP 500 includes standby letters of credit, whereas ISP 98 is specific to standby letters of credit.

DRAWING/PRESENTATION

Under ISP (Rule 3.13), if the last day for presentation is not a business day then presentation on the first following business day is considered timely. Under UCP (Sub-Article 44b), the extension of the last date of shipment and all similar dates are excluded from being extended if falling on a non-business day. Under ISP (Rule 3.14), if on the last business day for presentation the place for presentation is closed for any reason, then the last day for presentation is automatically extended to 30 calendar days after the office for presentation re-opens unless stipulated otherwise. There is no such provision in UCP (Article 17).

Under ISP (Rule 3.07), each presentation is considered a separate presentation. Making a non-compliant presentation or failing to make one of a number of scheduled or permitted presentations does not waive the right to make any further presentations or invalidate the standby credit. UCP (Article 41), on the other hand, stipulates that if drawing and/or shipments are not drawn within the period allowed for that instalment, the credit ceases to be available for that and any subsequent instalments, unless otherwise stipulated.

Under UCP 500 (Sub-Article 43a), documents must be presented in order no later than 21 days after date of shipment, and within the expiry date, unless stipulated otherwise. In ISP 98 there is no such provision.

EXAMINATION OF DOCUMENTS

UCP (Article 13a) states that banks must examine all documents, as stipulated and presented, with reasonable care. Under ISP (Rule 4.03), presentations are examined for consistency only to the extent provided in the standby.

Under UCP (Article 43a), the supporting documentation is time bound (ie banks will not accept documents presented to them more than 21 days after date of shipment unless stipulated otherwise), whereas under ISP there is no such restriction unless it is otherwise stated.

TRANSFER

UCP (Sub-Article 48g, h) stipulates that a transferable credit can be transferred once only and that the amount, the expiry date, the unit price, the last date for presentation and the shipment period can be reduced or curtailed. *ISP* (Rule 6.02) stipulates that a standby that states that it is transferable without further provision means that the drawing rights may be transferred in their entirety more than once and may not be partially transferred.

Originality

ISP (Rule 4.15, cii) stipulates that a document which appears to have been reproduced from an original is deemed to be an original if the signature or authentication appears to be original. This is a significant departure from the provisions of UCP (Sub-Article 20b).

The standby credit has some advantages compared with a guarantee in that it is issued with an independent set of rules, has a determinable expiry date and has no requirement demanding the return of the original instrument. However, compared with a documentary credit in cases where physical shipment of goods is involved, the standby has the disadvantage that there is no obligation on the bank to examine the original documents as these would have been forwarded by the beneficiary to the applicant either directly or through the banking system. The standby credit may require *copies* of shipping and other documents as evidence that the shipment took place. In many other cases the standby may require only a simple demand for payment accompanied by a draft and copy invoice.

A major risk in standby letters of credit concerns original documents which may be required not being presented to the bank, which will then not be in a position to examine them for 'conformity'. Another equally important risk is the possibility of a fraudulent or false claim being made. Fraudulent documents are not unknown in documentary credits but the possibility of a fraudulent claim is much greater in a standby. Full due diligence on the parties involved will help in reducing this risk.

Finance for Trade

George Curmi, Brocur Limited

BANK OVERDRAFT

The bank overdraft in its traditional form is one potentially useful form of trade finance both for exporters and importers. Although very flexible in operation, it suffers from the fact that it is payable on demand and not necessarily related directly to the receivables of the intended operation.

BILL FINANCE

Finance can be obtained, with recourse to the drawer, in respect of bills of exchange sent through the banking system on collection, whether D/A or D/P documentary collection. This form of finance is directly linked to the bills of exchange in question. Progress of the operation can be traced through the banking system and the advance liquidated on receipt of proceeds from the collecting bank.

RED CLAUSE DOCUMENTARY CREDITS

The origin of red clause credits lies in the Australian wool trade and the appellation 'red clause' derives from the original custom of printing the clause in red at the end of the credit. As well as its use in the wool trade, the red clause credit is sometimes used in commodity trades where the practical logistics are similar and the beneficiary needs to bring together a given quantity of stock to make shipment, such as in the oil, coffee, cocoa, cashew nut and other commodity trades.

Such credits authorize the confirming or nominated bank to make advances to the beneficiary in order to enable the beneficiary to buy the produce locally and thus make shipment. Such advances are typically made against presentation of the beneficiary's simple receipt, possibly accompanied by an invoice and an undertaking to present all documents stipulated in the credit in due course. The extent of the advance permissible would be stated in the red clause and the balance, representing the value of the goods, less the red clause advance, would be paid to the beneficiary on presentation of the documents stipulated in the credit, in accordance with terms of the credit.

The extent of the advance would vary according to the agreement reached between buyer and seller when negotiating their contract, but could vary from 50 per cent to almost the full value of the credit.

From a risk point of view, the beneficiary can be fully covered (depending on the agreed value of the advance against the actual cost of the produce), whereas the applicant is totally exposed for the amount of the red clause. In practice, this is little more than an advance payment situation within the mechanism of the documentary credit and there could be a risk of the goods not being shipped in full or not being shipped at all. Fullest enquiries regarding the beneficiary are essential.

GREEN CLAUSE CREDITS

The green clause credit is a development of the red clause credit. As in a red clause credit, it authorizes the confirming or nominated bank to make advances to the beneficiary, but in this case more tangible evidence of the existence of the goods is required. Thus an advance may be made to the beneficiary against presentation of a simple receipt accompanied by warehouse warrants or warehouse receipts for the stated produce, in a recognized independent warehouse in the name of a bank. The existence of the goods, and their packing and quality, can therefore be verified; the extent of this verification being dependent on the documentation required by the green clause. The balance of the value of the goods due is claimed by the beneficiary on presentation of the documents stipulated in the credit.

The risk to the applicant is very much reduced in this case although there is still the risk that the goods are not shipped on time or even shipped at all. Should this occur, the goods could be sold to an alternative buyer in order to repay the green clause advance but there is still a risk that a loss could ensue.

FORFAITING

The practice of forfaiting began in the 1960s at which time buyers, mainly of capital goods and commodities, demanded longer periods of credit than banks and other financial institutions were generally able to provide on a non-recourse basis. Forfaiting transactions, therefore, originally involved debts arising from commodity trade transactions and still apply to such transactions, as well as to the sale of capital goods. The maturity of debt instruments can vary from a few months to several years.

Forfaiting can be defined as the purchase, without recourse to any previous holder, of debt instruments due to mature at a future date, which arise from the provision of goods or services. In practice, most transactions tend to relate to goods rather than services. The debt instruments usually forfaited are bills of exchange or promissory notes. These must be accepted by a multinational company of undoubted status or guaranteed by the addition of a 'per aval' endorsement by a bank or government organization acceptable to the forfaiter. (The 'avalization' of a bill of exchange consists of an endorsement 'per aval' on the back of the bill, usually given by bankers or other acceptable endorsers, at the specific request of the bank's customer or drawee. This endorsement guarantees that the bill of exchange will be paid on presentation.)

Obligations arising out of documentary collections (D/A) can be sold on the *a forfait* market as can documentary credit obligations, although in the latter situation this would logically be applicable to cases of unconfirmed documentary credits emanating from banks in countries not necessarily classed as the best risk. Forfaiting transactions tend to be large value ones although small transactions, eg tens of thousand of US dollars or pounds sterling, are not uncommon.

In a typical transaction, an exporter would have contracted to supply a plant to an overseas buyer for several million pounds sterling or US dollars. This could involve the supply of goods as well as services, eg commissioning and training. Payment would be made over a period of five years, for example, with payment starting at the beginning of the second year and phased over six-month intervals, the last payment being due at the end of the sixth year. The importer would then provide the exporter with promissory notes or bills of exchange issued or avalized by the Ministry of Finance in the importer's country, drawn at 12 months, 18 months and so forth from an agreed date. The exporter would then sell the instruments to a forfaiting company at a discount which would reflect the cost of money over the period, the country risk and the forfaiting company's margin.

The advantages to the exporter are that the interest rate over the period is fixed, the cash flow is positive and the risk of collecting payment under the respective instruments has been passed on to the forfaiter.

EXPORT FACTORING

Export factoring should also be given serious consideration in appropriate circumstances. This allows the exporter to hand copies of all its invoices drawn on the overseas buyers to a specialist international factoring company. These debts would be purchased by the factoring company, often without recourse. The factoring company would undertake the functions of credit control, thereby eliminating the need for the exporter to cover credit insurance, collect the debts, and may also advance the exporter with funds to a high proportion of the invoice value. Foreign exchange risks will also be taken on by the factoring company. There are a great variety of schemes offered by factoring companies, many of which are owned by banks.

LEASING

Leasing tends to be applicable to high value capital goods, such as aircraft, ships and possibly also machinery. Buyers of such equipment may not have the ability to finance the purchase or may not wish to do so. The leasing company would intervene, purchase the equipment from the manufacturer and lease it to the overseas buyer. The manufacturer would therefore be able to produce the goods, comforted by the intervention of the leasing company. However, the buyer would need to demonstrate that the cash flow generated by the operation for which the capital goods are required will meet the payments required by the lessor.

PRE-SHIPMENT FINANCE

A manufacturer or trader may have agreed with its buyer that a documentary credit be opened for the sale of particular goods. However, the manufacturer may not have the necessary finance to manufacture, or the trader the finance to buy, the goods covered by the documentary credit. Their bank could be approached to provide the necessary pre-shipment finance in order to allow the goods to be made or bought. Such finance would be a form of bridging finance to cover the short period in question. The financier may need to have control over the goods as soon as they are manufactured or bought, until such time as they are shipped and proceeds of the incoming letter of credit paid.

STOCK FINANCE FOR IMPORTERS

Importers buying goods abroad and stocking them for eventual resale on the domestic market may require import finance and stock finance. This facility can be provided either by banks or other specialist trade financiers. The financier in question could open the import documentary credit on behalf of the trader, keep control over the stock and collect the receivables from the trader's customers, or provide finance for existing stocks and also provide a factoring or invoice financing facility. Covering both elements would no doubt be essential.

Identifying Risks and Risk Management

George Curmi, Brocur Limited

There can be few international trading operations that are completely risk free and, although it may not be possible or cost effective to eliminate risk entirely, it should certainly be possible to reduce it to a negligible or acceptable level. In order to do so, it is necessary first of all to identify the risks relating to a particular operation or trade, then decide how to manage and mitigate these risks.

Every business will have its own list of important parameters requiring consideration, but the following will be a suitable starting point for most international traders buying or selling to another country. It covers some of the many points that most companies will want to be clarified in order to determine whether to transact the business and what payment mechanism to use:

- *Country risk*: Is the other country politically stable?
  Is credit insurance/political risks insurance available?
  What is the country rating?
  Could there be imposition of exchange control restrictions, shortage in the availability of foreign exchange, import/export licensing problems either at the buyer's or the seller's end?
- *Customer risk*: Has due diligence been effected and completed?
  Is the customer experienced and able to perform?
  Will the customer's financial instruments be issued by acceptable banks and will they be confirmed?
  Is the customer 'credit insurable'?
  Is the financial strength/status of the customer adequate?
  Could there be any problem with the supply of the commodity, or product (eg drought, crop damage, crude oil supply, refinery problem, market volatility)?

Can this be covered by appropriate insurance?

- *Contract of sale*: Are the terms 'normal' terms in the trade? If not, why not?

  Are the payment period and terms acceptable?

  Are any import/export licences required and, if so, have they been, or can they be, obtained?

  Under what law and jurisdiction will the contract be drawn?

  Is that law acceptable?

  Has provision been made for arbitration, eg International Chamber of Commerce (ICC) arbitration?

  Has appropriate legal advice been taken?

- *Internal control*: Can the company handle the business in terms of value (internal limit), performance, complexity, manpower?

  Is the payment period acceptable (cash management)?

The following section will consider the risks attached to different methods of payment.

ADVANCE PAYMENT

The seller

To the seller advance payment represents minimum risk as payment is received in full in advance and there is no financial risk to mitigate. The seller should, however, ensure that proper performance under the terms of the contract is possible.

The buyer

To the buyer, this situation represents maximum risk as payment would have been made in advance of any goods being received. Risk mitigation options could include:

- visiting the seller and making enquiries to ensure the existence of the goods, their quality and quantity;
- undertaking an independent inspection of the goods, if appropriate;
- asking the seller for a performance guarantee;
- ensuring the contract includes a provision for compensation in case of non-performance;

- insuring against political risks covering the imposition of export or other trade controls or embargoes relating to the seller's country.

OPEN ACCOUNT

The seller

This situation is at the other end of the spectrum for the seller and represents maximum risk, as the goods would have been despatched and no monies received. Risk mitigation options could include:

- ensuring that the buyer is well known to the seller;
- full due diligence on the buyer and the obtaining of references, notwithstanding knowledge of the buyer;
- ensuring the contract between the seller and the buyer includes provision for remedy or compensation in the event that the proceeds are not remitted in the timeframe agreed, as well as assurance that such compensation or remedy can be enforced;
- giving consideration to the export factoring of invoices drawn on the buyer (which may incorporate an element of credit insurance) into consideration;
- adequate insurance of the goods;
- giving consideration to political risks insurance covering the imposition of import controls in the buyer's country, embargoes, foreign exchange restrictions and other impediments to the remittance of proceeds.

The buyer

The buyer, by contrast, is in full control and in a minimum risk position. The buyer's position is to ensure that the goods are sold as agreed and that proceeds are remitted to the seller within the specified period.

DOCUMENTARY COLLECTIONS

Documents against acceptance (D/A)

The main advantage here is that the seller forwards the documents and the accompanying drafts to the buyer through the banking system, and that the documentary collection is subject to a defined procedure. As was mentioned previously, if the documents include a full set of original documents of title, and the documents are to be released to the buyer against acceptance only, then there is control of the goods, at least in theory, until the documents are released. As soon as documents are released against acceptance by the buyer, control of the goods is lost and the only security the seller has is the buyer's acceptance.

The seller

The position of the seller is a relatively weak one as the buyer may not accept the draft and collect the accompanying documents. If the buyer accepts the drafts and collects the documents, there is still a danger that he may default at the time payment is due, and in the meantime control of the goods would have been lost. Risk mitigation options are given below.

If the drafts are not accepted:

- ask the collecting bank to store and insure the goods with a view to returning them to the seller, or to finding another buyer;
- sell the goods at auction;
- note and protest the draft.

In all cases, the seller could suffer considerable loss, particularly if the goods are perishable, have been specially manufactured or are goods/commodities subject to large fluctuations in price.

If the drafts are accepted, and control of the goods is to be lost:

- Ask the collecting bank to add its 'per aval' endorsement to the acceptance. This condition would have to be agreed with the buyer in advance. It will give the seller the guarantee of payment at maturity of the draft and also give the seller the option to offer the avalized draft to the forfaiting market (depending on the value and tenor) and thus obtain finance without recourse. Forfaiting would have the added advantage of improving the cash flow situation, without recourse.
- Obtain credit insurance, covering buyer default, on the understanding that the buyer is of sufficient standing to make this possible. There will however be a time delay from the time buyer default (usually protracted default) is proven until the time payment can be made to the seller. The cost of such insurance must be taken into account as well as the fact that

this would probably not cover the full value of the drafts, and would typically cover say 80 per cent to 85 per cent of the value of the collection.

- Export factoring is another option, but this method of finance is likely to be with recourse and also would not usually cover more than 80 per cent to 85 per cent of the value of the invoices.
- Note and protest.
- Consider legal action against the buyer in the event that the draft is not paid at maturity. This, however, is not really mitigating the risk at the outset but reacting if the loss is potentially real.

In both of these cases full sets of documents of title should be sent through the banking system, failing which there can be no control over the goods. The seller should also ensure that the appropriate import licences are in the possession of the buyer and the requisite exchange control authorization obtained as mentioned earlier.

The buyer

The buyer is in a comparatively strong position with regard to acceptance, or otherwise, of the drafts and accompanying documents. He is, however, at risk with regard to the specification and quality of the goods and can mitigate against this risk by appropriately worded contracts, quality inspection and a request for performance guarantees.

Documents against payment (D/P)

This is a comparatively more secure situation for the seller in that the goods will be released only against payment. Therefore, control of the goods will be retained until such time as payment is obtained (on the assumption that full sets of documents of title are included in the collection). However, if the goods are not taken up by the buyer, a scenario similar to the D/A can be reverted to as the mitigation options are similar.

DOCUMENTARY CREDITS

Revocable credits

Revocable credits are rarely used and are best avoided.

Irrevocable credits – unconfirmed

The buyer is committed to pay and the seller has the undertaking of the issuing bank, but not the confirmation of a local bank. The risk to the seller lies in the standing of the issuing bank and in the country risk. If both are undoubted, there is no need for further mitigation of risk. If not, however, the seller (the beneficiary) should attempt to mitigate the risk by requesting that the confirmation of an acceptable bank (probably the bank that has already advised the credit) be added to the credit. If that is not possible, for a variety of reasons, a silent confirmation could be sought.

A further option is to seek to forfait a banker's acceptance under an unconfirmed credit. In London, such an acceptance would probably be that of a non-UK bank, typically with a subsidiary or branch office in London, where the country risk would be higher than a European bank, for example. If it is the intention of the seller to follow that route, enquiries should be made in advance to ensure that forfait of the appropriate paper is possible, although it must be appreciated that such situations are fluid and can change at any time. The price of such a procedure would probably be higher than having a confirmed credit in the first place.

Irrevocable credits – confirmed

This is an evenly balanced situation in that the seller is assured of payment and the buyer, through the banking system which gives evidence that the goods have been shipped, is assured of receiving shipping documents. However, as was mentioned earlier, absolute clarity is essential in the terms of the credit, the nature of the documentation required, the issuers of any specific documentation, the originality or otherwise of particular documents and how this originality is to be identified or determined[1]. The seller should

---

[1] A recent ICC decision stated that:

Banks examine documents presented under a letter of credit to determine, among other things, whether on their faces they appear to be original. Banks treat as original any document bearing an apparently original signature, mark, stamp or label of the issuer of the document, unless the document itself indicates that it is not original. Accordingly, unless a document indicates otherwise, it is treated as original if it:

a) appears to be written, typed, perforated or stamped by the issuer's hand;
b) appears to be on the document issuer's original stationery; or

scrutinize all these points in detail *as soon as the credit is received*, clarify any matters that need to be clarified immediately and ensure that all the terms can be complied with. Any amendments should be requested at this stage.

Red clause credits

The buyer is obviously in a high risk situation. There seems no obvious risk-mitigating solution other than a performance guarantee, but that is only likely to cover part of the risk. However, appropriate due diligence should have been carried out. The seller must be very well known to the buyer. The seller is of course in a favoured position, similar to an advance payment, having been able to draw a substantial proportion of the cost as an advance.

Green clause credit

The existence of the goods can be verified as can the quality. As the goods are stored to the order of a bank, the buyer's risk is much reduced and the only probable risk-mitigating action would be to come to some alternative arrangement for the shipment of the warehoused goods in the event that, for whatever reason, the seller does not ship them.

Transferable credits

The risk to the beneficiary (the seller) in a transferable credit is the perform-ance risk of the second beneficiary. Given that the credit is transferred in a form identical to the original, with a few exceptions as mentioned earlier, the seller (now the first beneficiary) is dependent on the transferee (the second beneficiary) to ship the goods in accordance with the terms of the credit, which will reflect the terms of the contract between the buyer and the first beneficiary. Any failure to perform will reflect on the first beneficiary, who would not be able to claim the expected difference between the original credit and the transferred part and would also have paid the transfer fees.

---

c) states that it is original, unless the statement appears not to apply to the document presented (eg because it appears to be a photocopy of another document and the statement of originality appears to apply to that other document).

See also legal precedents section.

The risk to the buyer is different. The buyer would be relying on the seller (the first beneficiary), on whom due diligence would have been carried out and enquiries made. If the seller then transfers the performance of the obligation to supply to another party, the buyer is suddenly confronted with an unknown party as the supplier. The goods may be essential for a particular purpose and the seller will have to satisfy the buyer of the certainty of supply. Some buyers refuse to issue transferable credits precisely because of the uncertainty this procedure creates. There is also the problem of disclosure; the details of the second beneficiary could, in error, be disclosed to the applicant of the original credit which could, of course, cause tremendous problems.

Back-to-back credits

This is probably the most difficult situation in which to minimize risks because there are two independent credits – one opened in favour of a trader covering the commodity sold by the trader to an end buyer, and the other opened by order of the trader in favour of the trader's supplier, with both credits covering the same commodity.

Both credits should have matching terms. They should also both be available at the counters of the same bank, as previously discussed. This would be the best risk-mitigating position, if it can be achieved, in order to ensure the checking of documents, their application to the respective instruments and timing.

In commodity transactions generally, and particularly so in oil transactions, letters of indemnity covering the absence of original shipping documents are frequently used. Given the speed and logistics of oil operations, compared with general cargo and other commodities, it is understandable that standby credits are, and are likely to remain, more common in oil trading transactions than in others. Considerable care therefore must be exercised in determining the circumstances when standby credits or indemnities can be accepted.

A parallel, but not identical, risk is incurred if the trader receives an incoming documentary credit on CIF terms and needs to open separate documentary credits for the FOB value, insurance and freight. This is not usually acceptable to banks.

GENERAL

In all the above situations the risk, and the possibility of mitigating the risk, in documentary credit and other payment mechanisms has been considered from the point of view of the buyer and the seller. It is important however not to forget the lender who, by providing facilities to a customer – be it the buyer or the seller – can be put at considerable risk if the payment mechanism is not secure and if the whole risk process is not adequately managed and mitigated.

CURRENCY FLUCTUATION

Although the topic of foreign currency management is fully covered in Part Three, this section cannot be complete without referring to currency fluctuations. If the currency used for payment is not that of the trader or that used for the receipt of proceeds, there is a risk that the rate of exchange of the 'foreign' currency may fluctuate against the trader's own currency, thereby creating either a loss or realisable profit.

In essence, the currency exposure created by such a situation is redressed only when the exposure is 'hedged' by the purchase or sale of a currency matching the contract in amount, currency and in value date for the receipt of payment in 'foreign' currency. A 'hedge' is, therefore, the creation of another foreign currency exposure identical to the first exposure, but with the reverse position.

In such a situation, the exposure could be 'long' (ie an exposure caused by a future receipt) or 'short' (an exposure caused by a future payment). Both situations relate to the currency of the exposure, the amount of the currency and the time of future payment or receipt. For a hedge to be perfect and fully effective, it must be identical in currency, amount and value date to the original contract.

Trade Finance and Export Credit Schemes

George Curmi, Brocur Limited

The consideration of adequate credit insurance cover under an appropriate scheme is invariably an integral part of an exporter's trade finance and risk mitigation strategy. It may also serve as a sales tool by enabling the exporter to increase sales on terms more advantageous to the buyer, expand into new markets and take advantage of cyclical selling periods, while simultaneously reducing substantially the risk of non-payment by the buyer.

Credit insurance is essentially about protection against bad debts, whether commercial or political. Consequently, a credit insurance policy can be considered to be a management tool that helps to improve and consolidate a company's credit management procedures and systems. As a result of the protection that credit insurance affords, it helps to give the lending institution supporting the exporter the comfort it requires and therefore assists funding, enabling certain export operations to be financed and carried out.

Export credit schemes are provided by two main categories of insurer: government-sponsored/run agencies and private sector commercial insurance companies. In general, the former tend to provide longer-term cover, eg for projects, and the latter shorter-term cover. However, there is often considerable overlap and this division is certainly not an absolute or a strict one.

Risks covered by export credit insurance fall into two main types:

- commercial risks, which encompass credit risks as well as financial risks;
- political risks.

COMMERCIAL RISKS

Credit risks

Credit risks would include risks to contracts entered into with foreign companies (eg contract frustration and repudiation, embargo) as well as risks to receivables (eg buyer default, insolvency, non-payment). In cases where it is necessary to manufacture or purchase goods to special order, it may also be necessary to cover:

- pre-credit, pre-export finance or pre-shipment/delivery risks that could take place from the date of entering into a contract and occur prior to shipment or delivery. This could include:
    - the risk relating to the loss occasioned by the insolvency of the buyer during the period of manufacture;
    - the loss resulting from the insolvency or default of the supplier, preventing the exporter from fulfilling the export contract, thus creating the additional cost of finding and paying for alternative supplies or manufacturing facilities;
    - damages that may be claimed because of the exporter's inability to fulfil the contract as a result of the supplier's default or insolvency and/or the unavailability of alternative supplies or manufacturing facilities;
    - the loss of any advance payment that may have been made by the exporter to the supplier as a result of the supplier's default or insolvency;
  Pre-export finance insurance cover could incorporate elements of both commercial and political risks, eg contract frustration, embargo, licence cancellation, supplier contract termination, non-delivery of goods and war.
- revenue and financial risks, including:
    - trade disruption;
    - *force majeure*, eg the interruption of supplies to an oil refinery or other manufacturing or processing plant, with obvious consequential losses);
    - unfair calling of 'on demand' guarantees.

POLITICAL RISKS

Although the cliché 'turbulent times' may be as relevant now as it ever was, the fragmentation of certain political blocs, the growth and realignment of others, the ensuing volatility in world currencies and prices, as well as in political situations, calls for particular prudence by an exporter in ensuring that as many avenues as possible are fully insured. Political risks are a very real feature of international trade and project work, particularly in the current global environment. Political risks insurance, therefore, has a very real role in helping to mitigate these risks.

The following are some of the many risks that can be covered in most cases by brokers with underwriters at Lloyd's of London, and specialist international insurance companies and brokers. Where applicable some risks may also be covered by the appropriate export credit agencies, private credit insurers and multilateral agencies. Some of the risks apply mainly to traders with shorter-term situations to cover and others to companies with longer-term investments such as manufacturing plants, processing plants or other operations in many parts of the world:

- risks to foreign earnings, including currency inconvertibility, exchange transfer, selective and discriminatory taxation, restrictions on the remittance of dividends and profits;
- embargo, the introduction of a law or decree which prevents the export of the insured goods from the country of the supplier to the country of the buyer;
- licence cancellation, eg the cancellation, suspension or non-renewal of a licence with the consequence of preventing the insured goods being shipped from the country of the supplier to the country of the buyer;
- risks to foreign assets such as expropriation, confiscation, nationalization, deprivation, forced abandonment, sabotage, terrorism and war damage;
- risks to overseas personnel such as kidnap, extortion, detention, emergency repatriation.

These examples may make for uncomfortable reading, but are nevertheless situations that can be very real and therefore need to be considered. Many, if not all, of the above risks can be mitigated by risk transfer to the credit insurance and political risks insurance markets.

From a trader's or an investor's point of view, the transfer of risk to the insurance market enables a transaction to be carried out which might otherwise prove to be commercially unattractive. It has the added advantage of helping to free capacity for other new business. From a lender's point of view, any potential losses arising from a borrower being unable to meet obligations due under financing facilities made available are mitigated to a considerable degree by appropriately chosen political and credit insurance cover.

EXPORT CREDIT AGENCIES

The following is a list of some of the major export credit agencies. In addition to these, there are, as previously mentioned, many highly reputable and professional non-governmental and private insurance groups that provide an extremely valuable range of insurance products, both credit and political.

Europe and Scandinavia

Austria	Oesterreichische Kontrolbank AG (OeKB) Website: www.oekb.co.at
Belgium	Office National du Ducroire/ National Delcrederedienst (ONDD) Website: www.ondd.be
Croatia	Croatian Bank for Reconstruction and Development (HBOR)
Czech Rep.	Export Guarantees Development Corporation (EGAP) Website: www.egap.cz
	Czech Export Bank (CEB) Website: www.ceb.cz
Denmark	Eksport Kredit Fonden (EKF) Website: www.ekf.dk
Finland	Finnvera Oy/PLC (Finnvera) Website: www.finnvera.com
	FIDE Ltd (FIDE) Website: www.fide.fi
France	Compagnie Francaise d'Assurance pour le Commerce Exterieure (COFACE) Website: www.coface.com + www.coface.fr

	Direction des Relations Economiques Exterieures – Ministere de l'Economie – (DREE)
Germany	Hermes Kreditversicherungs – AG (HERMES) Website: www.hermes-credit.com
	Gerling Credit Insurance Group (CGIG) Website: www.gerling.com
Greece	Export Credit Insurance Organisation (ECIO)
Hungary	Magyar Exporthitel Biztosito Rt (MEHIB) Website: www.mehib.hu
Italy	Sezione Speciale per l'Assicurazione del Credito all'Exportazione (SACE) Website: www.isace.it
Netherlands	Nederlandsche Creditverzekering Maatschappij NV (NCM) Website: www.ncm.nl
Norway	The Norwegian Guarantee Institute for Export Credits (GIEK) Website: www.giek.no
Poland	Korporacja Ubezpieczen Kredytow (KUKE)
Portugal	Compania de Seguro de Creditos SA (COSEC)
Slovenia	Slovene Export Corporation (SEC)
Spain	Compania Espagnola de Seguros de Credito a la Exportacion SA (CESCE) Website: www.cesce.es

	Secretaria de Estado de Comercio (SEC)
	Compania Espanola de Seguros y Reasseguros De Credito y Caucion SA (CESCC) Website: www.creditoycaucion.es
Sweden	Exportkreditnamnden (EKN) Website: www.ekn.se
Switzerland	Export Risk Guarantee (ERG) Website: www.swiss-erg.com
United Kingdom	Export Credits Guarantee Department (ECGD) Website: www.ecgd.gov.uk

Outside Europe and Scandinavia

Argentina	Banco de Inversion y Comercio Exterior (BICE)
Australia	Export Finance and Insurance Corporation (EFIC) Website: www.efic.gov.au
Bermuda	Exporters Insurance Company
Canada	Export Development Corporation (EDC) Website: www.edc.ca
China	The People's Insurance Company of China
Colombia	Segurexpo de Colombia (Segurexpo)
Cyprus	Trade Department of the Ministry of Commerce, Industry and Tourism of the Republic of Cyprus
Hong Kong	Hong Kong Export Credit Insurance Corporation
India	Export Credit Guarantee Corporation of India (ECGC) Export-Import Bank of India (Eximbankindia) Website: www.eximbankindia.com

Indonesia	Asuransi Ekspo Indonesia (ASEI)
	PT Bank Export Indonesia (BEI)
Israel	Israel Foreign Trade Risks Insurance Co (IFTRIC) Website: www.iftric.co.il
	Israel Discount Bank (Discount bank) Website: discountbank.net
Japan	Export-Import Insurance Department Ministry of Economy Trade and Industry Website: www.meti.go.jp/english/index.html
	Japan Bank for International Co-operation (JBIC) Website: www.jbic.go.jp
	Nippon Export and Investment Insurance (NEXI) Website: www.nexi.go.jp
Korea	Korea Export Insurance Corporation (KEIC) Website: www.keic.go.kr
	The Export Import Bank of Korea (Korea Eximbank) Website: www.koreaexim.go.kr
Malaysia	Malaysia Export Credit Insurance Berhad (MECIB) Website: www.mecib.com
Mexico	Banco National de Comercio Exterior SNC (Bancomext) Website: bancomext.com
New Zealand	EXGO (EXGO) Website: exgo.co.nz

Oman	Oman Export Credit Agency – Oman Development Bank (ECGA)
Russian Federation	Export Import Bank of the Russian Federation (Eximbank Russia)
Singapore	ECICS Credit Insurance Ltd (ECICS)
South Africa	Credit Guarantee Insurance Corporation of Africa (CGIC) Website: www.creditguarantee.co.za
Sri Lanka	Export Credit Insurance Corporation (SLECIC)
Taiwan	Taipei Export Import Bank of China (TEBC)
Thailand	Export Import Bank of Thailand (Thai Exim)
Trinidad and Tobago	Export Import Bank of Trinidad and Tobago (Eximbank Trinidad and Tobago)
Turkey	Export Credit Bank of Turkey (Turk Eximbank)
United States	Export-Import Bank of the United States (Exim Bank) Website: www.exim.gov
	Overseas Private Investment Corporation (OPIC) Website: www.opic.gov
Uzbekistan	Uzbekinvest National Export-Import Insurance Company (UNIC)

It is interesting to note that in January 2001 a cooperation agreement was negotiated between the Export Credit Guarantee Department (ECGD) of the United Kingdom and the Export-Import Bank of the United States (Ex-Im Bank) providing UK and USA companies with a 'one stop shop' service when companies from both countries are bidding jointly for overseas projects. The agreement is the Ex-Im Bank's first such cooperation agreement with a counterpart export credit agency. ECGD started cooperation agreements in the 1990's and this is their 23rd such agreement.

Avoiding Problems with Documentary Credits: Some Legal Precedents

*Stephen Tricks, Partner, Clyde & Co., London and
George Curmi, Brocur Limited*

In Chapter 4.2 we discussed the use of the documentary credit as a payment instrument in international trade. In most cases the documentary credit works as intended, but occasionally disputes reach the English Courts. No one involved in international trade, whether as importer, exporter or a bank wants to be involved in a legal dispute, but one has a better chance of avoiding a dispute if one is aware of the potential problems. In this section we shall look at the some of the issues raised in recent cases on the following topics:

- discrepancies;
- the time for inspection of the documents and notification of rejection;
- what constitutes an original document?;
- deferred payment credits.

These issues are, of necessity, described only very briefly. If a problem arises that cannot be resolved quickly, it is often worth obtaining legal advice before it develops into a major dispute.

DISCREPANCIES

Article 13a of UCP 500 reads:

> Banks must examine all documents stipulated in the Credit with reasonable care, to ascertain whether or not they appear, on their face, to be in compliance with the terms and conditions of the Credit. Compliance of the stipulated documents on their face with the terms and the conditions of the Credit shall be determined by international standard banking practice as reflected in these

Articles. Documents which appear on their face to be inconsistent with one another will be considered as not appearing on their face to be in compliance with the terms and conditions of the Credit.

Therefore, when a beneficiary of a credit, usually the seller, presents the documents to a bank, the bank must check that the documents meet the requirements of the credit and are not inconsistent with one another. Since the bank is concerned only with the documents and not with the goods themselves, it is important that the documents precisely match the requirements of the credit. This is known as the doctrine of strict compliance. For instance, if the credit calls for 'Coromandel groundnuts', it is not sufficient to submit bills of lading for 'machine-shelled groundnut kernels'. Even if such descriptions are interchangeable in the trade, the bank is not required to be familiar with trade terminology.

The bank should be particularly concerned with checking the commercial invoice, transport document and insurance documents. If the credit calls for any other documents to be presented, Article 21 of UCP 500 provides that the credit should stipulate by whom such documents are to be issued and their wording or data content. If the credit does not stipulate these details, banks will accept such documents as presented, provided that the content of such documents is not inconsistent with any other stipulated document presented.

Within this framework the English courts will allow some exceptions to the doctrine of strict compliance. For instance, a typographical error that does not significantly affect the description of the goods or the identification of one of the parties to the transaction will not be a discrepancy. But problems can arise if the instructions in the credit are not sufficiently precise. In *Kredietbank v Midland Bank* the credit called for a survey report issued by 'Griffith Inspectorate'. The beneficiary presented a report issued on headed paper of Daniel C. Griffith (Holland) BV, with the printed notation at the foot 'Member of the Worldwide Inspectorate Group'. Midland Bank rejected the document. The court decided that Midland Bank should have accepted the document because it was reasonably clear that the credit required a report by a Griffith company, which was a member of the Inspectorate group. Although the bank had to pay the credit, this case was testing the boundaries of what is a discrepancy. The issue would not have arisen if the surveyors' name had been set out correctly and in full in the credit.

Further, when checking subsidiary documents, such as packing lists, the bank is not expected to carry out its own detailed calculations based on the information in the packing lists to see if there is a discrepancy with the nature and quantity of the goods described in the commercial invoice. In *Credit*

Industriel et Commercial v China Merchants Bank, where the credit covered a shipment of logs of varying grades, the issuing bank rejected the documents after the checker performed various calculations that showed differences between the percentage of logs of each grade on the invoice with the percentages shown in the packing list. The court said that the variance was not immediately apparent from the face of the documents and so was not a discrepancy. In any event the variance was within the tolerances permitted by the credit.

As mentioned in Chapter 4.2, the ICC has developed the concept of international standard banking practice mentioned in article 13a quoted above by publishing a document entitled 'International Standard Banking Practice' in January 2003. This is a guide to the approach adopted by banks worldwide to the examination of documents. It is too soon to say how the courts will interpret this publication, but it will almost certainly be taken into account in arguments over what does and does not constitute a discrepancy.

THE TIME FOR INSPECTION OF THE DOCUMENTS AND NOTIFICATION OF REJECTION

Article 13b of UCP 500 states:

> The Issuing Bank, the Confirming Bank, if any, or a Nominated Bank acting on their behalf, shall each have a reasonable time, not to exceed seven banking days following the day of receipt of the documents, to examine the documents and determine whether to take up or refuse the documents and to inform the party from which it received the documents accordingly.

UCP 400, the precursor of UCP 500, also required the bank to examine the documents within 'a reasonable time', but the reference to seven banking days was a new insertion in UCP 500. It is a common misapprehension that banks now have seven banking days in which to examine the documents. This is not correct. The test is still 'a reasonable time'. It may be shorter than seven banking days, but it cannot exceed seven banking days. Ultimately, it is up to the Court to decide what is a reasonable time, but the Court will take into account a number of factors, such as the location of the bank, the size of its trade finance department, the number of documents and any exceptional circumstances such as staffing shortages, very large and unusual volumes of business and breakdown of equipment. All these may affect a bank's operational efficiency. In *Bankers Trust Co v. State Bank of India*, a dispute concerning UCP 400, the Court of Appeal in London took into account the practice of UK clearing banks of issuing a rejection notice within three banking days of the receipt of the documents. The court decided that Bankers Trust Co in London should have been able to check the documents, comprising 967 pages, presented to it by State Bank of India within three banking days and that a rejection nine days after receipt was too late. Bankers Trust Co therefore lost the right to reject the documents and was ordered to pay the sum due under the Credit. English courts will still apply a similar test to 'a reasonable time' under UCP 500.

It is for the issuing bank, and not the applicant (ie the buyer) to decide whether the documents comply with the Credit. The issuing bank is entitled to ask the applicant whether it is prepared to waive any discrepancy, but it is not entitled to delegate responsibility for checking the documents to the applicant. Under Article 14c of UCP 500, if the bank chooses to approach the applicant for a waiver of any discrepancy, this does not extend the bank's time for checking and accepting or rejecting the documents.

Under Article 14d of UCP 500, once the bank has decided to reject the documents, it must give notice of rejection without delay, but no later than the close of the seventh banking day following receipt of the documents. The notice should be given to the person from whom the bank received the documents, ie an intermediate bank or the beneficiary, and should be given by telecommunication or, if that is not possible, 'by other expeditious means'. The rejection notice must identify all the discrepancies on which the bank relies in refusing the documents. The bank must also state whether it is holding the documents at the disposal of the presenter or returning them to him. Again it is important to note that, once the bank has decided to reject, it must do so immediately. The reference to close of business of the seventh banking day is a long-stop to cover the unusual position that the reasonable time for checking the documents may have taken up to seven banking days.

In *Seaconsar v. Bank Markazi* (a case under UCP 400) the bank decided to give notice of rejection on Friday but did not send the notice of rejection until the following Tuesday. The Court of Appeal held that the delay may have been too long, but eventually allowed the rejection to stand because there was insufficient evidence of what had happened on the Monday.

There are therefore two distinct requirements. The first is for the bank to check the documents within a reasonable time and make a decision on whether to accept or reject. The second obligation is for the bank to give prompt notice of its decision in the correct form. If the bank fails to comply with either obligation, it will lose the right to reject the documents and will have to pay the beneficiary (or the intermediate bank), even if the documents contained discrepancies.

WHAT CONSTITUTES AN ORIGINAL DOCUMENT?

A documentary credit will often call for specific documents to be provided in one or more originals with several supporting copies. In the case of Bills of Lading, this normally does not present a problem, because it is traditional for carriers to mark original Bills of Lading clearly as 'original' and copies as 'non-negotiable copy'. However, problems may arise with other types of document, particularly those prepared using modern document processing systems, where it may be difficult to distinguish the original from the copies.

Article 20b of UCP 500 reads:

> Unless otherwise stipulated in the Credit, banks will also accept as an original document(s), a document(s) produced or appearing to have been produced:
>
> By reprographic, automated or computerized systems;
> As carbon copies;
>
> Provided that it is marked as original and, where necessary, appears to be signed.
>
> A document may be signed by handwriting, by facsimile signature, by perforated signature, by stamp, by symbol, or by any other mechanical or electronic method of authentication.

In *Glencore v. Bank of China* the Bank of China rejected a presentation of documents because the beneficiary's certificate as required by the Credit was not marked 'as original' under Article 20b of UCP 500. The certificate in question had been generated on the seller's word processing system and photocopied several times. At that point it was impossible for the naked eye to distinguish which of the various copies was the original from the word processor and which were photocopies. The beneficiary signed one of the copies (but not necessarily one prepared on the work processor) in blue ink. He submitted this as the original with the others making up the required number of copies. The Court of Appeal in London held that the signature was not sufficient to meet the requirement for an original document under Article 20b, and in particular the words.

> Provided that it is marked as original <u>and</u> where necessary appears to be signed.

Therefore, on the basis that the document had been produced or appeared to have been produced by a reprographic, automated or computerized system, it should have been both marked as 'original' and signed. The signature did not convert a copy into an original document.

A similar problem arose in *Kredietbank v. Midland Bank*. The document in question in this case was an insurance policy. The policy was produced on a word processor and issued in original and duplicate. The 'original' was printed on the insurance company's headed notepaper and bore a blue logo as well as an identifying watermark. It did not bear the word 'original' but did contain a clause stating 'this policy is issued in original and duplicate'. The duplicate was a photocopy of the original and was marked 'duplicate'. Midland Bank rejected the documents on the basis that the original policy was not marked 'original'.

The Court of Appeal said that the *Glencore* decision did not apply to documents that clearly would have been accepted as originals under UCP prior to 1984, because UCP 400 extended the classification of original documents by including documents prepared by reprographic, automated or computerized systems. It was therefore not necessary for the insurance policy with the blue logo and watermark to also be marked 'original'.

At about the same time as the Court of Appeal was considering the *Kredietbank* case, the ICC published a 'decision' in July 1999, which expressed concern at the confusion over the marking of original documents and set out what it considered to be the correct interpretation of Article 20b of the UCP 500 as follows:

> Banks examine documents presented under a Letter of Credit to determine, among other things, whether on their face they appear to be original. Banks treat as original any document bearing an apparently original signature, mark, stamp, or label of the issuer of the document, unless the document itself indicates that it is not original. Accordingly, unless a document indicates otherwise, it is treated as original if it:
>
> i.   Appears to be written, typed, perforated, or stamped by the document issuer's hand; or
> ii. Appears to be on the document issuer's original stationery; or
> iii. States that it is original, unless the statement appears not to apply to the document presented (eg because it appears to be a photocopy of another document and the statement of originality appears to apply to that other document.)

The decision went on to say that a hand-signed document would be treated as an original document, whether or not some or all of the document was pre-printed or produced by reprographic, automated or computerized systems.

Despite the ICC's attempt to clarify the position, this decision still left some doubt as to whether a hand-signed document would be acceptable unless it was an 'obvious original' as discussed by the Court of Appeal in the *Kredietbank* case.

The issue of original documents surfaced again in the case of *Credit Industriel et Commercial v China Merchants Bank* in 2002. China Merchants Bank (CMB) had issued a letter of credit for a consignment of African logs. The French supplier presented the documents to Credit Industriel et Commercial (CIC), who agreed to negotiate the credit and so acquired the right to be reimbursed by CMB. CMB rejected the documents for various reasons, one of which was that the packing list, certificate of quantity and certificate of quality were not originals. These three certificates appeared to have been produced by a computer-controlled printer or photocopier, rather than by a conventional typewriter. Each document contained a stamp of the supplier's name, address and telephone number with an ink signature. The Court was given no specific evidence as to how the documents were produced. The Judge had to reconcile the previous Court of Appeal decisions in the *Glencore* and *Kredietbank* cases, as well as decide whether or not to take account of the ICC decision on original documents.

The Judge heard evidence from expert bankers on behalf of both parties and concluded that documents such as the ones in question would have been accepted as originals by banks prior to the introduction of UCP 400. Therefore, in accordance with the *Kredietbank* decision, such documents should still be accepted as originals, even if not stamped 'original'. The Judge suggested that the *Glencore* decision would, however, still apply to documents known or appearing to be copies. If it was intended to use such copies as originals, they must be marked 'original'.

The Judge went on to consider the ICC decision and said that it was appropriate for the ICC to try to resolve any difficulties or ambiguities in the interpretation of UCP 500. The decision was said to reflect international standard banking practice, and should be accepted as such.

Although the *CIC v CMB* case, coupled with the ICC decision, has significantly reduced the risk of banks rejecting a document not marked 'original' (at least as a matter of English Law), that risk has not been removed altogether. There remains an element of doubt for those documents, particularly photocopies, which may fall under the *Glencore* ruling. If there is any doubt about the acceptability of a document, the simplest step for the seller to take is to stamp the document 'original' in coloured ink, as well as signing it if required to do so.

DEFERRED PAYMENT CREDITS

The *Banco Santander v Banque Paribas* case considered whether, in a confirmed deferred payment credit in which the confirming bank had discounted its own payment undertaking, the risk resulting from fraud on the part of the beneficiary should be borne by the confirming bank or by the issuing bank. A deferred payment letter of credit had been issued by Paribas and was advised and confirmed by Santander. The credit was available by deferred payment at 180 days after the date of the bills of lading. The beneficiary presented documents to Santander and asked the bank to discount the sum that would be due on the maturity date. Santander found the documents to comply with the terms of the credit and paid the discounted sum. It then took an assignment of the beneficiary's rights under the credit and forwarded the documents to Paribas.

Prior to the maturity date Paribas informed Santander that the documents included false or forged documents. Therefore, Paribas refused to reimburse Santander on the grounds that fraud had been discovered prior to maturity. It was acknowledged that Santander was not aware of the alleged fraud at the time it accepted the documents and discounted its deferred payment undertaking.

The case went to trial to decide on preliminary issues as to the liability of Paribas to reimburse Santander on the assumption that the beneficiary had been fraudulent. Both the High Court and the Court of Appeal decided in favour of Paribas.

The Court of Appeal said that, in its position as assignee of the beneficiary's rights against Paribas under the credit, Santander could be in no better position than the beneficiary. If the fraud would have entitled Paribas to decline payment to the beneficiary, it also entitled Paribas to decline payment to Santander. Further, the Court of Appeal said that Santander had no right to reimbursement by Paribas under UCP 500 because, in agreeing to discount the beneficiary's claim, Santander was acting outside the mandate given to it by Paribas under the credit.

There seems little doubt that, had fraud not been alleged, Santander would have been entitled to reimbursement from Paribas at maturity of the deferred payment undertaking and not before. Furthermore, if Santander had asked Paribas for authority to 'discount' its deferred payment undertaking, it would have been covered. If the credit had called for the presentation of bills of exchange, Santander would have been covered by the Bills of Exchange Act 1882. The conclusion must be, therefore, that if a bank elects to pay its deferred payment undertaking early (that is before the maturity date), it does so at its own risk, unless it specifically requests authority from the issuing bank to do so.

ACKNOWLEDGEMENT

We would like to thank Claude Mifsud for his support and many helpful suggestions on the first edition of this chapter.

Part 5

International Trade
Development Issues

Researching International Markets

Jonathan Reuvid

THE MARKET RESEARCH REVOLUTION

During the past five years the Internet has totally transformed the methodology for research into international markets, as it has the provision of information in so many diverse business and educational fields.

Nowhere is the metamorphosis more apparent than in 'desk' phases of market research. Here, the conventional approach of programming internal marketing department staff or hiring market research (MR) professionals to scour available sources such as public business libraries, business school papers, chambers of commerce information files, government export department and trade association records, trade and business journals and others has given way to surfing the websites of information providers at source and clicking on to online databases.

The revolution did not occur overnight. Initially, the readier availability of in-depth information about markets and industries was the offspring of late 1980s and early 1990s IT developments which enabled hard copy publishers and research or news agencies themselves to store vast amounts of information electronically on disk for resale on a report-by-report basis or by subscription. By 1995, for example, Reuters had developed and was marketing a direct link news service, available by subscription through PCs with a search engine, enabling subscribers to enter keywords (eg 'automotive' together with 'Korea') which would generate on screen, in reverse date order, all the Reuters news clippings relating to the keyword combination (ie the Korean automotive industry). The subscriber had the additional facility of being able to print out these newsflashes in date sequence.

By today's standards, such groundbreaking services seem cumbersome, but they sounded the death knell for MR agencies' desk research services.

Clients could now carry out their own desk research and, for this primary phase of MR, agency services have become increasingly redundant.

Similarly, background economic data and econometrics on a country by country basis, the essential elements of local commercial and employment law, regulatory procedures and constraints for market entry and tax, audit and accountancy regimes can all be investigated now online. New subscription services for developing markets, starting with Central and Eastern Europe, are planned for early 2002 introduction by the publishers of this book.

THE WWW IS NOT ENOUGH

However, the limitations of the Internet as an effective MR medium need to be understood by all those engaging in international trade. At the most basic level, MR online is often not quite the user-friendly exercise which aficionados of Internet surfing may lead you to expect. Although research engines have become increasingly sophisticated they can be tedious to use, with some promising websites yielding disappointingly incomplete or stale information.

A really useful website should enable the researcher to investigate progressively from the general to the particular, but information is often not arranged in that way or not displayed sequentially. Sometimes, there is a lack of 'granularity' in the data available. For example, an exporter of electronic components for, say, security alarm systems may be able to identify that there is a growing domestic demand for security alarms in a given developing country and for imported electronic componentry in general, but it is unlikely that confirmation can be made of the demand for imported components for security alarm manufacture without direct enquiry.

Fortunately, the Internet era has been accompanied by the e-commerce explosion. In addition to the opening up of international trade to electronic transactions (see Chapters 5.5 and 5.6), the ubiquitous e-mail provides a formidable tool which takes desk research into the second phase of selected respondent enquiry. Having identified lists of potential customers or procurement sources, the exporter or importer can now communicate effectively with them online in order to establish shortlists of targeted customers or suppliers. Transmitting by e-mail with attachments, buyers and sellers can generate enquiries against technical specifications and drawings, study manufacturing processes and quality manuals, carry out credit checks, place orders and execute all the documentary routines necessary to ensure shipment and delivery and to close out the transaction. The worldwide purchasing networks of global automotive manufacturers operate as business-to-business (B2B) facilitators, collapsing time and distance barriers and replacing cumbersome marketing and procurement routines with more cost-effective solutions.

Of course, much of this 21st century business activity could have been accomplished in the last 20 or so years by inter-office facsimile (fax) communication, and so it was. The reasons why the e-mail is so much more effective than the fax are rooted in its immediacy and the personal nature of its communication. Firstly, e-mails are normally transmitted on a person to person (or persons) basis between sender's and receiver's PCs. Unlike the hard copy fax, which can be conveniently re-routed within office systems and may insulate the addressee from the need to respond promptly, e-mails received personally demand a rapid response. Secondly, responding to e-mails is not as onerous as replying by fax; only the lowest level of typing skills are required to reply immediately. Thirdly, the informality of language in common e-usage also helps to facilitate communication. For MR direct enquiry from would-be supplier to potential customer or vice versa, e-mail transmissions are an exceptionally effective medium of communication.

DIRECT EXPOSURE

When entering new markets, of which neither the company nor any of its management has previous direct experience, there is no substitute for visiting the market as an integral part of the evaluation process. It is perfectly possible to build export sales or develop reliable import sources, especially of raw materials and industrial products, through the e-commerce and remote trading routines described here and in Chapters 5.5 and 5.6. However, hands-on experience becomes necessary to assess thoroughly the potential for significant penetration of a targeted foreign market. Equally, the qualification of a foreign factory as a supply chain partner delivering to original equipment manufacturer's (OEM) specifications (as opposed to a less quality and performance-sensitive vendor) demands some physical contact. In Chapter 5.2, face to face meeting is also commended as an essential step in the final process of selecting and appointing agents and distributors.

Exporters seeking to evaluate markets for consumer products can develop intelligence remotely on consumer preferences and buying patterns, channels to market and the retail environment, local packaging preferences, sales promotion and publicity, even competitors' strengths and weaknesses. But, somehow, this never seems enough to convey fully the flavour of the market, or to craft how the exporter's own products may be positioned most effectively.

However closely the consumer shopping scene in developed markets or the urban centres of developing countries may conform to an ubiquitous global pattern, there remain cultural differences which give each market some individual character. These differences can only be recognized and diagnosed from the personal experience of visits to the marketplace.

In the same way, although the conduct of business in most parts of the world has converged and generally conforms to international standards of best practice, mindsets still diverge sharply. Business people's perceptions of each other's country, its product and service performance may be conditioned by outdated past experience or reputations. For an enduring involvement in any foreign market as buyer or seller, these differences should be understood and factored into forward planning.

Participation in outward-bound trade missions is a good way of making another country's first acquaintance. The trip and its programme will be well-organized; travel and accommodation will be arranged for you; and, usually, the cost is relatively modest, since most trade missions are, to some degree, subsidized.

Such visits give useful first exposure to the market, but the experience needs to be treated with some degree of caution: local companies to which visitors may be introduced will be carefully selected by the hosts – perhaps on grounds of excellence, but just as likely because they are in need of export customers or, in the case of developing countries, of foreign direct investment. It is generally unwise to rush into relationships with trading partners encountered through trade missions, unless they have also been shortlisted through supporting desk research.

Visiting trade fairs is another useful way of evaluating the marketplace and the strengths and weaknesses of foreign and domestic competition. However, participation as an exhibitor is an expensive exercise for exporters and may be money ill spent unless desk research and initial exposure to the market has persuaded you that there is probably a demand for your company's products.

MR AGENCY SERVICES

Serious players in export markets for consumer products, aiming to achieve market penetration, need to enlist MR agency support, as they would in home markets, from surveys to establish consumer profiles and brand awareness, to focus groups for product and packaging design and to pre-launch product placement tests.

In developed and many emerging markets the services of international MR agencies or of strong local agencies, accredited by the leading multi-national advertising agencies and their local partners, are available. In developing countries, it is not uncommon for the branded international MR agencies to subcontract fieldwork, including focus groups, to reputable local MR firms. When research is subcontracted, the commissioning client is advised to demand access to the reports of the local agencies that carried out the work and, where appropriate, direct access to the consultants responsible for the work. All qualitative research, particularly focus group findings, are best communicated at first hand.

EXECUTIVE SUMMARY

The recommendations of this chapter apply equally to companies of any size planning or already engaged in regular international trade in one or more foreign markets:

- Develop an in-house market research unit responsible for carrying out ongoing desk research into all foreign markets in which the company is already engaged or has identified a potential interest for future trading.
- Depending upon the level of activity, the unit may be staffed full-time by employees dedicated to the task, by marketing department staff with other day-to-day responsibilities or by part-time employees contracted on an assignment basis – perhaps by first degree university researchers or second degree business school students. There is a prerequisite for advanced skills in Internet and other information source data extraction.
- Ensure that the appropriate senior management gains sufficient first hand exposure to the foreign markets in which the company has a serious commercial interest and intends to gain penetration or develop as a major product source.
- Outward trade missions may be a cost-effective means of getting to know the business environment of a foreign market, but be alert to the possibility that the potential customers and suppliers visited may not be representative of the market as a whole.
- As a part of the ongoing research programme, participate in the hosting of inward trade missions too. Compare and contrast the offerings and presentations of visiting foreign company managers with the reality of their businesses at home.

- When commissioning formal market research from MR agencies, make a point of accessing the reports of the consultants who actually carry out the research and meeting with them to discuss their findings, whenever circumstances permit.

Engaging in international trade used to be considered a pioneering activity in which intrepid salesmen and procurement managers set forth into uncharted territories armed only with a few local contacts, perhaps a sheaf of random enquiries and their travellers' cheques. Successful outcomes to such excursions, even into the 1990s, were as much a matter of good fortune as the result of informed planning except for larger companies with substantial research budgets and a willingness to invest heavily up front in MR. Happily, the Internet has brought sophisticated desk research and market analysis within reach of the smallest company. There are no excuses now for ill-informed and unplanned forays into international markets.

5.2

Appointing Export Agents and Distributors

Jonathan Reuvid

Before entering an overseas market seriously, the first important decision which a potential exporter needs to take is a choice of the most appropriate sales and distribution channel. Unless the exporter has decided to set up and staff a representative or branch office or form a local subsidiary company at the outset, it needs to appoint an agent or distributor to represent the company as its intermediary in each export market as the decision to enter is taken.

Branded franchise network operators have a different choice between granting a master franchise for a country or territory, which in turn appoints a network of franchisees, or of appointing the franchisee network direct itself. The remit of this chapter follows that of the book; therefore the focus is on exporters of manufactured products and services, referred to collectively in this chapter as 'goods', for whom the choice lies between appointed sales agents or distributors as the preferred intermediaries.

CHOOSING THE FORM OF INTERMEDIARY

We assume that the company has already researched the market, or has some export experience of servicing local customers' orders. In either case, its management has acquired sufficient market knowledge to make a reasoned judgment as to the kind of intermediary its business needs.

Agents

Working as an independent contractor on commission, the foreign sales agent's task is to gain orders for his Principal's goods and convey them to the Principal. The exporter normally has the responsibility of delivering the product to the customer, which may be discharged by the company's forwarding agent.

The agent is normally not restricted to selling one company's goods, but is restricted territorially. A territory can be a well-defined geographical area, or it could be a specific market within a geographical area – eg the retail trade or mail order houses – in the case of consumer products. Alternatively, there may be no specific geographical limitation but the territory may be defined by the way in which the product is delivered – eg by e-commerce online for books or consumer services.

The typical characteristics of an agent and his role are the following:

- The agency may be a company or firm or a sole trader and is usually a national of the specific market, having some expertise in the product sector.
- The agent is responsible in the territory assigned to him for:

    - research;
    - promotion;
    - selling;
    - order getting;
    - customer care;
    - problem solving, etc.

Sometimes the agent is responsible, after acceptance of an order by the exporter, of calling the order off the forwarding agent's local warehouse and confirming delivery schedules. Sales agents may also take on the task of debt collection from customers who have exceeded their credit terms.

- The agent receives a Commission from the company on sales in his territory, usually between 5 and 10 per cent, which should be based on the exporter's Ex-Works price to the customer and payable only after receipt of full payment by the customer. (It is common practice to pay advances of commission to agents against invoices to customers, which are recoverable in the event of failure to pay.)
- Usually, the agent does not handle the goods sold and does not have any authority to commit its Principal contractually beyond accepting an order.

The benefits of an agent are his fast start-up capability and low fixed cost for the Principal. The disadvantages are concerns over the degree of commitment, the lack of control over his commercial actions and the cost penalties of termination in many countries (as under EU Law).

The status of the sales agent varies considerably from country to country. In Germany, for example, the qualified technical sales agent representing component manufacturers, often an engineering graduate himself, commands respect from original equipment manufacturing (OEM) customers in industries such as automotive. His relationship with the customer, involving interface with designers, specifiers and the quality assurance function, as well as procurement and purchasing, is far from the conventional 'order-taking' role of sales representatives serving customers in the retail chain.

DISTRIBUTORS

By contrast with the sales agent, the foreign distributor acts as a principal, buying and selling manufactured products for his own account, on his own terms, although in close consultation with the exporter. In effect, he is the exporter's direct customer, although not the end-user. Delivery is made through the distributor, which manages the local customer relationship directly. Subject to local competition law, which in the EU outlaws exclusive distribution agreements except for categories of product where block exemption has been granted, the distributor is normally restricted territorially. He may be restricted from selling competitors' products by e-commercial terms of the distribution agreement, is usually trained by the exporter and easier to monitor than the sales agent. The distributor is usually a better channel to market than the agent for technically complex finished product requiring after-sales service and repair facilities or for marketing-intensive products.

Usually an incorporated firm, the distributor:

- purchases goods from the manufacturer and resells into the territory, sometimes as a sole distributor, at a profit;
- makes a profit from marking up the discounted price at which he purchases the goods from the exporter to the agreed market price;
- performs all the agent's tasks plus:

  - stocking goods and parts;
  - pre- and after-sales service;
  - sales administration;
  - local deliveries;
  - installation;
  - maintenance and repairs;
  - credit control and payment collection.

Distributors' discounts vary from sector to product sector. Typically, industrial goods discounts might allow for 15 to 25 per cent mark-ups, whereas consumer goods discounts, which must provide for retailers' margins, may allow for mark-ups of over 50 per cent.

Higher distributors' margins also reflect the additional services which they perform over and above those of an agent, and the greater financial risk.

THE SELECTION PROCESS

Whatever agent/distributor combination a company has chosen to appoint, it should never appoint an intermediary without developing a clear specification of the role to be filled and then checking thoroughly that the appointee has the necessary attributes to perform the role.

Exporters should remember that for some national markets with strong regional characteristics it may be appropriate to appoint more than one distributor with clearly defined territories or a single distributor with several supporting agents.

Given the density and size of most West European markets, the appointment of more than one distributor may be sensible for companies intending to provide truly responsive product after sales service. Again in Germany, where qualified technical agents often specialize in one or two industries only, the preferred arrangement for, say, an electronic components manufacturer may be to appoint one agent whose 'territory' is automotive OEMs, and one that concentrates on domestic appliance manufacturers.

Generally, when one or more agents are appointed for a territory which is serviced by an exporter's appointed distributor, the distributor's selling responsibilities are diminished and its margin is reduced by the amount of the agent's commission.

SELECTION CRITERIA

Having established a long list of candidates by reference to the databases of trade associations and published directories, by soliciting recommendations from existing customers and other exporters or from direct approaches received from the territory, the exporter will apply his own selection criteria to each candidate. The criteria will commonly include the following:

- *Compatibility vs competition*

  While familiarity with the same kind of product brings benefits in terms of market knowledge and potential customer contacts, the appointment of an agent or distributor already selling a competitor's products seems a certain recipe for failure. Replacing an existing competitor whom the agent has served with past success may seem attractive, but if the reputation and the quality of the previous product line were poor, the agent's past association could be a handicap. There is also a loyalty factor; some customers will react unfavourably to an agent who changes Principals.

  A more promising scenario is the appointment of an agent who is already selling complementary but non-competing products successfully to market sectors which the exporter has targeted; again, it is important that the complementary products handled are not of inferior quality to the exporter's.

- *Commercial capability*

  Candidates will need to demonstrate a high level of market knowledge in terms of the exporter's competition, the purchasing and procurement functions of major target companies and personal contacts within those targeted sectors.

  Marketing skills and promotional expertise will be assessed against their attendance at trade fairs, effective use of trade media, local press and, where appropriate, direct mail.

  Administrative capability may be judged against quality of customer relations management, use of IT, showrooms and, in the case of potential distributors, their logistical capability against warehousing and transport facilities.

- *Technical capability*

  The best evidence for a prospective agent or distributor's capability to provide the technical expertise necessary to sell and service an exporter's products is success in the same market sector with comparable products. The technical qualifications of management and staff and in-house training activity are also relevant.

- *Financial status*

  The normal credit reference routines and reviews of trading history, balance sheets and capital adequacy should be undertaken. In the case of countries where there is no statutory requirement to file annual audited accounts, information held in government bureau offices may be accessed on payment of fees to search agencies.

It may not be possible to evaluate all these characteristics in advance of a visit to a prospective agent/distributor's place of business, but a first assessment can be made on these criteria sufficient to establish a shortlist of candidates. Hopefully, the screening process will yield a shortlist of three or four candidates from which the exporter will be able to make a satisfactory final selection. It is essential that a personal visit to each shortlisted candidate's place of business is made before entering into an agency or distribution agreement. Only through a site visit and face to face discussion can an exporter verify desk research findings on a candidate's capabilities and assess selling ability, enthusiasm, professionalism, integrity and other personal attributes.

At this stage only should the exporter allow subjective judgements to influence his decisions. If there are two possible candidates at final selection, which both meet the objective criteria, it is acceptable for management to choose the one it likes the look of best. But remember, you don't have to like your carefully selected agent/distributor personally for the relationship to work.

TERMS OF AGREEMENT

However confident the exporter may be in his final choice, it should be sure to grant only a trial period of representation (typically 12 months) until he is certain that the right choice has been made. Therefore, a company's written agreement with a new agent/distributor should include a specific termination date.

Essential terms

The agreement should define the following:

- products;
- territories;
- commission rates/discounts;
- credit and payment terms;
- the Principal's duties and responsibilities;
- the agent/distributor's duties and responsibilities;
- use of copyright and ownership of Intellectual Property Rights;
- limits of the agent/distributor's authority;

- product and commercial liabilities to customers;
- length of the agreement and provisions for termination;
- law governing the contract (jurisdiction);
- provisions for disputes resolution.

Even if the initial engagement is provisional, it should be the subject of a full written agreement, not just for the company's protection or to enforce compliance, but also to clarify for both parties exactly what is being agreed.

Critical issues

Many agents/distributors receive statutory legal protection (particularly throughout the European Union where Single Market law applies). Exporters must take particular care in their agency/distributor agreements to provide for the following:

- A fixed duration for the agreement, subject to formal renewal by both parties. Compensation may be payable to an agent following cancellation of an agreement with no fixed duration.
- While in English Law the longest period of notice to agents is three months for all contracts that have run for more than three years, the notice provision is extended in other countries (eg under German Law the longest period is six months in respect of contracts that have run for more than five years).
- Quantitative definition of minimum performance levels as the basis for terminating the appointments of non-performing intermediaries. (Without definition it is very difficult to establish the level of non-performance.)
- Claims for indemnities upon termination of an agency agreement in most jurisdictions and under English Law for compensation instead or as well. Under most jurisdictions indemnities are calculated as an annual percentage of the agent's commission, calculated on past earnings over up to five years. In some jurisdictions (eg Germany) an agent who agrees to refrain from competition with the Principal after termination is entitled to reasonable compensation throughout the period of the restriction.

Competition law and distribution agreements

Ordinary relationships between Principal and agent are unlikely to be caught in EU competition rules. However, distribution agreements, unless drafted carefully, may contain restrictions which infringe Article 85 (1) of the Treaty of Rome. Restrictions on a distributor not to sell competing products when granted an exclusive territory, not to serve certain categories of customer who fail to satisfy the manufacturer's requirements, or to purchase supplies of a specific product from one source only are not uncommon and are *prima facie* infringements. Where a block exemption does not apply and the parties are unwilling to remove the restrictions, the agreement may apply to the Commission for individual exemption under Article 85 (3). Where the parties' total market shares are 5 per cent or less, EC competition rules may not apply.

International Freight Management and Logistics[1]

Jonathan Reuvid (BIFA)

THE EXPANDING ROLE OF THE FREIGHT FORWARDER

Traditionally, the freight forwarder acted merely as the agent of the principal or shipper, arranging transport as an intermediary and referred to as a 'shipping and forwarding agent'. In this limited role, the agent's activities were confined to production of the necessary documentation for transport, payment and customs clearance. Today, the freight forwarder's role is more comprehensive, providing valuable and knowledgeable advice, as well as the expedition of freight services, to the international trading and logistics management community.

The drivers of change in the freight forwarder's role have been threefold. Initially, the arrival of the container and the roll-on/roll-off ferry revolution predisposed exporters and importers alike towards seamless door-to-door transport operations around the world. Then, new opportunities for intermodal transportation developed through the increasing significance of airfreight, and in the case of the UK and Continental Europe, the opening of the Channel Tunnel, which continue to collapse time barriers in global trade. Finally, the introduction of e-commerce made international trading online a reality, with the development of regulations and procedures for electronic documentation clearing the way for paperless bank transactions.

Through these evolutionary changes a new type of market is emerging for the information age, with a new breed of logistics services solutions

---

[1] The content of this chapter is drawn from material provided by the British International Freight Association (BIFA) and articles and presentations given by its Director General, Colin Beaumont, whose assistance is gratefully acknowledged.

affecting not just freight forwarding professionals but also their customer base of shippers and logistics managers. The outsourcing of logistics management has now become an attractive option for many manufacturers engaged in the import of components and assemblies and the export of finished product, or vice versa. Even the core activities of masterminding the trouble-free movement of goods internationally on behalf of the exporter and importer, such as purchase order expediting, managing suppliers and vendors and rationalizing gateways to produce optimal use of freight space, as well as the physical functions traditionally carried out in-house, eg inventory management, market customization or the labelling of goods, can be outsourced safely. Electronic communications, already implemented by the freight services industry, provide cargo tracking facilities for forwarder and client, the exchange of data by e-mail using electronic data interchange (EDI) or web-based technology.

THE CLASSIFICATION OF FREIGHT FORWARDERS AND THEIR FUNCTIONS

There are over 1,200 members of the British International Freight Association (BIFA) and they account for more than 85 per cent of UK business. However, BIFA estimates that there are more than 2,000 companies operating as freight fowarders in the UK alone.

There is no typical freight forwarding company, but the different types of company can be divided roughly into three categories:

- *Local companies*: generally small single-office firms that tend to deal with clients in their immediate local area, or operate at seaports or airports concentrating on particular types of traffic.
- *National companies*: have offices in the major ports and airports throughout the country, as well as in the largest industrial conurbations. They may also operate services from their own warehousing or handling depots. Such national companies often have overseas agents or correspondents in markets where they commonly trade.
- *International companies*: have their own offices overseas and offer a wide range of worldwide services.

Some international and national freight forwarders classify themselves as 'non-vessel owning carriers' (NVOCs) to enhance the marketing of their service offering. However, irrespective of the classification, all freight forwarders provide one or more of the following services:

- road and rail distribution;
- maritime intermodal services;
- airfreight consolidation and forwarding;
- trade facilitation, customs broking and consultancy;
- logistics and supply chain management.

THE MOVEMENT OF GOODS

The main service provided by the freight forwarder, whether acting for an importer or exporter, is the movement of goods. From the forwarder's experience, he will advise on the cheapest, quickest and safest routeing, the best mode of transport, customs requirements, packing, insurance and the diverse regulations which apply in both the country of origin and the country of destination. The freight forwarder will bring specialist knowledge and skills to each of these areas.

Arranging transportation

Freight fowarders may be contracted to work for either the exporter or the importer and their key function is to arrange for the movement of goods between the two. They will book space on the ship, aircraft or other transport carrier and call forward the goods, or collect them, at the appropriate time. They will coordinate delivery to the buyer through their overseas agent. The mode of transport chosen will influence each of these actions.

Documentation

The preparation of the necessary formal documents is a crucial step in all international trade. The freight forwarder may undertake the task himself or advise the exporter. With the abolition of customs borders within the European Union (EU), trade between Member States has become much simpler, with reduced documentation. In addition, the development of e-business solutions enables information to be transmitted in a variety of ways, reducing the need to prepare hard copy documents.

Customs and excise

Under European Community and Member State legislation, importers and exporters are legally obliged to record and declare all third country goods which enter and leave the EU. Forwarders' services include the preparation of import and export entries. Since 1 January 1993, Customs clearance is not required for goods moving within the EU, although freight forwarders may be involved in other procedures, such as the collection, preparation and submission of statistical information. Goods exported to third countries are still subject to customs control, although systems continue to be simplified.

Payment of freight and other charges

The forwarder will accept and pay all charges on behalf of established clients. In this way, a trader requiring the services of airlines, shipping companies and other transportation and handling organizations will receive only one invoice from the forwarder. The forwarder will pass on credit facilities for these services which the client may not command, and will sometimes arrange to collect the amount of the seller's invoice for goods sold cash on delivery through overseas agents.

Packing and warehousing

Many forwarders provide a packing service for their clients which may be highly cost effective. Factors affecting the choice of packing are requirements for the protection of the goods together with their handling risks, the methods of transport used, the climates of the countries through which consignments will have to travel and the terrain. The forwarder may be better placed than the client to judge what packaging is most suitable. Usually, the forwarder will also be able to provide warehousing and allied functions, such as stock control, on a temporary or longer-term basis to those traders with limited space of their own.

Arranging insurance

Forwarders will have expert knowledge of cargo insurance and its complexities within the domain of underwriters – the professional risk-takers who accept the financial losses involved on payment of a premium, subject to certain terms and conditions. A trader will be able to access advice on the risks involved and the type of policy required. Many forwarders have excellent insurance terms which they have negotiated and offer the facility of 'open policy', ie cover for all consignments rather than on an individual shipment basis. In the event of loss or damage, the forwarder will provide assistance with the processing of claims to expedite settlement.

Consolidation, groupage and special services

Freight forwarders provide client benefits through their ability to group together consignments from several exporters and present them to a shipping company or airline as a single large consignment. In this way a forwarder can gain a much cheaper rate than an individual company and can offer the client a competitive tariff for his small consignment. 'Consolidation' is a term normally applied to airfreight; for surface freight the system is referred to as 'groupage'.

Consolidation can also provide added value at the other end of the delivery chain. For example, a forwarder will consolidate cargo in one country and despatch the full load to an agent in the destination country, who will de-consolidate on receipt, clear customs and deliver to the final con-signee. The forwarder may also be able to hold consignments at destination prior to delivery on receipt of payment from the importer. In this way, the vendor gains both an element of security and the assurance of minimum delay in delivery. The same capability can be applied to the benefit of an importer; the buyer at desination may use the forwarder to collect goods from many different suppliers in the country of export, thus avoiding the need to employ a separate purchasing agency.

However, when the forwarder offers a groupage or NVOC service, such as the carrier, the agency-only role ceases and advice to the client can no longer be regarded as impartial. When acting as the carrier, the forwarder does not charge a separate agency fee to the shipper but incorporates a return within the rating structure of the carrier service tariff.

THE DOCUMENTATION OF INTERNATIONAL TRANSPORT

International transport documents can be separated into three sectors:

- documents of carriage, including the airwaybill, bill of lading, consign-ment note etc;

- documents for customs and other regulatory bodies;
- commercial documents.

Documents of carriage

Bill of lading
The bill of lading is the central document of carriage for ocean shipment. In legal terms, it is a receipt for goods shipped, a document of title and evidence of the contract of affreightment. Possession of a properly completed negotiable bill of lading constitutes effective control of the goods.

The standard bill of lading (FBL) of the International Federation of Freight Forwarders Association (FIATA) is the most widely used multimodal transport document, recognized officially by both the United Nations Conference on Trade and Development (UNCTAD) and the International Chamber of Commerce (ICC). The issuing company assumes responsibility as a carrier and the FBL may be used for door-to-door transport or as a marine bill of lading.

Airwaybill
The primary document for the carriage of goods by air is the airwaybill. It serves as the contract between the shipper and the carrier for the carriage of goods, and also as a receipt of goods for shipment, a form of invoicing and a document for the import, export and transit requirement of customs.

Road consignment note
The CMR Convention, a set of legal articles which form the contract between the carrier and the shipper, governs the international carriage of goods by road. The CMR Convention prescribes the issue of a consignment note as evidence of the contract of carriage, the conditions of the contract and the receipt of the goods by the carrier.

Regulatory documents

International transport also requires regulatory documents, such as those for the declaration of goods at import and export to customs authorities, import and export licensing and the movement of dangerous goods.

Commercial documents

The commercial documents in a specific transaction will depend upon the nature of the consignment, methods of payment etc, and are likely to include invoices, insurance certificates, letters of credit and shipping instructions. Trade finance documentation and its terms are discussed at length in Part 4.

Commercial contracts are usually couched in 'Incoterms' – the set of international rules for the most commonly used terms in foreign trade. Incoterms were produced by the ICC to avoid the uncertainties of various interpretations of such terms that can give rise to costly and time-wasting misunderstandings, disputes and possible litigation. Originally published in 1936, Incoterms have since been amended. The *Preamble of the Incoterms* from the current edition (2000) of the ICC publication is reproduced in Appendix VII.

COMMUNICATING INSTRUCTIONS

Failure to follow correct procedures and good practice in international trade can cause problems and prove expensive. Good practice starts with giving all instructions in writing, on letterheads. Instructions may be transmitted by fax, telex and EDI as an alternative to shipping instruction forms, although it is prudent to follow this up with hard copy confirmation. Instructions should include:

- name and address of shipper and consignee;
- collection and delivery addresses (if different from above);
- consignment specifications including weight, measurements, content and value;
- insurance declaration (a positive statement, eg 'insurance not required');
- dangerous goods declaration (eg 'goods not hazardous');
- terms of shipment (eg 'CIF' or 'FOB');
- special instructions (eg letter of credit, payment terms).

Effective management of the transport chain is fundamental to successful trading. The freight forwarder and the client, acting in partnership, have a responsibility to keep each other informed at all times about any development which may affect the safe and timely delivery of goods, thereby eliminating uncertainty and minimizing risk.

Professional forwarders have responded to the challenge of the new techniques presented by e-business in terms of collecting and managing data from all parties and managing the supply chain. This activity includes tracking consignments and presenting the information electronically so that the shipper can keep overseas sales agents, distributors and customers fully informed.

5.4

Inspection and Certification of Goods

Gordon Hutt, formerly of SGS Group

All trade involves risk, both to seller and buyer, but international trade involves extra degrees of risk caused by different languages, regulations, documentation, business practices and manufacturing standards. Prevention is better than cure, and it is certainly much less expensive to ensure a consignment is correct before shipment than to rely on insurance. For more than 100 years, independent inspection and certification services have been evolving to provide more and more sophisticated aids to minimize normal commercial risks for both exporters and importers.

STANDARD CARGO SUPERVISION

The main commercial risks in international trade relate to:

- goods not matching the requirements of the order: the wrong sort, wrong size, wrong colour etc;
- goods which are unsatisfactory because they are of poor quality or are unsafe to use or consume;
- poor value, because the condition or presentation makes them unprofitable to the importer that is going to resell them;
- fraud, which may involve various types of documentary or shipment malpractice.

Using an accredited inspection agency is an effective and economical way to minimize or remove these risks. The safeguards provided by independent inspection have been endorsed by the World Bank and the WTO. For many basic commodities, such as grains, ores and oils, the standard contracts of sale make specific provisions for the involvement of independent inspectors to issue certificates to define the quantity and quality of the goods shipped. Many of the major international banks will also stipulate the use of inspection in their documentary credits.

A professional independent inspection will usually be one of two main types, commercial or statutory. The inspection process will be similar in both types but the scope of inspection, and the qualifications and expertise of the inspector, may be different.

Commercial inspections will relate to the terms of a contract between a buyer and a seller. The scope of the inspection, and the format of the report, will be determined either by the actual terms of the contract or by established trade practices. The inspector will usually be required to verify that the goods are in conformity with the specifications or dimensions described in the order and that the quantity ordered is complete and adequately packed for shipment. It may be necessary also for manufacturing quality or performance standards to be verified by further checks or tests.

Statutory inspections will be governed by the regulations or standards which relate to those particular products, irrespective of the terms of sale. In addition to quantitative assessment, the inspector will have to verify that the goods conform to the precise requirements of national or international standards. To do this, the inspector may need specific professional or technical qualifications. Examples of this kind of specialized inspection would include fabrics, garments, upholstery materials and floor coverings, where quality of materials and manufacture could be related to a whole range of British Standards. Chemicals, which might be contaminants, are subject to more vigorous checks, which may be extended to the sea freight containers or even the holds of the vessel. The strictest inspection methods are applied to medicines and foodstuffs, where the inspection sampling and testing procedures will often be defined by European or international standards, such as the ISO 4832:1991(E) for the enumeration of coliforms present in animal feed. Otherwise, the inspector uses training and experience to decide whether samples need to be drawn for reference or test. If so, a random sampling method will be used, which is based on BS 6001, MIL 10 5D, or similar. For reference and identification purposes, inspectors also use photography, nowadays often digital equipment, to meet the high speed reporting required to support the airfreight industry.

There are many companies which offer inspection services. The major companies, which can offer services through networks which cover the entire world, can offer the most sophisticated laboratory testing procedures and are members of the International Federation of Inspection Agencies (IFIA), which has its headquarters in the City of London. Members of IFIA are bound by a Code of Conduct which assures the integrity and independence of their work.

In addition to inspecting goods before shipment, or at the point of delivery, the major inspection companies (see Appendix 5.4.1) can also provide technical appraisals on prospective suppliers in any country of the world, can check production capacities and in-process quality, as well as advise on export or import regulations and supervision of packing, loading and container security.

Quality improvement

The quality of goods, especially consumer goods and particularly fresh or perishable goods, can be a matter of presentation or perception as much as specification. Fruit and cut flowers would be good examples.

During the last half-century, and especially since the introduction of wide-bodied jets on intercontinental routes, the inspection companies have been at the forefront of developments in storage and handling techniques which have made exotic tropical fruits commonplace in European supermarkets. With locally trained technical staff and well-equipped laboratories in many developing countries, the major inspection companies have played a large part in the development of new industries in Africa, SE Asia and the Far East. An example from Kenya, now one of the world's largest exporters of cut roses, is that the Fresh Produce Exporters Association of Kenya (FPEAK) appointed SGS Kenya, members of the world's largest inspection organization, to inspect all exports of horticultural produce from Kenya.

Inspection to combat counterfeiting

Counterfeiting has been a problem to international trade for centuries. In the last 20 years it has become worse. The costs to established manufacturers with internationally recognized brand names in the clothing, fashion and music recording industries are enormous.

It is a global problem. Estimates of the overall incidence of counterfeiting suggest that more than 6 per cent of total world trade involves fake goods. The UK Anti-Counterfeiting Group has put the costs at more than £600 billion a year.

Manufacturer organizations have come together when they see a common interest in protecting investments in research and marketing. Intellectual property law and international conventions have been strengthened and trademark regulations have been tightened. Engineers and designers strive to design products, packaging and documents which cannot be copied, but the counterfeiters won't give up while profits can be so lucrative.

Pre-shipment inspection companies are working quietly alongside those who are most vigorously trying to discourage the fraudsters. The three or four biggest inspection companies operate worldwide networks and have the management strength to maintain the integrity of their staff in the most difficult centres for the production of counterfeit goods. India, China and Taiwan have long ceased to be the main sources. Indeed, some well-known branded products from those countries have also been counterfeited.

With the opening of borders in the EU, and the emergence of newly independent states in the former Soviet Union, the counterfeiters have gained new production sources as well as better supply routes. A common manoeuvre is to ship the counterfeit goods to countries in Western Europe and then package them to give the impression they were, for example, 'made in England', and then export to developing countries where the apparent origin of the goods will be a cachet of quality and high standards.

In the recent past, SGS inspectors in the UK have stopped shipments going to Africa, the Far East and South America, which have included Leyland bus brake parts made in Malaysia, railway engine turbochargers made in Poland from obsolete drawings, counterfeit OTC medicines made in the former Yugoslavia, and Pierre Cardin luggage counterfeited here in Britain. All these cases had two things in common:

- they are produced with the deliberate intention of being passed off as the genuine product and sold as such;
- in terms of performance or durability they are inferior to the genuine product.

Attack can often be the best form of defence. If a company shows an aggressive anti-counterfeiting policy, most fraudsters will look for safer targets. A reputation for effective action takes time to build up, but the use of independent inspectors can provide support for further legal action and demonstrates visibly that serious counteraction is being taken. The ICC's International Maritime Bureau has endorsed the use of inspection to combat fraud of this type.

Counterfeiting is an insidious form of theft – the unauthorized use of a company's assets and goodwill. It is not known how often respectable companies have stood the cost of replacing counterfeit goods sent back by a complaining customer, simply to avoid damage to the good name of the brand. In spite of all that manufacturers can do to protect their products, people will always be tempted by the 'extra special offer' with no questions asked. Inspection can, however, make life that much harder for the counterfeiter, that much more risky, that bit less profitable. In that way, the deterrent effect provides practical and effective support for the development of legitimate trade.

INSPECTION FOR ECONOMIC DEVELOPMENT

For developing countries, two of the main economic priorities are revenue collection and the development of local industries. Throughout the postcolonial period of the last 50 years, these two priorities have also represented areas of risk in which many countries have been helped by the use of a special type of pre-shipment inspection service (PSI).

The use of a professional, independent inspection company as part of national economic management was pioneered in the mid-1960s by SGS for the Government of Zaire (now the Democratic Republic of Congo). Since that time other large inspection companies that are members of IFIA have introduced similar services. Around 30 countries are using PSI at present, and nearly 50 countries in total have used the system at some time in the last 30 years.

The original objective was simply to ensure that goods being imported were correct in terms of specification and quantity. In other words, the traditional cargo supervision services described in Standard Cargo Supervision above were being applied to all imports. For Zaire at that time, the aim was to ensure that export earnings from copper and cobalt were not at risk from production breakdowns.

However, within a few years, SGS had developed techniques of price comparison, to detect and prevent over-invoicing, which was being used as a mechanism to transfer funds illegally out of the importing country, an abuse known as 'Capital Flight' which could rapidly deplete the national foreign exchange reserve. During the 1970s, the rising inflation levels in Europe which followed the oil price increases imposed by OPEC, together with declining trends in major commodity prices, brought an increasing focus on the need to prevent hard currency being drained out of Africa.

During the mid-1980s, the increasing moves towards trade liberalization by African countries, the removal of exchange controls and the abolition of import licensing, resulted in a change of focus. The prime economic risk for developing countries was seen to be revenue collection and the control of inflation. In contrast with the industrialized countries of Europe and North America, the new nations of Africa and SE Asia were heavily dependent upon revenue from import duties and taxes. Commonly, as much as 40–60 per cent of government revenues are derived from this source.

The main obstacles to efficient revenue collection are generally seen to be:

- inefficiency, lack of training and corruption within the Customs Service;
- poor communications and inadequate or incomplete records;
- out of date or arbitrary valuation procedures.

This kind of situation fostered a climate which encouraged tax evasion through misclassification and deliberate under-invoicing. At the same time, it increased uncertainties and mistrust among exporters, which encouraged the addition of 'risk premiums' to invoice prices.

The role of the inspection agencies in national economic planning is generally threefold. First, to provide an independent expert opinion, based on physical checks of the goods before shipment, to assess whether the commercial documentation provides full and accurate information for the assessment of import duties and taxes. Secondly, to provide training for customs officials and staff in the development and operation of modern methods of record keeping, including computer-based systems. Thirdly, to help the country in the creation of more orderly and less bureaucratic systems for import monitoring, which will encourage more open competition for trade.

The effect of these PSI programmes, in many developing countries, has been enhancement of revenue collection which has led to rationalization of custom duty bands, the abolition of specific import licences, and a gradual lowering of effective rates of duty. One example is Indonesia. The country suffered from many of the problems previously described when it adopted a comprehensive PSI programme in 1985. At that time, the effective rate of import duty was 33 per cent and wholesale evasion and severe customs corruption limited actual receipts. When the programme of modernization was completed, and Indonesia took back full control of revenue collection in 1996, the annual revenue receipts had risen from $1460 million to $6639 million while the effective rate of duty had been reduced progressively to only 13 per cent.

Although the objective of these programmes is to assist the governments of importing countries, there is a benefit to the exporter. The inspection which is carried out, and the Clean Report of Findings (clean report) which is issued, are normally paid for directly by the importing country. There is no charge to the exporter. First, the inspection report provides independent verification that the consignment is in conformity with the order in terms of specification and quantity. Where necessary, it will also confirm that the goods meet any applicable quality standards and that they are safe to use. This protects the exporter against spurious claims of discrepancies from overseas customers. Second, the issue of the clean report involves checking the documentation. This means that errors will be referred back to the exporter for correction. It is well known that in nearly two-thirds of the transactions covered by a Letter of Credit, the exporter fails to obtain payment on first presentation of the documents because the bank finds an error. Where pre-shipment inspection has been carried out, that proportion is halved, according to several bank surveys. Third, the presentation of the 'clean report' by the importer is designed to facilitate import clearances and discharge of cargo, which should mean faster remittance of payments under non L/C arrangements. The security of the cargo is also improved because the evidence of the Inspection Certificate will usually mean that customs will not choose to apply further checks upon arrival.

The development of e-commerce

Over the last 25 years, international trade has experienced a revolution in both logistics and administration. In that time, the typewriter, the telex machine and Idem multi-page form sets have been replaced, first by the fax machine and the computer, and now by the scanner and e-mail. During the same time, air cargo has come to play a far more significant part in international trade, and large sections of the clothing, automotive, electrical, pharmaceutical and consumer durables manufacturing industries have moved from Europe and North America to the emerging nations of India, Asia and South America.

The convergence of these developments has produced a new type of business which is computer-based and is essentially international. It is similar in some ways to 'Catalogue Shopping', but the difference lies in the greater separation between the customer and the source of supply, which is usually going to be far distant.

This new business arena is still in its infancy, but it is growing strongly and the main centres for the production of goods supplied over the Internet are China, India and the other Far East 'tiger' economies.

For those new businesses to be successful in the long term, the customers have to be convinced they can be trusted: trusted to supply the goods which are ordered; trusted to supply goods which meet fully the customers' expectations of performance and value. In Europe, the focus is on consumer protection, in terms of safety, quality and durability.

In regard to these areas of public concern and customer confidence, the major inspection companies, in particular SGS and Bureau Veritas, have a very important role. Using their global networks of branch companies and trained inspection and laboratory staff in these countries, they are able to carry out detailed audits to establish, confirm and monitor the capabilities (and sometimes even the existence) of companies advertising their products on the websites of portals such as MeetChina.com, IndiaMart.com and Oneswoop.com. The rating given by the inspection company to a hitherto unknown factory in a distant country of supply not only gives potential customers an independent guarantee of satisfaction; it may also, in time, help that product to become a new worldwide market leader.

As international trade continues to evolve in the electronic age, the inspection industry will continue to develop new techniques to encourage and assist best manufacturing practices and improved logistical services to enable better products to be delivered faster, and to provide greater satisfaction, to more customers throughout the world.

APPENDIX 5.4.1 LIST OF PRINCIPAL UK INSPECTION COMPANIES

Alex Stewart (Assayers Ltd)
Alfred H Knight Holdings Ltd
Baltic Control Ltd
BIVAC International
Bureau Veritas
Control Union (UK) Ltd
Cotecna International Ltd
Gellatly Hankey Marine Services International Ltd
Inspectorate Griffith Ltd
Inspectorate Worldwide Services Ltd
Intertek Testing Services International Ltd
Lloyd's Register of Shipping, Industrial Division
Moody International Ltd
Petrak Services Ltd
Saybolt United Kingdom Ltd
SGS – Société Générale de Surveillance SA

5.5

Personal Liability for Offences Relating to Import and Export Controls

Amy Jackson, Laytons

In some circumstances, a company director can be held personally liable for an offence committed by his or her company under import or export controls. Such liability will flow from breaches of the national criminal law of a specific country, although other countries in the European Union (EU) or indeed elsewhere may have similar import and export controls.

The term 'import and export controls' is a collective term meaning restrictions or prohibitions on exportation and importation of certain goods or trading with particular countries. Exportation and importation under such controls are restricted in the UK, in that it is necessary to obtain a licence from the Secretary of State before exporting or importing certain goods, or trading with certain countries. If a company does not abide by such controls, by exporting restricted goods without a licence or importing prohibited goods such as an endangered species of parrot, for example, it can be prosecuted. If the offence is committed in the UK with the consent or connivance of, or is attributable to any neglect of, a director then he or she, as well as the company, may be held guilty of the offence and fined and/or imprisoned. It is therefore essential for directors to be aware of their potential liability if they are involved in the importation or exportation of goods. It should be remembered by directors of businesses involved in international trade that their failure to comply with import and export controls, either in their home country or overseas, can render them liable to prosecution in either jurisdiction. As such, for many years after an export or import control offence has been committed it may be impossible for the director to visit the relevant country to do any business without running the risk of facing prosecution, or even a term of imprisonment.

DIRECTORS' LIABILITIES IN GENERAL

Under the laws which regulate companies in general in almost all jurisdictions, a director can be held personally and sometimes criminally liable in respect of a wide range of company duties, eg in respect of filing accounts and returns. This is because although many legal requirements will be termed as a duty of the company, in reality the company acts through its directors. Furthermore, a director may be held criminally liable if he or she has knowingly or wilfully authorized the company to commit an illegal act such as theft or fraud. However, when the offence is serious, eg manslaughter arising when an employee is killed due to the company disregarding health and safety laws, a director can be charged simply if he or she was aware of the contravention, providing he or she was controlling the organization.

Under export and import controls in the UK, Her Majesty's (HM) Customs and Excise will usually only hold a director personally liable if the company exports or imports goods in contravention of the regulatory laws and the director was knowingly involved in evading the controls. However, in some cases it is sufficient for the director to have been negligent or reckless, eg by signing a declaration about the type of goods involved, if the facts set out in the declaration are later found to be false.

In order to appreciate the potential liability of a director in the area of exports and imports, it is necessary to outline the range of controls that exist.

WHAT EXPORT AND IMPORT CONTROLS APPLY TO COMPANIES IN THE UK?

Export and import control legislation affects the trading in a wide range of goods; import controls, however, do not exactly mirror export controls. It is essential that any company seeking to export or import goods seeks specific advice from the relevant government department to find out the exact controls that will apply. The following controls may apply, and are given as a general overview.

Export control regulations

The most prevalent controls are in the area of military equipment, technology and 'dual use' goods, ie goods which, though intended for a civil use, can actually be used to manufacture, among other things, chemical, biological or nuclear weapons or the missiles to deliver them. These regulations not only control the physical export of such goods, but also electronic transfers of technology. They are put in place pursuant to many international commitments, and are aimed at preventing the irresponsible transfer of arms or goods that can contribute to the development of weapons of mass destruction. In the UK, the relevant export controls in this area are contained in pieces of legislation such as the Export of Goods (Control) Order 1994 (as amended), the Dual Use Items (Export Control) Regulations 2000 and various other European laws which are directly applicable in English law.

There are also export controls that relate to other goods that are administered by the relevant governmental departments. These cover goods such as foodstuffs, antiques and protected species of wildlife.

Import control regulations

There are a number of import restrictions in place for security reasons in the areas of firearms and ammunition, nuclear materials, and chemical weapons. On a European Community (EC) level there are control regimes covering textiles and clothing, iron and steel and non-textile goods originating in China. The Department of Trade and Industry (DTI) administers most of these controls. There are also international environmental controls in place, which prohibit the import of goods that are harmful to the environment or of endangered species.

Trade sanctions

In addition to the controls outlined above, the United Nations (UN) imposes trade sanctions and arms embargoes. These prohibit or place restrictions on exports, imports, financial transactions, communications and transportation in certain countries. Such sanctions also prevent the giving of technical assistance or training relating to specified goods in such countries.

ENFORCEMENT OF IMPORT AND EXPORT CONTROLS

Although export and import controls in the UK are administered by governmental departments such as the DTI, they are all enforced by HM Customs and Excise. As well as having enforcement powers, eg to enter into business premises to carry out searches and seize unlawfully imported goods, if an offence is committed it can instigate legal proceedings against an offender which may result in a fine or imprisonment. Most offences are dealt with under the HM Customs and Excise Management Act 1979 (CEMA) which acts as a framework for the penalties that may be imposed. The severity of the penalty in each case will depend upon how potentially dangerous the goods are and whether the company knowingly committed the offence. Before turning to the specific offences that may be committed in respect of breaching import and export controls, it is useful to understand the range of penalties that may be applied.

Penalties

As a general rule, the following consequences will apply where an offence is committed:

- The goods will be forfeited.
- If the director is found to have been knowingly involved in the exportation of the goods, and it is proved that he or she intended to evade any restrictions or prohibitions, he or she may be arrested.
- If tried and convicted of an offence in the magistrates court, the offender may be fined up to £5000 or a sum of three times the value of the goods (whichever is greater) and/or imprisoned for up to six months.
- If tried and convicted of an offence in the Crown court, the offender may face an unlimited fine and/or up to seven years imprisonment. Although the penalty may be 'unlimited' by law it should be an amount which the offender is financially capable of paying.
- In some specific cases, such as the exportation of forged bank notes or drugs, the penalties will be higher. If convicted of exporting class A drugs, the offender faces life imprisonment.
- By virtue of the fundamental principle that one cannot benefit from one's own wrong-doing, any proceeds that arise from the commission of the offence, ie money from drug trafficking, will be confiscated. If the proceeds have already been invested elsewhere, ie in property, the court can order the offender to pay the amount equal to the property bought with the proceeds.

OFFENCES

The import and export controls set out which acts constitute an offence. The offences range from smuggling (knowingly acquiring or carrying prohibited or restricted goods with intent to evade the restriction or prohibition) to refusing to be searched when asked by an HM Customs and Excise officer. Import and export offences are generally committed where the director or company is actively involved in breaking the law. However, it is important for the director to bear in mind that even if he or she is not directly involved in the commission of an offence, he or she may still be held liable for some indirect involvement in the offence.

Conspiracy to commit an offence

It is an offence to conspire to commit an offence, even if the actual act is not carried out in the end. Therefore any attempt to, for example, export banned goods or avoid paying customs duties, regardless of whether the attempt is actually successful, will amount to the offence of conspiracy if two or more directors of a company agree to breach an import or export control. The offence of conspiracy is committed the moment the agreement to break the law is made. A person found guilty of conspiracy to commit an offence is liable to face the same penalties that would be awarded for the actual commission of the offence itself, which, in most cases of import and export offences, could be an unlimited fine and/or up to seven years' imprisonment.

Money laundering

It is also an offence for anyone to acquire, use or possess any property which they know to have been bought with the proceeds of any criminal conduct. This would include, for example, using property that was bought with proceeds arising from the sale of illegally imported drugs. This would come under the general offence of money laundering. The penalty for money laundering can be up to 14 years' imprisonment.

As outlined above, most offences will be treated under the general scale under CEMA, although in specific cases the penalties will differ. The main import and export control offences are set out below.

Offences in relation to exportation of prohibited or restricted goods

Exportation of goods in contravention of a prohibition or restriction

It is an offence to export goods where the exportation is contrary to a prohibition or restriction. An example is the exportation of military equipment to a country with which trade is banned under a trade sanction. The severity of the penalty for such an offence will depend upon whether the company was knowingly exporting a good in contravention of the law and the potential dangerous effect of the goods in question. The penalties will be those outlined above.

Refusal to allow search by HM Customs and Excise officer

It is an offence to refuse to show the goods being carried, make a declaration as to the goods, or to allow oneself to be searched (without reasonable excuse) if requested by an HM Customs and Excise officer. The maximum fine for this offence is £1000. However, the above penalties will apply if the goods are later found to have been exported illegally.

Offences in relation to improper importation

Smuggling and possessing unlawfully imported goods

Smuggling is the offence of knowingly acquiring or carrying goods that are subject to an import prohibition or restriction, with the intent to evade the restriction or prohibition. In a recent case, an importer was convicted of smuggling rare parrots contrary to the Convention against the International Trade in Endangered Species (CITES). The guilty party was sentenced to 2½ years' imprisonment and ordered to pay £5000 costs. This was the highest ever sentence given in the English courts for an offence under CITES.

It is also an offence to simply possess goods, where the possession is subject to a restriction; for example, it is an offence to possess certain firearms without a proper licence. Where HM Customs and Excise discover that goods have been imported illegally and the goods are subject to restrictions in relation to possession, it will often prosecute the offender under the offence of 'unlawful possession' as there is no need to prove that the offender intended to avoid the import controls.

The penalties stated above will apply unless there is specific legislation dealing with the specific goods being imported, eg if convicted of unlawfully importing seal skins the offender may face up to two years' imprisonment.

Offences relating to the non-payment of customs duty

Customs duty is a tax levied on goods imported into the European Community from third countries. There are a number of offences connected with the non-payment of customs duties:

- It is an offence to knowingly acquire possession of goods that are chargeable with a duty which has not been paid, where this is done with an intent to defraud HM Customs and Excise of the duty payable on the goods. The penalties are as set out under the CEMA above.
- If the company is the importer, it is an offence to knowingly engage in any conduct for the purpose of avoiding any duty or excise. This includes obtaining, without being entitled to it, any repayment rebate, drawback, relief or exemption from duty. Again, the penalties are set out in CEMA above;
- Even if the company has innocently failed to pay customs duties on imported goods, it may still be penalized in so far that HM Customs and Excise will seek to recover those unpaid customs duties after importation. In a recent case, an importer was ordered to pay £180,000 in unpaid customs duties. In that case the importer had innocently believed that there were no customs duties payable on the imported goods because the certificate of origin issued by the authorities in the exporter's country said that the goods came from Korea. Such goods were classified in the customs code as being free of customs duties. However, it was later found that the exporter had lied about the origin and so HM Customs and Excise sought to recover the unpaid duties.

At present, penalties for failing to pay correct customs duties may be reduced or cancelled upon appeal although it is difficult to succeed. However, it is likely that during 2001 legislation will be enacted to implement a civil penalty regime in customs duties matters similar to those existing for value added tax (VAT). This will allow importers who transgress the rules and evade customs duty, in appropriate circumstances, not only to be dealt with outside the criminal law regime of customs but also, where relevant, to plead that they have a 'reasonable excuse' to avoid paying the civil penalty demand.

In considering whether the offender has a 'reasonable excuse' the court will be likely to ask two questions:

- Was the event which brought about the default beyond the person's control and could it not have been reasonably anticipated?

- Was the legal obligation to pay taken seriously and was there an intention to comply with the legal requirement?

HM Customs and Excise will not accept an insufficiency of funds or the failure of someone to whom a certain task was delegated (ie the task of paying the correct customs duties) as a 'reasonable excuse'.

Offences in relation to export and import licences

It is unlawful to import or export certain goods without a proper licence. As well as the offence of failing to obtain a licence where one is required, there are also less serious offences, such as making false statements when applying for a licence. In particular, company directors should be aware of the offences outlined below.

Making false statements
It is an offence to make, either knowingly or recklessly, a statement that is false in respect of an important fact in connection with an application for an import licence or an export licence. Similarly, it is an offence to either knowingly or recklessly make or sign a declaration addressed to HM Customs and Excise that is untrue with regard to an important fact. The maximum penalty for such an offence is a fine of £5000 and/or up to two years' imprisonment.

Failing to comply with a condition attached to a licence
There are conditions applied to export licences that require, for example, that certain notices be given to HM Customs and Excise and certain records kept when exporting goods. It is an offence to fail to comply with such conditions. It is a defence, however, if the condition that was not complied with had been modified without the importer's consent by the Secretary of State. Such offences will face the penalties under CEMA as outlined above.

CONCLUSION

It should not come as a real surprise to learn that company directors can be held personally liable where the company has committed an offence that has been committed with the consent, connivance, or was attributable to any neglect of the director – after all, a company acts through its directors.

However, given that a director can also be held liable for offences in which he or she has not been directly involved, any director should find out exactly which export or import controls may affect the company's business and properly supervise the importation and exportation of goods under such controls. Although the courts, in imposing penalties for import and export offences, are increasingly taking into account the commercial reality of this trade, it appears that, in order to avoid liability for a company breaching the law, a director must pass as a 'conscientious businessman'. In other words, directors should be able to demonstrate that the company takes its legal responsibilities under import and export controls seriously and fully intends to comply with them.

E-Commerce in World Trade

Åke Nilson, Chairman, ICC Electronic Commerce Project

BACKGROUND

We have all heard of the vast numbers and volumes involved in international trade, amounting to some US$5500 billion annually, with an estimated 7 per cent of these costs representing the administrative functions related to moving goods around the world. These administrative processes have traditionally been paper-based, slow and prone to error. Therefore anything that can help to make these information flows speedier and more efficient will result in great savings for all those currently involved in producing and moving the paper that controls the movement of the goods.

One major advance would be to convert the papers into their electronic equivalents, but to date the world of international trade has been relatively slow to adopt electronic trading techniques, due to a number of factors. Perhaps the most obvious is the nature of the business environment. Although the trade of a cargo of goods may involve just two parties, the buyer and the seller, many other parties need to become involved in the process of getting the goods from one part of the globe to another. These parties may include the shipping line, freight forwarder, the bank, Customs, an inspection company, the Chamber of Commerce etc, and until they are all able to carry out their parts in the trade electronically the overall cost savings and increased speed and efficiency do not begin to take effect.

The other issue that concerns those involved in trade, as with most other business-to-business (B2B) applications, is that of security. The values of the cargoes that are being shipped are generally high; the average cargo shipment is estimated to be worth US$30,000. The paperwork supporting the trade is also valuable, particularly when a negotiable bill of lading is involved, as it embodies the title to the goods. Therefore, there must be a way of signing and securing the electronic documents, so that the traders can prove who has the title to the goods at any one time, and this has not been a simple problem to solve in the electronic world. The security of the data itself is also at issue; for instance an exporter or importer, or indeed a shipping line, would not be happy for all its trade data to be accessible to its competitors.

The security issues can be solved in the electronic scenario with the use of digital security, within what is known as a 'public key' infrastructure (PKI). This involves each user being able to sign electronic documents with a digital signature. In order to create a digital signature, the signatory makes use of a cryptographic key pair, made up of a public and private key. He signs the document with his private key and the recipient of the document then uses the corresponding public key to check that the document is from the person in question, and that the message has not been tampered with in transit. The public key is certified by a Certification Authority (CA) which verifies the link between the key and a specific person by providing the user with a digital certificate. This digital certificate is a statement by the CA that a certain public key belongs to this person. A copy of this certificate is sent along with the signed message. Certain CAs will assume liability in connection with the certificates they are issuing, which means that the recipient also has recourse if something relating to the certificate goes wrong.

Using this digital technology does not, however, solve the issue of electronic negotiability. For a document such as the bill of lading it is important to know who is the holder of the original document at any one time, since it represents title to the goods. In an electronic environment there is no such thing as an original and, therefore, a different solution has to be sought. Bolero.net, which is a service offering a secure exchange for electronic documentation using digital security, also offers a title registry function to address the issue of negotiability. Here, a record is kept centrally of who is the holder of the electronic version of any active document. Requests for changes and updates to ownership can only be carried out by the current holder sending a relevant, digitally signed message to the registry. Therefore it is always clear who is the holder at any one time and the concept of negotiability is maintained. Bolero.net also offers a legal framework which puts the person issuing or holding the electronic bill of lading in the same position legally as if it were a paper document.

However, international trade is now waking up slowly to the possibilities that the Internet and electronic communication can offer. Starting at the beginning of the trade cycle when the deal is actually being set up, there are now several B2B exchanges. These are marketplaces for the trading of goods. Some are specific to one product, eg a commodity exchange for coffee, sugar, metals etc where, rather than there being an actual trading floor where the traders deal face to face, the Internet acts as a virtual exchange. Access to this particular type of service is likely to be limited to known traders who have signed up to the service. Other marketplaces use online auctions as a framework for the bidding for, and selling of, goods. Possibly the most prevalent type of service is the bulletin board, which offers a wide range of goods for sale over the Internet. Any trader interested in buying clicks on the relevant offer and can negotiate a deal with the person who is offering the goods.

The use of such virtual markets means that traders have much easier access to products, and a wider range from which to choose. Global information on the market is also much more freely available. However, the trader does not always know who he is trading with or whether they are trustworthy. As such, digital signatures and PKI can bring a greater security to the trade. When all parties have been registered by a reputable CA service as described above, the trader has some element of comfort that the party at the other end of the trade is who he says he is.

The next step of the process would be to agree a contract. The International Chamber of Commerce (ICC) in conjunction with Allagraf Limited is currently setting up a service to offer an online version of its International Model Sales Contract. This Internet version of the contract will enable the buyer or seller to select interactively the terms, Incoterms (the standard delivery terms for international trade) and customs codes required for the trade. The text that is automatically produced, once all terms have been input, can then be accessed and amended by the other party to the trade, if necessary. Digital security will enable the electronic document to be signed by both parties so that it need never exist in paper form. It is also the intention that the interactive contract system be available as an adjunct to B2B exchanges, so that traders can negotiate a suitable international sale contract once they have agreed the deal.

For services covering the physical transport of goods from one place to another, there are web-based services provided by businesses known as 'shipping portals.' Although some of these shipping portals only offer information and news on the shipping industry, some also offer the trader the opportunity to arrange some or all of the services he needs to ship, inspect and insure the goods electronically. Although it is likely in the current climate that some of these services will not survive and that there will be much consolidation, those portals with a solid business model for bringing in revenues by offering a value-added service to the parties of the international trade will be able to expand and prosper.

Depending on the terms and conditions and financing of the trade, a number of documents (20 on average) will be needed. These will cover the paperwork involved in the shipping, invoicing, insurance, inspection and customs clearance, among other things. These documents come from different sources and have to be collected together and sent in parallel with the cargo, so that they are available for release of the cargo at the port of destination. Having all this documentation on different pieces of paper originating from the different parties often leads to discrepancies, inefficiencies and delays.

Bolero.net is a service that has been set up to offer a secure exchange for electronic documentation relating to international trade. The commercial bolero.net service was set up by the Society for Worldwide Interbank Financial Telecommunication (SWIFT), the banks' network and the TT Club, a mutual transport insurer. Bolero.net has recently announced that it has raised a further US$50 million to accelerate the growth of the service, which will help to cut out the inefficiencies involved in paper trade documentation. This service, however, is not just offering a technical solution; there is also a rulebook to which the users have to sign up, and this provides a legally secure framework. Rigorous registration processes and the use of digital security add up to the bolero.net system being secure enough for seven out of the world's top ten banks, as well as major trading houses such as Mitsui and Marubeni and carriers such as K Line, Cosco and Evergreen, to sign up to use it as a central part of their trade documentation processes.

Due to their involvement in the finance of many of these international trades the banks are very interested in anything that will cut down on the administration and reduce the number of errors that occur in the documentation. They see bolero.net as a way of achieving this. There are also new organizations which aim specifically at providing the actual trade finance process as an electronic service. TradeCard offers a payment settlement solution to allow B2B marketplaces to offer their customers end-to-end transaction services, using digital security technology. This is particularly aimed at small and medium-sized organizations. It is currently available for transactions between Hong Kong, Korea, Taiwan, Singapore, Canada and the USA and is expected to expand its services to Japan by early 2001 and to China, Western Europe and Latin America by late 2001.

Some more recent announcements of services in this space are CCEWeb's @GlobalTrade service, which bills itself as 'the first fully open and secure system for completing and financing trade deals over the Internet'. It is due to run a pilot between April and August 2001 (to be launched in the autumn) with major participants from the world of international trade and will be launching a commercial service in the autumn of 2001.

Meanwhile Citigroup, Enron Broadband Services, i2 Technologies Inc, S1 Corporation and Wells Fargo and Company have also announced the formation of a company to streamline buying, selling and facilitating payments in B2B commerce. The company called FinancialSettlementMatrix.com intends to offer a complete and open payments system to those e-marketplaces allowing buyers and sellers to access services provided by any of the participating banks or financial services companies.

When all these electronic services covering the different parts of trade become widely available and used, it will be possible for an exporter or importer to carry out a seamless secure electronic trade process from the start of a trade to the finish. All the requisite documents can be produced automatically, thus cutting down on errors, and transmitted electronically to make the whole process far faster and more efficient. The increased accessibility that the Internet offers to all businesses will enable those who have previously not sold their goods internationally to do so and, with the electronic services available to support these trades, to do so more effectively.

THE ROLE OF THE ICC IN E-COMMERCE

The ICC is *the* world business organization – the only global voice for business. Since its establishment in 1919, businesses around the world have been looking to the ICC to promote their interests, and also to create a stable set of rules within which to trade.

Among the ICC's best known sets of rules are Incoterms and UCP 500, the standard practices under which banks handle documentary credit transactions. The ICC also supports international trade through its Court of Arbitration, by setting policies in fields varying from maritime transport through environmental concerns to taxation. And of course, it is also active in e-commerce.

The ICC's role representing international business makes it ideally placed to look at the issues that e-Commerce raises and to put in place some guidelines as to how its members, and commerce in general, can benefit from using e-commerce, while minimizing the risks. Therefore, in 1994, the ICC launched its Electronic Commerce Project (ECP) with the objective of creating global trust in electronic trade transactions by defining best business practices for the digital age. The ECP takes input from many of the other commissions of the ICC, since the issues of e-commerce cover all industry sectors. These commissions include banking technique and practices, telecommunications and information technologies, financial services and insurance, and transport and international commercial practice. The ECP has attempted to work in areas which do not overlap with work being carried out by other national and international organizations.

There are Working Groups concentrating on different areas such as information security, e-terms, electronic trade practices and the Model Sales Contract.

The InfoSec Group has released a first edition of the *GUIDEC* (General Usage for Internationally Digitally Ensured Commerce) which is available from ICC Publications and over the ICC website. This document sets out harmonized definitions and rules for the use of electronic authentication techniques, including digital signatures and certificates. It is widely referred to as one of the first truly global pieces of business self-regulation of electronic commerce. This has now been updated and a new version was completed in March 2001. The same Group is also producing the *Pofec* (Principles of Fair Electronic Contracting) which is a set of guidelines for automatic contracting between communicating computer systems. A first draft of this was presented at the next general meeting of the ECP in May 2001.

The E-Terms Group has been working on a project to provide an online repository of electronic trading terms and rules for reference by those involved in international trade. The project is now looking for sponsors to turn it into a commercial reality.

The Electronic Trade Practices Working Group is working on best practice for e-commerce traders: this is the area most closely related to the activities of the world of trade finance and international trade initiatives such as the bolero.net service.

The final group currently working in this area is a group of legal experts (which includes the Chairman of the Commission on International Commercial Practice) that, as described above, is defining how the ICC's Model International Sale Contract could be made available over the Internet so that those involved in international trade can make and negotiate their own specific contracts according to the terms and conditions required.

Outside the Electronic Commerce Project, the ICC Banking Commission has spent some time in discussing what it should do in relation to the electronic world. The UCP 500 and its predecessors are a set of rules on documentary credits which has been developed by this Commission. It has been drafted with the paper world in mind and the Banking Commission has, after much consideration, now decided that it should put together an electronic supplement which looks specifically at the electronic issues related to documentary credits. This would be called the eUCP, and be annexed to the ICC's rules on letters of credit UCP 500. This project was discussed at the meeting of the Banking Commission held in Istanbul on 21 and 22 November 2000. The eUCP Working Group has developed a first draft which will be voted on by the ICC Banking Commission at its meeting in November.

These are all projects which aim at supporting and underpinning the move of world trade into the electronic era. They have begun to offer a framework under which those involved in the sale and transport of goods worldwide can work and have the same level of comfort that they have in using the traditional paper methods. In much the same way as the ICC has its publishing arm to produce, sell and distribute the rules and guidelines that are produced by its membership in paper form, the intention is for the ICC to become involved in the marketing and distribution of the new electronic products such as the Interactive Model International Sale Contract, and the repository for e-terms.

Appendices

Appendix I

Membership of Regional Trading Groups

ANDEAN: Bolivia   Columbia   Ecuador
           Peru   Venezuela

APEC:

Australia	Brunei Darussalem	Canada
Chile	Hong Kong	China
Indonesia	Japan	Republic of Korea
Malaysia	Mexico	New Zealand
Papua New Guinea	Peru	Philippines
Russian Federation	Singapore	Taipei, Chinese
Thailand	USA	Viet Nam

ASEAN:

Brunei Darussalem	Cambodia	Indonesia
Lao PDR	Malaysia	Myanmar
Philippines	Singapore	Thailand
Viet Nam		

CEFTA:

Bulgaria	Czech Republic	Hungary
Poland	Romania	Slovenia
Slovak Republic		

EUROPEAN UNION:

Austria	Belgium	Denmark
Finland	France	Germany
Greece	Ireland	Italy
Luxembourg	Netherlands	Portugal
Spain	Sweden	United Kingdom

MERCOSUR:

Argentina	Brazil	Paraguay
Uruguay		

NAFTA: Canada   Mexico   USA

SAPTA: Bangladesh   Bhutan   India
          Maldives   Nepal   Pakistan
          Sri Lanka

Six East Asian traders:

Hong Kong	China	Malaysia
Republic of Korea	Singapore	Taipei Chinese
Thailand		

Appendix II

Least-developed Countries (LDCs)

Afghanistan	Angola	Bangladesh	Benin
Bhutan	Burkina Faso	Burundi	Cambodia
Cape Verde	Central African Rep.	Chad	Comoros
Dem. Rep. of Congo	Djibouti	Equatorial Guinea	Eritrea
Ethiopia	Gambia	Guinea-Bissau	Guinea
Haiti	Kiribati	Lao PDR	Lesotho
Liberia	Madagascar	Malawi	Maldives
Mali	Mauritania	Mozambique	Myanmar
Nepal	Niger	Rwanda	Samoa
Sao Tome & Principe	Sierra Leone	Solomon Islands	Somalia
Sudan	Togo	Tuvalu	Uganda
Tanzania	Vanuatu	Yemen	Zambia

Appendix III

International Chamber of Commerce (ICC) National Committees and Groups

Note: in some cases where the ICC does not have a separate website we have, in some cases, supplied the website for the local Chamber of Commerce.

ICC ALGERIA

c/o Chambre Algerienne de Commerce et d'Industrie (CACI)
Palais Consulaire, 6 Boulvard Amilcar Cabral
16003 Algiers
Algeria
Tel: +213-21 966666
Fax: +213-21 969999
Contact: Mohamed Chami, Secretary General

ICC ARGENTINA

c/o Camara Argentina de Comercio
Avenida Leandro N. Alem 36
C 1003 AAN Buenos Aires
Argentina
Tel: +54-11 53009097
Fax: +54-11 53009036
E-mail: iccargentina@cac.com.ar
Website: www.cac.com.ar
Contact: Herberto Hugo Karplus, Secretary General

ICC AUSTRALIA

Level 3, North Tower, Rialto Towers
525 Collins Street
3000 Melbourne
Australia

Tel: +61-3 86082072
Fax: +61-3 86082547
E-mail: publications@iccaustralia.org
Website: www.iccaustralia.org
Contact: Michael Pryles, Acting Chair

ICC AUSTRIA
Wiedner Hauptstrasse 63
A-1045 Wien
Austria
Tel: +43-1 501053701
Fax: +43-1 501053703
E-mail: icc@wko.at
Website: www.icc-austria.org
Maximilian Burger-Scheidlin, Executive Director

ICC BAHRAIN
P.O. Box 248
Bahrain
Tel: +973 227306
Fax: +973 212937
E-mail: a.rahim@bahrainchamber.org.bh
Website: www.bahrainchamber.org.bh
Contact: Abrahim Mohamed Ali Zainal, Chair

ICC BANGLADESH
Dhaka Chamber Bldg (Ground Floor)
65–66 Motijheel C/A, P.O. Box 3861
1000 Dhaka
Bangladesh
Tel: +880-2 9557478
Fax: +880-2 9557429
E-mail: iccb@citechco.net
Website: www.icc.bwbo.org/iccbd.htm
Contact: Mohammed Zafar Hamid, Secretary

ICC BELGIUM
c/o Fédération des Entreprises de Belgique
Rue des Sols, 8
1000 Bruxelles
Belgium
Tel: +32-2 5150899
Fax: +32-2 5130494
E-mail: cci@vbo-feb.be
Website: www.icc.wbo.be
Contact: Donatienne de Cartier d'Yves, Attachée

ICC BRAZIL
Avenida General Justo, 307-8° Andar
20021-130 Rio de Janeiro , RJ
Brazil
Tel: +55-21 25326015
Fax: +55-21 25442821
E-mail: icc@cnc.com.br
Website: www.cnc.com.br
Contact: Ernane Galvêas, Secretary General

ICC BURKINA-FASO
c/o Chambre de Commerce, d'Industrie et d'Artisanat
01 B.P. 502+E67
Ouagadougou 01
Burkina Faso
Tel: +226 306114
Fax: +226 306116
Website: ccia-bf@cenatrin.bf
Contact: Oumarou Kanazoé, President

ICC CAMEROON
c/o CCIMA
B.P. 36
Yaounde
Cameroon
Tel: +237 9842077
Fax: +237 2213077
E-mail: icc cmr@hotmail.com
Contact: Francis Elandi, Secretary General

CANADIAN COUNCIL FOR INTERNATIONAL BUSINESS
Delta Office Tower, Suite 501
350 Sparks Street
Ottawa, Ontario K1R 7S8
Canada
Tel: +1-613 2304562
Fax: +1-613 2307087
Website: www.ccib.org
Contact: Alex Lofthouse, Director, Policy

ICC CARIBBEAN
P.O. Box 499
Columbus Circle, West Moorings
Port of Spain
Trinidad W.I.
Tel: +1-868 6376966
Fax: +1-868 6377425
E-mail: chamber@chamber.org.tt
Website: www.chamber.org.tt/icc_publishers
Contact: Michelle Fournillier, Secretary

ICC CHINA
c/o China Chamber of International Commerce (CCOIC)
1, Fu Xin Men Wai Street
Beijing 100860
China
Tel: +86-10 6804 1275
Fax: +86-10 6802 3554
E-mail: hfli@public.east.cn.net
Website: www.icc-china.org
Contact: Li Haifeng, Executive Director

ICC COLOMBIA
c/o Camara de Comercio de Bogota
Carrera 9, N° 16-21 - P.O. Box 29824
Santa Fe De Bogota
Colombia
Tel: +57-1 3810324
Fax: +57-1 2842966

E-mail: asesorri@ccb.org.co
Website: www.ccb.org.co
Contact: Andres Lopez Valderrama, Secretary General

ICC COSTA RICA
c/o Camara de Comercio de Costa Rica
Opposite Publicidad Garnier, Barrio Tournon
San Jose
Costa Rica
Tel: +506 2210005 ext 122
Fax: +506 2569680
E-mail: cci@camara-comercio.com
Website: www.camara-comercio.com
Contact: Marcela Chavarria Pozuelo, Secretary General

ICC CROATIA
Rooseveltov trg 2
10000 Zagreb
Croatia
Tel: +385-1 4561555
Fax: +385-1 4828380

ICC CUBA
c/o Cámara de Comercio de la Rep. de Cuba
Calle 21 Esq. a A, N° 661, Vedado
Ciudad de la Habana
Cuba
Tel: +53-78 312404
Fax: +53-78 333042
E-mail: ccicuba@camara.com.cu
Website: www.camaracuba.com
Contact: Sara Marta Diaz Rodriguez, Secretary General

ICC CYPRUS
c/o Cyprus Chamber of Commerce
P.O. Box 21455
38, Grivas Dighenis Av & 3 Deligiorgis Str.
Nicosia
Cyprus

Tel: +357 22889800
Fax: +357 22669048
E-mail: chamber@ccci.org.cy
Website: www.ccci.org.cy
Contact: Panayiotis Loizides, Secretary General

ICC CZECH REPUBLIC
Freyova 27
190 00 Praha 9
Czech Republic
Tel: +420-2 24096018
Fax: +420-2 24096251
E-mail: icc@icc-cr.cz
Website: www.icc-cr.cz
Contact: Vladimir Prokop, Executive Director

ICC DENMARK
c/o Danish Chamber of Commerce
Börsen
1217 Copenhagen
Denmark
Tel: +45 70131200
Fax: +45 70131201
E-mail: mail@iccdanmark.dk
Website: www.iccdanmark.dk
Contact: Lars Krobaek, Secretary General

ICC ECUADOR
Av. Francisco de Orellana y Victor Sicouret
Ed. Centro Empresarial "Las Cámaras", piso 3
Guayaquil Casilla 09-01-7515
Ecuador
Tel: +593-4 2682771
Fax: +593-4 2682725
E-mail: iccecuador@lacamara.org
Contact: Augusto Alvarado Garcia, Executive Director

ICC EGYPT
c/o Fed. of Egyptian Chambers of Commerce
4 Falaky Square
Cairo
Egypt
Tel: +20-2 7951835
Fax: +20-2 7945872
E-mail: icceg@hotmail.com
Contact: Abdel Sattar Eshrah, Executive Secretary General

ICC FINLAND
World Trade Center Helsinki
Aleksanterinkatu 17, P.O. Box 1000
00100 Helsinki
Finland
Tel: +358-9 669459
Fax: +358-9 69696647
E-mail: icc@wtc.fi
Website: www.iccfin.fi
Contact: Timo Vuori, Secretary General

ICC FRANCE
9, rue d'Anjou
75008 Paris
France
Tel: +0142651266
Fax: +0149240639
E-mail: cnfcci@dial.oleane.com
Contact: Marie Psimènos de Metz-Noblat, Secretary General

ICC GEORGIA
1, Nutzubidze Street
380077 Tbilisi
Georgia
Tel: +995-32 251436
Fax: +995-32 537123
E-mail: icc@icc.ge
Contact: Saba Sarishvili, Secretary General

ICC GERMANY
Mittelstrasse 12–14
50672 Cologne
Germany
Tel: +49-221 2575571
Fax: +49-221 2575593
E-mail: icc@icc-deutschland.de
Website: www.icc-deutschland.de
Contact: Angelika Pohlenz, Secretary General

ICC GHANA
c/o Ghana National Chamber of Commerce & Industry
P.O. Box 2325
Accra
Ghana
Tel: +233-21 662427
Fax: +233-21 662210
E-mail: gncc@ncs.com.gh
Contact: Salathiel Doe Amegavie, Secretary General

ICC GREECE
27 Kaningos Street
10682 Athens
Greece
Tel: +30-210 3810879
Fax: +Fax: +30-210 3831189
E-mail: iccgr@otenet.gr
Contact: Alexandros Modiano, Secretary General

HONG KONG
China Business Council of ICC
12th Floor, Kwong Fat Hong Building
1 Rumsay Street
Sheung Wan
Hong Kong
Tel: +852 29730006
Fax: +852 28690360
E-mail: general@icchkcbc.org
Website: www.icchkcbc.org
Contact: Anthony Chan, Secretary

ICC HUNGARY
Kossuth Lajos tér, 6-8
1055 Budapest
Hungary
Tel: +36-1 4740043
Fax: +36-1 4740042
E-mail: hun.icc@axelero.hu
Website: www.icc.co.hu
Contact: Lajos Kustos, Secretary General

ICC ICELAND
House of Commerce
Kringlan 7
103 Reykjavik
Iceland
Tel: +354 5107100
Fax: +354 5686564
E-mail: icc@chamber.is
Website: www.chamber.is/iccis.htm
Contact: Lara Solnes, General Manager

ICC INDIA
Federation House
Tansen Marg
New Delhi 110 001
India
Tel: +91-11 23738760
Fax: +91-11 23320714
E-mail: iccindia@iccindiaonline.org
Website: www.iccindiaonline.org
Ashok Ummat, Executive Director

ICC INDONESIA
Menara Kadin Indonesia
Jalan H.R. Rasuna Said, X-5, Kav. 2-3
Jakarta 12950
Indonesia
Tel: +62-21 5274284
Fax: +62-21 5274286
Contact: Sugihono Kadarisman, Executive Director

ICC IRAN
254, Taleghani Avenue
Room 504, 5th Floor
Tehran
Iran (Islamic Republic of)
Tel: +98-21 8306127
Fax: +98-21 8308330
Website: icciran2000@yahoo.com
Contact: Hadi Dastbaz, Secretary General

ICC IRELAND
17 Merrion Square
Dublin 2
Ireland
Tel: +353-1 6612888
Fax: +353-1 6612811
E-mail: info@chambersireland.ie
Website: www.chambersireland.ie
Martina Diegmann, Executive

ICC ISRAEL
84, Hahashmonaim Street
P.O. Box 20027
Tel Aviv 61200
Israel
Tel: +972-3 5631048
972-3 5619027
E-mail: icc@chamber.org.il
Website: www.chamber.org.il
Contact: Itzhak Y. Kashiv, Secretary General

ICC ITALY
Via Venti Settembre N.5
00187 Rome
Italy
Tel: +39-06 42034301
Fax: +39-06 4882677
E-mail: icc.cci.italia@flashnet.it
Website: www.cciitalia.org
Amerigo Rutilio Gori, Secretary General

ICC JAPAN
Taisho Seimei Hibiya Bldg 5F
1-9-1 Yuraku-Cho, Chiyoda-ku
Tokyo 100-0006
Japan
Tel: +81-3 32138585
Fax: +81-3 32138589
E-mail: icc@iccjapan.org
Website: www.iccjapan.org
Contact: Shigeo Hashimoto, Secretary General

ICC JORDAN
P.O. Box 940170
Amman 11194
Jordan
Tel: +962-6 5665492
Fax: +962-6 5685997
E-mail: international_chamber@nets.com.jo
Contact: Amin Husseini, Secretary General

ICC KOREA
Gateway Tower Bldg.
12, Dongja-dong, Yongsan-gu
Seoul 140-709
Korea (Republic of)
Tel: +82-2 3163541
Fax: +82-2 7579475
Email: 07978@korcham.net
Website: www.korcham.net
Contact: Seung-Woon Kim, Secretary General

ICC KUWAIT
P.O. Box N° 775
Safat
Kuwait
Tel: +965 805580
Fax: +965 2404110
E-mail: natik@kcci.org.kw
Website: www.kcci.org.kw
Contact: Majed Jamaluddin, Secretary General

ICC LEBANON
c/o Beirut Chamber of Commerce & Industry
G. Haimari Str., E. Abdel-Nour Bldg.
Achrafieh-Sassine, P.O. Box 11-1801
Beirut
Lebanon
Tel: +961-1 200437
961-1 321220
E-mail: iccleb@sodetel.net.lb
Contact: Carla René Saadé, Secretary General

ICC LITHUANIA
Vokieciu Str. 28/17
2001 Vilnius
Lithuania
Tel: +370-5 2121111
Fax: +370-5 2122621
E-mail: info@tprl.lt
Website: www.tprl.lt
Contact: Algimantas Akstinas, Executive Director

ICC LUXEMBOURG
31, Boulevard Konrad Adenauer
2981 Luxembourg
Luxembourg
Tel: +352 423939303
Fax: +352 438326
E-mail: direction@cc.lu
Website: www.cc.lu
Contact: Pierre Gramegna, Secretary General

ICC MEXICO
Edificio WTC, Oficina No. 20, Piso 14
Av. de las Naciones, 1 Colonia Napoles
03810 Mexico, D.F.
Mexico
Tel: +52-55 54882678
Fax: +52-55 54882680
E-mail: camecic@iccmex.org.mx

Website: www.iccmex.org.mx
Contact: Carlos Espinosa Castillo, Executive Director

ICC MONACO
c/o Chambre de Développement Economique
Imme Tel: +uble "Le Concorde", 11, rue du Gabian
98000 Monaco
Monaco
Tel: +377 97986868
Fax: +377 97986869
E-mail: info@cde.mc
Website: www.cde.mc
Contact: Jean-Pierre Fonteneau, Secretary General

ICC MONGOLIA
c/o Mongolia National Chamber of Commerce and Industry
MNCCI Building, Sambuu Str. 39
Ulaanbaatar 11
Mongolia
Tel: +976-11 312501
Fax: +976-11 324620
Email: tecd@mongolchamber.mn
Website: www.mongolchamber.mn
Contact: Mrs Oyunchimeg, Secretary General

ICC MOROCCO
201, Boulevard de Bordeaux
Appartement 505 - 5ème étage
20 000 Casablanca
Morocco
Tel: +212-22 225111
Fax: +212-22 225119
E-mail: icc@casanet.net.ma
Contact: Abderrahman Tazi, President

ICC NEPAL
Chamber Bhawan
P.O. Box 198, Kantipath
Kathmandu

Nepal
Tel: +977-1 230947
Fax: +977-1 229998
E-mail: iccnepalnc@wlink.com.np
Contact: Surendra Bir Malakar, Secretary General

ICC NETHERLANDS
Postbus 95309
2509-CH Den Haag
Netherlands
Tel: +31-70 3836646
Fax: +31-70 3819563
E-mail: info@icc.nl
Website: www.icc.nl
Contact: Wilko Gunster, Secretary General

ICC NEW ZEALAND
c/o Auckland Regional Chamber of Commerce and Industry
100 Mayoral Drive - P.O. Box 47
Auckland
New Zealand
Tel: +64-9 3096100
Fax: +64-9 3029919
E-mail: akl@chamber.co.nz
Website: www.chamber.co.nz
Contact: Michael Barnett, Secretary General

ICC NIGERIA
c/o Nigeria Employers, Consultative Association (NECA)
Elephant Cement House (6th Floor)
ASSBIFI Road - Central Business District
Aluasa- Ikeja, P.O. Box 2231, Marina
Lagos
Nigeria
Tel: +234-1 7742734
Fax: +234-1 4962571
E-mail: oshinowo@necang.com
Contact: O. A. Oshinowo, Secretary General

ICC NORWAY
Drammensvn. 30
P.O. Box 2483 Solli
0202 Oslo
Norway
Tel: +47 22541700
Fax: +472 22561700
E-mail: post@iccnorge.no
Website: www.iccnorge.no
Contact: Lisbeth Grondahl Kaarem, Secretary General

ICC PAKISTAN
V.M. House, West Wharf Road
P.O. Box No 4050
Karachi – 74000
Pakistan
Tel: +92-21 2311365
Fax: +92-21 2310602
E-mail: iccpak@cyber.net.pk
Website: www.iccpakistan.com
Contact: Javaid Basini, Secretary

ICC PERU
Avenida Gregorio Escobedo 396
Lima 11
Peru
Tel: +51-1 4634263
Fax: +51-1 4639629
E-mail: icc-peru@ccom.org
Contact: Monica Watson Aramburu, Secretary General

ICC PHILIPPINES
c/o Philippine Foundation for Global Concerns
43/F Philamlife Tower, 8767 Paseo de Roxas
Makati City 1226
Philippines
Tel: +63-2 8436536
Fax: +63-2 8454832
Contact: Antonio I. Basilio, Secretary General

ICC POLAND
c/o Polish Bank Association
Smolna 10A
00-375 Warszawa
Poland
Tel: +48-22 8222744
Fax: +48-22 8281406
E-mail: pawel@zbp.pl
Website: www.iccpolska.pl
Contact: Pawel Pniewski, Secretary General

ICC PORTUGAL
c/o Camara de Comercio e Industria Portuguesa
Rua das Portas de Santo Antao, 89
1150-266 Lisboa
Portugal
Tel: +351-21 3463304
Fax: +351-21 3224052
E-mail: icc@port-chambers.com
Contact: Joao Mendes de Almeida, President

ICC QATAR
P.O. Box 15213
Doha
Qatar
Tel: +974 4418181
Fax: +974 4809775
Email: iccqatar@qatar.net.qa
Contact: Samir Fakhouri, Secretary General

ICC ROMANIA
2, Octavian Goga Boulevard
Bucharest 3
Romania
Tel: +40-21 3229516
Fax: +40-21 3229517
E-mail: dre@ccir.ro
Website: www.ccir.ro
Contact: Mariana Lodroman, Secretary

ICC RUSSIA

3rd Floor, Office 342
17/1 Kotelnicheskaya Nab.
109240 Moscow
Russian Federation
Tel: +7-095 7205080
Fax: +7-095 7205081
E-mail: iccadmin@iccwbo.ru
Website: www.iccwbo.ru
Contact: Tanya Monaghan, Secretary General

ICC SAUDI ARABIA

c/o Council of Saudi Chambers of Commerce
P.O. Box 16683
Riyadh 11474
Saudi Arabia
Tel: +966-1 4053200
Fax: +966-1 4024747
E-mail: council@saudichambers.org.sa
Website: www.saudichambers.org.sa
Contact: Talal A. Arif, Executive Director

SENEGAL

Centre d'Arbitrage de Mediation et de Conciliation
Chambre de Commerce, d'Industrie & d'Agriculture
1, Place de l'Indépendance, B.P. 118
Dakar
Senegal
Tel: +221 8236515
Fax: +221 8234898
E-mail: centarbi@sentoo.sn
Contact: Amadou Dieng, Permanent Secretary

ICC SERBIA AND MONTENEGRO

Terazije 23
31000 Uzice
Serbia and Montenegro
Tel: +381-11 3248123
Fax: +381-11 3248754

E-mail: cooperation@pkj.co.yu
Website: www.pkj.co.yu
Contact: Olivera Kiro, Secretary General

ICC SINGAPORE
c/oSingapore Business Federation
19 Tanglin Road - #10-01 to 07
Singapore 247909
Singapore
Tel: +65 68276828
Fax: +65 68276807
E-mail: info@sbf.org.sg
Website: www.sbf.org.sg
Contact: David Chin, Executive Director

SLOVAK CHAMBER OF COMMERCE AND INDUSTRY
Gorhéko 9
816 03 Bratislava
Slovakia
Tel: +421-2 54433291
Fax: +421-2 54131159
E-mail: sopkurad@sopk.sk
Website: www.icc-nc.sk
Contact: Peter Mihók, President

ICC SLOVENIA
Dimiceva 13
1504 Ljubljana
Slovenia
Tel: +386-1 5895000
Fax: +386-1 5898100
Contact: Andrej Friedl, Secretary General

ICC SOUTH AFRICA
P.O. Box 213
Saxonwold 2132
South Africa
Tel: +27-11 4463800
Fax: +27-11 4463850
Contact: James Lennox, Secretary

ICC SPAIN
Avinguda Diagonal, 452–454
08006 Barcelona
Spain
Tel: +34-93 4169300
Fax: +34-93 4169301
E-mail: iccspain@cambrabcn.es
Website: www.cambrabcn.es
Contact: Luis Solá Vilardell, Secretary General

ICC SRI LANKA
141/7 Vauxhall Street
Colombo 02
Sri Lanka
Tel: +94-1 307825
Fax: +94-1 307841
E-mail: iccsl@ltnet.lk
Website: www.iccsl.lk
Contact: Gamini Peiris, Chief Executive Officer

ICC SWEDEN
Västra Trädgardsgatan 9
P.O. Box 16050
103 27 Stockholm
Sweden
Tel: +46-8 4408920
Fax: +46-8 4113115
E-mail: icc@icc.se
Website: www.icc.se
Contact: Tell Hermanson, Secretary General

ICC SWITZERLAND
c/o Economiesuisse
Hegibachstrasse 47
Postfach 1072
8032 Zurich
Switzerland
Tel: +41-1 4213450
Fax: +41-1 4213488

E-mail: info@icc-switzerland.ch
Website: www.icc-switzerland.ch
Contact: Florent Roduit, Secretary General

ICC SYRIA

c/o Federation of Syrian Chambers of Commerce
Engineers Bldg, 12/F, Off. 1201, Maysloon St.
Damascus
Syrian Arab Republic
Tel: +963-11 2450495
Fax: +963-11 2450496
E-mail: iccsyria@net.sy
Contact: Abdul Rahman Attar, Chair

TAIWAN

Chinese Taipei Business Council of ICC
7th Floor, No. 85, Section 4
Ba De Road
Taipei105
Taiwan
Tel: +886-2 25288833
Fax: +886-2 27425342
E-mail: service@cieca.org.tw
Contact: Shin-Yuan Lai, Secretary General

ICC TANZANIA

7th Floor, Haidery Plaza Building
Ali Hassan Mwinyi Road, P.O. Box 163
Dar-Es-Salaam
Tanzania
Tel: +255-22 2119353
Fax: +255-22 2119360
E-mail: hq@ipp.co.tz
Contact: Agapitus L. Nguma, Secretary General

ICC THAILAND

Board of Trade of Thailand Building, 3/F
150/2 Rajbopit Road
BANGKOK 10200

Thailand
Tel: +66-2 2210555
Fax: +66-2 2255475
E-mail: admin@iccthailand.or.th
Website: www.iccthailand.or.th
Contact: Sawitree Ratanachand, Managing Director

ICC TOGO
c/o CCI du Togo
Angle Avenue de la Présidence
Avenue Georges Pompidou
B.P. 360, Lome
Togo
Tel: +228 2212065
Fax: +228 2214730
E-mail: ccit@rdd.tg
Contact: Yazas Egbarè Tchohou, Secretary General

ICC TUNISIA
1, rue des Entrepreneurs
Tunis 1000
Tunisia
Tel: +216-71 341607
Fax: +216-71 354744
Email: ccitunis@planet.tn
Contact: Moncef Kooli, Secretary General

ICC TURKEY
Atatürk Bulvari N°149
06640 Bakanliklar-Ankara
Turkey
Tel: +90-312 4178733
Fax: +90-312 4171483
E-mail: icc-tr@tobb.org.tr
Contact: Demet Ariyak, Executive Director

ICC UKRAINE
c/o Ukrainian League of Industrialists & Entrepreneurs
34 Khreschatik Street

01001 Kiev
Ukraine
Tel: +380-44 2244273
Fax: +380-44 2263152
E-mail: office@iccua.org
Website: www.iccua.org
Contact: Volodymyr Mykhaylov, Secretary General

ICC UNITED KINGDOM

12 Grosvenor Place
London SW1X 7HH
United Kingdom
Tel: +44-20 78232811
Fax: +44-20 72355447
Website: www.iccuk.net
Contact: Richard C.I. Bate, Director

US COUNCIL FOR INTERNATIONAL BUSINESS

1212 Avenue of the Americas
21st Floor
New York , NY 10036
United States
Tel: +1-212 3544480
Fax: +1-212 5750327
E-mail: info@uscib.org
Website: www.uscib.org
Contact: Peter M. Robinson, Senior Vice President

ICC URUGUAY

c/o Cam. Nat. de Com. y Servicios del Uruguay
Rincón 454, 2° piso - Casilla de Correo 1000
Montevideo
Uruguay
Tel: +59-82 9161277
Fax: +59-82 9161243
E-mail: gerencia@adinet.com.uy
Website: www.comaradecomercio.com.my
Contact: Claudio Piacenza, Secretary General

ICC VENEZUELA
c/o Camara de Comercio de Caracas
Calle Andrés Eloy Blanco N° 215
Los Caobos
Caracas 1050
Venezuela
Tel: +58-212 5718831
Fax: +58-212 5782456
E-mail: dianadroulers@iccvenezuela.org
Website: www.venezuela.org
Contact: Diana Droulers, Secretary General

Appendix IV

Banking Groups With Trade Finance Interest by Region

(The under-mentioned list represents a selection of banks known to have an interest in trade finance activity as at the time the list was compiled. A number of very important banks may not appear on this list as, according to the information available, they did not appear to have a significant interest in trade finance at the time. This activity may, in some cases, be limited to the respective bank's head offices and may not be available at their overseas branches)

WESTERN EUROPE / EASTERN EUROPE AND SCANDINAVIA

Austria	Bank Austria-Creditanstalt
	Erste Bank der Oesterreichische Sparkassen
	Raiffeisen Zentralbank Oesterreich
Belgium	Banque Bussels Lambert
	Fortis Bank
	Belgolaise Bank
	KBC Bank
Cyprus	Bank of Cyprus
	Cyprus Popular Bank
	Turkish Bank (Northern Cyprus)
Czech Republic	Komercni Banka
Denmark	Danske Bank
	Unibank

Estonia	Hansapank
Finland	Merita- Nordbanken
France	BNP-Paribas
	Credit Agricole-Indosuez
	Credit Lyonnais
	Société Générale
Germany	Bayerische Landesbank Girozentrale
	BHF Bank
	Commerzbank
	Deutsche Bank
	DG Bank
	Dresdner Kleinwort Benson
	Hamburgisce Landesbank
	Hypovereinsbank
	Landesbank Baden Wurttemberg
	Norddeutsche Landesbank Girozentrale
	Westdeutsche Landesbank Girozentrale
Greece	Alpha Credit Bank
	EFG Eurobank Ergasias
	Egnatia Bank
Hungary	Hungarian Foreign Trade Bank
	OTP Bank
Ireland	Allied Irish Bank (GB)
	Anglo Irish Bank Corporation
	Bank of Ireland
Italy	Banca Antoniana Popolare Veneta
	Banco di Roma
	Banca Monte dei Paschi di Siena
	Banca Nazionale del Lavoro
	Banca Popolare di Milano
	Banca Popolare di Novara Scari
	Banco do Napoli
	Banco di Sicilia
	Sanpaolo IMI
	Unicredito Italiano

Latvia	Hansa Banka
	Universal Bank
	Parex Bank
Lithuania	Hansa Bankas
	Medicinos Bankas
	Vilniaus Bankas
	Parex Bank
Luxembourg	Banque Internationale a Luxembourg
	Brown Shipley & Co
Malta	Bank of Valletta
	First International Merchant Bank
Netherlands	ABN Amro Bank
	ING Bank Group
	KBC
	Rabobank International
Norway	Christiania Bank OG Kredit Kasse
Poland	Bank Handlowy w Warszawie
	PEKAO Bank SA
	BRE Bank (Commerzbank Group)
	WBK Bank (Allied Irish Bank Group)
	Bank Zachodny (Allied Irish Bank Group)
Portugal	Banco Comercial Portugues
	Banco Nacional Ultramarino
	Banco Totta y Acores
Romania	Anglo Romanian Bank
	Banca Comerciale Romana
Russia	Alfa Bank
	Moscow Narodny Bank
	Mosnar Bank
	Sberbank
	Gazprombank

| | Vneshtorgbank-Bank for Foreign Trade |
| | Ros Bank |

Spain
Banca March
Banco Bilbao Viscaya Argentaria
Banco Espanol de Credito
Banco Santander Central Hispano
Confederacion Espanola de Caja de Ahorros

Sweden
Skandinaviska Enskilda Banken
Svenska Handelsbanken
Swedbank

Switzerland
United European Bank
Credit Suisse First Boston
Habib Bank AG Zurich

United Kingdom
HSBC Bank Group
Lloyds TSB Bank
Barclays Bank
National Westminster Bank
Bank of Scotland
Royal Bank of Scotland
Standard Chartered Bank
Standard Chartered Grindlays
British Arab Commercial Bank
Equator Bank

MIDDLE EAST AND AFRICA

Algeria
Banque Commerciale et Industrielle d'Algerie
Albaraka Bank

Bahrain
Gulf International Bank
ABC Bank

Egypt
National Bank of Egypt
Arab African International Bank
Bank Misr

Ghana	Ghana International Bank
Iran	Bank Melli Iran
	Bank Mellat
	Bank Saderat Iran
	Bank Sepah
	Bank Tejarat
	Iran Overseas Investment Bank
Israel	Bank Hapoalim
	Bank Leumi
	FIBI Bank
	Israel Discount Bank
	United Mizrahi Bank
Jordan	Arab Bank
	Jordan National Bank
	Housing Bank
Kenya	Kenya Commercial Bank
Kuwait	National Bank of Kuwait
	United Bank of Kuwait
Lebanon	Banque Banorabe
	Beirut Riyadh Bank
	Byblos Bank
	Fransa Bank
Libya	Sahara Bank
Mauritius	Mauritius Commercial Bank
Morocco	Banque Marocaine pour le Commerce Extérieure
Nigeria	Afribank
	First Bank of Nigeria
	National Bank of Nigeria
	Diamond Bank

	Bank of the North Wema Bank
Qatar	Qatar National Bank
Saudi Arabia	Arab National Bank National Commercial Bank Riyadh Bank
Sudan	Sudanese French Bank Saudi Sudanese Bank National Bank of Umm Durman Animal Resources Bank
South Africa	ABSA Bank Henry Ansbacher & Co Nedcor Bank Standard Bank
Tunisia	Union Bancaire pour le Commerce et l'Industrie Banque Internationale Arabe de Tunisie
Turkey	Akbank AS Sebanci Bank Turkiye Ziraat Bankasi Tukiye Is Bankasi
United Arab Emirates	Emirates Bank International Mashreq Bank National Bank of Abu Dhabi National Bank of Dubai
Zambia	Zambia National Commercial Bank

FAR EAST AND AUSTRALASIA

Australia	Australia & New Zealand Banking Group Commonwealth Bank of Australia

	National Australia Bank
	Westpac Banking Corporation
Bangladesh	Sonali Bank
China	Bank of China
	Bank of Communications
	Industrial and Commercial Bank of China
Hong Kong	Bank of East Asia
	Dao Heng Bank
	Overseas Trust Bank
India	Bank of Baroda
	Bank of India
	State Bank of India
	Canara Bank
	Syndicate Bank
Indonesia	Bank Mandiri
	Bank Negara Indonesia
Japan	Asahi Bank
	Bank of Tokyo Mitsubishi
	Dai Ichi Kangyo Bank
	Sahura Bank
	Sanwa Bank
	Sumitomo Bank
	Tokai Bank
Korea (South)	Cho Hung Bank
	Korea Development Bank
	Korea Exchange Bank
	Korea First Bank
	Shinhan Bank
Malaysia	Bumiputra Commerce Bank
	Malayan Banking Berhad

Pakistan	Allied Bank of Pakistan
	Habib Bank
	National Bank of Pakistan
	United Bank
Philippines	Philippine National Bank
Singapore	DBS Bank
	Oversea-Chinese Banking Corporation
	United Overseas Bank
Sri Lanka	Bank of Ceylon
Taiwan	Chang Hwa Commercial Bank
	First Commercial Bank
	Hua Nan Commercial Bank
Thailand	Bangkok Bank
	Siam Commercial Bank
	Thai Farmers Bank

THE AMERICAS

Argentina	Banco de la Nacion Argentina
Bermuda	Bank of Bermuda
Brazil	Banco do Brasil
	Banco de Estado de Sao Paulo
	Banco Mercantil de Sao Paulo
Canada	Bank of Montreal
	Royal Bank of Canada
	Scotia Bank
	Toronto Dominion Bank
Colombia	Banco Cafetero

Cuba	Havana International Bank

Jamaica	National Commercial Bank

USA	American Express Bank
	Bank One
	Bank of America
	Bank of New York
	Chase Manhattan Bank
	Citibank
	Riggs Bank
	State Street Bank

OTHER FINANCIAL INSTITUTIONS

The International Monetary Fund

MULTILATERAL AND REGIONAL DEVELOPMENT BANKS

The World Bank Group
International Finance Corporation
Multilateral Investment Guarantee Agency
International Development Association
International Bank for Reconstruction and Development
International Centre for the Settlement of Investment Disputes
African Development Bank
Asian Development Bank
Caribbean Development Bank
Central American Bank for Economic Integration
Inter-American Development Bank Group
North American Development Bank
The Nordic Development Fund/The Nordic Investment Bank
The Islamic Development Bank
The OPEC Fund for International Development
The European Investment Bank
The European Bank for Reconstruction and Development
The International Fund for Agricultural Development

With the process of privatization gaining pace in Eastern Europe, many local banks have combined forces with international bank groups with a view to increasing and reinforcing their international operations. Poland has, to date, been at the forefront of this process with some 60 per cent or more of Polish banks having merged or been taken over by international bank groups.

Many European and American international banks also operate under their own names in most countries in Eastern Europe. These are not listed individually here.

Appendix V

Examples of Letters of Credit

Irrevocable Confirmed Documentary Credit Advice

<table>
<tr>
<td>Name of Advising Bank
The American Advising Bank
456 Commerce Avenue
Tampa, Florida

Reference Number of Advising Bank: 2417

Place and date of Notification: January 14, 1994, Tampa</td>
<td>Notification of Irrevocable
Documentary Credit</td>
</tr>
<tr>
<td>Issuing Bank:
The French Issuing Bank
38 rue François 1er
Paris, France</td>
<td>Beneficiary:
The American Exporter Co. Inc
17 Main Street
Tampa, Florida</td>
</tr>
<tr>
<td>Reference Number of the Issuing Bank:
12345</td>
<td>Amount:
US$100,000. – One hundred thousand U.S. Dollars</td>
</tr>
</table>

We have been informed by the above-mentioned Issuing Bank that the above-mentioned Documentary Credit has been issued in your favour. Please find enclosed the advice intended for you.

Check the Credit terms and conditions carefully. In the event you do not agree with the terms and conditions, or if you feel unable to comply with any of those terms and conditions, kindly arrange an amendment of the Credit through your contracting party (the Applicant).

Other information:

☐ This notification and the enclosed advice are sent to you without any engagement on our part.

☒ As requested by the Issuing Bank, we hereby add our confirmation to this Credit in accordance with the stipulations under UCP 500 Article 9.

The American Advising Bank

Irrevocable Confirmed Documentary Credit

Name of Issuing Bank The French Issuing Bank 38 rue François 1er 75008 Paris, France	**Irrevocable** **Documentary Credit** Number 12345

Place and Date of Issue: Paris, 1 January 1994 **Applicant:** The French Importer Co. 89 rue du Commerce Paris, France **Advising Bank:** Reference No The American Advising Bank 456 Commerce Avanue Tampa, Florida	**Expiry Date and Place for Presentation of Documents** Expiry Date: May 29, 1994 Place for Presentation: The American Advising Bank, Tampa **Beneficiary:** The American Exporter Co. Inc. 17 Main Street Tampa, Florida ⇦ **Amount:** US$100,000. - one hundred thousand U.S. dollars

Partial shipments [X] allowed [ ] not allowed Transhipment [X] allowed [ ] not allowed [ ] Insurance covered by buyers **Shipment as defined in UCP 500 Article 46** From: Tampa, Florida For transportation to: Paris, France Not later than: May 15, 1994	**Credit available with Nominated Bank:** The American Advising Bank, Tampa [X] by payment at sight [ ] by deferred payment at: [ ] by acceptance of drafts at: [ ] by negotiation Against the documents detailed herein: [X] and Beneficiary's draft(s) drawn on: The American Advising Bank

Commercial Invoice, one original and 3 copies

Multimodal Transport Document issued to the order of the French Importer Co.
marked freight prepaid and notify XYZ Custom House Broker Inc

Insurance Certificate covering the Institute Cargo Clauses and the Institute War
and Strike Clauses for 110% of the Invoice value endorsed to The French Importer Co.

Certificate of Origin evidence goods to be of U.S.A. Origin

Packing List

Covering: Machinerie and spare parts as per pro-forma invoice number 657
dated December 17, 1993 – CIP INCOTERMS 1990

Documents to be presented within [14] days after the date of shipment but within the validity of the Credit.

We hereby issue the irrevocable Documentary Credit in your favour. It is subject to the Uniform Customs and Practice for
Documentary Credits (1993 Revision, International Chamber of Commerce, Paris, France, Publication No. 500) and engages
us in accordance with the terms thereof. The number and the date of the Credit and the name of our bank must be quoted
on all drafts required. If the Credit is available by negotiation, each presentation must be noted on the reverse side of this
advice by the bank where the Credit is available.

This document consists of [1] signed page(s)   The French Issuing Bank

Advice for the Beneficiary

© Copyright 1993. International Chamber of Commerce/Chambre de Commerce Internationale

ICC Guide to Documentary Credit Operations for the UCP 500
ICC Publication No. 515 pp. 46–47 – ISBN 92.842.1159.X
Published in its official English version by the International Chamber of Commerce.
Copyright © 1994 – International Chamber of Commerce (ICC), Paris.
Available from: *ICC Publishing S.A.,* 38 Cours Albert 1er, 75008 Paris, France or *ICC United Kingdom*, 14/15 Belgrave
Square, London SW1X 8PS, United Kingdom.

Appendix VI

Incoterms

These preambles neither constitute the full text of *Incoterms 2000* nor a summary of them. They only present selected features of Incoterms.

EXW*
EX WORKS
(. . . named place)

'Ex works' means that the seller delivers when he places the goods at the disposal of the buyer at the seller's premises or another named place (ie works, factory, warehouse, etc) not cleared for export and not loaded on any collecting vehicle.

This term thus represents the minimum obligation for the seller, and the buyer has to bear all costs and risks involved in taking the goods from the seller's premises.

However, if the parties wish the seller to be responsible for the loading of the goods on departure and to bear the risks and all the costs of such loading, this should be made clear by adding explicit wording to this effect in the contract of sale. This term should not be used when the buyer cannot carry out the export formalities directly or indirectly. In such circumstances, the FCA term should be used, provided the seller agrees that he will load at his cost and risk.

FCA
FREE CARRIER
(. . . named place)

'Free Carrier' means that the seller delivers the goods, cleared for export, to the carrier nominated by the buyer at the named place. It should be noted that the chosen place of delivery has an impact on the obligations of loading and unloading the goods at that place. If delivery occurs at the seller's premises, the seller is responsible for loading. If delivery occurs at any other place, the seller is not responsible for unloading.

This term may be used irrespective of the mode of transport, including multimodal transport.

'Carrier' means any person who, in a contract of carriage, undertakes to perform or to procure the performance of transport by rail, road, air, sea, inland waterway or by a combination of such modes.

If the buyer nominates a person other than a carrier to receive the goods, the seller is deemed to have fulfilled his obligation to deliver the goods when they are delivered to that person.

FAS*
FREE ALONGSIDE SHIP
(. . .named port of shipment)

'Free Alongside Ship' means that the seller delivers when the goods are placed alongside the vessel at the named port of shipment. This means that the buyer has to bear all costs and risks of loss of damage to the goods from that moment.

The FAS term requires the seller to clear the goods for export. THIS IS A REVERSAL FROM PREVIOUS INCOTERMS VERSIONS WHICH REQUIRED THE BUYER TO ARRANGE FOR EXPORT CLEARANCE.

However, if the parties wish the buyer to clear the goods for export, this should be made clear by adding explicit wording to this effect in the contract of sale.

This term can be used only for sea or inland waterway transport.

FOB
FREE ON BOARD
(. . . named port of shipment)

'Free on Board' means that the seller delivers when the goods pass the ship's rail at the named port of shipment. This means that the buyer has to bear all costs and risks of loss of or damage to the goods from that point. The FOB term requires the seller to clear the goods for export. This term can be used only for sea or inland waterway transport. If the parties do not intend to deliver the goods across the ship's rail, the FCA term should be used.

CFR
COST AND FREIGHT
(. . . named port of destination)

'Cost and Freight' means that the seller delivers when the goods pass the ship's rail in the port of shipment.

The seller must pay the costs and freight necessary to bring the goods to the named port of destination BUT the risk of loss of or damage to the goods, as well as any additional costs due to events occurring after the time of delivery, are transferred from the seller to the buyer.

The CFR term requires the seller to clear the goods for export.

This term can be used only for sea and inland waterway transport. If the parties do not intend to deliver the goods across the ship's rail, the CPT term should be used.

CIF**
COST INSURANCE AND FREIGHT
(. . . named port of destination)

'Cost, Insurance and Freight' means that the seller delivers when the goods pass the ship's rail in the port of shipment.

The seller must pay the costs and freight necessary to bring the goods to the named port of destination BUT the risk of loss of or damage to the goods, as well as any additional costs due to events occurring after the time of delivery, are transferred from the seller to the buyer. However, in CIF the seller also has to procure marine insurance against the buyer's risk of loss of or damage to the goods during the carriage.

Consequently, the seller contracts for insurance and pays the insurance premium. The buyer should note that under the CIF term the seller is required to obtain insurance only on minimum cover. Should the buyer wish to have the protection of greater cover, he would either need to agree as much expressly with the seller or to make his own extra insurance arrangements.

The CIF term requires the seller to clear the goods for export.

This term can be used only for sea and inland waterway transport. If the parties do not intend to deliver the goods across the ship's rail, the CIP term should be used.

CPT
CARRIAGE PAID TO
(. . . named place of destination)

'Carriage paid to . . .' means that the seller delivers the goods to the carrier nominated by him but the seller must in addition pay the cost of carriage necessary to bring the goods to the named destination. This means that the buyer bears all risks and any other costs occurring after the goods have been so delivered.

'Carrier' means any person who, in a contract of carriage, undertakes to perform or to produce the performance of transport, by rail, road, air, sea, inland waterway or by a combination of such modes.

If subsequent carriers are used for the carriage to the agreed destination, the risk passes when the goods have been delivered to the first carrier.

The CPT term requires the seller to clear the goods for export.

This term may be used irrespective of the mode of transport including multimodal transport.

CIP**
CARRIAGE AND INSURANCE PAID TO
(. . . named place of destination)

'Carriage and Insurance paid to . . .' means that the seller delivers the goods to the carrier nominated by him, but the seller must in addition pay the cost of carriage necessary to bring the goods to the named destination. This means that the buyer bears all risks and any additional costs occurring after the goods have been so delivered. However, in CIP the seller also has to procure insurance against the buyer's risk of loss of or damage to the goods during the carriage.

Consequently, the seller contracts for insurance and pays the insurance premium.

The buyer should note that under the CIP term the seller is required to obtain insurance only on minimum cover. Should the buyer wish to have the protection of greater cover, he would either need to agree as much expressly with the seller or to make his own extra insurance arrangements.

'Carrier' means any person who, in a contract of carriage, undertakes to perform or to procure the performance of transport, by rail, road, air, sea, inland waterway or by a combination of such modes.

If subsequent carriers are used for the carriage to the agreed destination, the risk passes when the goods have been delivered to the first carrier.

The CIP term requires the seller to clear the goods for export.

This term may be used irrespective of the mode of transport, including multimodal transport.

DAF*
DELIVERED AT FRONTIER
(. . . named place)

'Delivered at Frontier' means that the seller delivers when the goods are placed at the disposal of the buyer on the arriving means of transport not unloaded, cleared for export, but not cleared for import at the named point and place at the frontier, but before the customs border of the adjoining country. The term 'frontier' may be used for any frontier including that of the country of export. Therefore, it is of vital importance that the frontier in question be defined precisely by always naming the point and place in the term.

However, if the parties wish the seller to be responsible for the unloading of the goods from the arriving means of transport and to bear the risks and costs of unloading, this should be made clear by adding explicit wording to this effect in the contract of sale.

This term may be used irrespective of the mode of transport when goods are to be delivered at a land frontier. When delivery is to take place in the port of destination, on board a vessel or on the quay (wharf), the DES or DEQ terms should be used.

DES
DELIVERED EX SHIP
(. . . named port of destination)

'Delivered Ex Ship' means that the seller delivers when the goods are placed at the disposal of the buyer on board the ship not cleared for import at the named port of destination. The seller has to bear all the costs and risks involved in bringing the goods to the named port of destination before discharging. If the parties wish the seller to bear the costs and risks of discharging the goods, then the DEQ term should be used.

This term can be used only when the goods are to be delivered by sea or inland waterway or multimodal transport on a vessel in the port of destination.

DEQ*
DELIVERED EX QUAY
(. . . named port of destination)

'Delivered Ex Quay' means that the seller delivers when the goods are placed at the disposal of the buyer not cleared for import on the quay (wharf) at the named port of destination. The seller has to bear costs and risks involved in bringing the goods to the named port of destination and discharging the goods on the quay (wharf). The DEQ term requires the buyer to clear the goods for import and to pay for all formalities, duties, taxes and other charges upon import.

THIS IS A REVERSAL FROM PREVIOUS INCOTERMS VERSIONS WHICH REQUIRED THE SELLER TO ARRANGE FOR IMPORT CLEARANCE.

If the parties wish to include in the seller's obligations all or part of the costs payable upon import of the goods, this should be made clear by adding explicit wording to this effect in the contract of sale.

This term can be used only when the goods are to be delivered by sea or inland waterway or multimodal transport on discharging from a vessel onto the quay (wharf) in the port of destination. However, if the parties wish to include in the seller's obligations the risks and costs of the handling of the goods from the quay to another place (warehouse, terminal, transport station, etc) in or outside the port, the DDU or DDP terms should be used.

DDU***
DELIVERED DUTY UNPAID
(. . . named place of destination)

'Delivered duty unpaid' means that the seller delivers the goods to the buyer, not cleared for import, and not unloaded from any arriving means of transport at the named place of destination. The seller has to bear the costs and risks involved in bringing the goods thereto, other than, where applicable, and 'duty' (which terms includes the responsibility for and risks of the carrying out of customs formalities, and the payment of formalities, customs duties, taxes and other charges) for import in the country of destination. Such 'duty' has to be borne by the buyer as well as any costs and risks caused by his failure to clear the goods for import in time.

However, if the parties wish the seller to carry out customs formalities and bear the costs and risks resulting therefrom as well as some of the costs payable upon import of the goods, this should be made clear by adding explicit wording to this effect in the contract of sale.

This term may be used irrespective of the mode of transport but when delivery is to take place in the port of destination on board the vessel or on the quay (wharf), the DES or DEQ terms should be used.

DDP****
DELIVERED DUTY PAID
(. . . named place of destination)

'Delivered duty paid' means that the seller delivers the goods to the buyer, cleared for import, and not unloaded from any arriving means of transport at the named place of destination. The seller has to bear all the costs and risks involved in bringing the goods thereto including, where applicable, any 'duty' (which term includes the responsibility for and the risks of the carrying out of customs formalities and the payment of formalities, customs duties, taxes and other charges) for import in the country of destination.

Whilst the EXW term represents the minimum obligation for the seller, DDP represents the maximum obligation.

This term should not be used if the seller is unable directly or indirectly to obtain the import licence.

However, if the parties wish to exclude from the seller's obligations some of the costs payable upon import of the goods (such as value-added tax: VAT), this should be made clear by adding explicit wording to this effect in the contract of sale.

If the parties wish the buyer to bear all risks and costs of the import, the DDU term should be used.

This term may be used irrespective of the mode of transport but when delivery is to take place in the port of destination on board the vessel or on the quay (wharf), the DES or DEQ terms should be used.

*Variants of Incoterms

In practice, it frequently happens that the parties themselves by adding words to an Incoterm seek further precision than the term could offer. It should be underlined that Incoterms give no guidance whatsoever for such additions. Thus, if the parties cannot rely on a well-established custom of the trade for the interpretation of such additions they may encounter serious problems when no consistent understanding of the additions could be proven.

If for instance the common expressions 'FOB stowed' or 'EXW loaded' are used, it is impossible to establish a worldwide understanding to the effect that the seller's obligations are extended not only with respect to the cost of actually loading the goods in the ship or on the vehicle respectively but also include the risk of fortuitous loss of or damage to the goods in the process of stowage and loading. For these reasons, the parties are strongly advised to clarify whether they only mean that the function or the cost of the stowage and loading operations should fall upon the seller or whether he should also bear the risk until the stowage and loading has actually been completed. These are questions to which Incoterms do not provide an answer: consequently, if the contract too fails expressly to describe the parties' intentions, the parties may be put to much unnecessary trouble and cost.

Although Incoterms 2000 do not provide for many of these commonly used variants, the preambles to certain trade terms do alert the parties to the need for special contractual terms if the parties wish to go beyond the stipulations of Incoterms.

EXW	the added obligation for the seller to load the goods on the buyer's collecting vehicle;
CIF/CIP	the buyer's need for additional insurance;
DEQ	the added obligation for the seller to pay for costs after discharge.

In some cases sellers and buyers refer to commercial practice in liner and charterparty trade. In these circumstances, it is necessary to clearly distinguish between the obligations of the parties under the contract of carriage and their obligations to each other under the contract of sale. Unfortunately, there are no authoritative definitions of expressions such as 'liner terms' and 'terminal handling charges' (THC). Distribution of costs under such terms may differ in different places and charge from time to time. The parties are recommended to clarify in the contract of sale how such costs should be distributed between themselves.

Expressions frequently used in charterparties, such as 'FOB stowed', 'FOB stowed and trimmed', are sometimes used in contracts of sale in order to clarify to what extent the seller under FOB has to perform stowage and trimming of the goods onboard the ship. Where such words are added, it is necessary to clarify in the contract of sale whether the added obligations only relate to costs or to both costs and risks.

As has been said, every effort has been made to ensure that Incoterms reflect the most common commercial practice. However, in some cases – particularly where Incoterms 2000 differ from Incoterms 1990 – the parties may wish the trade terms to operate differently. They are reminded of such options in the preamble of the terms signalled by the word 'However'.

**The 'C'-terms require the seller to contract for carriage on usual terms at his own expense. Therefore, a point up to which he would have to pay transport costs must necessarily be indicated after the respective 'C'-term. Under the CIF and CIP terms the seller also has to take out insurance and bear the insurance cost. Since the point for the division of costs is fixed at a point in the country of destination, the 'C'-terms are frequently mistakenly believed to be arrival contracts, in which the seller would bear all risks and costs until the goods have actually arrived at the agreed point. However, it must be stressed that the 'C'-terms are of the same nature as the 'F'-terms in that the seller fulfils the contract in the country of shipment or dispatch. Thus, the contracts of sale under the 'C'-terms, like the contracts under the 'F'-terms, fall within the category of shipment contracts.

It is in the nature of shipment contracts that, while the seller is bound to pay the normal transport cost for the carriage of the goods by a usual route and in a customary manner to the agreed place, the risk of loss of or damage to the goods, as well as additional costs resulting from events occurring after the goods having been appropriately delivered for carriage, fall upon the buyer. Hence, the 'C'-terms are distinguishable from all other terms in that they contain two 'critical' points, one indicating the point to which the seller is bound to arrange and bear the costs of a contract of carriage and another one for the allocation of risk. For this reason, the greatest caution must be observed when adding obligations of the seller to the 'C'-terms which seek to extend the seller's responsibility beyond the aforementioned 'critical' point for the allocation of risk. It is of the very essence of the 'C'-terms that the seller is relieved of any further risk and cost after he has duly fulfilled his contract by contracting for carriage and handing over the goods to the carrier and by providing for insurance under the CIF- and CIP-terms.

The essential nature of the 'C'-terms as shipment contracts is also illustrated by the common use of documentary credits as the preferred mode of payment used in such terms. Where it is agreed by the parties to the sale contract that the seller will be paid by presenting the agreed shipping documents to a bank under a documentary credit, it would be quite contrary to the central purpose of the documentary credit for the seller to bear further risks and costs after the moment when payment had been made under documentary credits or otherwise upon shipment and dispatch of the goods. Of course, the seller would have to bear the cost of the contract of carriage irrespective of whether freight is pre-paid upon shipment or is payable at destination (freight collect); however, additional costs which may result from events occurring subsequent to shipment and dispatch are necessarily for the account of the buyer.

If the seller has to provide a contract of carriage which involves payment of duties, taxes and other charges, such costs will, of course, fall upon the seller to the extent that they are for his account under that contract. This is now explicitly set forth in the A6 clause of all 'C'-terms.

If it is customary to procure several contracts of carriage involving transhipment of the goods at intermediate places in order to reach the agreed destination, the seller would have to pay all these costs, including any costs incurred when the goods are transhipped from one means of conveyance to the other. If, however, the carrier exercised his rights under a transhipment – or similar clause – in order to avoid unexpected hindrances (such as ice, congestion, labour disturbances, government orders, war or warlike operations) then any additional cost resulting therefrom would be for the account of the buyer, since the sellers obligation is limited to procuring the usual contract of carriage.

It happens quite often that the parties to the contract of sale wish to clarify the extent to which the seller should procure a contract of carriage including the costs of discharge. Since such costs are normally covered by the freight when the goods are carried by regular shipping lines, the contract of sale will frequently stipulate that the goods are to be so carried or at least that they are to be carried under 'liner terms'. In other cases, the word 'landed' is added after CFR or CIF. However, it is advisable not to use abbreviations added to the 'C'-terms unless, in the relevant trade, the meaning of the abbreviations is clearly understood and accepted by the contracting parties or under any applicable law or custom of the trade.

In particular, the seller should not – and indeed could not, without changing the very nature of the 'C'-terms – undertake any obligation with respect to the arrival of the goods at destination, since the risk of any delay during the carriage is borne by the buyer. Thus, any obligation with respect to time must necessarily refer to the place of shipment or dispatch, for example, 'shipment (dispatch) not later than . . .'. An agreement for example,

'CFR Hamburg not later than. . .' is really a misnomer and thus open to different possible interpretations. The parties could be taken to have meant either that the goods must actually arrive at Hamburg at the specified date, in which case the contract is not a shipment contract but an arrival contract or, alternatively, that the seller must ship the goods at such a time that they would normally arrive at Hamburg before the specified date unless the carriage would have been delayed because of unforeseen events.

It happens in commodity trades that goods are bought while they are at sea and that, in such cases, the word 'afloat' is added after the trade time. Since the risk of loss of or damage to the goods would then, under the CFR- and CIF-terms, have passed from the seller to the buyer, difficulties of interpretation might arise. One possibility would be to maintain the ordinary meaning of the CFR- and CIF-terms with respect to the allocation of risk between seller and buyer, namely that risk passes on shipment: this would mean that the buyer might have to assume the consequences of events having already occurred at the time when the contract of sale enters into force. The other possibility would be to let the passing of the risk coincide with the time when the contract of sale is concluded. The former possibility might well be practical, since it is usually impossible to ascertain the condition of the goods while they are being carried. For this reason the 1980 United Nations Convention on Contracts for the International Sale of Goods article 68 stipulates that 'if the circumstances so indicate, the risk is assumed by the buyer from the time of the goods were handed over to the carrier who issued the documents embodying the contract of carriage'. There is, however, an exception to this rule when 'the seller knew or ought to have known that the goods had been lost or damaged and did not disclose this to the buyer'. Thus, the interpretation of a CFR- or CIF-term with the addition of the word 'afloat' will depend upon the law applicable to the contract of sale. The parties are advised to ascertain the applicable law and any solution which might follow therefrom. In case of doubt, the parties are advised to clarify the matter in their contract.

In practice, the parties frequently continue to use the traditional expression C&F (or C and F, C+F). Nevertheless, in most cases it would appear that they regard these expressions as equivalent to CFR. In order to avoid difficulties of interpreting their contract the parties should use the correct Incoterm which is CFR, the only worldwide-accepted standard abbreviation for the term 'Cost and Freight (. . . named port of destination)'.

CFR and CIF in A8 of Incoterms 1990 obliged the seller to provide a copy of the charterparty whenever his transport document (usually the bill of lading) contained a reference to the charterparty, for example, by the frequent notation 'all other terms and conditions as per charterparty'. Although, of course, a contracting party should always be able to ascertain all terms of his contract – preferably at the time of the conclusion of the contract – it appears that the practice to provide the charterparty as aforesaid has created problems particularly in connection with documentary credit transactions. The obligation of the seller under CFR and CIF to provide a copy of the charterparty together with other transport documents has been deleted in Incoterms 2000.

Although the A8 clauses of Incoterms seek to ensure that the seller provides the buyer with 'proof of delivery', it should be stressed that the seller fulfils that requirement when he provides the 'usual' proof. Under CPT and CIP it would be the 'usual transport document' and under CFR and CIF a bill of lading or a sea waybill. The transport documents must be 'clean', meaning that they must not contain clauses or notations expressly declaring a defective condition of the goods and/or the packaging. If such clauses or notations appear in the document, it is regarded as 'unclean' and would then not be accepted by banks in documentary credit transactions. However, it should be noted that a transport document even without such clauses or notations would usually not provide the buyer with incontrovertible proof as against the carrier that the goods were shipped in conformity with the stipulations of the contract of sale. Usually, the carrier would, in standardized text on the front page of the transport document, refuse to accept responsibility for information with respect to the goods by indicating that the particulars inserted in the transport document constitute the shipper's declarations and therefore that the information is only 'said to be' as inserted in the document. Under most applicable laws and principles, the carrier must at least use reasonable means of checking the correctness of the information and his failure to do so may make him liable to the consignee. However, in container trade, the carrier's means of checking the contents in the container would not exist unless he himself was responsible for stowing the container.

There are only two terms which deal with insurance, namely CIF and CIP. Under these terms the seller is obliged to procure insurance for the benefit of the buyer. In other cases it is for the parties themselves to decide whether and to what extent they want to cover themselves by insurance. Since the seller takes out insurance for the benefit of the buyer, he would not know the buyer's precise requirements. Under the Institute Cargo Clauses drafted by the Institute of London Underwriters, insurance is available in 'minimum cover' under Clause C, 'medium cover' under Clause B and 'most extended cover' under Clause A. Since in the sale of commodities under the CIF term the buyer may wish to sell the goods in transit to a subsequent buyer who in turn may wish to resell the goods again, it is impossible to know the insurance cover suitable to such subsequent buyers and, therefore, the minimum cover under CIF has traditionally been chosen with the possibility for the buyer to require the seller to take out additional insurance. Minimum cover is however unsuitable for sale of manufactured goods where the risk of theft, pilferage or improper handling or custody of the goods would require more than the cover available under Clause C. Since CIP, as distinguished from CIF, would normally not be used for the sale of commodities, it would have been feasible to adopt the most extended cover under CIP rather than the minimum cover under CIF. But to vary the seller's insurance obligation under CIF and CIP would lead to confusion and both terms therefore limit the seller's insurance obligation to the minimum cover. It is particularly important for the CIP-buyer to observe this: should additional cover be required, he should agree with the seller that the latter could take out additional insurance or, alternatively, arrange for extended insurance cover himself. There are also particular instances where the buyer may wish to obtain even more protection than is available under Institute Clause A, for example insurance against war, riots, civil commotion, strikes or other labour disturbances. If he wishes the seller to arrange such insurance he must instruct him accordingly in which case the seller would have to provide such insurance if procurable.

***Customs clearance

The term 'customs clearance' has given rise to misunderstandings. Thus, whenever reference is made to an obligation of the seller or the buyer to undertake obligations in connection with passing the goods through customs of the country of export or import it is now made clear that this obligation does not only include the payment of duty and other charges but also the performance and payment of whatever administrative matters are connected with the passing of the goods through customs and the information to the authorities in this connection. Further, it has – although quite wrongfully – been considered in some quarters inappropriate to use terms dealing with the obligation to clear the goods through customs when, as in intra-European Union trade or other free trade areas, there is no longer any obligation to pay duty and no restrictions relating to import or export. In order to clarify the situation, the words **'where applicable'** have been added in the A2 and B2, A6 and B6 clauses of the relevant Incoterms **in order for them to be used without any ambiguity where no customs procedures are required.**

It is normally desirable that customs clearance is arranged by the party domiciled in the country where such clearance should take place or at least by somebody acting there on his behalf. Thus, the exporter should normally clear the goods for export, while the importer should clear the goods for import.

Incoterms 1990 departed from this under the trade terms EXW and FAS (export clearance duty on the buyer) and DEQ (import clearance duty on the seller) but in Incoterms 2000 FAS and DEQ place the duty of clearing the goods for export on the seller and to clear them for import on the buyer respectively, while EXW – representing the seller's minimum obligation – has been left unamended (export clearance duty on the buyer). Under DDP the seller specifically agrees to do what follows from the very name of the term – **D**elivered **D**uty **P**aid – namely clear the goods for import and pay any duty as a consequence thereof.

Incoterms 2000*
ICC Publications No 560 – ISBN 92.842.1199.9
Published in its official English and French versions by the International Chamber of Commerce, Paris.
Copyright © 1999 – International Chamber of Commerce (ICC)
Available from: *ICC Publishing S.A.*, 38 Cours Albert 1er, 75008 Paris, France or *ICC United Kingdom*, 14/15 Belgrave Square, London SW1X 8PS, United Kingdom
*Incoterms is a protected ICC trademark.
Full information on the Incoterms can be found on the Internet at www. incoterms.org.

Appendix VII

ICC Publications

Code	Language(s)	Title
INCOTERMS		
620	E-F	ICC Guide to Incoterms 2000
617	E	Incoterms 2000: a Forum of Experts
616	E	Incoterms 2000 Multimedia Expert (CD ROM)
614	E-F	Incoterms 2000 Wall Chart (per pack of 10 copies)
589	E	Incoterms 1990 Questions and Answers
560	EF-ED-ES	Incoterms 2000
417/4	EFDSI	Key Words in International Trade – 4th edition
INTERNATIONAL TRADE AND CONTRACTS		
650	E-F	Force Majeure Clause and Hardship Clause 2003
646	E-F	ICC Model Distributorship Contract (sole Importer distributor) – 2nd edition
644	E-F	ICC Model Commercial Agency Contract – 2nd edition
641	E	Guide to Export-Import Basics – 2nd edition
634	E-F	ICC Model Short Form Contracts: International Commercial Agency / Int. Distributorship
624	E	International Commercial Transactions 2nd edition
623	E	A to Z of International Trade
619	E-F	The ICC Model Occasional Intermediary Contract
557	E-F	ICC Model International Franchising
556	E-F	ICC Model International Sale Contract
546	E	Transfer of Ownership in International Trade
478	French only	Guide to Penalty and Liquidated Damages Clauses

DOCUMENTARY CREDITS

645	E-F	International Standard Banking Pratice – ISBP
639	E	ICC Guide to the Eucp
633	E	Documentary Credit Law throughout the world
632	E	Collected Opinions of the ICC Banking Commission 1995–2001
613	E	Opinions of the ICC Banking Commission 1998–99
596	E	Opinions of the ICC Banking Commission 1997
590	E-F	ISP98 – International Standby Practices – The Rules
575	E	ICC Guide to Bank-to-Bank Reimbursements
565	E	Opinions of the ICC Banking Commission (1995-1996)
551	E	ICC Uniform Rules for Bank-to-Bank Reimbursements – a Commentary
525	E-F	ICC Uniform Rules for Bank-to-Bank Reimbursements under Documentary Credits
525	E-S	ICC Uniform Rules for Bank-to-Bank Reimbursements under Documentary Credits
516	E	ICC Standard Documentary Credit Forms for the UCP 500
515	E	ICC Guide to Documentary Credit Operations for the UCP 500
511	E	Documentary Credits: UCP 500 and 400 Compared – 1993 Revision
500/3	E-F	eUCP Supplement for Electronic Presentation of Documentary Credits – Leaflet (Pack of ten)
500/2	E	UCP 500 + eUCP (2002 book format)
500	ED-ES-ER	ICC Uniform Customs and Practice for Documentary Credits (1993 Revision)
494	E	Opinions of the ICC Banking Commission (1989–1991)
469	E	Opinions of the ICC Banking Commission (1987–1988)
459	E	Case Studies on Documentary Credits for UCP 400 (Vol. 1)
434	E-F	Opinions of the ICC Banking Commission (1984–1986)

951	E	Annual Survey of Letters of Credit 2001
950	E	ISP98 and UCP500 compared
947	E	ISP98 – International Standby Practices – The Commentary

BANKING TECHNIQUES AND FINANCE

645	E-F	International Standard Banking Pratice – ISBP
631	E	User's guide to ICC Uniform Rules on Demand Guarantees
593	E	Bills of Exchange – 3rd edition
582	E	Trading and Investing in Emerging Markets
572	E	Managing Interest Rate Risk
561	E	ICC Guide to Collection Operations for URC 522
550	E-F	Uniform Rules for Collections – a Commentary
547	E	Bank Guarantees in International Trade (1996 updated edition)
522	E-F	ICC Uniform Rules for Collections (URC 522)
522	ED	ICC Uniform Rules for Collections (URC 522) – (1995 revision)
510	E	Guide to the ICC Uniform Rules for Demand Guarantees
503	E-F	Model Forms for Issuing Demand Guarantees
497	E	Funds Transfer in International Banking
458	E-F	ICC Uniform Rules for Demand Guarantees
458	ES	ICC Uniform Rules for Demand Guarantees
325	E-F	Uniform Rules for Contract Guarantees (1978)

INTERNATIONAL ARBITRATION

808	E-F	ICC Rules of Arbitration (2001 edition)
649	E-F	Rules for Expertise
647	EF	Collection of ICC Arbitral Awards 1995–2000
642	E-F	The UNIDROIT Principles of International Commercial Contracts
640	E-F	ADR – International Applications
627	E-F	Arbitration, Finance and Insurance
612	E-F	Arbitration in the next decade
609	E	International Commercial Arbitration in Asia
598	E	Improving International Arbitration – The Need for Speed and Trust

595	E	Annotated Guide to 1998 Arbitration Rules
594	E	ICC Arbitration (3rd edition)
592	E	Resolving International Intellectual Property Disputes
586	F	Règlement d'arbitrage – actes de la conférence
567	EF	Collection of ICC Procedural Decisions (1993–1996)
564	E-F	The Status of the Arbitrator
553	EF	Collection of ICC Arbitral Awards Vol. III (1991–1995)
537	E	International Commercial Arbitration in Europe
519	F	Mesures conservatoires et provisoires en matière d'arbitrage international
514	EF	Collection of ICC Arbitral Awards (1986–1990)
949	E	Dispute Resolution in Asia – 2nd edition
948	E	International Commercial Law
946	E	Guide to the New ICC Rules of Arbitration

BUSINESS LAW AND PRACTICE/INTERNATIONAL LAW

624	E	International Commercial Transactions (2nd edition)
576	E	Business Law in China: Trade, Investment and Finance
546	E	Transfer of Ownership in International Trade
490/3	EF	Global Competition and Transnational Regulations
480/8	EF	New Technologies: Their Influence on International Audiovisual Law
480/6	EF	Due Process and Anti-Competitive Practice
480/5	EF	Competition Law and Information Based Services
480/3	EF	Competition and Arbitration Law
480/2	F	Les commissions illicites
440/6	F	L'exécution des sentences arbitrales
440/5	E	International Contracts for Sale of Information Services

COMMERCIAL FRAUD AND COUNTERFEITING

651	E	Arbitration : Money Laundering, Corruption and Fraud
953	E	Private Commerce Bribery

652	E	Fighting Corruption 2nd edition
648	E	Preventing Finance Instrument Fraud – The Money Launderer's Tool
643	E	Trade Finance Fraud
630	E	Anti-Counterfeiting Technology Guide
608	E	Enforcement Measures against Counterfeiting and Piracy
585	E	Money Laundering
574	E	Countering Counterfeiting
554	E	Counterfeiting in China

ART TRADE AND LAW

| 532 | EF | Legal Aspects of International Trade in Art (Vol. 5) |
| 513 | EFS | International Art Trade and Law (Vol. 4) |

ELECTRONIC COMMERCE

| 945 | E | Electronic Commerce in Practice (ISP) |

INSURANCE

627	E-F	Arbitration, Finance and Insurance
536	E	ICC Guide to Uniform Rules for Contract Bonds and Model Forms
524	E-F	ICC Uniform Rules for Contract Bonds

TRANSPORT

| 481 | E-F | UNCTAD/ICC Rules for Multimodal Transport Documents |

ENVIRONMENT/MARKETING AND ADVERTISING

| 483 | E | ICC Guide to Effective Environmental Auditing |
| 468 | E-F | Environmental Auditing |

PERIODICALS

| DCI | E | Documentary Credits Insight – subscription 4 issues/1 year |
| BUL | E-F | The ICC International Court of Arbitration Bulletin (Go to www.iccbooks.com) |

Key to languages:
E: English – F: French; EF: bilingual English-French; ED: bilingual English-German; ES: bilingual English-Spanish

These publications and other titles are available from your local ICC National Committee or through the ICC business bookstore: www.iccbooks.com

Appendix VIII

Institute of Export Recommended Reading Lists for the Diploma and Advanced Certificate in International Trade

DIPLOMA IN INTERNATIONAL TRADE

The references below are a selection of recent publications relevant to each subject. They have been subdivided by overall topic area in order to aid reference. It should be noted that this is not intended to be a comprehensive reading list. They have been selected as interesting and – in some cases – provocative reading.

General Export Management

Dictionary of International Business Terms, Capela J., Barron's Business Dictionaries.
International Business, 2nd edition, Bennett R., Financial Times, Prentice Hall.
Management, 3rd edition, Bennett R., Financial Times, Pitman Publishing.

International Marketing Planning

Consumer Behavior and Marketing Action, Assael, H., PWS-Kent Publishing.
Elements of Export Marketing and Management, Branch, A.E., Chapman and Hall.
International Marketing Management, Jeannet, J.P. and Hennessey, H., Houghton Mifflin.

International Marketing Strategy and Management, Gilligan, C. and Hird, M., Croom Helm.
International Marketing, Cateora, P.R., Irwin.
International Marketing, Gilligan, C. and Hird, M., Routledge.
International Marketing, Terpstra V. & Sarathy R., Dryden Press.
Introduction to International Business, El-Kahal, S., McGraw-Hill.
Marketing Management, Analysis, Planning, Implementation and Control, Kotler, P., Prentice Hall.
Strategic Marketing Communications, Smith P., Berry C. & Pulford A., Kogan Page.

Management of International Trade

Export Practice & Management, Branch A., Thomson Learning.
International Business, Bennett R., Pearson Education Ltd.
International Financial Management, Cheol S *et al*, Irwin/McGraw Hill.
International Purchasing Handbook, Ashley J., Director Books.
Trading in the Global Currency Market, Luca C., Prentice Hall Press.

International Logistics & Purchasing

Handbook of Logistics and Distribution Management, Rushton A. & Oxley J., Kogan Page.
International Logistics, Wood D, *et al*, Chapman & Hall.
International Purchasing Handbook, Ashley J., Director Books.
The Importer's Handbook, Butler J., Prentice Hall.

ADVANCED CERTIFICATE IN INTERNATIONAL TRADE

The following textbooks and other publications have been chosen by the examiners as recommended reading material. Those titles in bold are listed as priority reading.

General

Schmittnoff:Export Trade, D'arcy, Murray & Cleave, Sweet & Maxwell.
INCOTERMS, ICC United Kingdom.

The business environment

The Business Environment, Institute of Export.
Business Law, 7th Edition, Abbot K.R. & Pendlebury, Contavuum.
Charlesworth Business Law, 16th Edition, Dobson P., Sweet & Maxwell.
Principles of Law Relating to Overseas Trade, 1st Edition, Kouladis N.,
   Blackwells.

Finance and international trade

Finance and International Trade, 2nd Edition, Institute of Export.
Finance of International Trade, 5th Edition, Watson A.J.W., Bankers Books.
Guide to Documentary Credit Operations for UCP 500
Principles of International Trade and Payments, 1st Edition, Briggs P,
   Blackwells.
Uniform Customs and Practices for Documentary Credits (UCP 5000), ICC
   United Kingdom.
Uniform Rules for Collections (URC 522)
Uniform Rules for Demand Guarantees

Operating in the global economy

Operating in the Global Economy, 2nd Edition, Institute of Export.
An Introduction to Modern Economics, 5th Edition, Hardwick P. Langmead
   J. & Khan B., Pearson Education.
International Marketing Strategy, 4th Edition, Bradley F., Prentice Hall
   Europe.
International Marketing, 2nd Edition, Bennett. R., Kogan Page.
International Marketing, 3rd Edition, Walsh L. S., Pearson Education.
International Marketing, Paliwoda S., Butterworth & Heinemann.
Marketing Research, 2nd Edition, Kent R., ITB Press.

International physical distribution

International Physical Distribution, 2nd Edition, Institute of Export.
International Trade Procedures and Management, 4th Edition, Walker A.G.,
   Butterworth-Heinemann.
Principles of International Physical Distribution, 1st Edition, Sherlock J.,
   Blackwells.

The Merchant's Guide, Millennium Edition, Richardson J.W., P&O Nedlloyd.
Understanding the Freight Business, 4th Edition, Down D.E., Micor Freght
  UK Ltd.

Institute of Export, Export House, Minerva Business Park, Lynch Wood,
Peterborough PE2 6FT. Tel: + 44(0)1733 404400; Fax: + 44(0) 1733 404444;
E-mail: education@export.org.uk; Website: www.export.org.uk.

Kogan Page International Business Publications

The Handbook of International Trade
A Guide to the Principles and Practice of Export
Consultant Editors: Jim Sherlock and Jonathan Reuvid
Published in association with the Institute of Export

Based on the syllabus of the Institute of Export's new certificate exams (launched in 2002) this important new book is both a 'textbook' for students of international trade and a handbook for practitioners. It aims to provide a thorough understanding of the issues involved in developing and managing overseas trade and to keep practitioners up-to-speed with current best practice.

Opening with a description of the structure of the global economy and the dynamics governing world trade, the book moves on to be a practical guide to the principles and practice of export trade, covering: international marketing (from research to distribution); the law relating to international trade; the export order process (from quotation to contract); international transport; customs controls; risk management; and export finance. Finally there is a section looking at the prospects and likely future development of global trade.

£29.95 Paperback 0 7494 4414 5 400 pages 2004

A Business Guide to EU Enlargement
Trade and Investment Opportunities in Europe and the Candidate Countries
Consultant Editors: Chris Ollington and Jonathan Reuvid

Much has been made of the benefits or otherwise of EU membership for the new members but nothing has been written about how the new members will affect the political and social landscape of the EU. Will traditional blocs be torn down and new ones built or will the traditional ties that bind many of the countries become even stronger? How will the new members affect moves towards tax harmonization? Will the new members affect the labour markets of the respective countries? How will the increased size of the EU affect EU funding? And what about the future – where does Europe begin and end – who will be in the next tranche of countries seeking membership?

This book takes each new member country in turn and examines how it stands, economically, politically and socially. These country reports include key facts, econometric data, the political structure, macroeconomic analysis, economic outlook and key industries etc. All the information a potential investor or company seeking a new market needs to know before looking at making more in-depth research.

£50.00 Hardback 0 7494 4082 1 336 pages 2004

IoD European Business Handbook
10th Edition
Consultant Editor: Adam Jolly

'This handbook should be on your desk, not on your shopping list.'
Sales and Marketing Management

Markets across the EU are moving decisively towards a free market model. E-commerce, global competition, privatization, the euro and enlargement are fundamentally changing the way in which European companies are structured and run. Yet for ambitious enterprises seeking to develop business across Europe, there remain multiple obstacles, risks and costs. Drawing on the Institute of Directors' unrivalled experience of working with entrepreneurs, *The European Business Handbook* reviews how best to structure and implement European business models.

Designed to appeal to a wide audience of business readers in both established and growing companies, the *IoD European Business Handbook* will provide a practical source of reference and advice on developing and resourcing business across Europe.

£40.00 Paperback 0 7494 3975 0 296 pages 2003

The Handbook of Country Risk 2004–2005
A Guide to International Business and Trade
Coface

'A useful and interesting book for those in international business who need to make decisions based on risk or for managers of risk strategies.'
Business in Africa

The worldwide panorama presented in the latest edition of *The Handbook of Country Risk* provides an invaluable reference tool with which to understand and evaluate market potential from either an investment or an export credit standpoint.

The volume offers two levels of information. First come transcripts of presentations made at the annual conference on country risk organized by Coface, the world leader in the field of export credit insurance, providing comment from both the company's own experts and leading specialists at international institutions.

The second level consists of the profile section, providing over 140 up-to-date profiles of emerging countries with comment on risk appreciation, market analysis, potential and perspectives, plus all manner of relevant facts and figures.

£45.00 Paperback 0 7494 4198 4 436 pages 2004

Directory of International Direct and E-Marketing
A Country-by-Country Sourcebook of Providers, Legislation and Data
Seventh Edition
Published in association with FEDMA and DMA

'The only definitive guide.'
Financial Times

'A very useful addition to the business bookshelf.'
Marketing Magazine

'This book teaches you in a few hours what it took experts like Reader's Digest and Time-Life years of trial and error and millions to discover'
Drayton Bird

The only guide you need for planning direct marketing campaigns is now even bigger! This acknowledged industry bible offers a comprehensive directory of over 10,000 DM and e-service providers worldwide, along with expert advice from leading practitioners on the latest industry developments.

£95.00 Paperback 0 7494 3977 7 944 pages 2003

GLOBAL MARKET BRIEFINGS SERIES

Global Market Briefings is the ultimate country-by-country information resource for managers, analysts, entrepreneurs and consultants engaged in international business, investment and market development around the world. Initially launched with six titles, this groundbreaking new series has rapidly extended to cover over 15 countries of interest to the global business community.

The series not only provides the most up-to-date information on important business issues; it also draws the expertise of leading professional firms with 'on-the-ground' local experience for authoritative advice, analysis and commentary on what economic and political developments really mean.

Comprehensively supported by its own dedicated website (www.global marketbriefings.com), each book in the series comes complete with a unique username and password giving instant access to the online service. Users can access the material from the book, wherever in the world they may be travelling, as well as regular updates, additional information and in-depth reports on developments in the respective country since the book was published.

Each volume comprehensively covers:

- the business investment environment;
- the legal structure and business regulations;
- finance, accountancy and taxation;
- background to the market and market potential;
- business development;
- the climate for foreign investment;
- regional and sector profiles;
- key industry and business sectors;
- information on operating an enterprise, property ownership and residence, employment and HR issues.

Contributors to the series include:

Deloitte & Touche, Bank Austria Creditanstalt, CMS Cameron McKenna, Groupe Coface, HSBC, Merchant International Group, Standard & Poor's, International Chamber of Commerce; Raiffeisen Bank; UK Trade & Investment; Allen & Overy; Ernst & Young; Denton Wilde Sapte; Herbert Smith; PricewaterhouseCoopers; Coca Cola; DuPont.

Doing Business with China
4th Edition
Consultant Editors: Jonathan Reuvid and Li Yong
Published in association with China's Ministry for Foreign Trade and Co-operation (MOFTEC), Cable and Wireless and HSBC

'A unique, timely and comprehensive guide'
Business Horizons

'An awesome reference guide... one of the best books on generating revenues in China.' *Ulster Business*

£95.00 Hardback 0 7494 3911 4 800 pages 2003

Doing Business with Croatia
2nd Edition
Consultant Editor: Marat Terterov and Visnja Bojanic
£50.00 Hardback 0 7494 4075 9 320 pages 2004

Doing Business with Cyprus
Consultant Editor: Philip Dew
£50.00 Hardback 0 7494 4140 2 320 pages 2004

Doing Business with the Czech Republic
4th Edition
Consultant editors: Jonathan Reuvid and Marat Terterov
Published in association with CzechInvest
£50.00 Hardback 0 7494 3838 X 432 pages 2002

Doing Business with Estonia
Consultant Editor: Marat Terterov
Published in association with Enterprise Estonia and the Headman Osborne Clarke Alliance
£50.00 Hardback 0 7494 3841 X 256 pages 2003

Doing Business with Hungary
3rd Edition
Consultant Editor: Jonathan Reuvid
Published in association with Trade Partners UK and CMS Cameron McKenna
£50.00 Hardback 0 7494 3514 3 304 pages 2002

Doing Business with Kazakhstan
3rd edition
Consultant Editor: Marat Terterov
Published in association with Trade Partners UK and the Kazakhstan Ministry of Foreign Affairs
£50.00 Hardback 0 7494 3990 4 304 pages 2004

Doing Business with Latvia
Consultant Editor: Marat Terterov
Published in association with the Latvian Development Agency
£50.00 Hardback 0 7494 3842 8 256 pages 2003

Doing Business with Libya
2nd Edition
Consultant Editors: Jonathan Wallace and Bill Wilkinson
Published in association with Trade Partners UK, Shell Petroleum and the Libyan Academy of Graduate Studies

'This handbook should be on the desk of anyone with business dealing in Libya.'
Gulf Business

'Now that UN sanctions have finally been lifted, and US sanctions must be under review, many companies will be taking a fresh look at the Libyan market. Information is hard to find, and this handbook is the best possible introduction.'
Oliver Miles CMG, Former British Ambassador to Libya

£50.00 Hardback 0 7494 3992 0 304 pages 2004

Doing Business with Lithuania

Consultant Editor: Marat Terterov
Published in association with the Lithuanian Development Agency
£50.00 Hardback 0 7494 3843 6 344 pages 2003

Doing Business with Malta

Consultant Editor: Marat Terterov
Published in association with Malta External Trade Corporation and Malta
Financial Services Authority
£50.00 Hardback 0 7494 3993 9 304 pages 2003

Doing Business with Poland

4th Edition
Consultant Editors: Marat Terterov and Jonathan Reuvid
Published in association with the Polish Agency for Foreign Investment
£50.00 Hardback 0 7494 3840 1 450 pages 2002

Doing Business with Russia

3rd Edition
Consultant Editor: Marat Terterov
Published in association with Trade Partners UK, the Russo-British Chamber
of Commerce and the American Chamber of Commerce in Russia
£50.00 Hardback 0 7494 3839 8 592 pages 2003

Doing Business with Slovakia

Consultant Editor: Jonathan Reuvid
£50.00 Hardback 0 7494 4073 0 288 pages 2003

Doing Business with Slovenia

Consultant Editor: Jonathan Reuvid
£50.00 Hardback 0 7494 4074 0 256 pages 2004

Forthcoming titles will cover:

Germany
Kuwait
Saudi Arabia
United Arab Emirates
Turkey

Jordan
Serbia & Montenegro
Ukraine

Other Doing Business with. . . titles
Invaluable for any company wishing to invest or trade in these flourishing
markets, these books are essential purchases for finance, sales and marketing
directors and company export departments.

Doing Business with South Africa
5th Edition
Consultant Editor: Jonathan Reuvid
£65.00 Paperback 0 7494 3374 4 432 pages 2001

Doing Business with Egypt
Consultant Editor: Marat Terterov
£40.00 Paperback 0 7494 3428 7 352 pages 2001

Doing Business with Georgia
Consultant Editor: Marat Terterov
£40.00 Paperback 0 7494 3516 X 352 pages 2001

Doing Business with the United Arab Emirates
Consultant Editors: Phillip Dew and Anthony Shoult
£40.00 Paperback 0 7494 3171 7 302 pages 2000

Doing Business with Turkey
Consultant Editors: Paul Cheeseright and Mehmet Oktemgil
£40.00 Paperback 0 7494 2954 2 352 pages 1999

Doing Business with Germany
3rd Edition
Consultant Editor: Jonathan Reuvid
£40.00 Paperback 0 7494 3558 5 352 pages 1999

Doing Business with India
Consultant Editors: Roderick Millar and M S Chandramouli
£47.50   Paperback 0 7494 2924 0 352 pages 1999

Doing Business with Saudi Arabia

Consultant Editors: Anthony Shoult and Sami Salman
£40.00 Paperback 0 7494 3701 4 508 pages 2002

WORLD OF INFORMATION SERIES

The World of Information series of five annual Regional Reviews, now in its 28th year, provides the context, trends and recent history essential to an understanding of global events. Each review covers, country by country, its region's developments and challenges in a readable uniform presentation.

Each year world experts are commissioned to give their objective assessment of the politics and economics of every country and territory in the world. This expertise has made the Reviews a primary reference source for business people and academics, researchers, government and diplomatic officials, international organizations and agencies.

Each Review contains:

- expert and timely analysis of recent events;
- country profiles covering history, political structure, demography, media, economy, industrial sectors and geography;
- regional developments and challenges;
- key Facts and Key Indicators boxes highlight essential information for each country listed;
- risk assessment boxes indicate the economic and political situation;
- business Directory highlights important contact details and useful Internet sites;
- business guides include entry requirements, travel links, working hours, public holidays and health precautions.

Africa Review 2003/04

The Economic and Business Report

The only reference work of its kind to cover the whole continent, the 25th edition provides specific data for 55 countries and covers key issues within the region. Specific issues include the water crisis, the economic and social impact of AIDS, the effects of Western trade barriers and subsidies on agriculture, and analysis of the future opportunities for African oil-producing nations.

£50.00 Paperback 0 7494 4065 1 288 pages 2003

Americas Review 2003/04
The Economic and Business Report

This edition provides both an analytical overview of the region and specific data for each of its 53 countries. It is the only reference work of its kind to cover all the Americas, North and South, plus all the Caribbean states and South Atlantic. Country-by-country economic and business reports are combined with analysis of regional issues such as the impact of debt on the region, the stability of the Latin American banking sector and the effects of recent political changes on the pan-American free-trade zone.

£50.00 Paperback 0 7494 4064 3 320 pages 2003

Asia and Pacific Review 2003/04
The Economic and Business Report

The only English language publication to cover the whole Asia and Pacific region, the 21st edition provides both an analytical overview of the region and country-by-country economic and business reports for each of the 60 countries within it. Specific regional issues covered include the threat of terrorism, the impact of deflation on the region's economy and the successes and failures of micro-credit within the region.

£50.00 Paperback 0 7494 4063 5 320 pages 2003

Europe Review 2003/04
The Economic and Business Report

The 15th edition covers the whole of Europe and includes 49 countries from Gibraltar to Georgia, Andorra to Azerbaijan. Regional issues covered include Foreign Direct Investment and which European countries have attracted the least and most, the response from both national governments and the EU to the movement of refugees within the region, and the impact of EU enlargement.

£50.00 Paperback 0 7494 4067 8 320 pages July 2003

Middle East Review 2003/04
The Economic and Business Report

The 27th edition now includes all the Central Asian states and comprises 32 country profiles. Regional issues are also covered and include analysis of the growth of Islamic banking, the impact on regional political and economic affairs by ex-Soviet Central Asian gas and oil producing nations, and the significance of terrorist activity in the region.

£50.00 Paperback 0 7494 4066 X 256 pages 2003

Appendix X

Contributors' Contact Details

Clyde & Co
51 Eastcheap
London
EC3M 1JP
Tel: +44 (020) 7623 1244
Fax: +44 (020) 7623 5427

Deloitte & Touche Customs & International Trade Group
Hill House
1 Little New Street
London
EC4A 3TR
Tel: +44 (020) 7303 3604
Fax: +44 (020) 7303 4780

Derrick Edwards
2, Brampton Court
Stockbridge Road
Chichester
West Sussex
P019 2PD

Brocur Limited
No 3 The Homestead
Waterfall Road
London
N11 1LH
Tel: +44 (020) 8368 3884
Fax: +44 (020) 8361 0312
Website: www.brocur.com

George Curmi
No 3 The Homestead
Waterfall Road
London
N11 1LH

ICC United Kingdom
12 Grosvenor Place
London
SW1X 7HH
Tel: +44 (020) 7823 2811
Fax: +44 (020) 7235 5447
Website: www.iccuk.net

ICC Switzerland
Handelskammer
c/o Economie Suisse
Hegibachstrasse
47 Case Postale 1072
Ch-8032
Zurich
Switzerland
Website: www.icc-switzerland.ch

The Institute of Export
Export House
Minerva Business Park
Lynch Wood
Peterborough
PE2 6FT
Tel: +44 (01733) 404 400
Fax: +44 (01733) 404 444
Website: www.export.org.uk

King & Spalding International LLP
City Place House
55 Basinghall Street
London
EC2V 5DU
Tel: +44 (020) 7551 7500
Fax: +44 (020) 7551 7575
Website: www.kslaw.com

Laytons
Carmelite
50 Victoria Embankment
Blackfriars
London
EC4Y 0LS
Tel: +44 (020) 7842 8000
Fax: +44 (020) 7842 8080
Website: www.laytons.com

Marinade Limited
1 Gainsford Street
London
SE1 2NE
Tel: +44 (020) 7378 1171
Fax: +44 (020) 7403 9820
Website: www.marinade.ltd.uk

John Merrett
Solicitor (England and Wales)
14–16 Belgrave Square
London SW1P 8PS

SGS UK Limited
Global Trade Solutions
217–221 London Road
Camberley
Surrey
GU15 3EY
Tel: +44 (01276) 69 1133
Fax: +44 (01276) 69 1155

SGS Group (Switzerland)
SGS Société Générale de Surveillance SA
1 Place des Alpes
P O Box 2152
Ch-1211
Geneva 1
Switzerland

Index

NB: page numbers in *italic* indicate figures or tables